Mary Bernard

Catherine Merridale is the author of the critically acclaimed *Night of Stone: Death and Memory in Twentieth-Century Russia.* The professor of contemporary history at the University of London, she also writes for the *London Review of Books, New Statesman,* and the *Independent.*

Also by CATHERINE MERRIDALE

Night of Stone:
Death and Memory in Twentieth-Century Russia

★ Praise for IVAN'S WAR ★

"[A] breathtaking, sweeping, yet well-balanced and finely tuned study."
—Omer Bartov, *The Times Literary Supplement* (London)

"Catherine Merridale has done something very unusual. The Soviet war effort has been described many times but her book tells the searing story from the bottom up. Her account of the sufferings of the Red Army soldiers and their families is unlikely to be bettered."
—Robert Service, author of *Stalin: A Biography*

"[A] profoundly empathic work of history."   —*Newsday*

"The story of the war has never been told before from the standpoint of the common Soviet soldier.... Most touchingly, [Merridale] finds immediate testimony of what the war was like in the letters and diaries of frontline soldiers.... It is to Merridale's great credit that she lets us listen to what her veterans had to say."
—Sheila Fitzpatrick, *The New York Times Book Review*

"A powerful work of research and writing...Merridale shatters myth after myth."   —*San Antonio Express-News*

"This book is the raw and bleeding version.... A tightly edited, well-paced, and very readable account."   —*The Seattle Times*

"Merridale succeeds admirably in fashioning a compelling portrait, helped immensely by her talent as a writer."   —*Foreign Affairs*

"An impressive work of history, managing to give a sense of the amazing hardships of the *frontoviki*'s experience." —*The New York Sun*

"Merridale accomplishes a great deal in her extraordinary new book. She has crafted a top-notch social history of the Red Army during World War II from memoirs, newly opened archives, and two hundred interviews with veterans. This is a new story. Highly recommended."
—*Choice*

"Marvelous...*Ivan's War* is full of the type of information that will make you find someone to tell." —*Richmond Times-Dispatch*

"This is an inventively researched and evocatively written study of the Soviet soldier on the blood-ridden Eastern Front. Using freshly available archival materials, as well as sparkling interviews with a vanishing generation of veterans, Merridale has provided an empathetic and realistic portrait of the men and women who, more than any other combat soldiers, brought down the Third Reich."
—Norman M. Naimark, author of
The Russians in Germany and *Fires of Hatred*

"Utterly gripping and beautifully written." —*The Moscow Times*

"[A] harrowing and deeply compassionate portrait." —*Library Journal*

"Merridale's new book is excellent. This unique, strikingly original account of the Red Army in World War II is a first-rate social history as well as an important military study, and a stellar example of the combination of oral history with standard archival research. It makes the soldiers of the Red Army come alive."
—Stanley Payne, Hilldale-Jaume Vicens Vives
Professor of History, University of Wisconsin–Madison

IVAN'S WAR

Life and Death in the Red Army, 1939–1945

CATHERINE MERRIDALE

Picador

A Metropolitan Book
Henry Holt and Company
New York

www.picadorusa.com

Picador® is a U.S. registered trademark and is used by
Henry Holt and Company under license from Pan Books Limited.

For information on Picador Reading Group Guides,
as well as ordering, please contact Picador.
Phone: 646-307-5629
Fax: 212-253-9627
E-mail: readinggroupguides@picadorusa.com

All illustrations, except those otherwise acknowledged, are courtesy of
the Russian State Archive of Cinema, Recording, and Photography, Moscow.

Designed by Meryl Sussman Levavi

Library of Congress Cataloging-in-Publication Data

Merridale, Catherine, [date]
    Ivan's war : life and death in the Red Army, 1939–1945 / Catherine Merridale.
        p. cm.
    Includes bibliographical references and index.
    ISBN-13: 978-0-312-42652-1
    ISBN-10: 0-312-42652-6
    1. Soviet Union. Raboche-Krest§'ìnskaëì Krasnaëì Armiëì—History—World War, 1939–1945. 2. World War, 1939–1945—Campaigns—Eastern Front. 3. Soldiers—Soviet Union—Social conditions—20th century. I. Title.

D764.M395 2006
940.54'217—dc22

                                                            2005050457

First published in the United States by Henry Holt and Company
First Picador Edition: February 2007

10 9 8 7 6 5 4 3 2 1

To my father,
Philip Merridale

CONTENTS

★

ILLUSTRATIONS

★

IVAN'S WAR

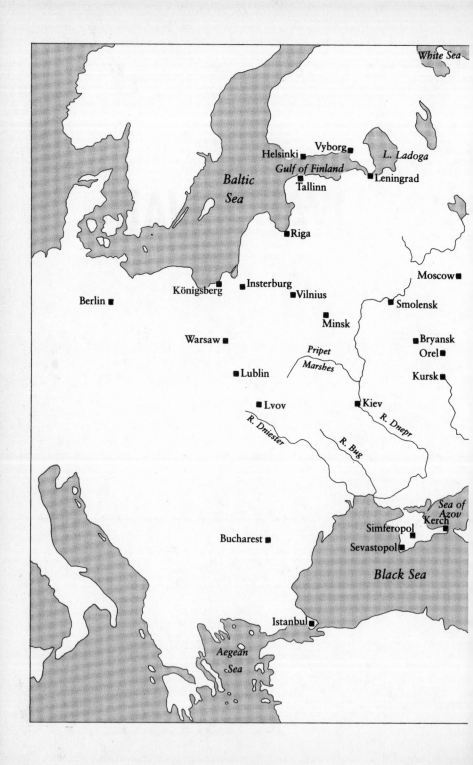

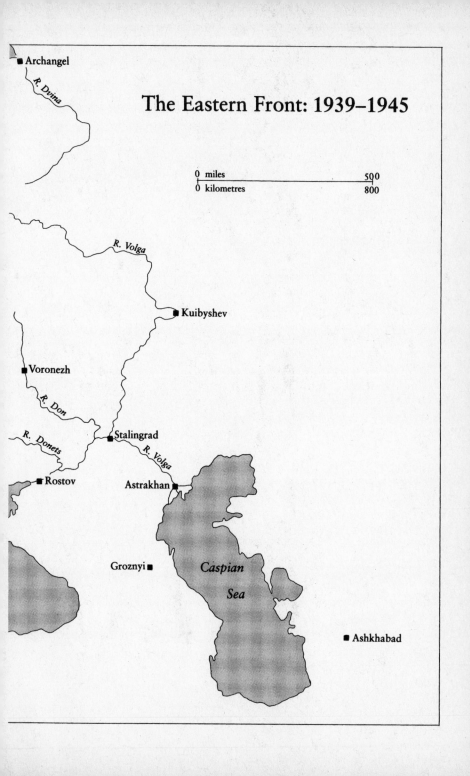

The Eastern Front: 1939–1945

Introduction

TRUE WAR STORIES

★

There is no shade in the center of Kursk in July. Achieving this required an effort, for Kursk stands on some of the richest soil in Russia, the black earth that stretches south and west into Ukraine. Wherever there is water here there can be poplar trees, and all along the roads that lead to town the campion and purple vetch climb shoulder high. The land is good for vegetables, too, for the cucumbers that Russians pickle with vinegar and dill, for cabbages, potatoes, and squash. On summer Friday afternoons the city empties rapidly. Townspeople go out to their dachas, the wooden cottages that so many Russians love, and the fields are dotted with women stooping over watering cans. The tide reverses on weekdays. The countryside flows inwards to the city. Step away from the center and you will find street vendors hawking fat cep mushrooms, homemade pies, eggs, cucumbers, and peaches. Walk around behind the cathedral, built in the nineteenth century to celebrate Russia's victory over Napoleon Bonaparte, and there are children squatting on the grass beside a flock of thin brown goats.

All this exuberance is banished from the central square. A hundred years ago there were buildings and vine-clad courtyards in this space, but these days it is all tarmac. The weather was so hot when I was there that I was in no mood to count my steps—two football fields or three?—but the square is very, very large. Its scale bears no relation to the buildings on its edge and none at all to local people getting on with life. Taxis—beat-up Soviet models customized with icons, worry beads, and fake-fur seat covers—cluster at the end nearest the hotel. At half-hour intervals, an old bus, choking under its own weight, lumbers toward the railway station, several miles away. But living things avoid the empty, uninviting space. Only on one side, where the public park begins, are there trees, and these are not the shade-producing kind. They are blue-gray pines, symmetrical and spiky to the touch, so rigid that they could be made of plastic. They stand in military lines, for they are Soviet plants, the same as those that grow in any other public space in any other Russian town. Look for them by the statue of Lenin, look near the war memorial. In Moscow you can see them in a row beneath the blood-red walls of the Lyubyanka.

This central square—Red Square is still its name—acquired its current shape after the Second World War. Kursk fell to the advancing German army in the autumn of 1941. The buildings that were not destroyed during the occupation were mined or pitted with shots in the campaign to retake the place in February 1943. Many were ripped apart one bitter winter when the fuel and firewood ran out. Old Kursk, a provincial center and home to about 120,000 people in 1939, was almost totally destroyed. The planners who rebuilt it had no interest in conserving its historic charm. What they wanted of the new Red Square was not a space where local people could relax—there were few enough of them left, anyway—but a parade ground for an army whose numbers would always swamp the city's population. In the summer of 1943, well over a million Soviet men and women had taken part in a series of battles in Kursk province. The rolling fields that stretch away toward Ukraine saw fighting then that would decide not only Russia's fate and even that of the Soviet Union but the outcome of the European war. When that war was over, the heart of the provincial city was turned into an arena for ceremonies of similarly monstrous size.

Whatever measure you decide to take, this war defied the human sense of scale. The numbers on their own are overwhelming. In June

1941, when the conflict began, about six million soldiers, German and Soviet, prepared to fight along a front that wove more than a thousand miles through marsh and forest, coastal dune and steppe.[1] The Soviets had another two million troops already under arms in territories far off to the east. They would need them within weeks. As the conflict deepened in the next two years, both sides would raise more troops to pour into land-based campaigns hungry for human flesh and bone. It was not unusual, by 1943, for the total number of men and women engaged in fighting at any time on the eastern front to exceed eleven million.[2]

The rates of loss were similarly extravagant. By December 1941, six months into the conflict, the Red Army had lost four and a half million men.[3] The carnage was beyond imagination. Eyewitnesses described the battlefields as landscapes of charred steel and ash. The round shapes of lifeless heads caught the light like potatoes turned up from new-broken soil. The prisoners were marched off in their multitudes. Even the Germans did not have the guards, let alone enough barbed wire, to contain the two and a half million Red Army troops they captured in the first five months.[4] One single campaign, the defense of Kiev, cost the Soviets nearly 700,000 killed or missing in a matter of weeks.[5] Almost the entire army of the prewar years, the troops that shared the panic of those first nights back in June, was dead or captured by the end of 1941. And this process would be repeated as another generation was called up, crammed into uniform, and killed, captured, or wounded beyond recovery. In all, the Red Army was destroyed and renewed at least twice in the course of this war. Officers—whose losses ran at 35 percent, or roughly fourteen times the rate in the tsarist army of the First World War—had to be found almost as rapidly as men.[6] American lend-lease was supplying the Soviets with razor blades by 1945, but large numbers of the Red Army's latest reserve of teenagers would hardly have needed them.

Surrender never was an option. Though British and American bombers continued to attack the Germans from the air, Red Army soldiers were bitterly aware, from 1941, that they were the last major force left fighting Hitler's armies on the ground. They yearned for news that their allies had opened a second front in France, but they fought on, knowing that there was no other choice. This was not a war over trade or territory. Its guiding principle was ideology, its aim the annihilation of a way of life. Defeat would have meant the end of Soviet power, the genocide of Slavs and Jews. Tenacity came at a terrible price: the total number of Soviet lives that the war claimed exceeded twenty-seven million. Most of these were civilians, unlucky victims of deportation, hunger, disease, or direct violence. But Red Army losses—deaths— exceeded eight million of the gruesome total.[7] This figure easily surpasses the number of military deaths on all sides, Allied and German, in the First World War and stands in stark contrast to the losses among the British and American armed forces between 1939 and 1945, which amounted to fewer than a quarter of a million for each. The Red Army, as one recruit put it, was a "meat-grinder." "They called us, they trained us, they killed us," another man recalled. The Germans likened the process, dismissively, to mass production, but the regiments kept marching, even when a third of Soviet territory was in enemy hands.[8] By 1945, the total number of people who had been mobilized into the Soviet armed forces since 1939 exceeded thirty million.[9]

The epic story of this war has been told many times, but the stories of those thirty million soldiers are still unexplored. We know a great deal about British and American troops, and they have become the case studies for much of what is known about combat, training, trauma, and wartime survival.[10] But when it comes to the war of extremes along the Soviet front, perversely, most of what we know concerns soldiers in Hitler's army.[11] Sixty years have passed since the Red Army triumphed, and in its turn the state for which the Soviet soldiers fought has been swept away, but Ivan, the Russian rifleman, the equivalent of the British Tommy or the German Fritz, remains mysterious. Those millions of conscript Soviet troops, for us, the beneficiaries of their victory, seem characterless. We do not know, for instance, where they came from, let alone what they believed in or the reasons why they fought. We do not know, either, how the experience of this war changed them, how its inhuman violence shaped their sense of life and death. We do not know how soldiers talked together, what lessons, jokes, or folk wisdom they shared. And we have no idea what refuges they kept within their minds, what homes they dreamed of, whom and how they loved.

Theirs was no ordinary generation. By 1941, the Soviet Union, a state whose existence began in 1918, had already suffered violence on

A soldier's farewell to his wife and children, Don Front, 1941

an unprecedented scale. The seven years after 1914 were a time of unrelenting crisis; the civil war between 1918 and 1921 alone would bring cruel fighting, desperate shortages of everything from heating fuel to bread and blankets, epidemic disease, and a new scourge that Lenin chose to call class war. The famine that came in its wake was also terrible by any standards, but a decade later, in 1932–33, when starvation claimed more than seven million lives, the great hunger of 1921 would come to seem, as one witness put it, "like child's play." [12] By then, too, Soviet society had torn itself apart in the upheaval of the first of many five-year plans for economic growth, driving the peasants into collectives, destroying political opponents, forcing some citizens to work like slaves. The men and women who were called upon to fight in 1941 were the survivors of an era of turmoil that had cost well over fifteen million lives in little more than two decades.[13]

"The people were special," the old soldiers say. I heard this view expressed dozens of times in Russia, and the implication was that torment, like a cleansing fire, created an exceptional generation. Historians tend to accept the assessment, or at least to respect the evidence of stoical endurance and self-sacrifice on the part of an entire nation. "Material explanations of Soviet victory are never quite convincing," writes Richard Overy in his authoritative history of Russia's war. "It is difficult to write the history of the war without recognising that some idea of a Russian 'soul' or 'spirit' mattered too much to ordinary people to be written off as mere sentimentality."[14] "Patriotism," the veterans would shout at me. "You will not find it among our young people now." This may be true, but few have reflected on the motivation of soldiers whose lives had been poisoned by the very state for which they were about to fight. Few wonder, too, what insights future soldiers might have gleaned from parents or from older comrades who had survived other wars, seen other Russian governments, or learned the way to stay alive by watching just how others died. The soldiers' stories are a web of paradox, and sixty years of memory have only added to the confusion.

There is, of course, a long-standing official version of it all: the Soviet Union's hero myth. You can find it carved into stone on any Soviet war memorial, and it has been described in countless wartime songs. One of its classic expressions is an epic poem about the fictional soldier Vasily Tyorkin, which won a Stalin Prize for its author, Aleksandr Tvardovsky, in 1944. In this version of the myth, as in the songs and paintings of the time, the soldier is an ideal everyman.[15] He is simple, healthy, strong and kind, far-sighted, selfless, and unafraid of death. He almost never dwells on the dark side of the war. Indeed, his gaze is turned toward the future, a bright utopia for which he is prepared to sacrifice his life. If he gives in to emotion at all—and he is human, so there has to be some—it is the maudlin, sentimental sort. He likes his poetry to rhyme, and he likes silver birch trees, Russian maidens, and the certainty of simple kinds of love. Were he to die, as millions did, his loved ones and his comrades would grieve, but there would be no swearing, smoking, stench, or guts. Above all, there would be no hint of panic, failure, or doubt to cloud the story, let alone the suggestion that this might be a man who looted the cities that his army came to liberate.

The Tyorkin poem was a favorite with soldiers. They liked the plain rhythms and the gentle pace, the homespun Russian language and the patriotic theme. They also seemed to enjoy the euphemistic treatment of warfare, for they would help perpetuate it. For decades, well into the 1990s, the war veterans talked and wrote like a breed apart. They knew the way they liked their war to be—or rather, how to make memory safe, to defuse the shared horror—and they built civilian lives by keeping to the agreed script. Their favorite authors were war writers, but no Soviet book on the war ever mentioned panic, self-mutilation, cowardice, or rape. Official censorship, which banned the work of writers like Vasily Grossman for describing soldiers' fear, worked hand in hand with the survivors' need to tame the clamor of their past.[16] Collective memory was used to soothe, not to recall; the war generation reconnected with the time of its own youth like former boy scouts sharing camping tales. On public holidays the veterans would raise a glass, remember friends, and then join in the singing of their favorite wartime songs, the sound-track of pain and disaster turned to pathos.

I set out to write this book with the aim of reaching beyond the myths in search of what another writer from another war has called "true war stories."[17] The idea began as I completed a different work, a study of death and bereavement that dealt principally with Stalin's victims. I had talked to veterans for that project and longed to find out more about the silences that lay behind their tales. I also wanted to explore the double-edged quality of their self-esteem as soldiers, for though Red Army veterans are always portrayed as victors and continue to regard themselves this way, most were also the victims of one of the cruelest regimes of modern times. They handled guns, and were empowered to use them, but they had grown up in a world where citizens lived in the shadow of arbitrary and humiliating state violence, and when their soldiering was done they would return to it. Their contribution, as a group, was acknowledged, but much of what they fought for—more open government, for instance, and an end to fear—would never come to pass. It was ironic that their state should have instilled in them a sense of pride so powerful that few could see how thoroughly it disinherited them.

The project followed naturally from my earlier work, then, but because it concerned the war I could not have begun it until recently. The crumbling of the single-party state, as Soviet Communism collapsed, loosened the grip of the official tales on people's minds, allowing a wider range of memories to surface. It is now possible to say—and think—things that were taboo in the days of Soviet power. The restrictions on researchers are also easing all the time. Documents that were once closed to scholars—and therefore also denied to Soviet collective memory—have been declassified in their millions. This book could not have been written without the bundles of soldiers' letters, the reports of the military and secret police, the army's own internal notes about morale. It was illegal for soldiers to keep diaries at the front, but there were those who ignored the regulations, and I was able to read dozens of surviving texts, some in the original pencil manuscript. I also found and studied the reports of witnesses, for this war was fought, until its last months, entirely on Soviet soil, through villages and farmyards where civilians were still attempting to live. I traveled to the battle sites, to Kursk, for instance, and also to Sevastopol, Kerch, Kiev, Istra, Vyaz'ma, and Smolensk, and in each place I tried to find out who had fought, what they had done, what local people saw. In the old days of Soviet rule, this would have been impossible.

But something else has changed, more subtle and more crucial than travel and archival restrictions. In Soviet times, the war was not a topic for right-thinking scholarly research. My friends at Moscow University in the 1980s viewed it with a mixture of boredom—for they had to hear about it all too frequently—and horror, mainly at the way that genuine memories of death and struggle had been turned into a patriotic myth. The war seemed to belong to a corrupt and ideologically bankrupt state. Like the ungainly secondhand furniture in our cramped student rooms, it was too recent to be history, too large entirely to avoid. But generations change, and young people who are growing up in Russia now have never known Soviet power. Few can remember dreary state parades or the enforced piety of nationalist myths of war, and this means that they can be free to ask new questions. A renewed interest in the Soviet Union's war, shorn of much of the cant of the last half century, is sparking new research, new conversations, and new writing.[18] Sometimes the veterans themselves, freed from Soviet culture's prim constraints, have also started to revisit and rethink their war. Most of the people whom I met had shelves that were bowing under hardback books—new histories, new memoirs, reprints of classified commands.[19]

In 2001, at the very beginning of my work for this book, I applied to teach some history classes in Russian schools. In each case, I asked the teenage students what historical subject they would most like to see revived and researched. Without hesitation, they all talked about the Second World War. "Those old people," one girl said, "they really had something special. I wish I had listened to my grandmother's stories more carefully while she was still alive." Other children whose relatives had survived agreed to help me approach them and also to collect some of their stories. Several of the testimonies that shaped this book were the result of that collaboration. Some blossomed into contributions to the essay competitions that the Moscow-based human rights association Memorial has run for several years. Together, they constitute an informal archive of the human experience of war.[20]

In all, about two hundred veterans provided interviews for this book. Most talked to me directly, alone or with one of the assistants present who helped to locate them and put them at their ease.[21] We were sometimes conscious of awkwardness, of a restraint that might have been the result of my foreignness or of my lack of military experience. It did not always help to be a woman, either. To address all this, I asked a colleague, a Russian army veteran and professional interviewer, to conduct some interviews on his own. Aleksei Shimchuk went back to his home in Kaluga and spent a summer talking to old soldiers, many of whom he had known since childhood. We found that some constraints still held, such as the taboos about sex and death that separate the war generation from our own. We also found—all of us—that the weight of years and of the patriotic myths, of a self-image that was manufactured for the soldiers in the very midst of war, was hard to lift now, in people's extreme old age. Nonetheless, some interviews turned into friendships, dialogues that lasted over several years. Problems that no written archival source could answer were solved or transmuted over tea and vodka, Georgian wine. But though the veterans talked vividly of love, food, travel, countryside, and weather, and though they happily recalled the friends they made, few could return to the world of combat itself.

This constraint, I would find, is not unique to Soviet troops. John Steinbeck, who visited Russia just after the war, had seen battle himself. But even he—like almost every other soldier who reflects on combat—was aware that certain things, and battle most of all, remain beyond communication. As soldiers are withdrawn from operations, Steinbeck explained, they are physically and emotionally weary and tend to escape into sleep. "When you wake up and think back to the things that happened," he continued, "they are already becoming dreamlike. You try to remember what it was like, and you can't quite manage it. The outlines in your memory are vague. The next day the memory slips further, until very little is left at all. . . . Men in prolonged battle are not normal men. And when afterwards they seem to be reticent, perhaps they don't remember very well."[22] Soviet soldiers' letters, and the testimonies of the survivors today, tell this same story almost every time. Perhaps there are some aspects of violence where lack of memory is a boon. I have used every source I could find, from testimony to poetry, police reports to scarred woodland, to try to reconstruct the universe of war. I have also used accounts from Hitler's army, for sometimes an enemy perceives more than combatants of the other side. But in the end some silences reflect the truth more closely than pages of prose.

Others, however, are merely frustrating. There is still much resistance in Russia (though less in most other former Soviet republics) to reinterpretations of the war. Commemoration is an industry of sorts, and many of the beneficiaries resent inquiries about fact and detail as they prepare for large-scale parades and solemn memorial ceremonies.[23] The Russian government, too, has an interest in preserving a good memory of war, for the victory over Fascism remains the greatest achievement that modern Russia can claim. Accordingly, research into the conflict is not encouraged. There have been worries about potential reparations suits, about the possibility of European demands for the return of looted art, but these are not the real core of the issue. The point is that commemoration comforts the survivors and raises national morale. It also helps to bolster faith in the armed forces at a time when all the evidence points to moral neglect and gathering financial crisis. And secrecy can be a habit. The Ministry of Defense still guards its massive archive city at Podolsk, near Moscow. The main reason, probably, is fear of exposing systematic evidence of official brutality, or of cowardice, or even of organized mutiny. But there do not need to be reasons. For a state body whose power relies on its inaccessibility, secrecy is also an end in itself.

The other archives remain veritable treasure houses, although in these, too, there was much that I was not allowed to see. Sometimes the censorship was primitive. In some cases, the forbidden pages in a file were simply sealed in a brown paper envelope and secured with paper clips. Sometimes entire runs of files were closed. The rules appeared capricious. In one archive, it was permitted to make notes about desertion, but not to write down the offending (and dead) soldiers' names. In another, statistics about drunkenness were off-limits. Meanwhile, in a third, it was possible to read about the drunkenness and desertion of an entire regiment, names and all, and the staff happily brewed tea and unpacked biscuits while I took my notes. The Ministry of Defense is supposed to monitor all wartime documents, and it certainly keeps a close watch on its own holdings, but its rules often conflict with the generous laws on access that govern the archives of the Russian Federation. Even the ministry, moreover, has no direct control over policy in the former Soviet territories that are no longer part of Russia itself.

The search for Ivan, the Red Army soldier, involved more than one journey, then, and sometimes the most obvious paths had been deliberately blocked. The enterprise also demanded an effort of imagination. Before I could begin to find the true Ivan, I had to make sure that I was not looking for an image of myself. A young recruit to Stalin's army would have grown up in a world so alien to my own that I would have to start with that, with the landscape, the language, family, education, fear, and hope. A state that claimed to be remaking human souls, as Stalin's did, had to have left its mark on every youth; their mental universe was touched, if not entirely shaped, by it. The Red Army was many millions strong, and its ranks included conscripts and volunteers, ordinary men and women, as well as professional soldiers. In many ways, it was a reflection of the society from which it sprang, and its fortunes mirrored the strengths and weaknesses of that lost world. My book had to take account of records, tables, and what might be called competing master narratives of war, the stories that emerged as the smoke cleared. But it would also have to include several hundred individual stories, those of the diarists, compulsive letter writers, memoirists, widows and orphans, survivors. My friend the archivist in Moscow chuckled when I looked daunted. As ever, he could see the humorous side of an ambitious plan. "You wrote Life and Death or whatever it was," he commented. "Now you want to write *War and Peace*."

★

The Soviets were not the only people to create an Ivan myth. The Nazis, with their passion for racial labeling, had their own ideas about the Slav in uniform. For Goebbels, Soviet soldiers were a "red horde," half-Asiatic savages who threatened Europe's way of life. German wartime intelligence was necessarily more scientific. Nazi military observers made their notes by watching combat, interviewing their own men, and questioning the prisoners they took.[24] But though they admired Russian tank crews, took comfort when the infantry lacked training, and envied the men's willingness to die, even practically minded spies could not avoid the language of biology. "The two large[st] groups" within the Red Army, Great Russians and Ukrainians, "absorbed the same racial elements, the product of which they represent today," a German officer wrote. "In this racial mixture there can be traced a weak Germanic blood strain from the Gothic period and the Middle Ages. Of special importance, however, I consider the infusion of Mongol blood."[25]

These remarks might have had little more than antiquarian significance but for the readership they reached. For in March 1947, soon after the Third Reich collapsed, some of its former officers' racially based analyses of the Red Army were being dictated to members of the American intelligence service. The Soviets were no longer the allies of democracy by then. The Cold War was already tightening its grip, and policy makers in the United States of America needed to find out more about the superpower they faced. Even the humblest US soldiers required a briefing on their enemy's strengths and weaknesses. To help with the educational process, the U.S. Department of the Army prepared a pamphlet, *Russian Combat Methods in World War II*, the second part of which described "the peculiarities of the Russian soldier."

"The characteristics of this semi-Asiatic," the pamphlet begins, "are strange and contradictory." The captured Nazi officers had done their job. "The Russian," continued the pamphlet, "is subject to moods which to a westerner are incomprehensible; he acts by instinct. As a soldier, the Russian is primitive and unassuming, innately brave but morosely passive when in a group." At the same time, "his emotions drive the Russian into the herd, which gives him strength and courage." Hardship was no deterrent for these primitives. The Red Army's wartime endurance at Stalingrad was explained as a side effect of culture and those Asiatic genes. "It is no exaggeration to say that the Russian soldier is unaffected by season and terrain. . . . [He] requires only very few provisions for his own use." Finally, the Red Army could not be trusted to play by the rules. "The Germans found," the summary concluded, "that they had to be on their guard against dishonesty and attempts at deception by individual Russian soldiers and small units. . . . An unguarded approach often cost a German his life."[26]

Cold War commentaries like these, racist parentage and all, helped shape the image of Red Army soldiers for English speakers of the later twentieth century. Most combatants dehumanize their enemy. It is much easier to kill someone who seems entirely alien, whose individuality has gone. And Russia always seemed to be so difficult, even in the brief four-year spell when Stalin was the ally of democracy. Red Army soldiers might well be brave, "probably the best material in the world from which to form an army," in the view of one British observer, but their "astonishing strength and toughness" and "their ability to survive deprivations" were disconcerting, even in an ally.[27]

Setting the racist labeling aside, it remains true that Soviet soldiers served one of the most ambitious dictatorships in history and that most had been educated according to its precepts. Most, therefore, were more profoundly steeped in their regime's ideology than soldiers in the Wehrmacht, for Soviet propaganda had been working on its nation's consciousness for fifteen years by the time Hitler came to power in Berlin. Soviet citizens also tended to be more isolated from foreign influences, and very few (except, perhaps, the veterans of the First World War) would have had the opportunity for international travel. They shared a common language, a kind of lens that was engineered to show the world in the colors of Marxism-Leninism. But beyond that, the idea that Red Army soldiers were an undifferentiated horde, or even scions of one race, is simply wrong.

Russians were in a majority in the Soviet armed forces throughout the war. Ukrainians were the second-largest nationality. But the Red Army included scores of other ethnic groups, from Armenians to Yakuts, as well as large numbers of people who preferred to call themselves "Soviet," evading traditional categories in favor of a new sort of citizenship.[28] Conscripts included skilled workers, young men who could turn their acquaintance with industrial machines into an easy mastery of tanks. But though such people were the army's preferred recruits, its ranks also numbered boys from the villages, many of whom had never seen an electric light, let alone an engine, before they were called up. Recruits from desert and steppe regions had yet to see broad rivers, yet to learn to swim. They were the ones who drowned most quickly when the order came to wade through the Crimean marsh or storm across the icy Dnepr.

There were also wide variations in the soldiers' age. The majority of conscripts were born between 1919 and 1925, but older men, including tens of thousands in their forties, were also called up. These were the veterans who remembered the First World War, the men who had known what life under tsarism was like. Their mentality and expectations were entirely different from those of young lads straight from Soviet schools. Some even remembered different kinds of armies. That of the tsars had been hierarchical, its discipline severe, but in the 1920s there had been a brief experiment with classlessness, an attempt to build a people's army that was free of bombast, formality, and gold braid.[29] Men who remembered those experimental days were suspicious of drill, watchful, and quick to condemn (or even shoot) their inexperienced young officers. There never was a single army type. After a few months on the road with former peasants, small-time crooks, career soldiers, adolescents, and would-be poets like himself, one conscript, David Samoilov, concluded that "a people is not like the processed stuffing ready for history's sausage machine. . . . A single language, culture, and fate give rise to characteristics that many seem to share, the things that we call national character. But in reality a people is a multiplicity of characters."[30]

If Soviet culture was not capable of turning out a single type of man, there could be grounds for suspecting that war itself might be. It is hard to conceive of individuality against a background of industrialized slaughter, or even to imagine sensitivity where so much would have been obliterated by smoke, stench, and deafening noise. Brutalization—or, as the historian Omer Bartov has it, barbarization—is the word that springs to mind.[31] And yet these soldiers, like any others, had dreams and aspirations of their own, ambitions that ranged from promotion or Communist Party membership to a bit of leave, some new boots, or a German wristwatch. They continued to write their letters home, to notice the weather, the varying landscapes, the health and breed of local pigs. They made friends, too, and exchanged stories from back home, rolled cigarettes, stole vodka, learned new skills. The front was not merely a theater of death. Paradoxically, for those who survived, the war presented a new world, one they would not have seen if they had stayed on the farm. The German army went through the reverse process, marching into a land that struck former workers from Bavaria or Saxony as primitive, barbarous, unlit, unheated, and unwashed. Where some detachments of the Wehrmacht motored to the front, initially, from Paris, the best Red Army soldiers often came from villages where travel meant a five-day walk to town. Some of the riflemen who ransacked Berlin, drinking old cognac out of Meissen cups, had never set foot in a train before the army and this war.

Comparisons with other armies do more than suggest the things that were specific in the Red Army's culture. They also point to themes that Soviet sources may not highlight on their own. One question, which no writer born in Stalin's world would even think to ask, is what made any Soviet soldier fight. Combat motivation, like national character, was an issue that preoccupied military experts in the United States in the 1950s. The result was a theory about small-group loyalty, the notion that men give their best in battle if they have "buddies," "primary groups" that, unlike ideology or religion, truly command their love.[32]

The notion eventually inspired new policies on training and using reserves, and it has become conventional wisdom for social psychologists
and policy makers alike. But the Red Army does not readily fit the mold.
To be sure, battalions would train together behind the lines whenever
they were joined by new reserves—or that, at least, was the plan. But
when the rates of loss were high, when the average front-line tour of
duty for an infantryman before he was removed by death or serious disability was three weeks, the small groups seldom lasted long.

High casualty rates afflicted the Wehrmacht as well, and it has
been suggested that the place of primary groups in German lines was
taken by ideology on the one hand and fear on the other.[33] Fear played
its part in the Red Army, too, although men who were more afraid of
German guns than of their own officers initially were too terrified to
fight. Ideology also featured centrally in Soviet soldiers' lives. These
men had been shaped to see themselves not merely as citizens in uniform but as the self-conscious vanguard of a revolution, the spearhead
of a just war. But how effective ideology could be in motivating them,
and how it jarred or scraped against older beliefs, including religion
and traditions of nationalism, remains an open question. Communist
rhetoric may have contributed a certain zeal, but it was not accepted
universally. Nor was the godlike status of Stalin. In the 1930s, the
leader's name, in capitals, had appeared in pamphlets, newspapers,
and posters everywhere that Soviet people looked. His face loomed
out of wartime newspapers and pamphlets, too, and his name was
spelled out on the painted banners that were strung between birch
trees to hallow soldiers' meeting places in the open air. But it is another matter to read allegiance into Stalin's ubiquitous presence, least
of all among troops at the front line. "To be honest about it," the poet
Yury Belash wrote later, "in the trenches the last thing we thought
about was Stalin."[34]

To some extent, training built men's confidence when ideology
failed to convince and comfort them. In 1941, Soviet recruits faced the
most professional fighting force the continent had ever seen. By 1945,
they had defeated it. Between those dates, there was a revolution in Red
Army soldiers' preparation, in military thinking, in the use and deployment of technology, and in the army's relationship to politics. These

changes, which were central to the Soviet triumph, affected every soldier's life, and many wrote and spoke about them. For some, training was irksome, especially when, in deference to the Soviet fascination with American styles of management, the methods used resembled preparation for production lines. But the tide turned, Stalingrad held, and the Red Army's progress after 1943 suggested that its training methods were increasingly effective. How much they resembled German methods, how much the two sides learned from each other, is one question. Another is the place of party rhetoric, of Communist belief, in this most technical of fields.

Finally, there is a problem on which almost every Soviet source is silent. Trauma, in the Red Army, was all but invisible. Even the toll that the war took on soldiers' family lives was seldom discussed.[35] Shock, and the distress of all that the men witnessed at the front, was virtually taboo. There can have been few battlefields more terrible than Stalingrad, Kerch, or Prokhorovka and few sights more disturbing than the first glimpse of mass extermination, of Babi Yar, Maidanek, or Auschwitz. But Soviet accounts say nothing about trauma, battle stress, or even depression. Mental illness, even among troops, is scarcely mentioned in contemporary medical reports. In the guise of heart disease, hypertension, or gastric disorders, it haunts postwar hospital records without getting specific attention. The question is not so much whether Red Army soldiers suffered the torments of stress as how they viewed and dealt with them.

Linked to the issue of psychology is the long-term problem of the soldiers' adaptation to the peace. In four short years, Red Army veterans had turned into professionals, skilled fighters, conquerors. There would be little call, while Stalin lived, for the qualities they had developed. The journey home could be as confusing as a soldier's long-forgotten first few weeks in uniform. For many, the confusion continued in the decades to come. The process of adjustment could encompass family problems, poverty, depression, alcohol abuse, violent crime. Perhaps the survivors' ultimate victory should be measured, in their old age, by their achievement of a kind of ordinariness, by the sharing of tea and sweets, pictures of grandchildren, homegrown tomatoes from the dacha. That triumph, the least spectacular but most enduring, is part of the uniqueness of this generation, an aspect of the special quality that the schoolchildren who helped to inspire this book could sense but did not name.

★

It is a Friday evening in mid-July and my assistant, Masha Belova, and I have an invitation to tea. We have been working in Kursk's local archive, reading about the chaos that gripped the province as the front drew near in 1943. The documents tell a confusing tale. The army's advance was a trail of liberation, but not everyone was pleased when the soldiers arrived, ransacking homes for food, demanding horses to transport their guns. And then there was the danger in the streets, not only the shelling but the looting, mugging, and the unexploded mines. After nine hours of documents like these, the war seems real and the quiet afternoon a dream; it always takes a while to readjust. But it is hard to stay solemn for long once we have left the square. The building we are visiting stands in a courtyard shaded by plane trees. Windows are open on every floor, some swagged with drying laundry, some crowded with tomato plants or marigolds in plastic tubs. A man in a tracksuit is fixing his car. Another is watching, spitting the husks of sunflower seeds into an arc around his feet. The woman we have come to see is waiting by the stairs. We take off our shoes by her front door and pad through to the living room.

Valeriya Mikhailovna was born near Kursk in 1932. She is a village woman, the daughter of peasants, and when she speaks her accent is guttural, the consonants slurred, a hybrid of Russian and Ukrainian. "It was terrible," she says, "frightening. God forbid! Dear girls, good girls, what can I tell you about the horrible war?" She is sitting on a low stool opposite us and as she starts to tell her story she begins to rock. "They came, I don't remember when. There were tanks, the tanks came by, and there were planes, German planes, our planes. The whole sky was black. God forbid! The tanks were on fire, they were burning. And the bombs were flying. There were battles raging, battles. I was nine years old. People were crying, everyone was crying, Mother was crying. My dear girls." She rocks, she smiles, and then her face grows stern again. "There were bodies lying everywhere. Our conditions were so bad, so bad. There were prisoners of war. We saw them. Our father was taken, he was a prisoner of war. Mother was still young and pretty, it was terrible. You cannot imagine. It was cold. I remember there was ice. They took the wounded soldiers to our barn. And the wounded soldiers were all crying, Let us die, let us die. They put them in our barn. And then, dear girls, they came and took the clothes from the dead ones. Their shirts and coats. They took them and they put them on. Without even washing them or anything, God forbid!"

Valeriya Mikhailovna is not rich, but her flat has electricity and gas and she owns a black-and-white television that probably works most of the time. She also has a job; she is not living in some isolated forest hut. When she talks, however, her words come out in the authentic cadence of the village, the peasant village of a hundred years ago. Catastrophes come from the blue, the people suffer, God forbids. The narrative rolls in blank verse, punctuated by that refrain—good girls, my dear girls, God forbid! The mothers of the boys who fought Napoleon no doubt spoke in the same rhythm, weaving their stories on a warp of repetition. Like theirs, this fable recognizes fate, it designates the good and bad, it offers details to substantiate its truths. The Austrian soldiers were good people, kind. The Finns were the worst; even the Germans were afraid of them. The Germans hated the cold, dear girls. They hated the winter, they were afraid of it. When it was warm, they liked to look for eggs, they liked their eggs and lots of milk. But the Germans, they bombed us, they burned our homes, they were here for two years. It was very frightening.

Valeriya Mikhailovna's face is full of concern for us. She wants us to understand, she wants us to get whatever it is that we have come for. She has told this story many, many times, but she is trying very hard to make it come alive. How much of what she is saying is based on her own memory and how much is drawn from local folklore is impossible to say. But there is a moment when the rhythm breaks, when all her years and later stories fall away and she is standing in her mother's hut beside the door. I have asked her to tell us about the moment when the Red Army recaptured her village. "We lived near a bridge," she begins. "The Germans blew it up because they were retreating. We watched them going by, going by. They were retreating from Voronezh. They took everything. They took our food, our pots." She pauses. "We weren't expecting ours. But there was a knock on the door. Mother said it would be some kind of German. But it was one of ours . . ." Valeriya Mikhailovna starts to cry. But she is smiling, too, and she hugs herself and shakes her head, apologizing for the pause. "He picked me up. He was one of ours. They came, they knocked on our door. They picked me up. They were knocking, and they said, 'We have come.'"

"I always cry when I remember them," she tells me later as we drink our tea. "They were ours. I could not believe it." The little girl may well have cried in 1943. But then, as she explains, "They could not stay, of course." The liberators were on their way, and all that remained was a snapshot in her memory, a soldier from her own side at the door. Sixty years of propaganda have altered the grander stories of the war, but the eleven-year-old Valya's joy cannot be faked. As I listen to the tape of her story I can almost hear the shuffle of heavy boots, the deep voices, Russian being spoken without fear. The men that she so skillfully conjured for me are no longer ordinary peasants. In her account, they are more like the heroes of a Russian epic tale.

Local people talking to Red Army soldiers, September 1943

"There's nothing much for us in that one," Masha commented as we walked home. "She was very nice, but she didn't really see anything, did she?" Compared with some of the other interviews we had recorded, hers was indeed lacking. That very morning we had spent an hour arranging to hear the memories of local veterans, including one or two who could have known the soldier who knocked on Valeriya's door in 1943. We had listened to others describing the day they were called up, their experiences of training, their first battles, the German soldiers they had killed. A few days earlier, at Prokhorovka, which is where the fiercest tank battle of the whole war took place, a veteran had described his terror as the fields of ripening corn caught fire around him and the horizon burst into flame. Valeriya Mikhailovna was younger than most war veterans, she had not been a soldier, and she was a woman.

It was only as I thought about her interview later that night that I realized how crucial it had been. Without it, in fact, nothing that the soldiers said had a real context. For most of the soldiers Valeriya knew had come precisely from her world. Nearly three-quarters of the Soviet infantry in World War II had started life as peasants. Their horizons had been no larger than Valeriya Mikhailovna's, their mental universe as tightly bound by God and soil. The stories of their lives could easily have been as repetitious—cycles of harvest, winter, death, and hardship, the main events dealt to them, not within their power. But then the army took them and their world would change forever.

For many, what awaited was a mutilating wound or death. But that is not the whole tale of this war. The paradox is chilling, but nonetheless it remains true that foot soldiers on the Soviet side, if they survived, could genuinely talk of progress. Those who lived would meet foreigners, German, Italian, Polish, Rumanian, Hungarian, Finnish, even possibly American. They would fight beside Soviet citizens who did not speak their Russian language, some of whom, the Muslims, invoked Allah, not Stalin, before battle. They would see and handle new machines, learn to shoot, learn to drive, learn to strip parts out of heavy guns and tanks. They would also become adepts in black market trade and personal survival. As conquerors in the bourgeois world they would use its fine china for their meat, drink its sweet Tokay wine till they passed out, force their masculine bodies on its women. By the war's end, they would have gained a sense of their own worth. But even as they entered villages like Valeriya's, so like their own lost peacetime homes, they would have sensed the extent of their transformation, the distance each had traveled since their first call-up.

The people who greeted them had seen their fill of violence as well. The German occupation was far worse than Valeriya's memory describes. Even in the villages, Communists and Jews were hanged, women raped, and men—such as there were—shipped off to work as slave labor in Hitler's Reich. The Red Army would free them from all that, but it would also make demands, forcibly evacuating some people from front-line zones, requisitioning precious food and goods, destroying crops and buildings. A survivor would know this, and there are papers in the archive that describe the civil strife, the crime and anger. But Valeriya's emotion when she saw that tall Russian at the door was not the product of propaganda, even in retrospect. It reflected a hope, an act of faith, the loyalty that Russians felt toward their own, a gratitude that still feeds many veterans' hearts.

Valeriya Mikhailovna never traveled. Her schooling was interrupted by the war and she never managed to complete it, remaining in the province of her birth. The Soviet system under which she spent her adult life did not indulge its citizens with information. An old person now, she has not had the chance to buy and read the glossy magazines that crowd the bookshop windows of the new Russia. She has the same curiosity about outsiders, the same sense of the exotic, as a new soldier might have had in 1943. "Tell me about England," she asked. I wondered if she wanted to know about Tony Blair, to talk, as many veterans had, about the war in Iraq. "Do you have a sea?" she began. I explained that England was part of a group of islands. We had several seas. "But tell me," she continued, smiling warmly over her own cups and saucers, "is it all right for food in England? Can you get everything you need?" She wanted to make up a parcel for me with some bread and cucumbers. It is the custom when a journey starts.

ONE

MARCHING WITH REVOLUTIONARY STEP

★

Whenever people think that they will have to fight a war, they try to picture what it will be like. Their stories seldom correspond to reality, but forecasting is not the purpose. Instead, the idea that the boys will soon be back or that the enemy will be destroyed with surgical precision, like the myth that it will all be over by Christmas, serves to foster a confident, even optimistic, mood at times when gloom might be more natural. In 1938, as the momentum for large-scale war gathered, the citizens of Stalin's empire, like Europeans everywhere, attempted to allay their fears with comforting tales. The Soviet vision of future conflict was destined to inspire a generation of wartime volunteers, but the images were created deliberately, by a clique of leaders whose ideology had set them on the path to international hostilities. The favored medium of communication was the cinema. The epic struggle of utopia and backwardness played out in moving pictures, black and white, with stirring music swelling on the soundtrack. At other moments, Soviet people opened their newspapers to columns of portentous diplomatic reportage; their country was preparing for battle. But though the news available to citizens was full of threat, films were designed to inculcate the view that the people's vanguard, the Red Army, was certain to triumph, and very quickly, too.

The greatest epic of the time was Sergei Eisenstein's *Alexander Nevsky*, an anti-Fascist parable of Russian victory over German invaders. Although it is set in the thirteenth century, in the age of Slavic princes and Teutonic knights, Eisenstein's great spectacle, released in 1938, makes direct reference to the politics of the 1930s, even to the point of adding swastikas to some of the Teutonic knights' shields and standards. The message was not one that Soviet audiences, attuned to every nuance of state-controlled propaganda, would miss. For all its deliberate sermonizing, however, the film, which boasted a musical score by Sergei Prokofiev, endured as a classic of Soviet cinema. Inferior productions with similar themes stood the test of time less well. But in the 1930s their audiences were rapt. And while, on the surface at least, *Alexander Nevsky* was set in the deep past, for moviegoers who preferred to look forward, another film, Efim Dzigan's *If There Is War Tomorrow*, also released in 1938, foretold Russia's victory in the face of a future invasion, the one that kept people awake at nights.

Efim Dzigan set out to reassure. The impact of his hour-long film was created by blending fictitious action with clips of genuine newsreel, splicing documentary footage into an unfolding fantasy of effortless victory. The message—resolute and stoical but also full of hope—was strengthened by the repetition of a musical refrain with words by the popular songwriter Vasily Lebedev-Kumach.[1] *If There Is War Tomorrow* struck so live a chord with Soviet audiences that they went on watching it even after the real war began. By the winter of 1941, the invader had overrun a third of Soviet territory. The planes that droned across Dzigan's black-and-white screen had been destroyed, the tanks burned out, the brave soldiers corralled in prison camps. It was no longer possible to dream that this war would be over soon. That winter, the audiences crowding into old schoolrooms and empty huts included evacuees from Ukraine and Smolensk, people whose homes were now in German hands. Huddled together, relying on one another's breath for warmth, they needed patience as the hand-cranked dynamo was turned. All the same, a spell seemed to be cast.[2] This film was not about the war but about faith. That faith, and the images that sustained it, was part of what defined the generations that would bear the brunt of Russia's war. In the terrible years ahead, people would hum the music from the film to keep their spirits up. As they marched across dusty steppe, as they strummed guitars by the light of a campfire, it would be Lebedev-Kumach's song that soldiers often sang.

The film's action begins in a fairground, probably the newly opened Gorky Park, Moscow's Park of Culture and Rest. The Kremlin towers are visible in the distance, each topped with a glowing electric star. It is night, but the city is full of jollity, with Ferris wheels and fireworks and young people strolling about with ice creams in their hands. This is the socialist paradise, and it is a place of well-earned leisure, happy couples, brightly colored food. There is an innocence about it, crimeless, sexless, blandly without sin. In this land, Stalin and his loyal aides do all the worrying so that the children of the revolution can be free. But their freedom is under threat. The film cuts to the Soviet border, where Fascist troops, antlike, are climbing into tanks. There is no chance that we will sympathize with them. These are not the seductive species of villain but absurd buffoons. Their officers wear large mustaches, look pompous, and move with the bowlegged gait of cavalrymen. The infantrymen crawl, the airmen stoop. Throughout the action, they speak German, but they are more like cartoon Prussians from a children's book than genuine leather-booted Nazis. Even the swastikas on their helmets and collars are slightly eccentric. This is picture-book Fascism, not the real thing.

The invasion takes place at night. It could be frightening, and we may briefly worry for the stout young woman who is making soup a stone's throw from the front, but border guards hold the aggressor at bay. Our housewife joins the men, throwing off her apron and taking her place in the line of skillful gunners, proving that patriots can turn their hands to anything. Unfortunately, this is just the beginning of a series of perfidious attacks. The next comes from the air. The Fascist biplanes buzz with menace, but danger is averted for a second time. Soviet planes, a fleet of shining new machines, take to the skies, and at this point the audience should recognize the aces who have rushed to pilot them. There is Babushkin, the hero of an arctic rescue mission several years before, and Vodopyanov and Gromov, star aviators, their names printed across the screen in case we did not manage to identify their faces right away. The 1930s were the age of heroes, and pilots were the true elite. In a scene whose irony would become apparent three years later, when the Luftwaffe mounted its devastating attacks of June and July 1941, the famous aces run audacious raids into the Fascists' lair, destroying enemy aircraft on the ground and flying home without a single loss.

And now it is the Red Army's own turn. The volunteers stream in from every corner of the Soviet land. There is an old man with a gray beard in the line for recruitment. He fought against the White general Anton Denikin in the civil war and he wants another crack at the enemy. He holds a fist toward the screen, assuring us that the villains "will remember this from last time." The Fascists, like the Whites, have become the sworn enemies of right-thinking citizens everywhere. But not all citizens are fit to fight, and we now learn that front-line service is to be regarded as a privilege. Working and waiting are the lot of older people and the very young. Some women will remain at home, too, but others, every bit as trained and warlike as the men, line up in uniform, jaws set, prepared to do great deeds. It is not just Russians who come forward. The commissar for defense, Kliment Voroshilov, appears in his best uniform and appeals to the peoples of the east, the Uzbeks in particular. Hard-bitten men in sheepskin hats respond at once. Voroshilov's speech becomes a turning point for everyone. Soon Soviet troops will attack, driving the Fascists from their trenches. The war is going to be fought on the aggressor's soil, and it is going to be won.

The story never gets more frightening than that. Whenever Soviet forces engage with the enemy, the Fascists end up running for their lives. Not all the fighting is high-tech, and in fact the biggest set-piece battle in the film involves cavalry and bayonets, but there is no blood. Indeed, there is only one serious wounding. Its victim is a member of a tank crew who joined up in the first wave, together with his brother, and set off eagerly for adventure. The men—accompanied by a pretty young nurse—spend a few moments trundling happily along in their Soviet tank, a surprisingly spacious vehicle with a cabin that looks like the inside of a trailer. They could be heading off on holiday, even at the point when their machine grinds to a sudden halt. Our hero, smooth and cheerful as a young Elvis Presley, is undaunted. He grabs a handy wrench and climbs out through the hatch. There is a bang, the sound of a man at work, and though we cannot see the actor we can hear him whistling the theme song as he puts the problem right. But then the music stops in a flurry of gunfire. Inside, the brother's face sets in a mask of grief. A couple of seconds of suspense follow, accompanied by violins, so we may catch our breath in expectation of a tragedy. But Stalin's children need not cry for long. The young man's hand has been hurt, but that is all. Once he has climbed back in and the nurse has bandaged him, he is as good as new. The whole crew starts the song again, and off they go to win the war.

The story ends in Berlin. Soviet planes, wave after wave of them, are flying in formation like so many wild geese. They are not dropping bombs. Their payload is made up of leaflets calling on the population to put down their arms and join the international proletarian socialist revolution. The message is timely, for on the ground a large meeting is already under way. The workers in this other land are preparing to break the chains of capitalism. Slogans fill the screen. War, we are told, will lead to the destruction of the capitalist world. The fighting will not take place on Soviet soil. These reassuring messages are backed up by fanfares and more banners. The audience is smiling; it is saved. As the music fades, another slogan reminds us that the price of freedom is to be prepared for war. To be prepared, that is, to ride to Berlin in a shiny tank, to be a handsome pilot or a pretty nurse, to point a gun at a healthy man and shoot him down without spilling a single drop of blood.

The dream of quick and easy victory might not have been so potent if it had remained confined to the big screen. It might not have been quite so devastating, either. The problem, by 1938, was that the fantasy had affected real strategic thinking. "Decisive victory at low cost" was not just a vision of the propagandists; it was the Red Army's official goal. Dzigan's script may have helped to inure citizens to war, but less constructively it was also the scenario for a generation of military thinkers. In 1937, when Stalin replaced his leading strategists with people chosen for their political, as opposed to purely military, distinction, a new approach to national security was adopted in Moscow. In the past, a good deal of planning had gone into strategies for defense. Now the entire orientation of Red Army training was directed at offensive operations. The plans and training exercises needed for prolonged defense were scaled down, as were the fledgling preparations for partisan operations inside Soviet territory.[3] The notion that the enemy would be repelled and beaten on his own soil was not just a romantic dream; from the late 1930s it was the centerpiece of Stalinist military planning.

It was as if a whole people shared a delusion. As Hitler and his generals were drilling the greatest professional army on the continent, Stalin's advisers seemed lost in fantasy. There had been dissident voices—powerful ones—but by 1938 the critics had vanished into the silence of the prison camps, the covert graves. If the Bolsheviks could win the civil war, the propagandists shrieked, if they could dam the Dnepr, banish God, and fly to the North Pole, then surely they could keep the Fascist invader at bay. History, the ineluctable drive that was moving all humanity toward a common goal, was on their side, after all. The delusion was expressed in many other films of the era, including one that features yet more tanks. In this production, *The Tank Men*, the hero, Karasev, is ordered to make a reconnaissance raid across the enemy lines. But he decides to go beyond the call of duty. He engages the sinister enemy in battle, cripples a few machines, and then drives on toward Berlin. When he gets there, he pushes on into the Reichstag and takes Hitler prisoner. "Well done, Karasev," his mates applaud when he returns. "There's not a damn thing left for us to do!"[4]

In 1938, the audiences who watched these films would leave the hall and step into a real Russian night. The cheerful crowds and well-lit parks that people had seen on the screen would be nowhere in evidence. Instead, their path home would lead through bleak construction sites, along the muddy paths between poor peasant shacks, or past desolate streets where lights glimmered for just a few blocks before they gave in to the dark. Many would be going home to apartments so crowded that two families and three generations were packed into one room. Others, the young, might well be finding their way back to dormitories, barrack style, where dozens of boarders slept in rows. The revolution had not made these Russians rich. It had not even made their land the great industrial power of its own boast, although the rate of change was prodigious, the output staggering. But what distinguished them from other hard-pressed workers struggling to survive was the belief that they were the chosen. They might be hungry, ill-shod, crowded into slums, but they were working to transform the world. They had to win. That was the public face of Soviet culture, anyway.

★

The Soviet state was born in war. If any nation should have known the face of violence, it was this one. First there had been the tsar's war against Germany, in which more Russian soldiers died than those of any other European state.[5] The prospect of defeat in this, the First World War, along with the hardship that came with the war effort, sparked the riots of February 1917, the outburst of popular rage that toppled the tsar and swept a new government into power. But it took yet another upheaval, the Bolshevik coup under Lenin, to bring the tsar's exhausted troops back home. The Treaty of Brest-Litovsk, by which the new state dropped its former allies, Britain and France, in favor of a truce with Germany, brought peace for a few weeks at the beginning of 1918. Those servicemen who had not managed to desert rejoiced at the news that they no longer had to fight. But civil war followed, a conflict that blazed across the future Soviet world like a consuming fire, recalling soldiers to the colors and conscripting bystanders of every age. Its violence, more bitter even than conventional fighting, was only one aspect of this new war's cruelty. Wrecked towns and villages were also ravaged by epidemics—typhus in particular—while harvests failed and entire regions starved. By 1921, when the fighting ended in all but the last corners of the emergent state, most Soviet people knew exactly what war really meant.

The greatest promise of the new regime was peace. The word itself had been the most potent element in Bolshevik propaganda back in 1917, and there would be few things, in years to come, that Soviet people wanted more. But though the leaders talked conciliation, declaring that their long-term goal was nothing less than harmony and brotherhood, their policies set them on a collision course with the rest of the world. Marxism-Leninism assumed a prolonged war with capitalism, and while the struggle was certain to end with Communism's triumph, no one believed it would be bloodless. As the ultimate victory of Communism drew closer, the ideologists explained, its opponents would fight with ever more determination, clinging for dear life to the power and wealth they had amassed. Some kind of armed conflict was bound to erupt before the world reached its final state of brotherhood and plenty. More locally, there were still remnants of those same elements—bourgeois capitalism, imperialist oppression—to be overcome. The state, the self-appointed instrument of the people's will, set about extirpating them. Class war—a brand-new kind of violence—raged for the next decade. By 1938, its casualties approached fifteen million dead and many times that number homeless, broken, orphaned, or bereaved.

The prospect of a golden future and the fear that enemies were gathering to subvert it formed the carrot and stick of the Stalinist dictatorship. Opposition to aspects of official policy endured, and so did cynical evasion and crime. But this was no humdrum tyranny; it was a state that aimed to transform human lives. To some extent, a person's response depended on his age. The revolution was a watershed, and anyone who had a stake in the old world was likely to feel threatened by upheavals in the new. For older people, fear and hardship threw a chilling shadow over Communism's dawn, while memories of war and terror fostered cautious vigilance. But the young—the generation that would contribute the majority of soldiers after 1941—grew up learning the bright language of hope. Any schisms were largely concealed. For years before the war, the Soviet population had been trained to work as one. Each November and May, when it was time to celebrate the gains of revolution, the crowds turned out in their millions to march and sing. Stalin's image, reproduced on countless posters and banners, gazed down upon the spectacle of unity. In reality, the people who would form the core of the Red Army and fight the coming war were divided by everything from generation to class, ethnicity, and even politics. The thing that kept them together, molding them into a nation that remained distinct from any other, was their almost complete isolation from the outside world.

Within this sealed universe, the most contentious issue was the transformation of the countryside. The Soviet Union was still a country where four-fifths of the population came from villages. For generations, the sons of peasants had shouldered packs and tramped off to the cities in pursuit of work. But they often left wives and children behind, and almost all dreamed of returning one day, if only to die. The Russian countryside, or that of Ukraine, the Caucasus, the steppe, was a vision of motherland that anyone born there was bound to cherish. Its traditions, folklorists imagined, stretched back to the dawn of time. This was not true—Russia had changed dramatically even in the nineteenth century—but it was a comforting fantasy, especially for uprooted people who now worked at construction sites and in steel mills. For the peasants themselves, what mattered was their land, their stock, and the next harvest. In 1929, this whole economy and way of life would be turned upside down.

The Soviet government had decided that its agricultural sector was inefficient. Peasant farming, a culture ingrained even more deeply than religion, had to be streamlined, managed more efficiently, controlled. In the winter of 1929–30, police and volunteers spread out across the countryside to impose a second revolution, this time from above. Their aim was to create collectives, abolishing individual farms and setting up a system based on mechanized wage labor. To give it a more revolutionary bite, the campaign was cast as a new class war, and its enemies—the scapegoats of the coming agony—were identified as the wealthier peasants, the *kulaks*, a social category largely invented for the purpose. Kulaks were destined to lose everything: their stock and equipment, their homes, their civil rights, and frequently their lives. In the spring of 1930, the countryside came close to open war. In the years that followed, millions of those who worked the farms would flee to the cities, unable to support themselves on the irregular rations of grain that took the place of wages. Millions more would starve. By 1939, the rural population had declined from twenty-six to nineteen million households.[6] Of the men and women who had disappeared from the countryside, an estimated ten million were dead.

No policy would cause more anguish during Stalin's rule than collectivization, and none provoke so much opposition. It was a constant irritant despite the fact that its prime victims remained invisible. Famine victims were silent even as they died, while exiled kulaks were forced to vanish, largely, from the public gaze. Their lives and deaths in sparsely populated settlements to the far north and east were an irrelevance as far as Moscow was concerned. Kulaks were not even considered suitable candidates for army service. Their children, too, were treated as suspect. Members of the second generation tended to begin their military service working like slaves in labor battalions, building factories and digging rock, not fighting at the front.[7] But even supposedly loyal peasants, the surly, taciturn majority, included millions who resented the collectives and all the hardships they had brought. Many were hungry, overworked, disoriented. As the state requisitioned more and more grain from the countryside for sale abroad, families scattered like chaff. People were forced to live like vagabonds, moving around in search of food and work. When these sons of the village were called up, they made uncertain soldiers. At best, they resented and feared their arbitrary government. At worst, they waited for a chance to put things right.

The new collectives survived. They weathered the storm because enough people believed in them, and believed with sufficient passion to withstand the violence that attended their creation. During the campaign of collectivization, words seem to have blinded Stalin's activists to the reality before their eyes. A leaden language muffled other people's pain. "I did not trouble myself with why 'humanity' should be abstract," wrote one activist, the future Red Army officer, Lev Kopelev, "but 'historical necessity' and 'class consciousness' should be concrete."[8] "Historical necessity" called for armed gangs and mass arrests. The task of enforcement was assigned to secret police troops. The gangs included simple thugs as well as affectless professional bullies whose careers stretched back to tsarist times, but their vanguard was made up of real enthusiasts. "In the terrible spring of 1933 I saw people dying from hunger," Kopelev recalled. "I saw women and children with distended bellies, turning blue, still breathing, but with vacant, lifeless eyes. And corpses, corpses in ragged sheepskin coats and cheap felt boots, corpses in peasant huts. . . . I saw all this and did not go out of my mind or commit suicide. . . . Nor did I lose my faith."[9] The new Russia had staked its claim against the old.

Like the Red troops in Dzigan's film, the forces of the Stalinist regime were set to win. For one thing, the peasants, numerous as they were, remained remote, a population fragmented by distance, dialect, and their own misery. Decisions were taken in Moscow, not in some mud-locked village miles from the nearest road. In a democracy, dispossessed peasants might have formed a powerful faction, their protests stirring others to take up the cause. But a democracy would not have driven the peasants into collectives in the first place. Soviet power offered no outlet for protest: unless a person was religious, his choices were to nurture his resentment in obscurity or to embrace the new regime and hope for a better future. Religious faith offered an alternative set of beliefs for a large minority, but even the churches were powerless against the propaganda of this state, and all the more so because collectivization was accompanied by an assault on organized worship. Churches were closed, turned into barns and pigsties, priests arrested, believers exiled. And with religion shattered, no creed could stand up to the Communist worldview, no group sustain itself for long without collapsing under state pressure. The very depth of people's suffering increased their sense of isolation. As one survivor remarked, "Tragedy is not deep and sharp if it can be shared with friends."[10]

But repression alone could not have achieved the state's triumph, nor could the idealism of an elite of young activists. The Soviet state commanded real support among large numbers of ordinary citizens. Such people's fundamental motives were more positive than fear, more tangible than hope. "Life is getting better," the huge posters told them, "better and more joyful." Inch by inch, and almost shamefully, for millions it was. With Europe and America in economic depression, the Soviets could boast of full employment and rapid growth. A village boy who sought work in the towns would not be looking long. The older generation might not manage to adapt, but for the young the prospects seemed to be getting brighter. Moreover, as a worker in the Soviet state, a young man might bask in a patriotic pride. By 1938, the Soviet Union had the largest engineering industry in Europe. The proof was there for all to see in airships, dams, and polar icebreakers. Millions of tons of coal were dug from Soviet earth each year—166 million in 1940. "In all fields," *Pravda* wrote on the last New Year's Eve of peace, "our successes have been stupendous."[11] Readers would all have known about the tanks and planes. The Soviet state had more tanks at its disposal in 1941 than the rest of the world combined.[12] But more immediately, people could also point to improvements at home. Things had been so bad for so long, after all, that almost anything looked like progress.

Here was a paradox. Stalin's regime proclaimed its altruism, commanding its citizens to forsake private property. But one of its most potent selling points was the material prosperity it promised, an abundance that was measured, even in the censored newspapers, in terms of wristwatches and bicycles, not merely public goods. In consequence, although the papers did not usually mention it, a population already hardened by suffering and violence learned to look for opportunities at every turn. Even before the war, Soviet citizens could be resourceful when it came to trade, stockpiling, and the networking that makes black markets hum.[13] In the land of brotherhood, most people's first thoughts centered on themselves. Publicly, the rhetoric was all about collective happiness, but this was also pictured in material terms. Wristwatches, the symbol of modernity that people seemed to covet most, were still a dream for almost everyone. But one day, ran the tale, the factories springing up everywhere were bound to produce them. Lev Kopelev painted the future in similarly concrete terms. "The world revolution," he wrote, "was absolutely necessary so that justice would triumph." When it was over, there would be "no borders, no capitalists and no fascists at all. . . . Moscow, Kharkov and Kiev would become just as enormous, just as well-built, as Berlin, Hamburg and New York. . . . We would have skyscrapers, streets full of automobiles and bicycles," and "all the workers and peasants would go walking in fine clothes, wearing hats and watches."[14]

For the time being, the state provided citizens with small compensations that appeared to presage more, though the planners' choices could seem callously ironic. This was a land where children had been left to starve as famine raged in 1933, and many Soviet villages would remain sunk in poverty for decades to come; even the cities faced shortages of meat and butter, while bread rationing continued until 1935. The quality of mass-produced staples was always suspect, and there were constant rumors of dust or sand in the flour, gristle in place of meat. But Anastas Mikoyan, the minister responsible for food supplies, had plans to cheer things up for everyone who had a spare ruble to spend. His aim was to provide the people with irresistible snacks, so he focused the might of the planned economy on the task of processing frankfurters and ice cream. The Soviets had imported new mass-production methods from America and Germany, allowing fast food of a basic kind to be manufactured in prodigious amounts. There might not be fresh vegetables, there might not be much milk, but there would be ice cream for everyone. The new industry was portrayed as a harbinger of the good life that was soon to be. The more processed the food, moreover, the greater its supposed appeal for a generation hoping to transform the world. How could the Soviet people not be glad when they could eat not only plain but even cherry, chocolate, and raspberry ice cream?[15]

"We never went hungry." Those who grew up in the towns of the prewar years remembered only happiness. "And there was no crime, either." Their rosy view revealed more about the censored press and the romance of hindsight than about real life. Pilfering and theft were rife in the 1930s, while the exploitation of personal connections was often the only way to secure valuable goods.[16] One writer recalled standing in line all night outside a Moscow shop when his mother wanted to buy him a new suit. "Even so," he added, "we had to wait for five hours in the shop, emerging at 1:00 p.m." The suit itself had cost a month's wages.[17] But what mattered to people now was that they could actually buy suits. It had not been so long since there had been no goods of any kind for purchase, and soon there would be none again. Moreover, back in 1938, few people in the Soviet Union had the means to compare their quality of life with that of foreigners. Their leaders constantly told them that they lived in a better and more equal society, a place where the right kind of effort would soon deliver abundance for everyone. For all they knew—and most believed it—the lines in capitalist countries were even longer, the workers not permitted to wear suits at all.

Whatever else, the Soviet regime offered work. Not surprisingly, its most enthusiastic supporters were the people whose careers flourished in a fast-changing labor market. One of the best routes to a richer life, at least for those of humble origin, was military service. Even peasants (with the exception of kulaks) could make new futures for themselves this way. The first people to discover the opportunities that military service could offer under Soviet power were the tsarist conscripts who put their First World War experience at the disposal of the Red Army. Almost the entire officer elite of Stalin's army in the Second World War had started life as peasants and followed this route. Ivan Konev, one of the future heroes of Berlin, was born in the province of the Northern Dvina in 1897. He would have spent his days as a laborer in the local sawmill had he not been called up to fight in the tsar's war. Similarly, young Semen Timoshenko was fated to till fields in Odessa province until he was conscripted to serve as a machine gunner. In 1940 he would succeed Voroshilov as commissar for defense. Ivan Vasilevich Boldin, who played a conspicuous role in the first days of Hitler's invasion, was born in the Volga region and took his first job as a village baker just before the First World War. Even the greatest of them all, Georgy Zhukov, the marshal who claimed the laurels for Berlin, was born in a village, although he moved to Moscow as a youth to learn the cobbling trade.[18] Each of these men built their professional careers during the civil war. Their political convictions inclined them to fight for the Reds, and the army repaid them with promotion, fulfillment, and substantial quantities of cash.

Their efforts paved the way for other aspirants. Many professional soldiers, future officers, made careers despite the whirlwind that had swept through the villages of their birth. Kirill Kirillovich's story unfolds like a fable for the time. I listened to it in his flat in Moscow, a prestigious address a stone's throw from the Park of Victory and the Borodino Panorama Museum. He began with the war itself. He remembered that he was in Tallinn, the capital of the Soviet Union's newly acquired republic of Estonia, when the news came. Night after night that summer, German planes—Kirill remembered them as "Messers"—had flown over the port city.[19] The artillerymen in Kirill's unit obeyed their orders not to fire. But in the early hours of 22 June 1941 they received new instructions. "We were told to consider the situation a genuine state of war," Kirill recalled. "We were not afraid. I suppose it was our age. I wouldn't want to have to do it now. But I can truly say there was no fear. Perhaps we were just trained to be that way." The next few weeks were confused, sleepless, and demoralizing. "We had to prepare," Kirill told me, "for the surrender." He instantly corrected himself: "I mean for leaving Tallinn." The seaborne evacuation of Soviet troops from the Estonian capital was an operation that would later be described as "harrowing . . . a kind of Dunkirk without air cover."[20] Kirill insists that no one doubted that the Soviet side would win. They had been trained that way as well.

Kirill was twenty-one when the war started, but he was already a lieutenant, having been promoted at record speed as a result of his education. "I wanted to be independent," he said. "The military was a career. I went to a special artillery school." Students attended the usual classes, but there were extra sessions in the evenings and at weekends, when they were sent on exercises. "Most children did that kind of thing," Kirill explained, remembering the militaristic spirit of the 1930s, "but we did more of it. Mainly training with rifles." They also worked particularly hard at mathematics and at German, as if in conscious preparation for the war that everyone expected they would have to fight. "We knew it was coming," Kirill confirmed. Every newspaper and wall poster warned Stalin's people about Fascism, and so did every broadcast speech that talked about the world. "We saw the films. There was one I remember, the title was something like 'Professor Mamlok.' It was about what people would suffer under Fascism. It told us exactly what Hitler would do if he were in power here. We knew," he added, "about the Jews in Germany."[21]

Kirill was talented, but he was also lucky. The place he was sent was more than just a high school offering a bit of rifle practice. His fellow students included Timur Frunze, the son of the late commissar for war, as well as Sergo Mikoyan, son of the ice cream king, and even Vasily Stalin. These boys turned up with bodyguards and slipped away in smooth black cars at the end of class. It would be easy to assume that Kirill, like them, was born to privilege. But his story is complicated, poignant, and in many ways more typical of his generation. Kirill was neither wealthy nor secure. He did not come from Moscow or even from Russia, he did not speak the Russian language fluently, and when he arrived in the Soviet capital he was penniless. Listening to him, it is not hard to understand why soldiers of his kind were grateful to Stalin's regime. It is not hard at all to understand their loyalty in war.

Kirill was born in Dubrovno, a small town in rural Belarus, in 1919. His early memories are of the countryside: the horses that came down to the Dnepr River to drink as the sun set, the fields of flax and beets stretching away, the yellow dust in summer and the autumn mud. The whole community was poor. On Saturdays, the girls would walk to town barefoot, carrying their only pair of boots so that the leather would not get ruined. His family could not own land because they were Jews. Instead, his mother worked as a weaver at the local factory, which was the main employer, apart from farms, for miles around. Kirill's father had died of typhus just before the boy was born. He was his mother's only child. But there were half brothers and sisters, the children of his father's first wife, and it was one of these who brought the boy to Moscow. No one suspected that he would decide to train for the artillery, working all night to improve his arithmetic and languages, but a teacher noticed him and helped ease his path to the elite high school. When his family opposed his decision, all he could say was that he needed an education of some kind. There was no chance of that in Dubrovno. Children who stayed there would barely have learned to read and count before they had to join their parents at the mill.

With Kirill gone, his mother was left alone in the family house. Her idea was to join the others in Russia, but she kept delaying, insisting that it would take her some time to pack. Kirill dismissed her excuses, seeing instead the inertia, the fear of the unknown, that kept her from leaving home. "Mother was scarcely able to read," he explained. "It was like that in her village. Almost everyone was illiterate. She wrote me one letter after the war began. I could hardly make it out. The writing was so difficult. She said that she was going to leave, to come to Moscow to our sister. But she never did. She was there when the Germans came. I knew at the time what that would mean, but I waited till the war was over before I went back to find out." In 1941, Dubrovno's Jews were driven like cattle into the main square. When he revisited the place, Kirill asked people who had once been his neighbors to describe what had happened next, but no one chose to recollect the scene. All they could say was that the bodies, probably including his mother's, lay somewhere in an unmarked trench.

Kirill has reason, then, to thank the Soviet power that saved his life, trained and promoted him, and in some way avenged his mother's murder. He is nostalgic for the Soviet past, though not for Dubrovno or poverty. What he remembers is the discipline that formed him, the rewards for hard work, and his own faith in victory. He knew the system had its cruel side. He had seen plenty as a child. Dubrovno was not far from the Ukrainian border. The refugees from the successive famines there began to turn up after 1929. They brought their stories of collectivization, of the slaughter of animals, the looting, the fear. Soon after that, his own family, too, was hungry, though the potatoes they grew on a corner of land saved them from starvation. Nothing would shake the young man's faith in socialism. What he went on to witness in the war would make his belief firmer yet. He still thinks that collectivization brought more benefits than costs. The horses grew thinner, he remembers. People were hungry for a while. But all this was just a prelude. In time, the peasants would have tractors, each of which could do the work of a dozen men. One day there would also be hot water and electricity. Kirill was back in Tallinn later in the war. He saw what Nazi rule had done. He knew, and not from that visit alone, which system had destroyed his world and which rebuilt it brick by brick.

★

"Education has brought amazing results," a German officer discovered as he marched through Soviet territory in the summer of 1941. "On the wall of every Russian schoolroom I found a large map of Europe and Asia on which all of Russia was marked in bright red while the rest was shown without color. The insignificant size of the European peninsula was contrasted unmistakably with the vastness of Russia." Beyond the schoolrooms, he reported little skepticism in adults below the age of fifty. Only the very old or the religious dared to be critical of Soviet power. "I talked with many young soldiers," he reported, "farmers, laborers, and also women." All of their thinking was patterned along the same lines, and they were all convinced of the infallibility of that which they had been taught." Twenty years of schooling and propaganda seemed to have borne fruit. To the racist officer's surprise—for he considered Russians to be inert and long-suffering, more animal than man—the state had even instilled the need for "enthusiasm, initiative and vigor, the most essential prerequisites for great accomplishments not only in peace, but still more in war."[22]

What this German was observing was the impact of a national policy whose aim, for twenty years, had been to engineer new kinds of consciousness among the young. There was still widespread hardship, to say nothing of resentment of the collectives and of harsh working conditions in factories and on construction sites, but the crucial generations, the soldiers who would fight at Stalingrad and Kursk, were born into the Soviet system and knew no other. Though older people might never be reconciled to the new world, and younger ones might joke and make cynical remarks, the language and priorities of Soviet Communism provided the war generation with the only mental world they knew, not least because alternatives were excluded. Even the offspring of peasants, the most resentful section of the population, had no opportunity to develop a different political outlook, or not on a public scale. Children's training began from the moment they stepped through the door of nursery school. As future Soviet citizens, they would start to learn about the revolution as soon as they could pick out the Cyrillic letters forming Stalin's name. Where once their grandparents had chorused extracts from the Psalms, these children chanted lessons on the triumphs of electrification, science, and Communist morality. They also learned to be grateful that their elementary schools existed in the first place, for it was the Soviet regime, they were told, that cared to cultivate their literacy.[23] By 1941, there were 191,500 primary schools among the Soviet Union's villages and farms. Twenty-four million children were enrolled in them. If they worked hard, the best of them might be picked to join the 800,000 youngsters who were accepted at the country's 817 colleges and universities each year. The very fortunate might even win a place at one of the Red Army's special military academies.[24]

All children were taught that love for their motherland involved preparedness for future wars. While their parents were laboring to bring in the grain or working long shifts to help fulfill the nation's economic plan, they learned that military service would be an adventure, a privilege. It would mean taking up the banner of the revolution, continuing the struggle for which the heroes of their Soviet picture books had died. Some Nazis might have envied Soviet educators their task. For one thing, unlike Nazism, Communism had been in power for more than twenty years when the war came, so that several entire generations had lived under its influence. For another, there were no defeats to be explained, there was no stab in the back, as Germany claimed to have suffered in 1918, to avenge. The Soviets spoke only of success. But both regimes presented service—military or civil—as an honor to which the elite alone could aspire and portrayed death as something from which no hero would shrink. Such lessons motivated certain kinds of youth to train for war, whatever happened later on the battlefield.

Soviet students harked back to the civil war and celebrated the Communist Party as their inspiration and guide. The party in turn identified itself with military struggle, presenting the Red Army as its instrument of progress, weaving ideology and war together. Every child would learn about the army's record and in particular about the historic success of the Red troops against the massed ranks of the Whites. While other European children were reading about the Somme, Verdun, and Passchendaele, Soviet students learned about the Don Front and the struggle to save Petrograd. In their free time, they played at "Reds and Whites." The implication was that future conflict would be just the same and in particular that morality and ideological passion were the keys to victory. "Our teachers were the people who had taken part in the revolution, in the civil war," wrote one future Red Army combatant. His physics teacher always came to class in a soldier's uniform, complete with green tunic and gaiters.[25] It was his way of being prepared to take up a gun again, just as he had taken it up in 1918 when the revolution faced its crisis. The pupils he taught would never doubt that they lived in a beleaguered, embattled state. Many believed that their own happy lives depended on armed struggle and pure-hearted sacrifice.

In this way, schoolchildren—those from towns, at least—imbibed ideology and patriotism together, identifying field trips and sports clubs with the faces of Lenin and Stalin. When they volunteered to clear snow from the streets on their free days, they were inspired, in part, by faith in future progress. The altruism natural to young people was channeled into a sense of duty to the party. They studied, hiked, and trained to improve the world, to change it, to build a better one. "It was both possible and necessary to alter everything," a Muscovite, Raisa Orlova, recalled. "The streets, the houses, the cities, the social order, human souls." She believed firmly in the new life, a life in the future. It would start, "properly speaking," when she lived "in a new and sparkling white house. There I would do exercises in the morning, there the ideal order would exist, there all my heroic achievements would commence."[26]

Young adults had many opportunities to test their would-be heroism. The state was keen to acquaint them with weapons, drill, and maps. By 1938, the voluntary organization Osoaviakhim, which translates roughly as the Society for Air and Chemical Defense, had been training youngsters for more than a decade, its membership topping three million each year. Serious and hearty in what had become the Soviet tradition, the society offered classes in everything from marksmanship and map reading to first aid.[27] Young volunteers spent weeks in summer camps, embarking on forced marches, digging practice foxholes, and bandaging notional fractures of one another's healthy limbs. Osoaviakhim's members also led the way when the state needed money. They were the ones who painted campaign banners to raise the cash for building new planes, and on some paydays they would even stand outside factory gates, red armbands to the fore, to collect money from workers as they came off their shifts.

The dream that teenagers all shared was of powered flight. No other experience expressed that generation's fantasy of progress and modernity with quite the same intensity. For a time, in the early 1930s, the trademark craft was the dirigible, and youngsters campaigned for the cash to fund an airship named for tubby, smooth-faced Voroshilov, the defense commissar. Airships hung over Red Square on the anniversary of the Bolshevik revolution in November 1932, and more were planned as part of the new state's invincible defense. But by the late 1930s, it was the plane, albeit just a wooden biplane, and above all the parachute that inspired youths to take part in the military clubs. Parachute jumping became a national craze. Towers were built for practice jumps in many city parks. By 1936, there were over five hundred of them, backed up by 115 new parachute-training schools. Young Soviet citizens would make nearly two million jumps in that one year. The state-run *Krokodil*, a satirical magazine, even suggested that the bell towers of churches could be converted for the new sport.[28] Joking apart, it has been estimated that the Soviet population included more than a million trained parachutists at the end of 1940. It was ironic, one of many ironies, that parachute troops would prove marginal to the war effort when the crisis came.[29]

The craze for training camps was not purely about defense, at least as far as the young people who took part in them were concerned. Social activity of approved kinds was regarded as a sign of good citizenship. Young people who wanted to get on in the world knew that they had to join things, show their zeal. The elite of clubs was the *komsomol*, the young Communists' league, and anyone who aspired to a good career, or even to a place at university, would join it. Most joined anyway because it was a place to make new friends. "It was only later," a former officer recalled, "that I realized that in fact it was necessary for my career." This man, Lev Lvovich Lyakhov, studied geology before the war, a subject that he chose because, like so many others of his generation, he was entranced by travel and adventure. The komsomol and Osoaviakhim were well known for their good field trips. To grow up in these years was to enjoy the clutter of equipment, the collective discipline, the hiking boots and summer camps and marching with red flags. It was also a matter of gymnastics, and not just the physical kind.

Belonging was treated as a proof of faith. Lectures on ideology were so much a part of daily life that no one thought it odd to hear them in a social setting, including at an Osoaviakhim camp. The days of philosophical analysis and free debate were gone. Instead, youths who itched to try out their new skis or parachutes would have to sit through lectures on such exhortatory themes as "Let us strengthen the international links of the working class of the USSR with the working class of capitalism!"[30] The clumsy phrases sounded as ungainly in Russian as they do in translation, but these young people had grown up with them. The Russian language had evolved in step with Soviet man, losing the sharpness and elegance of the tsarist years. The multisyllabic Latinate slogans of the new regime were now as common as the garlic on a peasant's breath. Awkward acronyms—*partkom* for party committee, *komsomol* for the young Communists' league, *kolkhoz* for collective farm—were ordinary currency by 1938. Each linguistic innovation from the government gave rise to new slogans and longer words. Young people knew no other way.

Another acronym made sure that no one was tempted to ridicule it all. In 1917, Lenin's comrade Feliks Dzerzhinsky was put in charge of internal security in the new state. He assembled a secret police force with terrifying powers and called it the Extraordinary Commission, Chrezvychainaya Kommissiya in Russian, abbreviated to Cheka. It would go through several changes of title, although its fondness for murder, torture, and imprisonment without trial would remain the same. By 1938, and for the entire period of the war, it would be known as the NKVD, the People's Commissariat for Internal Affairs. Its main task was to enforce the state's will, and its victims included party members, army officers, intellectuals, and even loyal engineers. The NKVD was many things in one: police force, spy, and prison warden, provider of forced labor, judge, executioner, and burial service. It also had a para-military branch, which monitored dissension and indiscipline among soldiers, though certain detachments were also trained to fight. But in the last few years of peace, its main role was to run a system of surveil-lance, summary arrest, and state terror that would almost destroy the regime that it claimed to serve. Young komsomols and parachutists would have known of its work. Many of the arrests and even the death sentences were public. But protest was not possible, and nor, in any real sense, was discussion. There were no outlets for dissent, and critics would have found no public audience. "You become an accomplice even though you are an adversary," a former Bolshevik wrote later, "be-cause you are unable to express disapproval even if you are ready to pay with your life."[31]

Illegal arrests and mass executions had been state policy during the civil war. Thereafter, the scale of police terror was greatly reduced, at least for a decade or so. But in December 1934, the popular chairman of Leningrad's Communist Party committee, Sergei Kirov, was shot while working late in his office. His assassination was the pretext for a fresh campaign of fear. First came arrests and show trials in which leading fig-ures from Lenin's time were publicly disgraced and sentenced to death. These were followed by more secretive operations, including mass ar-rests and disappearances. Piles of bodies appeared in city-center ceme-teries, each victim having been shot at close range with a police gun.

The purges, in which tens of thousands of innocent people were arrested, imprisoned, tortured, and ultimately, in unnumbered cases, executed without trial, cast a shadow across all areas of public life. The armed forces were not immune, despite the certainty of war. In June 1937, the deputy minister of defense (and former chief of the general staff), Mikhail Nikolaevich Tukhachevsky, was arrested. Many of his senior aides, including several civil war heroes, were also implicated in the trumped-up case. The entire group was put on trial, found guilty, and sentenced to death on charges that included conspiracy and treason. No one believed the tales, but no one could express their disbelief out loud. Two years later, a local official in the city of Kursk was arrested for using old newspapers to protect the surface of his desk during a public meeting. One of them, dating from before the purge, showed a photograph of Tukhachevsky's face.[32]

While happy workers licked cherry ice cream, their revolution steeped itself in blood. To be an enemy of the people—a kulak, Trotskyist, foreign agent, parasite—was to be cast out of the community of true believers forever. Even those who escaped with their lives would pay a cruel price. By the end of the 1930s, the population of the Gulag, the network of NKVD prison camps and labor colonies, exceeded 1,670,000.[33] Those who remained at liberty, Stalinism's loyal sons and daughters, were bound together by shared awe, shared faith, shared dread. They sang the revolutionary anthems loudly, as if the sound might drown the protests or the echo of thousands of shots. And they tried to find ways of making sense of the unspeakable. "I regarded the purge trials of 1937 and 1938 as an expression of some farsighted policy," Kopelev wrote. "I believed that, on balance, Stalin was right in deciding on these terrible measures in order to discredit all forms of political opposition once and for all. We were a besieged fortress; we had to be united, knowing neither vacillation nor doubt."[34]

It was as if people could build walls in their minds. In private, they might have their own stories, their private doubts. But their public persona was deferential, Soviet, delighted to breathe the same oxygen that flowed into Comrade Stalin's lungs. "The sun shines on us in a different way now," ran a popular song. "We know that it has shone on Stalin in the Kremlin, too. . . . And however many stars there may be in the sky, there cannot be as many of them as there are thoughts in Stalin's brilliant head."[35] Irony, that staple of Second World War culture in Britain and the United States, was never part of Stalinism's public style.[36] Zhenya Rudneva, who would become a flying ace and die in 1944, kept a diary before the war. As she wrote: "In ten days it will be Constitution Day, in seventeen days, the elections to the Supreme Soviet of the USSR. . . . How can I not love my motherland, which gives me such a happy life?"[37]

People like Rudneva were not automatons. They all had stories, and they all had inner worlds. But they survived by learning to fit into the framework of the state, adopting individual routes toward the longed-for secure and productive life. It was far easier, as even the doubters found, to join the collective and share the dream than to remain alone, condemned to isolation and the fear of death. A veteran of Stalingrad told me about his own process of choice. Ilya Natanovich fought unflinchingly in 1943, remaining in the field until he was wounded so badly that he was left for dead. The courage that sustained him as he lay on the frozen steppe defies imagination, as does the pain he suffered from an arm and shoulder wound that never healed. He agrees that his Soviet identity, the optimism of Stalin's people, helped to build his resolve. But only months before this episode, Ilya Natanovich, an infantryman in Stalin's army, might easily have fallen victim to the purge. The problem was his background, although his sharp mind and sense of humor must have made things worse. It was never a good idea to be perceptive, let alone to laugh.

Ilya Natanovich was born in Vitebsk province, part of today's Belarus, in the summer of 1920. His father was a Bolshevik, but it was his mother's family, his aunts, who brought the color and excitement that made his childhood such fun. They would turn up without notice, blowing in from Warsaw or Moscow, talking as they stepped across the threshold. They would still be talking as he lay awake in his room, listening to the grown-ups laughing and arguing round the dinner table. On summer nights, as the dawn broke, someone might open the piano and then the songs would start—Russian songs, Jewish songs, anthems of the revolution. "I knew from my childhood that I was growing up in a family where interesting things were happening," he recalled. "Things connected to revolution."

Ilya's aunts had been involved in the revolutionary underground for decades. They were old hands by the time of Lenin's coup of 1917. One had worked in a secret revolutionary group in Baku, the oil port on the Caspian Sea. It was there that she encountered the young man who later gave himself the name Stalin. Ilya's own image of the future leader was shaped by a tale she liked to tell about his cruelty. One afternoon, she said, it must have been in April, sometime before 1904, she and a group of comrades were out for a walk. Their path lay by a river that had swollen after the spring thaw. A calf, newborn, still doubtful on its legs, had somehow become stranded on an island in the middle. The friends could hear its bleating above the roar of the water, but no one dared to risk the torrent. No one, that is, except the Georgian, Koba, who ripped off his shirt and swam across. He reached the calf, hauled himself out to stand beside it, waited for all the friends to watch, and then he broke its legs.

Ilya Natanovich lived half his life in that man's shadow. His father was the first to suffer directly. The Bolshevik revolutionary had made good, and by the 1930s he was a senior official in Stalin's government. The trappings of power included an apartment in Moscow and a new wife, younger than the first, childless, and unencumbered by loquacious relatives. Ilya and his mother and brother were installed in a separate residence, and it was this arrangement, probably, that saved their lives. In 1937, Ilya's father was arrested. He disappeared forever, and although his estranged family escaped the terror, they were tainted by their association with an enemy of the people. This burden, combined with young Ilya's Jewishness, dictated the choices available to the teenager. Advised by a sympathetic teacher to give up his plan to study at the prestigious foreign languages institute and instead to set his sights on a teaching career, Ilya pursued his studies at a humble college, avoiding even the komsomol for fear of unwelcome inquiries. When war broke out in 1941, his request to serve at the front was refused; he was sent to a building site in the Urals to help construct a factory. It was only when the army was in danger of collapse that he was permitted to transfer to the infantry, but although he fought at Stalingrad, he never managed to wipe the slate clean of his father's supposed shame. After the war, he took a job in the provincial city of Smolensk. It was a long way to a decent library—eight hours by train to his beloved Moscow—but he was inconspicuous, and that meant relatively safe.

Ilya Natanovich ought to remember Stalin with disgust. He ought to recall angry conversations around the table when those lively and observant aunts dropped by. But what the veteran remembers, with a smile of recognition, is an attitude that borders on religious faith. "When we heard him speaking on the radio," he explains, "and there was a pause, we used to whisper: There, Stalin's having a drink." The image may have come from Konstantin Simonov's famous novel, *The Living and the Dead*, where people who are listening to Stalin's greatest wartime speech in July 1941 catch their breath each time he takes a drink. Veterans' memories are often overlaid with images from books or films. The war was so long ago, after all. But then Ilya Natanovich remembers more. "It was like listening to the voice of God," he adds. "And I dreamed about him like a father. I dreamed, of course, about my own father as well. I still do. When the repressions started, I began to have some doubts. . . . I didn't believe that my father was guilty, or any of the other people I knew. But Stalin embodied the future. We all believed that."

"Our generation lived through 1937 and 1938," another veteran recalled. "We were witnesses to those tragic events, but our hands were clean. Our generation was the first to be truly formed after the revolution." This man had been at school when the first show trials were staged. He read about the purges on wall newspapers, the sheets of newsprint that were pinned up like posters for people to stand and read. Whatever his private thoughts, he kept his faith in the utopian cause. He believed, too, in the victory that had been described so vividly in the war films of 1938. The same faith would impel millions of young people to volunteer as soon as they heard the news of the invasion. Faith in the cause could make them fight, but faith was no defense against German shells. This was the generation that the war devoured. As this same veteran recalled, there were 138 young people in his rifle regiment. After their first battle, 38 were left, and ten days later there were only 5.[38] The state, with all its promises, had let them down. "They were prepared for great deeds," the historian Elena Senyavskaya remarked. "But they were not prepared for the army."[39]

TWO

A FIRE THROUGH ALL THE WORLD

★

The first real test for Stalin's Red Army came at the end of 1939. On 30 November, following a flurry of disputes about border security, Soviet troops invaded Finland. The campaign was to prove the first act in the Soviet Union's greatest war. It was a disaster. Within a month, nearly 18,000 men, almost half of those who had crossed into Finland that first day, were missing, captured, or dead. The slaughter was so terrible, and the panic that accompanied it so confusing, that it is difficult even now to establish just how many soldiers lost their lives in the short war that followed. The men were thrown headlong at Finnish guns. Tanks and their crews were shelled and burned, whole regiments of infantry encircled. Entire battalions of troops, the spearhead of the Red Army, were cut off from their reinforcements and supplies, while leaderless soldiers rioted in the face of starvation and cold. Tales of atrocities began to circulate. Men talked of Soviet corpses without penises or hands. Some had seen human faces with their tongues and eyes gouged out. When the war was over, the basis for many of these stories turned out to be the horror felt by inexperienced conscripts as they marched in succession, wave after helpless wave, over their own unburied dead, past corpses frozen, brittle, gnawed or torn apart by dogs.[1] Red Army losses—deaths—exceeded 126,000.[2] Nearly 300,000 more were evacuated because of injury, burns, disease, and frostbite.[3] Finland's losses in the war were 48,243 killed and 43,000 wounded.[4]

Sheer numbers—of men and heavy guns—told in the Soviets' favor in the end. Fresh troops were brought to the Karelian Front. A new assault, as crushing as a battering ram, destroyed the Finnish lines. As Europe plunged into conflict, Stalin was determined to secure the Soviet Union's northern borders, and to that end the forests to the north of the medieval city of Viipuri, today's Vyborg, were turned into a wasteland of charred metal and dead pine. The Finns capitulated in late March 1940. Readers of the Soviet daily newspaper, *Pravda,* would learn that justice had been done and that the war had put a stop to yet another threat to proletarian freedom. But even they might well have heard the rumors that returning soldiers spread, and outside Russia there were none who viewed the outcome as a victory for Moscow. Military planners in Hitler's Germany, their sights set on possible future war, were ready that spring with fat reports about the Soviet army's weakness.[5] An American correspondent in Stockholm concluded that the Soviet-Finnish war had "revealed more secrets about the Red Army than the last twenty years."[6]

The secrets that he had in mind were mainly about training, tactics, and equipment. Surveying the events of those four months with a military eye, a good spy would have noted that the Red Army had been tried and had failed on almost every count. Intelligence units had overlooked the existence of the line of fortified bunkers that blocked the infantry's advance. Even the Finns were surprised by the carnage that followed, the ease with which a few gunners could kill or terrify entire regiments of men. It helped, they found, that the Soviets were poorly equipped for arctic combat. In spite of their own cold winters, Red Army troops had not been trained to fight in the deep snow, and many were unnerved when Finnish ski troops loomed like ghosts out of the fog. They were also surprised to meet resistance. Later, as the first Soviet tanks broke through, the Finns were gratified by the success of their homemade antitank device, a bottle—usually an empty from Alko, the state alcohol monopoly—filled with kerosene and lit with a simple wick. The new missiles followed a prototype developed by Franco's troops in Spain, but it would be the Finns who gave them a name. In honor of the Soviet foreign minister, who featured most nights on Finnish radio that year, they were called Molotov cocktails. "I never knew a tank could burn for quite that long," a Finnish veteran recalled.[7]

An outsider would also have noticed that the Soviets' equipment—the tanks, shells, guns, and radio sets that the socialist planned economy had turned out with such fanfare over the past decade—was ill designed for real conditions. More seriously, young officers, often fresh from the classroom, lacked the imagination—and, failing that, the training—to coordinate its use. They also lacked supplies and spares. Whole regiments faced the Finns without food, ammunition, or boots. In January, Finnish troops reported taking prisoners who had kept themselves alive by tearing flesh from the carcasses of frozen horses or filling their mouths with snow. The wounded who were carried back to their own side often fared little better. The hospitals in nearby Leningrad were well equipped and lovingly staffed, but young men died of wounds, cold, and disease as they waited for the transport that would take them there.[8] Morale, the morale of the liberating army, the people's Red Army, was miserably low. "The whole thing is lost now," an infantryman from a Ukrainian battalion complained that December. "We're going to certain death. They'll kill us all. If the newspapers said that for every Finn you need ten Russkies [*moskalei*], they'd be right. They are swatting us like flies."[9]

The question of morale was one that fascinated foreign spies. To outsiders, the Red Army was an enigma. Everyone knew what Russian soldiers were supposed to be like. Tolstoy elaborated the stereotype after observing them in the Crimean War, and his masterpiece, *War and Peace*, was full of brave, stoical peasant sons, their hearts as great as Russia's vast steppe. These soldiers were the backbone of the army that had beaten Napoleon, the men who kept on fighting through the severest months of winter, and their image among foreigners changed little after 1812. "They probably provide the best material in the world from which to form an army," the British lieutenant-general Giffard Martel concluded after watching Soviet maneuvers as an invited visitor in the 1930s. "Their bravery on the battlefield is beyond dispute, but the most outstanding feature is their astonishing strength and toughness."[10]

Martel, like quite a few German observers of his vintage, was privileged to watch the Soviets on exercise, but he did not spend any time
among the ordinary men. It was one thing to observe a piece of drill or
a formal parade through Red Square and quite another to eavesdrop on
the private world within the barracks walls. If experts from abroad
heard anything, it was the view of officers, and handpicked officers at
that, since contact with a foreigner was not a casual affair in Stalin's empire. The outlook and opinions of the soldiers, the conscripts and the
career troops, remained inscrutable however much observers might pry.
As all outsiders found, no published sources offered any clue about the
soldiers' states of mind, and there was little to be learned from the enthusiasm of the crowds, the tens of thousands of civilians who turned
out to wave lilac branches on the streets each May. Two decades after
Lenin's revolution, the inner world of the Red Army was a mystery.

The Soviet state was so secretive about its armed forces that even
their social composition and age structure remained a matter of conjec-
ture. Outsiders who thought of investigating for themselves soon found
that their path was blocked. A foreigner could hardly move in 1930s
Russia without attracting attention. Spies who attempted to blend in
with the crowds could not even manage the new diet, let alone Soviet
manners. "You try to drink an ounce and a half of 40–50% vodka in
one gulp without practice," one agent complained, "or to smoke a cigarette with a cardboard mouthpiece."[11] The vodka made him cough, and
when he tried to chase it with hot tea he burned his fingers on the thin,
cheap glass in which it had been served. "Mistakes," an officer in the
German intelligence service noted, "could cost an agent his life."[12]

It was for these reasons that German officers seized on information coming out of Finland. Soviet prisoners of war seemed to offer a
healthy source of facts about real army life. But once again, the reports could be treacherous. Exhausted prisoners, as Germans interrogators would find at firsthand after 1941, would say almost anything
if they thought that it would save their skins. Their very suffering
clouded their minds. And the war against Finland was not a fair pre-
dictor of the Red Army's likely response to invasion on a massive
scale. Even the army that was fighting in the Finnish snow, the Red
Army of 1939, would be flooded, in 1941, by millions of new con-

scripts and volunteers, the patriotic youths who longed to do great deeds. The veterans of Finland were among the tens of thousands facing capture, death, and disability within weeks of Hitler's offensive. The old Red Army, the men of 1939, did not survive for long enough to fight at Stalingrad. But the story of this early disaster shows why the collapse was so swift and also just how far and fast that army could evolve when there was a real crisis, an invasion that threatened to engulf and destroy the motherland, men's families, the homes and landscapes that they loved.

The best clues to the soldiers' morale come from a source inside the army, not from outsiders. A network of political officers acted as agitators and teachers in every regiment. They also worked as the party's spies, which meant that someone was listening whenever groups of men gathered to talk. In their capacity as police agents, of course, these individuals were on the lookout for trouble. The army was one place, after all, where former peasants gathered in sufficient numbers for the weight of their discontent to coalesce, for factions to threaten to form. Political officers' reports are not unbiased, and the subjects of their interest were often spelled out for them by their paymasters in Moscow. Moreover, poor morale among the men reflected on political officers themselves, implying that their leadership was failing to inspire, and for this reason, too, the reports that they filed must be treated with caution. Each document is likely to begin with pages of enthusiastic nonsense. If these writers could be believed, the men had never been cleaner, happier, or more sober; their training always progressed well and they were all lice-free. These were all platitudes. In reality, it was a far cry from the Osoaviakhim and the parachute clubs to any barracks that held private soldiers, riflemen, in 1939. For all that, the political reports provide a rich and colorful account of soldiers' lives.

One thing that army and civilian worlds did share was propaganda. There was no escape from the lectures and slogans. Every soldier was taught that he was privileged to serve in the Workers' and Peasants' Red Army, a mouthful that the state abbreviated to its Russian initials, RKKA.[13] Recruits were also told that they were the standard-bearers of the future and the heirs of a heroic past. Whatever it was called upon to do, this was an army that would muster under banners colored red with martyrs' blood.[14] Language like this found its best audience in the training schools for officers. There it was possible to view a career in the army with real revolutionary pride. Some of the schools—Kirill Kirillovich's was one—were preparing a genuine professional elite, and some of the cadets could thank Stalin for their escape from poverty, their newfound skills, their hope. The Soviet Union was no longer a place where officers were drawn from distinct social elites. The family backgrounds of officer trainees and the mass of the men were often indistinguishable. But everything else was different, from education and prospects to political ideas. Among the men, especially the conscripts, the mood in the last prewar years is best described as sour resignation.

The resentment was muted, deadened by exhaustion, habit, and the fear of informers. But soldiers did not have to talk much, anyway. The memory of the war in the villages was still quite fresh. Some men had gone hungry themselves when the state seized peasants' grain; others were still getting letters from their families, still reading about shortages and fear. Collectivization did not need to be discussed, because it was as pervasive in the men's minds as the damp in their bones. At lecture time, no subject provoked more questions than the fate of Soviet farms. The army recruited peasants; sheer numbers made that necessary. The Soviet Union remained, up to the summer night when German forces crossed its borders, a place where most people had started life in village huts. Such folk had once made sterling servicemen, and sons of peasants were among the stars of Stalin's officer elite. But after 1929 it was taken for granted that the best soldiers would be drawn from families in the towns.[15]

Even the sons of workers, once in uniform, would soon become aware of collectivization's legacy. Although the Red Army was never used to drive peasants into the hated farms, its troops were asked to help in the fields at harvest time, replacing men and animals after they vanished into common graves. Farmwork would become a feature of the Soviet soldier's life: digging potatoes, herding pigs, mending equipment in the rain. The political officers who had to work among troops like this would not find much good news to write as they licked their pencils and prepared to report in 1939. "They tell us that collective farmers live well," one soldier was heard muttering. "In fact, they have nothing at all." "I'm not going to defend Soviet power," another conscript told a mate. "If it comes to it I will desert. My father was a fool to die in the civil war, but I'm not a fool. The Communist Party and Soviet power robbed me."[16] Another recruit told his comrades, after reading a letter from home, that he could not decide what to do. "I have to study," he said, "but I keep worrying about my family." "My family is starving," complained another. "Nothing else interests me."[17]

★

In 1939 the age for conscription was nineteen. The latest crop of new recruits, born at the end of the civil war, was drafted that September. Joining up was part of life, as traditional in Russian villages as wife beating and painted eggs. The army had always taken men. "The tsar commands and God permits," conscripts had grumbled in the First World War. In those days, military service, like famine, warts, and childlessness, was seen as punishment for sin.[18] A generation later the process had changed, but the men's fatalism was much the same. Soviet recruits were meant to pass some tests; the army wanted men who could read, although it did not always get them. As late as the end of the 1920s, psychologists had found that the vocabulary of the average infantryman ranged from five hundred to two thousand words.[19] At that time, too, some of these men had not been able to tell their officers who Stalin was, a finding that so shook the army's political administration that it had to be suppressed.[20] Political education was hastily stepped up, and by 1939 fewer recruits were failing reading tests and none was ignorant about the leader. But the most able were creamed off for work in the NKVD.[21] The army got the next-best ones.

Recruiting was a cumbersome process that usually dragged on for two or three months every year. In each district it fell to the local military soviets to sift and reject sick or insane men and to review claims for exemption. They also checked police records, for known enemies of the people were not trusted to bear arms. The young men who came before them after all these checks were not completely raw in military terms. All had been to some local school, and most knew their country needed to prepare for war. Some new recruits might even have clapped eyes on a rifle or a gas mask at a summer camp somewhere. They would certainly have listened to as many lectures on the Workers' and Peasants' Red Army as any teenager could take. This army could seem like a route to manhood, an adventure, and there were always youths who declared themselves proud to be called up. Not a few, especially in the cities, volunteered. But for the rest, the scenes at home were much as they had always been. The road still beckoned and the mothers wept. The men would gather up the few things they could carry—a couple of changes of underclothes, some sugar and tobacco—and stuff them into a canvas bag or cardboard case. And then they walked—for few had grander means of transport—to the recruitment point.

"Our military training began with a steam bath, the disinfection of our clothes, a haircut that left our scalps as smooth as our faces, and a political lecture," a recruit from this time remembered.[22] For many in the audience, the lecture would have echoed through a hangover. Young men were very often drunk by the time they arrived in their units. The drinking was a tradition, like many others, that dated from tsarist times.[23] It began before they left home and carried on for several days. The authorities may even have connived at it, since vodka stilled the men's anxieties more rapidly than group lectures or extra drill. Recruits might pass out on the train, the argument ran, but if they were unconscious it was easier to ship them off to any kind of hell.[24]

Bleary-eyed, then, and not quite certain where they were, the conscripts stood in ragged lines and waited to receive their gear. Whatever their civilian selves—sons of the village or of some factory or mining town—they would fold up the things in which they had spent their former lives and pull on dull green uniforms, the clothes of new identity. They stepped into rough woollen trousers and a jacket. They were also issued a belt, an overcoat, and boots. These things were theirs to wear and maintain every day. But their linen—an undershirt and pants—was issued on a temporary basis. They learned that they would hand these items in for regular, if not particularly frequent, laundering and that they would receive a clean set in exchange. In fact, they seldom got the same ones, or even a complete issue, back each time. It was a small humiliation, another thing, an intimate one, that they could not control.

Unless they brought their own, which some did, recruits were never given socks. This was an army that marched in footcloths, or *portyanki*.

Soldiers at the banya, *September 1941*

These strips of cloth, which wound around the feet and ankles, binding them like bandages, were alleged to protect against blisters. A veteran smiled at that idea. "I think socks would have been more comfortable," he said. But his words were just a whisper, not dissent. *Portyanki*, after all, were cheaper and less personal: one size would do for all. It took a while to learn to wrap them and the process caused delays and chaos at reveille for ages, but the strips of cloth were universal issue and they were used by men and women throughout the war. "They were the only things that made those boots they gave us fit," a woman veteran remembered. "And yes, we were glad to have the boots as well."

A senior sergeant teaches a young recruit to wrap footcloths

Only the officers were given handguns, usually Nagan revolvers, a design that dated from the 1890s. It was an officer's exclusive privilege, too, to get an army wristwatch. Privates got the bags and holsters, but much of the time they had nothing to put in them. Their tally of assorted empty luggage included a field bag, a bag for clothes, a bag for carrying biscuits, a strap for fastening their overcoats, a woollen flask cover, a bag for the things they had brought from home, a rifle sling, cartridge boxes, and a cartridge belt.[25] The weapons themselves, and even the ammunition rounds, were so precious that most men did not handle them until they took part in a field operation. But they were issued an army token—simultaneously their identity tag and proof of their new status—and a small kettle. The things that had a personal use were the most treasured. "Frontline soldiers would sometimes, in panicky re-treats, throw away their heavy rifles," wrote one veteran, Gabriel Temkin. "But never their spoons."[26] The men would lick them clean af-ter each meal and store them in the tops of their boots.

The new recruits would soon be looking for their beds. In this, as in so many other ways, the generation that joined in 1939 was out of luck. The army had been expanding rapidly. In 1934, it numbered about 885,000 officers and men. By the end of 1939, as the reservists were called up, that figure had grown to 1,300,000.[27] Among the many problems caused by the expansion was a housing crisis. Army regulations stated that each man should have a living space of 14.6 cubic meters, 4.6 square meters of which—think of six feet by eight—were to comprise the floor.[28] But this was optimistic talk. Even officers could not expect adequate quarters. "Collective farmers have a better deal than our officer corps," a Communist official in the Leningrad military district wrote in January 1939. The new arrivals described their conditions as "torture."[29] "It would be better for me to kill myself than to go on living in this hole," an officer recruit remarked. Complaining landed one cadet, who demanded "the quarters to which officers are entitled," in the guardhouse for three days. Tuberculosis rates among all ranks tended to rise in the year after they joined up, as did the incidence of stomach infections. In one barracks alone 157 cadets were taken to the hospital in their first ten days.[30]

Privates were also crowded into smaller-than-regulation space.[31] In fact, only the lucky ones would find they had a billet and a roof. The mobilization plan of 1939 was so ambitious that many turned up at their bases to discover that there was no barracks at all. In that case they could look around the town for accommodation of their own or sleep on the ground. Either way, they might have nothing under them but straw. The army provided blankets, but mattresses were always scarce and there were never enough plank beds for the swelling number of recruits. The straw, though warm, was an ideal refuge for lice.[32]

A stroll around the camp would not have cured a young man's hangover or his homesickness. Communal facilities of any kind were neglected in the Soviet Union. The culture of material goods had spawned a thriving black market. If something could be stolen, skimped on, or watered down, a huckster with the right contacts was always near at hand. Meanwhile, the shortages and management problems that dogged the centrally planned economy bore dismal fruit. A Communist party inspector visiting the Kiev military district in May 1939 found kitchens heaped with rubbish, meat stores stinking in the heat, and soldiers' dining rooms that still lacked roofs or solid floors. Moving across the yard toward the bathrooms, he noted that "the unclean contents of latrines are not removed, the surveyed lavatories have no covers. The urinals are broken. . . . The unit, effectively, has no latrine."[33]

The case was not unusual, as other reports showed. "Rubbish is not collected, dirt is not cleared," another note records. "The urinals are broken. The plumbing in the officers' mess does not work."[34] Hygienic measures were neglected everywhere. The slaughterhouse that provided soldiers in Kursk province with meat had no running water, no soap, no meat hooks, and no special isolator for sick animals. The staff who worked there had received no proper training and they had not been screened for infectious diseases of their own. Their filthy toilet was a few yards from the meat store, and like many others at the time it had no doors. "Even the meat is dirty," the inspector wrote.[35]

Food was a standing grievance everywhere. This is true of all armies, as budget catering and hungry men are on a fixed collision course, but the Soviet armed forces belong in a special class. However cold it was outside, the barracks kitchen would be rank and fogged with grease. Lunch—a soup containing sinister lumps of meat, served with black bread, sugar, and tea—steamed on wood stoves in giant metal pots. "At home," one conscript complained, "I used to eat as much as I needed, but in the army I have become thin, even yellow." "The grub is awful," reported another. "We always get vile cabbage soup for lunch, and the bread is the worst: it's as black as earth and it grinds against your teeth." In January 1939 alone there were at least five instances of groups of soldiers refusing to eat, striking in the face of another inedible meal. In the first three weeks of that month, army surgeons reported seven major outbreaks of food poisoning, the worst of which, involving rotten fish, left 350 men in need of hospital treatment.[36] Dead mice turned up in the soup in the Kiev military district; sand in the flour, fragments of glass in the tea, and a live worm featured on menus elsewhere.[37] Disabling diarrhea struck 256 men in March when the tea they were served turned out to have been brewed with brackish lukewarm water.[38] A young conscript from the Caucasus republic of Georgia—a region famous even then for its good food—deserted after a few weeks in Ukraine, leaving behind a note that singled out the Soviet army diet. "I am going back to the mountains," he concluded, "to eat good Georgian food and drink our wine."

One answer was to grow food on the army's land. Here was one thing that former peasants could really be asked to do. As historian Roger R. Reese records in his account of prewar army life, "By the late summer of 1932, one regiment already had more than two hundred hogs, sixty cows, more than one hundred rabbits and forty beehives."[39] Nothing had changed by 1939. The soldiers dug potatoes and cut hay, they milked cows, and they slaughtered pigs.[40] The work could be heavy, dirty, and cold, so field duties were sometimes used as punishment. In all cases, farming took the men away from their military training and distracted them from the real purpose of their army service. But everyone's priority was filling empty stomachs, and successful regimental farms made a real difference to the men's diet. They also helped to lift morale. This was a time when almost everyone—not only soldiers but collectivized peasants and even some communities of workers—was going hungry. While brightly painted new kiosks sold ice cream to the masses, most people were still forced to scrape and save to buy staples like butter and meat. The soldiers had a guaranteed allocation, even if the quality was poor. It is a bleak commentary on Soviet life, but Reese himself concludes that "despite their poor accommodations, officers and soldiers generally had a slightly higher standard of living in the 1930s than the rest of Soviet society."[41]

The point was that the soldiers did not have to forage. They did not have to walk for miles, as their parents might, or exchange their wedding rings for food. Instead, they could expect to be issued with most of what they needed. They also had access to a network of closed military stores, the ZVK. While goods at any price were scarce on the open market, Red Army men could buy, if their local store were reasonably run, a range of luxuries that included matches and tobacco, thread, razors, toothbrushes, and pens. Like everything else in the Soviet Union, however, experience varied from place to place. Sometimes the stores were badly managed or the storekeepers corrupt. Sometimes the stores themselves were little more than barns. And everyone complained about the shortages. There never was enough tobacco, and butter seemed to vanish within hours.

Soap, too, was a scarce item, and many soldiers mention that they never had the means to clean their teeth. Running water, after all, was only to be had on the occasions when the barracks bathroom worked. For a real wash, the soldiers knew they had to visit the steam baths, the famous Russian *banyas*. This ritual was not purely for comfort. A hot bath (and a change of clothes) every ten days was the minimum needed to keep typhus-bearing lice at bay. But *banyas* were usually in town, perhaps a half hour's march away. One man remembered bathing every fortnight, others that they bathed no more than once a month.[42] When war broke out in 1941, new conscripts would complain about the dirt that made them itch and stink and brought them out in boils. But the old hands were used to it. In peacetime, the life of Red Army soldiers was mostly about getting used to things. Whatever notions a young conscript may have had about Soviet life—and some had nurtured schoolboy dreams, however garbled, of opportunity and social justice—the army narrowed them and rubbed them coarse.

Another source of misery in many soldiers' lives was crime. Military warehouses and stores always attracted local crooks. Pilfering was common in army kitchens despite the unappealing quality of the food. Cooks were often accused of selling the meat and fats that should have gone to thicken the soup. But kitchens were merely the last link in a chain that stretched back to the warehouses and transport trains. Small thefts—a typical case involved fifty meters of footcloth material—were daily events.[43] If there was a chance, perhaps because of troop movements, to evade the police, there were livings to be made on a much grander scale, too. "Our checks in the units have shown that the supply workers connive in theft if they are not directly involved in it themselves," a 1941 report declared. In one district, "583 greatcoats, 509 pairs of boots, and 1,513 belts have disappeared." Among the other frequently stolen goods was food.[44]

The army, then, was certainly a training ground, but some of what it taught would find no place in any decent service manual. As the men dug their potatoes or joined teams working on the barracks roof, they may have wondered when their formal army work might start. They would, in fact, find little time to practice at being real soldiers, not least because their ideological training was never supposed to slip. In each of their ten-hour working days, men would attend at least one class about politics—a lecture on Stalin's analysis of capitalism, perhaps, or a question-and-answer session about the moral qualities of the ideal officer. Ideology was not regarded as an adventitious growth on army life, or even as a mere morale booster, equivalent to religion. In these last years before the war, the Soviet state cast soldiers in the role of propaganda ambassadors. As the people's vanguard, its sword and defender, they were supposed to represent right thinking for society as a whole. Part of the idea was that conscripts would return to their civilian lives and act as models, examples in word and deed. But first they had to be transformed. To be a decent soldier—let alone, for the minority, a Communist—a person had to be sober, thoughtful, chaste, and ideologically literate.

The party built a regime of its own within the army's ranks to work upon men's minds. Its interests were represented by an organization called PURKKA, the political administration of the Red Army. Among the most powerful operators at the top of this unmilitary structure was Lev Mekhlis, a sinister figure identified more with covert arrests than with soldiering. Mekhlis had served as editor of the official newspaper, *Pravda*, but it was as Stalin's close friend and henchman that he was feared and widely disliked in military circles. His influence on the Red Army would be a baleful one, and his removal, in 1942, signaled a turning point in the culture of the general staff. But in 1939, the army still labored under the burden of constant political interference. For the regular soldiers, this aspect of life was ruled by political commissars, who operated at the regimental and battalion level, and political officers— the Soviet term is *politruk*—who worked within the companies and lower units. A second tier included young Communists, komsomols, whose representatives among the men were known as *komsorgs*.

As well as working as the party's spy, an individual *politruk* was likely to combine the functions of a propagandist with those of army chaplain, military psychiatrist, and school prefect. "The *politruk*," the army's orders stated, "is the central figure for all educational work among soldiers."[45] The range of topics they taught was wide indeed. *Politruks* were present at classes in target shooting, drill practice, and rifle disassembly. They were the individuals who typed up individual

scores, noting how many men were "excellent" in any field and invent-
ing excuses for the many who were not. They wrote monthly reports on
their units' discipline, on morale, and on "extraordinary events," including desertion, drunkenness, insubordination, and absence without
leave. They were also the men behind the party's festivals, including the
anniversary of the October Revolution (which, since the calendar itself
had been reformed, now fell on 7 November each year), Red Army Day
(23 February), and the workers' carnival on the first of May. Enlisted
men looked forward to these holidays. The lecture they had to sit
through from the *politruk* was just a prelude, after all, to a bit of free
time and some serious drinking.

A *politruk* who really thumped the propaganda drum was bound to
meet resistance. It is impressive that some—earnest, ambitious, or just
plain devout—tried everything to mold their men according to the
rules. They kept up a barrage of discussions, meetings, and poster campaigns. They read aloud to the troops in their spare time, usually from
newspapers like the army's own *Red Star*. Some managed small li-

A political officer reads to the troops, 1944

braries, and almost all ran propaganda huts where posters were designed and banners hung. Political officers in all units taught basic literacy, too, as well as investigating complaints and answering the men's questions about daily life. Their work was never easy. Like every other type of officer, the *politruks* battled with shortages. "We do not have a single volume of the works of Lenin," one man informed his commissar in 1939. Worse, units that were bound for Finland discovered that they had no portraits of the leader, Stalin. "Send urgently," a telegram commanded.[46] Although they seem absurd in retrospect, some of these *politruks* and their younger comrades, the *komsorgs*, believed in their mission and made real sacrifices in its name. Maybe a few soldiers appreciated their presence in 1939; they would do, some of them, in the confusion of the Second World War. But more looked at the *politruks'* clean boots, smooth hands, and unused cartridge belts and sensed hypocrisy.

The *politruks* were hated, too, because they had an overall responsibility for discipline. Denunciations often originated with them, and it was usually their reports that brought the military police, the Special Section, into a messroom or barracks. Their obligation to inform was in direct conflict with another of the *politruks'* roles, which was to foster an atmosphere of mutual trust. "Revolutionary discipline is the discipline of the people, bound solidly with a revolutionary conscience," their regulations read. "It is based not on class subordination but on a conscious understanding of . . . the goals and purpose of the Workers' and Peasants' Red Army."[47] Some soldiers may have found that shared values like these built networks of political comradeship, but the culture of double standards, of secret denunciations and hypocritical demands, was hardly conducive to the group spirit that an army requires. Soldiers and officers who needed to rely on comrades absolutely in the event of an attack—whose lives depended on sentries, on gunners, and above all on their mates—soon found that fluency in Marxism-Leninism was no guarantee of steadfastness under fire. For the next three years, however, the *politruks* talked on. Communists were reliable, the argument went. Shared ideology ought to be quite enough to reassure a man that the soldier beside him would cover his flank when the shooting started. Known enemies would be removed. The party would take care of everything.

Even in peacetime the system had floated on a morass of false piety. The *politruks*—like party members everywhere—included plenty of poor role models, including little empire builders who controlled the vodka and the girls. "Junior *politruk* Semenov must be turned over to a military tribunal," ran a telegram of 1940. "He is morally corrupt. . . . He continues to drink, bringing the name of an officer into disrepute." Semenov had been discovered that week with a prostitute, helpless, in the bottom of a trash can.[48] But more evaded censure than were ever caught. It fell to the men to express the views that echo back to us through the political officers' own reports. "If I end up in combat," an infantryman told his Communist neighbor, "I'll stick my revolver in your throat first." "The first person I'll shoot will be *politruk* Zaitsev," threatened another conscript as he packed for Finland. Two young deserters whose unit was also bound for the north were locked up when they were returned to base. "As soon as we get to the front," one of them said, "I'll kill the deputy *politruk*."[49] It may have been to spite the party that soldiers daubed swastikas on their barracks walls. The fact that many *politruks*, whose education tended to be better than the average, were Jews was probably a factor, too. Reports from early 1939 noted the "antisemitic remarks and pro-Hitler leaflets" that some *politruks* had found among the men.[50]

Tensions and resentments of this kind were a large part of the reason for the Red Army's unpreparedness for war. But the nature of the soldiers' combat training also had a part to play. With ideology so prominent in the men's schedule each day, extra hours had to be found to accommodate conventional forms of training. In 1939 the "study day" was ten hours long, and after March 1940, following the Finnish disaster, it was increased to twelve. "I don't have time to prepare for all this studying," a recruit complained. "I don't even have time to wash."[51] In fact, the only skills that most recruits had time to learn were very basic ones. The men were taught to march, to lie down or jump up on command, and, most exhaustingly, to dig. They learned to get up and to dress in minutes, winding the long cat's cradle of their footcloths as they chewed on their first hand-rolled cigarettes. The drill might appear pointless, but at least it was the first step to real soldiering, to reflexlike obedience and greater physical strength. If there had been the time—to say nothing of the clarity of command—to build on it, things might have worked out better for the men. But political meddling constantly undermined their confidence, and lack of time limited the skills that they were able to learn.

All infantry must learn to shoot. The Russian word for foot soldier translates as rifleman. The rifle in question, at this stage, was a magazine-fed, bolt-action model with a bayonet. Its design dated from the 1890s, but it was reliable and trusted by the men. The problem was that even when the factories in Tula and Izhevsk stepped up production after 1937, there were not enough guns available for every recruit to handle. Spare parts were another problem.[52] The men who faced the Finns in 1939 had often trained for weeks with wooden replicas, enough perhaps to learn some drill, to try the handling when lying down or kneeling in a trench, but hopeless when it came to taking aim, to testing weight or balance in your hand. It was the same with tanks, where cardboard training replicas were sometimes used. And though Soviet factories had produced a world-class submachine gun, Vasily Degtyarev's PPD, it took the Finnish war to persuade Stalin of its value in the field. Suspicion prevented wider deployment. Until the end of 1939, the smart new guns were reserved for military police, and all the army's stock was locked away.[53]

Not surprisingly, reports from military camps painted a dismal picture of training and its effectiveness. Large numbers of recruits, both officers and men, regularly failed to meet expected standards of rifle competence.[54] Accidents, too, were alarmingly frequent. Even during daytime training there were instances of soldiers firing randomly when they were drunk. There was no reason, after all, to be in top form all the time, for this was an army where men who turned up for parade were often left to sit around and wait.[55] As any faith in their officers that they still nurtured ebbed away, bright soldiers learned to turn their time to better use. "You'll never teach me anything," observed a Ukrainian conscript. "I slept at my post and I'll go on sleeping."[56] In March 1939, an enterprising group of men sent a detachment out on horseback every morning to work in the local wood yard. The pay that each received was then divided up, although a part was reserved, tactfully enough, for the political officers.[57]

The raw recruits of 1938 and 1939 would also learn from older generations. In 1939 the reserves were called up in preparation for campaigns in Poland, the Baltic, and Finland. These mature men, sometimes in their late thirties or early forties, arrived already smoldering with wrath. They had been forced to leave their jobs and families behind, to go back to an army most had worked hard to forget. Their resentment was seldom far below the surface. "It's worse in the army than doing forced labor on the Baikal-Amur railway," one grumbled to his mates. Some harked back to the Red Army in its democratic years, the early 1920s, when they talked to officers through clouds of cheap tobacco smoke and treated orders as the signal for a general debate. The memory rankled like a broken promise. "Red Army discipline is worse than under the old tsarist regime," the veterans complained. The young heard all of this and learned. "We'll only get leave when we're dead."[58]

★

Potential officers, the future elite of the Red Army, could hope for a better deal than this. A select group began their training while they were still at school. Others started as privates and made their way up by impressing superiors with their political convictions and practical skill. As the army grew in the 1930s, the demand for new cadets increased as well. "No calling is higher than the calling of the Workers' and Peasants' Red Army," went the Communist slogan. "No profession is more honored than the profession of commander in this army."[59] In fact, it was only after 1934 that infantry platoon commanders began to make more money than blue-collar workers in Soviet factories.[60] Only the elite could expect the trappings of power and wealth enjoyed by senior managers and politicians in the civilian world. But poor pay was no deterrent to enthusiasts. The army offered the romance of adventure, travel, and good comradeship. It did not matter if cadets came from poor peasant huts or urban apartments. As they pored over their lessons in languages, mathematics, field tactics, and history, officer trainees were embarking on solid careers.

At least, that was the hope until the end of 1936. True, the shortages and physical misery that beset their men could affect junior officers as well. It was hard enough to get things done in an army that was perennially short of greatcoats, boots, and guns. But those were irritations, and good Communists ignored them unless they were specifically working to relieve the hardships of their troops. Far more oppressive, from 1937, was the constant fear of political error. Stalin's purge of the political and military elite, which began that spring and continued through the months to come, would change officer culture for the worse. One of the highest-profile victims, after all, was Tukhachevsky, the chief of the general staff himself.[61] The charges that he and his colleagues faced included treason, so a sentence of death was inescapable. Where formerly the victims of political repression had been civilians, this time a trial had sent a shudder through the military establishment.

Tukhachevsky's arrest was the first act in a process of state-directed terror that would subordinate the army, and the defense sector in general, to new forms of political control. The upheaval would lead to changes in strategy, for Tukhachevsky's plans for defense in depth were discredited by his personal downfall, leaving the general staff to plan for an offensive war in 1941. At the time, however, the question of strategy in a hypothetical conflict seemed trivial beside the fear that blew like a whirlwind through the officer corps. Between 1937 and 1939, a little over 35,000 army officers were removed from their jobs. By 1940, 48,773 people had been purged from the Red Army and Fleet. In the last three years of peace, 90 percent of military district commanders lost their jobs to subordinates, leaving recruitment, training, supply, and the coordination of troop movements in turmoil on the very eve of war.[62] Morale, too, lay in ruins as professional soldiers struggled to save their careers.

An officer who lost his job was not necessarily imprisoned, still less shot. Even those who were arrested by the NKVD—about a third of those discharged—were sometimes reinstated, and Reese has calculated that even in the hardest year no more than 7.7 percent of the Red Army's leadership were discharged for political reasons.[63] By 1940, some 11,000 men had returned to army posts. But the purge made every officer's work more difficult. In the first place, it was clear that no one's job—or life—was guaranteed. Among the military stars of the Great Patriotic War were several men, including Konstantin Rokossovsky, the victor of Kursk and Königsberg, who had done time in prison cells and camps. From 1937 on, there was no doubt that every aspect of the army's work, including purely military matters like training and the deployment of hardware, was of interest to the party. On the eve of the German invasion, its representatives dogged every step that officers would take. The entire culture of leadership had been undermined. Instead of taking pride in responsibility, an officer was well advised to dodge the limelight and to pass the buck. Cadets learned very little about inspiring their men in field conditions. The party hacks, the *politruks*, were supposed to take care of that.

It was a classic recipe for stress. Young officers, their minds already racing with the party's teachings on responsibility and sacred trust, were given tasks that they had not been trained to execute and then, as if in mockery of their efforts, the commissars obstructed them through relentless pettifogging. The pitfalls of bureaucracy were just as terrifying, for these trainees, as the threat of a visit from the secret police. In 1939, well after the worst years of the military purge, the suicide rate among cadets and junior officers was scandalous. "Fear of responsibility" was one of the most frequent reasons distilled from their farewell notes. For those who were prone to despair, poor diet and miserable living conditions might well destroy the last reserves of their morale. One junior lieutenant had been living in an earth dugout for months by the time his nerve gave way. As a young Communist, a komsomol, he could not condemn the political system. Instead, as he put it in his final note, "I am not able to go on living this hard life. . . . I love my country and I would never betray it. I believe in an even better future, when a bright sun will shine on the whole world. But here there are enemies who sit and threaten every step an honest commander tries to take. I have decided to take my own life, even though I am but twenty-one years old."[64]

Political involvement, and purging in particular, made it harder to recruit, train, and retain new officers. The shortage of skilled specialists of every kind had reached crisis proportions by 1940. As the army expanded, reaching a total strength of over five million by the summer of 1941, its need for officers grew desperate. According to its own estimate, the officer corps was short by at least thirty-six thousand on the eve of the German invasion, and when the wartime mobilization began, this figure leapt to fifty-five thousand.[65] Translated into real lives, this meant that men and women had to fight under the leadership of youths who had no battlefield experience. But even in the 1930s, before the army had to fight, cadets were being forced out of staff colleges before they had finished their training. In 1938, Voroshilov ordered ten thousand of them to take their commissions in advance of graduation.[66] These were twenty-two-year-olds whose relations with their seniors— fathers and teachers—had been confined to following, not leading. When they had to deal with a regiment of men in their thirties, they risked becoming objects not of reverence but of contempt.

Men in the ranks were quick to spot incompetence. While the culture of purging and denunciation did a lot to damage officers' prestige, their ineptitude was fatal. The Soviet army was supposed to be comradely and open. It did not use the barking noncommissioned officers so central to the British and American systems. Instead, junior officers, backed up (or undermined) by political representatives, were charged with drill and training. The results were predictable. "If they send me to the front," remarked a young recruit as he contemplated mobilization for Finland, "I'll sneak off into the bushes. I won't fight, but I will shoot people like our unit commander Gordienko."[67] Among the most common breaches of discipline in the army before 1941 was rudeness or insubordination toward junior officers.[68]

Politics affected everything an officer might do. The *politruks* and commissars shadowed regular officers, insisting that their own concerns—class consciousness, the inculcation of Communist values— be given priority over military issues. Resistance, or even discourtesy, might cost an officer his job. The arrangement was absurd. In 1939, even Mekhlis was inspired to denounce it.[69] New regulations were introduced the following year, in the wake of the Finnish disaster, to enhance purely military authority and entice officers to stay. The condition of their quarters was one of the issues that was slated for reform. Status, the thinking went, needed the emphasis of privilege. "The company commander," as reformers put it, "should be given the tallest horse."[70] It was a step—one of many steps—that would help young officers to do their jobs. But no one suggested the most radical change, which would have been to dispense with the tangling web of politics. Each time the issue of parallel authority was raised, the answer was a compromise, a shift of emphasis that left the party's influence intact.

★

Nothing stretched the creative powers of the *politruks* more than the job of explaining the news. Looking at Soviet foreign policy in the last few months of peace, one almost feels sorry for them. Most troops were not sophisticated men, and many could not read a paper for themselves, but even a semiliterate drunk would have noticed a curious change of policy in 1939. On 23 August the Soviet foreign minister, Vyacheslav Molotov, signed a nonaggression pact with Nazi Germany. Red Army men had been forced to sit through sermons on the threat of Fascism for a decade. Now, suddenly, they were told that the Germans had become their allies. On Stalin's sixtieth birthday in December 1939, the telegrams of congratulation included one from Adolf Hitler. The Führer included his best wishes "for the happy future of the friendly people of the Soviet Union."[71]

Neither civilians nor troops knew what to think about the news of the pact. When their turn came to explain it, political staff were forced to draw upon the revolutionary rhetoric of historic progress. It was always possible to talk of international proletarian solidarity, and the German working class held a special place in Soviet imaginations, not least because its industry was so admired. But the idea of a treaty with Hitler could only be a shock. Cadets in one staff college thought the story was a spoof.[72] Elsewhere, a *politruk* simply gave up when someone asked him if the next war would be an imperialist one. "There's no point," he answered, "in counting imperialist wars. . . . When the war's over, a [party] congress will convene, and they'll tell us what type of war it was."[73] Left to themselves, the soldiers started cracking jokes based on the rhyme between German foreign minister Ribbentrop's surname and the Russian word for ass.[74]

The Red Army was also about to engage in some unusual operations. A secret clause in the Nazi-Soviet pact of August 1939 provided for the partition of Poland between Germany and the Soviet Union and also for the future division of the Baltic states of Latvia, Lithuania, and Estonia. The ink was hardly dry before the Germans invaded Poland from the west, and just over two weeks later, on 17 September, the first Soviet troops crossed into the country's eastern provinces. Germany's act of aggression prompted Britain and France to declare war on 3 September, but Poland was doomed. Warsaw fell to the Germans on 28 September, by which time the two armies, German and Soviet, had overrun the rest of the country from opposite directions. The Red Army drew up along its new boundary, confronting its ally for a prolonged interlude of uneasy cooperation. Its soldiers became an occupation force, assuming the part of liberators while daily confronting the hatred of the population among which they were stationed. The experience would be repeated the following June, when the Soviets continued their advance northwards to the Baltic, adding several million more unwilling citizens to Stalin's western empire.

In 1939, Stalin's priority was to establish a secure new border before the Wehrmacht managed to alter the map a second time. Red Army troops along the new front line engaged in a token show of comradeship with equally skeptical German counterparts. Prisoners were exchanged. Behind the new border, soldiers were detailed to go from house to house in search of hidden weapons. "Diversionary bands" of Polish nationalists, the remains of the Polish army, were rounded up, as were any outspoken or respected members of local communities.[75] Tens of thousands of Polish soldiers, including reservists who had been called up only weeks before, were interned in prison camps. On Stalin's orders, more than twenty thousand of these would be murdered between March and May 1940. The execution of four thousand Polish officers in the forests near Katyn, to the west of Smolensk, was carried out by secret police, as were parallel shootings near Kharkov and Tver. The murders were covert, though local people heard volleys of gunfire for hours, night after night. But while they were kept ignorant of specific events, regular soldiers knew that the state that they represented, and whose policy they were enforcing every day, was not offering deliverance to fraternal peoples.

Stalin's military advisers had considered the most likely problems in advance. The troops detailed for Poland and the Baltic were given special lectures. They were told that their efforts would bring security and happiness to the people of the new territories. But they were also left in no doubt that the new border would protect their own homelands and safety. The troops who went into the Baltic states of Latvia, Lithuania, and Estonia were handpicked, "politically reliable, . . . provided with the best food, weapons, and ammunition."[76] "I am proud," one of these heroes said, "that I have been granted the honor of standing in the front line of the defense of our motherland." Meanwhile, the propagandists wove stories with happy endings for readers to celebrate. "The working people of western Ukraine and western Belorussia have greeted the Red Army with great joy and love," a report to the troops related. "The progress of units of the Red Army unfolds like a people's festival. The inhabitants of the towns and villages, as a rule, come out to greet them in an organized way and dressed in their best clothes. They throw flowers in front of the advancing soldiers. . . . 'Thank you, dear comrades,'" they were alleged to have said. "'Thank you, Stalin. We have been waiting for you and now you have come.'"[77]

The liberation was not entirely a charade. Some people, and especially the region's Jews, had good reason to prefer Soviet to Nazi rule. But even they would soon find that the Red Army was not the selfless sword of revolution that it pretended to be. To soldiers from the Soviet Union, European towns like Lvov and Grodno were a consumerist paradise. Life was suddenly pleasant again, even if few soldiers could afford to join the locals for a beer or a long night of jazz. "They sit for hours," one envious Soviet officer wrote home, "nursing a beer and smoking cigarettes."[78] To prevent breaches of the law, the army had issued the soldiers involved in the occupation a small allowance in cash. But there was just too much to spend it on. If the locals would not sell their goods for kopecks, the troops used threats to get the things they saw. They plundered simple cottages in search of loot. Favorite items included watches and pens, but even wooden doorknobs enjoyed a brief vogue.[79] Some veterans remember to this day how men from the Baltic occupying force sent clothes and money to their wives at home; for them, the borderlands were full of treasure. When an infantryman was arrested for buying a collection of anti-Soviet jokes in a Latvian bookshop he was overheard remarking that the capitalists knew how to live.[80]

Regular Red Army men were relatively benign as an occupation force. Worse was to come in the new provinces. To harmonize the new regions with the rest of Soviet territory, the NKVD was sent in to collectivize all private farms. Protesters, the latest crop of kulaks, were arrested and deported on goods trains heading east. At the same time, amid the turmoil of a social revolution and a coming war, the military soviets arrived to start recruiting men. The army's need for soldiers had become insatiable, and the new populations—above all those in frontier states—were obliged to contribute their quota like everyone else. Some politicians also hoped that military service would turn the sons of capitalist families into upstanding Soviet citizens. Either way, recruitment was an urgent matter, demanding quick and decisive work. The fact that the new soldiers would disrupt the culture and morale of serving troops was not considered until far too late.

From 1940, thousands of nineteen-year-olds from the former Polish territories of Ukraine and Belorussia joined units in the Kiev, Leningrad, and Bryansk military districts. In recognition of their likely impact, they were deployed in small groups of fifteen or so per company.[81] Their command of the Russian language was a problem, for many spoke and wrote only Ukrainian or Polish. But it was not comprehension that made them difficult to teach. Unlike the young men whose minds had been formed under Soviet power, these people came with recent memories of a very different world. Even the ones who felt grateful for Soviet protection against Germany—for few believed that Stalin's pact would last—brought with them doubts about the newly formed collective farms. They all had questions about politics. Some had witnessed the mass arrests of "enemies" that followed Soviet occupation, for NKVD troops were never far from the front line.[82] And some, joining the army of a state that propagated atheism, nurtured a deeply held religious faith.

The commissars were overwhelmed. "A significant number of them are religious," they reported. "Some wear crosses that they refuse to remove even in the *banya*."[83] One officer discovered that some of his newest men began "their letters home with the words *Long live Jesus Christ*. One soldier received an icon in the mail from his mother in front of which, before going to sleep, he prays."[84] Youths like these came from villages where the faithful held vigils in church at Easter. Some had neighbors whose religious beliefs forbade them even to bear arms.[85] It was a mistake, the *politruks'* bosses advised, to forget that these new men were politically untested and possibly even hostile to the Soviet regime. They might even harbor nationalist dreams. In the clumsy, eerily Orwellian language of the time, one note warned that new conscripts "not rarely not only show unhealthy states of mind, complaining about the severity of discipline and the hardship of serving in the Red Army, but in some places are trying to form separatist groups."[86]

Such men may well have been behind the graffiti that often turned up on the walls of barracks in these final years of peace. Humor, not religion, was probably the most serious challenge to the *politruks'* authority. Graffiti of all kinds—"uncensored words," as the informers put it—was getting bolder everywhere. Busts of Lenin and Stalin—one of which was given goggling, froggy eyes by an anonymous hand—were sitting targets, as were political posters. Some *politruks* were tempted to give up. "There is no political work in this unit," a report scolded, and it turned out that the men had stopped even expecting it. As a recruit—a Russian this time—in a communications unit put it in March 1939, "The fascists have not done a thing to me; I see no point in fighting them. From my point of view, it makes no difference if we have Fascist or Soviet power. It would be better to die or run away than to fight for the motherland."[87]

★

This was the army that mustered to fight the Finnish war. It was not the monolith of later Soviet myth. Instead, it was a piece of work in progress, an assemblage whose military readiness was still under construction. The lines of men who stood before their *politruks* to hear their marching orders in November 1939 included fathers as well as sons. The older men had memories of tsarism and its last war; the young, heads full of cant, had little but their energy. They knew, in theory, why they were being asked to fight. The story was that Finnish Fascists had been threatening the border of the Soviet motherland. Like soldiers in the propaganda films, Red Army troops had to repel them fast. It would be a quick and easy task, or that, at least, was the story they were told. Those who believed it may have hoped that someone else would do the fighting for them. If victory were truly guaranteed, no individual would need to run much risk, after all, and history alone would ensure that justice prevailed. Meanwhile, there was a chance of travel and of duty done, or, failing those, a Finnish wristwatch and some decent booze. Whatever the men's hopes, however, the weather was turning colder. The boots and greatcoats they had brought would not stand up to a long war.

"The political-moral condition of the troops is generally good," the *politruks* wrote for their masters' benefit. It was their job to take care of morale in wartime. But what that meant, in the Soviet army, was very different from contemporary British or American notions of military psychology. The *politruks* were not concerned with individual minds: the burden was on the soldier to prove himself worthy of military life. If he showed cowardice or doubt, he was a betrayer of the motherland, a disappointment to its revolution. His individual rights and interests were unimportant. All that a *politruk* needed to do, on this model, was to make sure the men knew that theirs was a just cause. Soldiers who understood and truly believed in their task would need no further help because they would know that they were doing what their society—and the future of the proletarian revolution—required them to do.[88] There was no place in this regime for ego. The indicators of a healthy political-moral situation were not cheerfulness or individual mental health but the number of applicants for party membership, the willingness of men to volunteer for dangerous work, and the overall level of conformity with collective norms.

These ideas were neither strange nor alien to the young men whose job it was to fight in Finland. Soviet troops were not Americans, and to varying extents the ideas of the party had become their own—even if they joked about them. There were some who had no dearer wish than to defend the Soviet motherland. Their heroes were the airmen and explorers of the 1930s, their dream to be as skillful and as brave themselves. There were others, too, caught up in the enthusiasm of the times, who saw themselves as vanguard Communists, the heirs, perhaps, of the civil war fighters they had heard about in school. Such men might "beg" to serve on the front line. "I want to go into battle for the motherland

and Stalin," one soldier wrote, perhaps taking dictation from a *politruk*. He added, as many did, a formal request to join the party. "I will fight in the party spirit, as a Bolshevik."[89]

It was as if the movies had come to life. Twenty years after the Red Army's first campaigns, its troops had little idea of battle beyond the stock images of manliness, heroism, and self-sacrifice. The real demands of modern war, including calculated tactics, self-restraint, and a facility with sophisticated weapons, would have looked almost tawdry to this generation. It was reported with pride, for instance, that "the deputy political officer of the Fifth Battalion of the 147th Rifles led his men into an attack shouting, 'For the motherland and Stalin!'" He was among the first to catch a Finnish bullet.[90] Komsomols in another regiment mounted a spate of pointless raids in celebration of Stalin's birthday on 21 December. Still others pledged themselves always to complete training classes with full marks, as if any other outcome were desirable.

Good comradeship, the formation of what the sociologists who study other armies have described as "primary groups" among the soldiers, would have been a better way to improve both discipline and coordination.[91] A stronger sense of loyalty between the men would have built stronger trust. But close relationships between soldiers were not encouraged. They might be a sign of deviance, the spies worried—conspiracies in embryo. Thirteen of the forty-six rifle divisions that the Red Army fielded in Finland had been formed for less than a year by the winter of 1939–40.[92] The others tended, as was the policy at the time, to have been brought up to strength—peopled with strangers—in the last weeks before their mobilization for the front.[93] In place of long-established trust, the *politruks* nurtured these people's party spirit or, worse, a fabricated "friendliness." "The soldiers, commanders, and political workers in our regiment show courage, heroism, and a willingness to give one another friendly help during battle," ran one of their reports.[94] "Friendliness" of this kind was no substitute for professionalism, let alone mutual trust. These men had not trained together. "Friendly," perhaps, described the spirit of an artillery division that fired without orders near the Finnish village of Makela "to help the infantry keep its spirits up."[95] The next stage in that battle was mass panic.

Party spirit was no help when the men were afraid, either. Soviet soldiers in Finland were unprepared for the battlefields that their own weapons would create. Even their officers had no idea of the coordination that would be necessary to make use of infantry, big guns, and tanks.[96] Without a basic understanding of their role, soldiers found battles incomprehensible and terrifying. Some were frightened of their own shadows. An infantryman in the Seventh Army caused havoc one morning when he shrieked so loudly that his whole battalion took fright. He explained later that he had glimpsed his own face in a mirror and taken it for a Finnish sniper's. His scream disturbed the nearby signals unit, whose men started firing wildly, without orders, wasting precious bullets in the air. Not far away, members of the railway guard corps also heard the noise and joined in with more shooting of their own.[97] Belatedly, even desperately, political officers tried to instill some sense of fighting spirit in their men. Their priority, they agreed, should henceforth be field training, but the memoranda they wrote on the subject make pathetic reading. "It is too late and almost impossible to organize party-political work during battle itself," a senior commissar explained. Among the things that it was "too late" to tell soldiers who were in the field, he said, was how to lie down when the Finnish gunners opened fire.[98]

"They told us that the Red Army would smash the White Finns with a lightning strike," men started to complain by the new year, "but the end of the war is not in sight." They had come up against the Mannerheim Line, the Finnish bunkers that Soviet reconnaissance had overlooked. If they had been afraid before, their mood was closer now to sheer despair. The party's tale of easy victory had turned out to be false. "We're going to find these bunkers everywhere. We cannot even collect our injured and dead. The infantry cannot overcome emplacements like these."[99] A new brochure, *Three Weeks of Fighting the White Finns*, was hastily assembled, along with the more practical *Specific Problems of This War and How to Improve Our Effort*.[100] But the basic Soviet tactic did not change. Red Army troops were supposed only to attack. That approach suited the Finns, whose machine gunners slaughtered Soviet soldiers almost at their leisure. It helped that some senior Soviet officers regarded the use of camouflage as a sign of cowardice.[101]

The poor conditions played on everybody's nerves. Even in the first week of the war, the infantry suffered dozens of cases of frostbite. By the end of December 1939, the reported figure, which included only the men whose ability to fight was seriously impaired, had increased to 5,725.[102] At the same time, officers were reporting shortages of *valenki* (the traditional Russian felt boots), fur hats, footcloths, and winter jackets. To make matters worse, sometimes there was no hot food, not even tea, for days.[103] The temperature had plunged to an exceptional low for early winter, well below minus twenty degrees Fahrenheit, and many soldiers had come straight from the milder climate of Ukraine. But the cold should have been easy to predict. Karelia had been a province of the Russian empire back in tsarist times; conditions there were part of recent, living memory.

The men began deserting in the hundreds. Sometimes they simply walked away, taking advantage of what looked like mere confusion to find a fire and warm themselves, steal the supplies, or simply disappear.[104] One infantryman "surrendered" to the Finns on behalf of two entire battalions.[105] Not merely individuals, and not only private soldiers, but whole regiments abandoned their posts in this way. Sometimes they left their heavier weapons behind, allowing the Finns to help themselves to field guns, ammunition, and rifles. Deserters could escape unnoticed because no one knew who was responsible for whom. At the same time, the chaos all along the line gave men a chance to get their hands on any loot they found. One man stole bicycles to sell when he got home. Others preferred to stock up on thick winter gear. A *politruk* was caught with two leather coats, four suits, shoes, and a suitcase full of stolen children's clothes.[106]

Stalin's generals, as was their custom, adopted savage measures to bring their ragtag army into line. That winter, orders were given to shoot stragglers and deserters. According to its own figures, eleven deserters from the Eighth Army had been shot by early January.[107] Meanwhile, other soldiers had begun to shoot themselves. Cases of *samostrel*, self-inflicted wounds, increased alarmingly in the new year. There was not much else that desperate men could do. *Zagradotryady*—another new word for the Soviet lexicon—referred to the troops whose job it was to stand behind the lines and pick off any man who tried to run away. Unlike the regulars, they had machine guns for the job. The officers, however, faced NKVD firing squads. In January 1940 a string of tribunals sentenced scores of them to death for cowardice and failure. By the war's end that March, even the Soviet high command had begun to wonder if there might not be a better way to organize a war. Perhaps, one of their memoranda carefully suggested, "the highest form of punishment is being overused."[108]

A survivor of the Winter War, as the Finnish conflict was called, recalled the "dull apathy and indifference toward impending doom" that pushed men ahead when there was no alternative but death.[109] It was a far cry from quick victory and party spirit. Back in Moscow, reformers read of the "negative effect" that the men experienced when they found the frozen bodies of earlier waves of soldiers pushing out of shallow graves along the ice roads heading north. Tales of catastrophe pervaded the barracks where fresh soldiers were waiting for their battle orders. "I'm not going to Finland," a conscript in Kharkov told his *politruk*. "Two of my brothers are there and that's enough."[110] Shocked by the gulf between their expectations and the real war, Stalin's generals gathered in Moscow to consider a program of reforms. There was almost no time for thought. As these gentlemen pored over plans, the Germans were preparing an attack on France whose devastating swiftness would put an end to any hope of peace along the eastern front.

THREE

DISASTER BEATS ITS WINGS

★

June is a special month all over northern Europe. In European Russia and Ukraine, it is magical. Winter's bitter dark and ice are barely even memories, spring's mud and rain forgiven. Kiev's famous chestnut trees come into bloom, and so do Moscow's lilacs, Yalta's Judas trees. It is the month of the peony and the green willow, the month, in the north, of the white nights. Midsummer night fell on a Saturday in 1941. In Sevastopol, the home of the Soviet Union's Black Sea Fleet, it was, as naval officer Evseev remarked in his diary, "a wonderful Crimean evening." That Saturday, "all the streets and boulevards in the city were lit. The white houses were bathed in light, the clubs and theaters beckoned the sailors on shore leave to come inside. There were crowds of sailors and local people, dressed in white, packing the city's streets and parks. As always, the famous Primorskii boulevard was full of people out for a stroll. Music was playing. There were jokes and happy laughter everywhere on the evening before the holiday."[1] A week earlier, the Soviet foreign minister, Vyacheslav Molotov, had insisted that rumors of Germany's intention to break its pact with Moscow and launch an attack on the Soviet Union were completely without foundation.[2] The temptation to believe him must have been overwhelming.

One source of all the light across the city's twin harbors that night was the Upper Inkerman lighthouse. With its help, the German planes could navigate their way unerringly toward the port.[3] They came from the east, flying low out of the steppe, their route a great arc across Soviet space. They knew their targets in advance: the fleet, the warehouses, the antiaircraft guns. Soon the Black Sea reflected new lights from the shore: incandescent trails and flares, searchlights, the evil glow of a landscape on fire. "Are those planes ours?" someone asked Evseev as the sailors scrambled into boats to get back to their ships. "It must be another exercise." But his neighbor had been taking careful stock. "Our antiaircraft batteries are firing live rounds," he said. "And those bombs don't look at all like dummies." "So we're at war, then?" said a third. "But with whom?"[4]

Hundreds of miles to the north, along the new border in formerly Polish land, Red Army men were winding down for their free day on Sunday. Those who could get local leave had gone off to town, to cosmopolitan Lvov or Minsk, to get a decent meal and forget their worries. Colonel General D. G. Pavlov, the commander in chief of the western special military district, was at the theater. A comedy called *The Wedding at Malinovka* was playing to a full house at the officers' club in the Belorussian capital.[5] The good commander did not allow his enjoyment of the play to be disrupted by the news, brought by his intelligence chief, Colonel Blokhin, that German troops along the border appeared to be preparing for action. There were even some reports, Blokhin whispered, of shelling. "It can't be true," Pavlov replied, and pointed to the stage. It was time to get back to the play.[6] The whole army, in fact, was under orders to keep calm. Kamenshchikov, an officer in the western air defense force, was accompanied to the theater that night by his wife, son, and father, who had come up from their home in Stalingrad that week for a short summer break.[7] The four of them also watched the play through to the end and then returned to Kamenshchikov's quarters for supper and bed.

At nine o'clock that evening, while Pavlov was still at the play, a German sapper called Alfred Liskow stole across the Soviet lines.

Liskow was one of the few German internationalists whom Soviet troops would ever meet. Before his call-up in 1939, he had worked in a furniture factory in the Bavarian town of Kolberg, which is where he had become acquainted with the works of Marx and Lenin. That night he came to warn his proletarian brothers of their imminent danger. He told his Soviet captors that German artillery units along the border had orders to start shelling targets on the Soviet side within the next few hours. At first light, he continued, "rafts, boats, and pontoons" would be thrown across the Bug, the marshy river that divided German-occupied Poland from the Soviet sector to the east.[8] The attack on the Soviet Union was poised to begin with devastating force. Information of the same kind was relayed by deserters elsewhere on the land frontier. It was not news to the political leadership in Moscow. British and even Soviet intelligence had been warning of this plan for weeks. But Stalin had chosen to ignore the tales, and border troops had made no preparation for an imminent attack. As far as they were concerned, the deserters that night looked like provocateurs. One, a German from Berlin, was shot on that basis. Liskow himself was still under interrogation when mortars started ripping through the dark.[9]

It was Kamenshchikov's wife who woke him. Perhaps it was her inexperience, she said, but she had never heard so many planes flying above a town at night. Her husband assured her that what she was hearing were maneuvers. There had been lots of exercises lately. All the same he threw a coat over his shoulders and stepped outside to take a closer look. He knew at once that this was real war. The very air was different: humming, shattered, thick with sour black smoke. The town's main railway line was picked out by a rope of flame. Even the horizon had begun to redden, but its glow, to the west, was not the approaching dawn. Acting without orders, Kamenshchikov went to the airfield and took a plane up to meet the invaders at once, which is why, exceptionally among the hundreds of machines that were parked in neat formations as usual that night, his was brought down over the Bialystok marshes, and not destroyed on the ground.[10] By midday on 22 June, the Soviets had lost 1,200 planes. In Kamenshchikov's own western district alone, 528 had been blown up like fairground targets by the German guns.[11]

Unlike Kamenshchikov, Colonel General Pavlov had never even gone to bed. There had been an awkward briefing with a few staff officers straight after the play, and then, at one in the morning, he had been called to front headquarters for a telephone conversation. The man at the other end of the line in Moscow was the Soviet defense commissar, Semen Konstantinovich Timoshenko.[12] He was calling to check the situation of the border troops. "Well," he began, "how is it where you are? Quiet?" Pavlov replied that there had been considerable German activity at the front line, including a buildup of motorcycle regiments and special forces. "Just try to worry less and don't panic," Timoshenko replied. "Get the staff together anyway this morning, because something unpleasant may happen perhaps, but don't rise to any provocation. If there is a specific provocation, call me."[13]

Pavlov later recollected that he spent the next two hours with his senior officers. One by one they reported on their troops, on the dismal problem of supplies, and on their lack of readiness for battle. Some units had been dispersed on exercises, others needed stocks of fuel or ammunition, and all were more or less paralyzed by inadequate or poorly organized transport. The railways were still running on peacetime schedules, and almost every front-line regiment was short of motor vehicles. The army could not even requisition trucks, for there were almost no civilian cars in Stalin's Soviet Union. Pavlov and his men were still busy with these questions at 3:30 a.m., the moment scheduled for the German land assault. Coincidentally, it was also the time when Timoshenko called again. "He asked me what was new," Pavlov recalled. "I told him that the situation had not changed."[14] By then, a dozen cities in the borderlands had been engulfed in flames.

The Luftwaffe had flown high into Soviet territory earlier that night. At dawn they swept westward to bomb a string of strategic cities, including Bialystok, Kiev, Brest, Grodno, Rovno, and Kovno, as well as the Baltic ports of Tallinn and Riga. The land attack, the first phase in Germany's Operation Barbarossa, the planned conquest of Slavic land, began just as the eastern sky began to lighten. At 3:15 on 22 June, the Soviet border guards in charge of the bridge over the river Bug at Koden were summoned by their German counterparts to discuss "important matters." When they obediently appeared, they were machine-gunned by the advance guard of a German assault party. Arriving at the railway bridge at Brest, German sappers tore the crude explosives from its central pier and waved their men across.[15] By 5:30 Moscow time, which was when the German ambassador, von der Schulenburg, delivered his declaration of war to Molotov, Pavlov's command was under attack from thirteen infantry and five tank divisions, together with artillery and airborne cover.

Shock led to misreporting and confusion. Grodno was under such heavy air attack that the commander of the Soviet Third Army, V. I. Kuznetsov, had barricaded himself in a basement well before first light. But other messages talked of calm for a few hours more and even, in the case of Golubev's Tenth Army, of a successful repulsion of the German troops. By 7:00 o'clock, some officers were starting to report that they had lost contact with their men, that whole units had simply disappeared. As Pavlov would later tell his interrogators, "Kuznetsov informed me, with a tremble in his throat, that the only thing that was left of the Fifty-sixth Rifle Division was its number."[16] The men may have been dead or captured, or, like those of the Eighty-fifth Rifle Division, they may simply have fled south. Radio and telephone links were broken, messages and orders were not getting through. The answer was to send a trusted deputy to take control. That morning, Pavlov assigned Lieutenant General Ivan Vasilevich Boldin to the Tenth Army's headquarters in the border town of Bialystok. He was to fly there straight away from Minsk.

Whatever doubts Boldin may have had, he learned the truth that afternoon. His light aircraft came under German fire before he even reached the border, and when he landed on a dirt strip outside Bialystok someone told him that parachutists had been sighted coming down nearby. The atmosphere, as he recalled later, was "incredibly hot and the air smelt of burning." His main feeling, as he climbed into the one truck that the army had been able to requisition, was one of shock, of helplessness. The truck made slow progress through the bewildered lines of refugees. Most people were on foot, heading anywhere to get away from the noise and searing flames, but then came a small motorcade, led by a smart new ZIS–101. "The broad leaves of an aspidistra were protruding from one of the windows," Boldin observed. "It was the car of some local top official. Inside were two women and two children." Boldin looked at the group with undisguised disgust, suggesting tartly that they might have ditched the plant to make space for another human being. But as the women turned away in shame, a plane dipped low above the road and there were three cracks of machine-gun fire. Boldin managed to jump aside in time, although his driver was killed. In the ZIS–101 the women, the children, and the driver were all dead. As Boldin recollected, "Only the evergreen leaves of the aspidistra were still sticking out of the window."[17]

It would be evening before Boldin made contact with the Tenth Army. Like the frightened refugees, the troops had fled Bialystok that very day. The army's new headquarters were in the birch woods to the east and consisted of two tents with a table and chairs. A shaken General Golubev told Boldin that all his divisions had sustained terrible losses. His light tanks, elderly T–26s, had proved themselves good "only for firing at sparrows." The Luftwaffe had targeted the army's fuel dumps, aircraft, and antiaircraft guns. His men, he said, were fighting "like heroes," but they were powerless against an enemy like this. The Tenth Army, effectively, had been wiped out.[18]

The news was reported to Minsk as soon as a radio could be made to work. Pavlov would also learn that night that the Third Army had abandoned Grodno. Reports from Brest suggested that this city, too, was not likely to hold. The Germans had known exactly where to target their artillery and air strikes, beginning with the army's command centers and then aiming for railways and factories.[19] Pavlov responded with a stream of orders that read like a propaganda script. This was the Red Army, and it was not meant to retreat. Accordingly, the general ordered men he could not see or even contact to mount a bold counterattack. The aim, as ever, was to push the Germans back behind the frontier and defeat them on their own soil.[20] Weeks later, with his life in the balance, Pavlov would tell his interrogators that he was still thinking strategically at that stage, confident that Brest could be held and the tide of attack turned. But Boldin, who was ordered to mount an offensive on 23 June with forces that were either dead or hopelessly dispersed, considered that Pavlov was merely covering his back. He was rapping out the orders, Boldin thought, just to show Moscow that something was really being done. The culture of the purge, of empty gestures, lies, and fear, was still alive and well.

It was to Boldin's credit that he tried to organize the remnants of the Tenth Army to fight on 23 June. Within a few hours, their supplies of fuel and ammunition ran out. The two planes that they sent to Minsk begging for help were soon shot down. Like thousands of other Soviet troops, they were trapped in the spur of Soviet territory that would become famous as the Bialystok pocket, surrounded by German forces and cut off from their comrades and supplies. Boldin was lucky. He headed east toward Smolensk with a ragtag following of uniformed refugees. After nearly seven weeks of retreat and sporadic fighting in the woods, the general and 1,654 of his men were reunited with the main Red Army.[21] Pavlov, meanwhile, had been arrested, questioned, scapegoated for cowardice, and shot. Eight other senior officers, all of whom had been equally helpless in the face of Germany's attack that June, died with him. As the State Defense Committee noted on 16 July, the men were considered guilty of "lack of resolve, panic mongering, disgraceful cowardice, . . . and fleeing in terror in the face of an impudent enemy."[22] Failure in this war, whatever its cause, would be blamed on the moral bankruptcy of individuals like these. No one would mention the war plans that had no chance of succeeding, the untrained armies, or the breakdown of morale. They would not point out, either, that this was a war, at first, that Stalin had not permitted anyone to fight.

David Samoilov, the poet and future front-line soldier, described the shock everyone felt in those few days. "We were all expecting war," he wrote later. "But we were not expecting *that* war." As the fortress city of Brest began to burn and the garrison in charge of nearby Kobrin fled into the Pripet Marshes, the people of Moscow, more than a day's train ride to the east, relied on little more than rumor. The news did not become official till just after noon on the twenty-second. In those days, important radio announcements were broadcast in the public squares. Soon, indeed, the possession of a radio for private use would be outlawed altogether.[23] So people heard the news that Sunday as a crowd, standing in the midday sunshine with their faces turned toward the tin throats of loudspeakers. "Today, at four o'clock," the voice of their foreign minister, Molotov, announced, "without any declaration of war, and without any claims being made on the Soviet Union, German troops attacked our country." It was an outrage, but the speaker did not reveal the full scale of the disaster. The crowds were told that there were now "more than two hundred dead." It would be many years before they learned how great an understatement that had been. But the essence of the message was clear. "The government calls on you, men and women citizens of the Soviet Union, to rally even more closely around the glorious Bolshevik Party," Molotov went on, "around the Soviet government and our great leader, Comrade Stalin. Our cause is just. The enemy will be smashed. Victory will be ours."[24]

Every account of the war goes on to talk about the surge of patriotism that these words produced. War veterans remember their proud indignation still. "I was a boy, fifteen years old," one told me. "I had lived my whole life in a Siberian village. I'd never even seen Moscow. But still it came from somewhere, that patriotism. I knew that I would volunteer straightaway."[25] In every city in the land the would-be heroes stepped forward to fight. The scenes, again, were reminiscent of an epic film. The war that volunteers imagined they would have to wage was an illusion, too. The men's words, certainly, read like a 1930s script. "I lived through German rule in the Ukraine in 1918 and 1919," a gnarled collective farmer from Kursk province told the crowd. "We will not work for landlords and noblemen. We'll drive that bloodstained Hitler out bag and baggage. I declare myself mobilized and ask to be sent to the front to destroy the German bandits."[26] "The workers feel a profound patriotism," a secret police report agreed. "There have been significant numbers of applications to join the army from young people from the cities and the farms."[27] But the state did not leave anything to chance. Extra officers were drafted into the secret police that very night, and suspected counterrevolutionaries, including hundreds of foreign nationals, were arrested at once.[28]

The tight security was justified, for Stalin's people had cause to be angry and to demand facts. In his announcement, Molotov had reminded them that just a few hours earlier Germany had been the Soviet Union's ally in a pact "the terms of which were scrupulously observed by the Soviet Union." It was a deal with Fascism that the Soviet people had been suspicious of for two years. Now came the news of unprovoked attack. The natural response, apart from shock, was skepticism. Veterans of the civil war remembered the daily reports and public debates of that time and complained that they were getting no hard news. Many assumed—correctly—that the truth was much blacker than they were permitted to know.[29] Other people, dazzled by the prewar myth, believed the rumors that Germany was in retreat, that Warsaw had already fallen, that Ribbentrop had shot himself, and that the Red Army was heading for Berlin.[30] The fictions blossomed around the silence of one man. Stalin himself did not address the people until 3 July.

The truth about the people's mood in that first week is still hard to separate from the web of propaganda. No one, not even the NKVD, could measure the relative strengths of patriotism and panic, anger and mistrust. No one could predict what the crowds would do. One fear, that there would be a run on stocks of food and fuel, proved accurate. Police agents were posted around the capital to prevent looting. One of them remembered his watch on a macaroni factory in the Sokolniki district, a three-day vigil that ended in a violent confrontation with local people, including his own cousin. "I told him that I would shoot if he did not leave," the old policeman said. "I can still remember the look in his eyes. It was necessary and it was my job. I would have shot him without hesitating."[31] The country might have dissolved into civil war. But most reports from the first night described relative calm. Rubbing their eyes as the dawn broke, police informers scribbled down the good news first. Perhaps they even believed it.

On 24 June two state security officers in Moscow submitted a summary of the popular mood in the capital to their superior, counterintelligence chief V. S. Abakumov. In general, they noted, the city's working people had responded admirably, offering to work extra shifts and volunteering to train for civil defense. "We will put up with any hardships," one man declared, "to help our Red Army ensure that the Soviet people utterly destroys the Fascists." "We must be firmly organized and observe the strictest steadfastness and discipline," another pronounced. "Our indignation has no limits," affirmed a print worker. "Hitler has violated the sacred borders of the first socialist country in the world. . . .

We will win because there is no power in the world that can vanquish a people who have risen up in patriotic war."[32] The same reactions were recorded in provincial centers, including the city of Kursk. The Communist Party there called an emergency meeting at midnight on 22 June. Unusually, its report recorded, the members all showed up on time. "The feeling of unlimited love for their motherland, for the party, and for Stalin and the people's deep outrage and hatred of bestial Fascism were reflected in every speech the members made."[33]

This was the most important theme for everyone that June. The patriotic declarations read like excerpts from a script, but the emotions that lay behind them were powerful and real. Twenty years of meretricious talk, of Communist jargon, had furnished Soviet patriots with an impressive stock of wooden phrases. The younger generation knew no other language for this kind of thing. At the moment of greatest shock, it was natural that people would fall back on the sentences they had been trained to use, the notions of Stalinist collectivism and service. The crisis of the next few months would test the credibility of the official line. But it would also show how many people were prepared to risk their lives, to die, for their country and its future. "Anti-Soviet behavior," wrote Moscow's Comrade Zhigalov after his visit to the city's Paris Commune factory on 26 June, "is nonexistent."[34]

If Zhigalov had stepped outside the party cells and strongholds of the ethnic Russian working class, however, he might have filed a different report. In Moscow, the secret police were particularly interested in the views of citizens with German names. "Soviet power wasn't elected by the will of the people," a Muscovite named Kyun observed. "And now the people will have their say." "The peasants will greet the news of the war with joy," a woman called Mauritz allegedly remarked. "It will free them from the Bolsheviks and the collective farms they hate so much. Russia may be strong, but it isn't a problem for Germany."[35] These comments were recorded partly as a prelude to that night's arrests, but they were not uncommon anywhere. Beyond the cities such talk was likely to be overheard among older people, especially those who resented not just the collective farms but godlessness as well.[36] And then there was the problem of hostility to Russian rule itself. There were good Communists in every republic of the Soviet Union, and there were enemies of Fascism, too, and patriots who could not tolerate invasion. But although volunteers came forward almost everywhere to fight, there were also some who held back, quietly considering the possibilities that the turn of events might bring. Even in remoter places, such as Georgia, that were not under immediate threat, there was a sense that Moscow's crisis might, perhaps, prove to be someone else's opportunity.[37]

Meanwhile, the loyal Soviet masses threw themselves into a surge of volunteering. In Kursk province, 7,200 people applied for front-line military service in the first month of hostilities.[38] In Moscow, where recruitment centers were jammed around the clock, more than 3,500 applications were received in the first thirty-six hours.[39] People attended crisis meetings at their factories, they heard the patriotic speeches as a group, and then, also in groups, they trooped off to local recruiting stations, like boy scouts, to volunteer. The eager patriots were not exclusively male. Women—the reports always call them girls—also appeared, also in groups. They made a strange impression as potential troops. "They looked at my manicure and my little hat," a woman veteran recalled. "They said they wouldn't last if I was going to the front." Such women were sometimes accepted for training, often as nurses, but most were talked into enrolling as blood donors and staying at home.[40] Either way, the whole process took place in an atmosphere of trance. Few of the early volunteers had much idea what they were signing up to do.

People who did were often cynical. Onlookers with direct experience of army life doubted that public fervor would change anything on the front line. "Our leaders seem to think they'll conquer the German people through agitation," a veteran of the tsarist army remarked. "But it won't work at all. There's a lot of discontent in the Red Army."[41] Reservists could be doubtful about taking up arms again. That June, there were reports of suicide among young people eligible for service at the front, and several cases of deliberate self-mutilation were recorded by Moscow's police.[42] As the initial shock of Molotov's announcement faded, too, the patriotic trance began to lose its grip. "I'll only volunteer for mobilization when they mobilize everyone," a komsomol in Kursk was heard deciding with his friends. A rumor had just reached him that Kiev and Minsk were under fire. Though this was true, no one was supposed to believe it. The official disclaimers led cynics to despair. Clerks in government offices could be paralyzed by fear, while many more, re-signedly awaiting the arrival of the German troops, stayed home and found solace in a haze of drink.[43]

The trance soon faded for the new recruits as well. The Red Army had not changed overnight, and nor had its recruitment and supply structures. Prewar contingency plans for mobilization had allowed three days for organizing the call-up of those eligible for immediate front-line service. In the panic that midsummer, these guidelines were scrapped, and the Supreme Soviet ordered the process to be completed in twenty-four hours. The ensuing chaos would last until the following spring.[44] More immediately, the mass movement of troops became acutely dangerous in the front-line regions, up to 200 kilometers into Soviet territory, that the Luftwaffe already controlled. "The normal mobilization of remaining soldiers . . . was impossible," a report on the Eighth Army, based in the northwest, noted, "because most of the border divisions had lost their mobilization bases."[45]

Safe for a while behind the lines that summer afternoon, the volunteers of Moscow also found the army unprepared. Photographs of the recruitment process show crowds of young men and women pressed together around a junior officer's desk, waving their passports and pushing their mates aside like shoppers on the first day of a sale. The propaganda image suggests young men squaring off for immediate combat, as if they were ready to grab the nearest German by the scruff and throw him out of Russia straightaway. The truth was that raw volunteers—unlike reservists—would need to be assessed, equipped, and trained for some weeks before they faced their first Fascist. Their experience that day, after the first moments of glory and resolve, was usually prosaic. The officer in charge gave them a glance to weed the hopeless cases from the healthy young. Then came a quick check of their documents and then, for those who made the grade, a long wait. At this stage, as the veterans attest, there were not even medical examinations.

There were no barracks, food, or transport, either. Most recruitment stations were set up in local schools. When the suitable applicants had been selected and their papers stamped, they were in the army. They were no longer free. But there was nowhere warm or dry for them to go, and the authorities had not thought to provide food or entertainment while they waited. In Moscow they crowded into classrooms, they spilled into the streets, and they gathered on the platforms of the Belorussian station as if they hoped for trains to take them to the front. By the time the party's reporter arrived at the station to check on this group most had been there for several days. There were no beds, so they slept on the ground. Some had brought bread or biscuits with them, others had nothing at all to eat, but somehow they had all found a supply of vodka.[46] Reservists from the capital fared no better. The city was thronged with groups of men, several hundred at a time, just sitting waiting, talking, drinking, and reflecting on their fate. "A good many volunteers have a drunken appearance," the police primly observed.[47] It was traditional, of course, but this was war.

In places nearer to the front the new recruits waited less long, drank less vodka, and indulged their illusions not at all. Misha Volkov worked in Kiev's fast-growing metal industry. A married man with a small child, he had for years been mainly concerned about his fragile health. He suffered from a heart condition that his own taut nerves made worse, but his illness had not been serious enough to exempt him from military service years before, and he was recalled in the first round of mobilization that summer. On 24 June, he and a group of fellow junior officers were ordered to join a unit in Lvov. Volkov was so anxious to get on with his new task that he did not even spend a last night at home with his wife and daughter. The memory of his hasty departure for the barracks would haunt him for the next five years.

As Volkov worried himself to sleep in a strange bed on his first night in uniform, Lvov was burning. The members of the local NKVD, in preparation for their own retreat, spent their night murdering the inmates of its crowded jails.[48] Volkov knew none of this. His problem was to get there. His call-up papers included a pass that paid his train fare, but there were no special carriages or requisitioned seats. Like everyone else, he had to fight to get a place on the first train that looked as if it might make the twelve-hour journey west. Here was another piece of Stalinist logic. There was no guaranteed means of getting to Lvov, but failure to appear on time would count as desertion. The result, as always, was a desperate scramble. Volkov somehow managed to shove a dozen other conscripts aside. He hauled himself up the iron steps of a carriage, clutching at the folds of someone else's coat. But then he tripped. His boot slipped and he fell hard. He would have injured his back on the rails, he wrote to his wife, if another man had not already slumped across them, softening his fall. "It was my first incident," he wrote. It was a fitting prelude to the journey in the overcrowded train. "On the way," he went on, "we passed columns of refugees from Lvov and other cities in western Ukraine. They told us that there was street fighting in Lvov and that life in the city had come to a standstill."

Volkov and his friends soon came under bombardment, but "I was lucky again, because I'm still alive." When he arrived in Lvov, a city now in complete chaos, he discovered that the unit he was meant to join had fled toward the east. Again he faced a troubling dilemma. There was no sign of his commanding officer, but if he did not report for duty he would be counted as a deserter once again. He lingered in Lvov for three more days, but still no orders came. The street fighting was never far away, the shops were empty, and the nights macabre. The locals, many of whom were patriots for a free western Ukraine, were as likely to spit in a Soviet soldier's face as they were to offer him directions, let alone a meal. Finally Volkov decided to leave, taking the twenty men who seemed to be in his command. There was no one to help with advice or supplies. None of the men had even seen a map, for these were considered secret documents back then. All the recruits could do was head eastward, braving the constant shelling and machine-gun fire. "We walked without a break for forty-eight hours," Volkov told his wife. "There was nothing to eat, and we were very thirsty. We walked through ravines and woods, through mud, we fell into potholes. Ten people got left behind on the way; they didn't have the strength to go on." A hundred miles later, the remnants of his group arrived at Tarnopol and joined up with their main unit at last. "When I remember this," he wrote, "I still can't understand where I got the strength from, where I found the stamina, especially since I'd had no time to toughen up."[49]

Volkov's letter was written after he was safely reunited with the Red Army. For him, the story of those panic-stricken weeks ended well. But he knew how complete the insecurity had been. That June, he would not have been able to guess whether Lvov was the last stronghold the Germans held or, conversely, whether—as the leaflets dropped from

German planes announced—Moscow had fallen and Stalin was dead. His walk through the woods and hills of western Ukraine was a last act of faith. As a Jew, he may have known what kind of reception he would have met in German hands. To remain in Lvov, he may have guessed, would mean capture and certain death. Other soldiers at the front, including tens of thousands of ethnic Ukrainians and Russians, chose to surrender to the invaders rather than plunging eastward through the wild. Still others simply picked up their greatcoats and their heavy packs and walked back home. The choices of those first few days were lonelier than any they had ever made.

The turning point, for many, came on 3 July. That day Stalin finally addressed the Soviet people, reading from a script and pausing frequently, as if distressed, to drink from a glass at his elbow. The speech itself, beginning with its famous address to Soviet citizens as "brothers and sisters, friends," was a calculated break with Communist formality and a watershed in Stalin's relationship with his people. As a recent Russian history of the time affirms, it was a crucial moment for morale. "Although Stalin admitted that the country was in mortal danger," writes O. V. Druzhba, "this was better than the untamed fear of leaderlessness and betrayal."[50]

One of the few outsiders to witness it all was Alexander Werth, a journalist who was based in Moscow to report for the *Sunday Times*. In his great history of the war, written from notes that he made inside Russia, he described Stalin's performance as "extraordinary." Addressed as it was "to a nervous, and often frightened and bewildered people," the speech had a significant effect. "Until then, there had been something artificial in the adulation of Stalin; his name was associated not only with the stupendous effort of the Five Year Plans, but also with the ruthless methods employed in the collectivisation campaign and, worse still, with the terror of the purges. The Soviet people now felt that they had a leader to look to."[51]

The speech was indeed shrewd, admitting to the country's mortal crisis without breathing a word about the panic at the front. Stalin did not spell out the extent of the German advance, but he conceded that the enemy was "wicked and perfidious . . . heavily armed with tanks and artillery." There was also a deft admission of unpreparedness. "Soviet troops had not been fully mobilized," the people learned, "and had not been moved to the frontier" when "Fascist Germany unexpectedly and perfidiously violated the 1939 nonaggression pact." Such crumbs seem to have satisfied some members of an audience that hungered for real news. "The leader did not remain silent about the fact that our troops have had to retreat," a Moscow plastics worker commented. "He does not hide the difficulties that lie ahead for his people. After this speech I want to work even harder. It has mobilized me for great deeds." The call for volunteers to train for civil defense, as well as the injunction to tireless effort in the factories, seemed to inspire thousands of people and make them take heart. Others, encouraged by Stalin's assurance that the enemy would not prevail, declared that they were leaving for the front at once. "If our leader says that victory is certain, it means that we will win."[52]

The reports of improved morale and collective determination far outnumber those that describe dissension. For millions, Stalin's speech was the real start of patriotic struggle. Without their dedication and their faith, the war might have been lost within a year. But there were those who could not be soothed with slogans and fine words. The speech did not allay suspicion everywhere. Werth might not have known it—and he certainly could not have reported the fact—but Stalin's speech was met with bitter laughter in some quarters, even in the capital. People had learned to read between the lines whenever an official spoke. Now some of them gave in to their worst fears. "All this talk about mobilizing the people and organizing civil defense just goes to show that the situation at the front is absolutely hopeless," said one Moscow engineer. "It's clear that the Germans will take Moscow soon and Soviet power will not hold out." "It's too late to start talking about volunteers now," a woman muttered to friends in her office. "The Germans are practically in Moscow already." "Some kind of collapse is inescapable," another office worker said. "Everything that we have been building for twenty-five years has turned out to be a chimera. The collapse is obvious from Stalin's speech, from his desperate summons to the colors."[53]

The leader's words had even less impact in villages where people still distrusted Soviet power. In Kursk province, for instance, there were peasants who resented the order to dig tank traps and defense trenches. "Shoot me if you like," an angry woman told local police, "but I'm not digging any trenches. The only people who need trenches are the Communists and Jews. Let them dig them for themselves. Your power is coming to an end and we're not going to work for you."[54] "A war has started and people are going to get killed," a man told fellow villagers at a meeting. "I personally am not opposed to Soviet power, but I hate Communists."[55] "Your war hasn't anything to do with me," another told the party men. "Let the Communists fight."[56] Collectivization was one focus for this opposition to Soviet power, political repression another. "It's a good thing Hitler has invaded the Soviet Union," a woman whose husband was in prison commented that July. "They'll have to let the prisoners out."[57] Such views were amplified, in different ways, among members of the non-Russian ethnic groups.

The greatest test of Stalin's speech, however, was the reaction in the Red Army itself. Official Soviet histories and memoirs agree that many saw it as the first true ray of hope. "It is hard to describe the enormous enthusiasm and patriotic uplift" with which the speech was met, recalled front-line general I. I. Fedyuninsky. 'We suddenly seemed to feel much stronger. Where circumstances permitted, short meetings would be held by the army units."[58] These meetings, sometimes the first that *politruks* had dared to call since 22 June, provided an opportunity to discuss the gravity of the attack at last. Instead of lies and silences, the men now heard the kind of effort each of them would have to make if the invaders were to be driven from Soviet soil. A war that had been unreal until that point, like a play that had suddenly deviated from its script, became serious, the fear as well as the certainty of sacrifice more valid. In his war novel, *The Living and the Dead*, Konstantin Simonov recalled the men's response. "Stalin did not describe the situation as tragic," he has a wounded soldier muse. "The truth he told was a bitter truth, but at last it was uttered, and people felt that they stood more firmly on the ground." The speech, wrote Simonov, left its audience with "a tense expectation of change for the better."[59]

Accounts like this reflect the sense of awe that the catastrophe inspired. Stalin, like Churchill in Britain, understood, and responded to, the emotional intensity of the moment. But the "bitter truth" that Stalin told was far from accurate. Although thousands of troops were indeed "fighting heroically," tens of thousands more were missing or captured, striking out towards their homes or waiting in depots for transport to take them anywhere at all. Nor could the leader's speech help people stranded in mosquito-haunted marsh. Among these was a *politruk* called Nikolai Moskvin.

Moskvin's war had begun with the same fine words and lofty hopes as any other loyal citizen's, words written in the collective national trance. "I profoundly believe in the rightness of our cause," he wrote in his diary on 22 June. "I love my motherland, I will defend it to the last ounce of my strength, and I will not begrudge my life for my people." That night he kissed his family good-bye as they joined the long convoy of evacuees. He did not think they would be separated long. Two days later, he was with his regiment and preparing to defend Belorussia. But disturbing rumors of loss—850 planes and 900 tanks—soon began filtering east, and the shrewd *politruk* already guessed that these estimates would prove to be low. "Who tells the truth in wartime?" he wondered. Moskvin began to weigh the odds. "We'll win for sure," he still believed. "But the cost will be colossal." Ten days later, on 4 July, the truth had dawned. "Our situation is very bad," he wrote in despair. "How could it have turned out that we, preparing to fight on enemy soil, absolutely failed to consider that we might have to mount some kind of defense? Something was wrong with the doctrine of our armed forces."[60]

Moskvin's main job was to maintain morale. After a short delay, he received a transcript of Stalin's speech with instructions to read it to the men. But by this stage his regiment had little time for meetings. "No time to write," the *politruk* noted on 15 July. "It is possible that we are not completely defeated yet, but the situation is extremely difficult. . . . The enemy's aviation is destroying absolutely everything. The roads are littered with the bodies of our soldiers and the civilian population. Towns and villages are burning. The Germans are everywhere—in front, behind, and on our flank." A couple of new recruits from western Ukraine were calling on the men to surrender their arms. Their situation seemed hopeless enough. By 23 July, the regiment had been encircled. "What am I to say to the boys?" Moskvin asked in a scribbled note. "We keep retreating. How can I get their approval? How? Am I to say that Comrade Stalin is with us? That Napoleon was ruined and that Hitler and his generals will find their graves with us? . . . It seems that I didn't do a good job of convincing them," he added the next day. The previous evening, after his pep talk to the men, thirteen of them had slipped away into the forest.[61]

★

The Red Army collapsed in the first weeks of the war. This is no criticism of its individual troops. It is a statement about bureaucratic rule, coercion, lies, fear, and mismanagement. The problems were not new, nor were they unfamiliar. Lack of transport, for instance, which was identified by nearly every front-line officer as the reason the retreat turned into a rout that June, was a long-standing concern of units based along the Soviet border. "It is absolutely unknown to us where and when we will receive the motorized transport we need for newly mobilized units," the commander of an infantry division in the Fourth Army had written on 12 March 1941. That same month, another report found no unit with more than four-fifths of its required transport strength. Spare parts, fuel, and tires were impossible to guarantee.[62] Four months later, when the crippled armies of the western region needed transport to bring fresh reserves up to the front, they found themselves short by at least a third.[63]

Gabriel Temkin, a Jewish refugee from Hitler who would later fight in the Red Army, witnessed the impact of the transport shortage from his lodging near Bialystok. The soldiers he saw on their way to the front that first week made a depressing spectacle: "Some in trucks, many on foot, their outdated rifles hanging loosely over their shoulders. Their uniforms worn out, covered with dust, not a smile on their mostly despondent, emaciated faces with sunken cheeks. Equally miserable," he added, "were the small trucks pulling the vehicles with ammunition, food, and personal belongings."[64] The men's morale was desperately low. It was a matter of poor leadership, inadequate training, and lack of faith in their own cause, but the long marches and even longer bivouacs, sometimes in the open air, made the whole nightmare worse. "Sometimes," Fedyuninsky wrote of the retreating armies, "bottlenecks were formed by troops, artillery, motor vehicles, and field kitchens, and then the Nazi planes had the time of their life. . . . Often our troops could not dig in, simply because they did not have the simplest implements. Occasionally trenches had to be dug with helmets, since there were no spades."[65]

Other equipment was in short supply as well. The Germans genuinely feared Soviet bayonets, and the troops were encouraged to use them for that reason. The problem for many was that they had no other choice. That June, soldiers in Belorussia and Ukraine ran out of cartridges and bullets. Anastas Mikoyan recalled his government's surprise when it learned that the army had run out of rifles, too. "We thought we surely had enough for the whole army," he wrote in his memoir. "But it

Red Army soldiers receiving their supply of shells before battle, 1941

turned out that a portion of our divisions had been assembled according to peacetime norms. Divisions that had been equipped with adequate numbers of rifles for wartime conditions held on to them, but they were all close to the front. When the Germans crossed the frontier and began to advance, these weapons ended up in the territory they controlled or else the Germans simply captured them. As a result, reservists going to the front ended up with no rifles at all."[66] Retreating troops also abandoned all the things they could not carry, which included wounded men as well as Maxim guns.

The Red Army had been restructured in the last few months of peace. The debacle in Finland had provoked an initial program of reforms, but it was the fall of France in 1940 that inspired the general staff to focus on their preparations for land-based attack. If they should happen to be faced with a massive strike from German planes and tanks, they reasoned, knowing their German allies to be false friends, their strategy should incorporate the deployment of large antitank artillery brigades in support of their infantry. The huge formations must have looked impressive, but when the attack came in 1941 they were good for little more than show. The front line would soon be so broad that the best the large armored brigades could do was to huddle in their deep consolidated rows, unable to predict, or respond to, the movements of an enemy whose measure they had yet to take. Infantry divisions faced German tanks without the consistent support of their artillery. Since their air cover had also been utterly destroyed, many soldiers concluded that the backbreaking effort of Soviet industry in the 1930s, the pride of Stalin's revolution, was now as good as wasted, lost. The troops had been expecting to enjoy the science-fiction spectacle of their own machines in battle. Instead, they watched as the horizon filled with the fruits of German modernity. A new term—*tank fright*—was soon coined by the general staff to describe the conscripts' terrified response.[67]

The story might have been quite different. Soviet tanks should have been world beaters. Many had been tested during the civil war in Spain in 1936, and some designs had been refined as a result. The heavy KV model, named after Kliment Voroshilov, was a redoubtable machine, almost impervious to German fire in the early fighting; it would, indeed, provide the model for the Germans' own Tiger in 1943. The lighter, more maneuverable T–34 eventually proved itself the best field tank of the war. But at this stage the Red Army still had more BT light tanks in service, as well as the obsolescent T–26s and T–28s. These machines were old, and few had been reliably maintained. The KV had a tendency to break down anyway, but every model suffered from a shortage of spare parts, to say nothing of skilled mechanical attention. In 1941, nearly three-quarters of the Soviet Union's 23,000 tanks were thought to need rebuilding or capital repairs. They would not make it to the workshops that summer. More Soviet tanks were lost in 1941 through breakdown than through German fire, and overall the Soviets lost six tanks to every German one.[68]

The same story could be repeated for artillery in 1941. The Red Army was well equipped, but its sclerotic command structures deprived it of flexibility in field conditions. There were never enough men with the right skills to operate complex equipment, and the inexperienced officers who commanded them were unlikely to give them much chance to learn. Heavy guns of every kind were hoarded by officers for whom men might be cheap but new equipment was too valuable to lose.[69] Men, too, were easier to move. Tractors were sometimes used to drag the heaviest equipment into place, but horses were the main source of draft power. In 1941, the Red Army still used the civil war *tachanka*, a three-horse cart, to draw some of its lighter guns to the front line. But the horses were slaughtered with the men that year, and though the June grass had been sweet, forage for the survivors soon ran low. Food supplies were a problem along the entire front. Horses and men grew thinner at the same accelerated pace.

The other fatal logistical problem that summer was radio communication. Again, the difficulty came as no surprise. Poor field communications had dogged the Soviet army in the Finnish campaign, but plans to provide equipment and train new operators had not yet been fulfilled. The Red Army relied on wire far more than on radio. The system was inflexible and centralized. Tank drivers, for instance, were seldom in contact with their comrades, or even their commanding officers, on the battlefield. The radio operators who did work at the front had not been adequately trained. As a former SS officer recalled after the war, the Soviets "used only simple codes and we nearly always were able to intercept and decode their radio messages without any difficulty. Thus we

Artillery moving into firing position, Southern Front, 1942

obtained quick information on the front situation and frequently also on Russian intentions; sometimes I received such reports from our monitoring stations earlier than the situation reports of our own combat troops."[70] In 1941, some units were not even using code. At Uman that summer, vital messages from staff officers in the Sixth Army were conveyed in clear text. "What else are we supposed to do," a lieutenant inquired, "when they want everything sent without delay?"[71]

Finally, there was little prospect of help for weak and injured soldiers in these early months. The suddenness of the German attack preempted plans to move hospitals and medical supplies away from the front line. Then transport difficulties strangled their retreat. By 1 July 1941, the southwestern front could call on just 15 percent of its planned medical facilities. In the Tarnopol garrison hospital, which would have been the first point of call for Volkov and his tired crew, more than five thousand wounded and exhausted men were crowded into facilities intended for two hundred people within five days of the first attack.[72] On 30 June, a report marked "absolutely secret" cataloged the losses of one week. "In the course of military action none of the sanitary establishments located in the western parts of Belorussia were mobilized," it began. "As a result, the [western] front lacked 32 surgical and 12 infection hospitals, 16 corps hospitals, 13 evacuation points, 7 administrative centers for evacuation, 3 motorized sanitary companies, . . . and other medical facilities."[73] The equipment, drugs, and other supplies that these facilities controlled, the report added, had been destroyed in the bombing and fires; their staffs, too, frequently were dead.

The invader was not always invincible that June. The Wehrmacht rolled into the Russian steppe with more horses than tanks, and in a few weeks, its supply lines had begun to stretch and thin across the unimaginable miles. At times, Soviet troops came upon German infantry that had neither transport nor air cover. Fascists, they discovered, could panic just as easily as komsomols in the right conditions. But in those early days the Wehrmacht enjoyed support from a portion of the local population, especially as it had yet to reach ancient Russian or even long-held Soviet soil. Civilians in cities like Lvov had been baiting Red Army troops for months. "The Germans are coming, and they'll get you," they whispered in the narrow streets of the Galician town.[74] Now soldiers from the western provinces, as well as the thousands who despaired of resisting Germany's advance, turned tail, surrendered, or fled the front line. By July the reports were already piling up of soldiers who drew swastikas on their clothes, refused to fire on Germans, and talked admiringly of Hitler.[75]

Desertion rates were so high that no one could be sure of the numbers, let alone the breakdown of culprits by ethnic group. In three days at the end of June, NKVD special troops behind the lines on the southwestern front caught nearly seven hundred soldiers on the run. Elsewhere, five thousand men were caught fleeing one of the catastrophic battles of those first few days. But it probably was true that soldiers from the recently annexed western regions were the most likely to disappear. They were anxious for their families, for theirs were the first homes the Germans overran. And some of them deserted because they saw no reason to die for Soviet power. Four thousand "westerners" had fled the Twenty-sixth Army by 6 July, and in one unit eighty men had refused their orders to fire.[76] By 12 August the army's political administration considered the situation to be so dangerous that citizens of the western territories—Ukraine, Belorussia, and the three Baltic states—were specifically barred from serving in the new tank crews.[77]

All this translated into murderous confusion in the field. Neither Red Army men nor officers had expected this war. No battle followed a thoughtful preconceived plan. The men resented their officers, mistrusted their orders, and suspected that some of their own comrades were traitors waiting to desert. If they had paused to consider their reasons for fighting, they would probably have found that fear—fear of their officers, of the unknown, and of the secret police as much as of the German invaders—played a large part. Then came their rage against the entire world. At the front, lofty ideas of brotherhood and utopia seldom survived for long. But these same men were expected to go on fighting, without hope, day after day. The 117th Rifle Division of the Twenty-first Army, for instance, retreated, then fought repeatedly for weeks. By 6 July, it had reached the town of Zhlobin on the Dnepr River. There it fought one of the first engagements in the defense of Kiev, a doomed campaign that would cost the Twenty-first Army alone, by the most conservative estimates, well over a thousand lives each day.[78] The battle lasted for eight hours. At the end of it Zhlobin had fallen and the remnants of the division had withdrawn to the Dnepr's eastern bank.

In their retreat, the men had succeeded in destroying Zhlobin's bridge, buying more time for the next day, and they had also blown up eight enemy tanks. But their morale was low. They were exhausted, hungry, sleepless, already haunted by all that they had seen. Many were injured. The next day, as usual, they faced combat again. Their officers had no plan other than head-on attack. As on the previous day, and every succeeding day, the officers threw men at the German tanks. The troops' only morale booster was their unanimous roar, the terrifying "Hoorah!" that struck fear in their enemy. Apart from that, few soldiers had any weapon more effective than an 1890s rifle and a bayonet. Even Molotov cocktails were hard to obtain, since Moscow had yet to sign the order that would soon have women stuffing glass bottles with wicks at a rate of 120,000 a day.[79] At this stage, lacking bottles or bombs to throw, soldiers had only their bare hands. Wave after wave they ran into attack, for hours, always amid the din of German shelling, screaming, and the crunch of steel on bone.

It was a style of defense—hopeless and head-on attack—that ground entire divisions to dust. It sickened the men involved, especially those who had endured weeks of it already. At Zhlobin ten Communists threw their party cards away as soon as the firing started. At least one man shot himself in the leg in an attempt to escape from combat altogether. A soldier said to be Georgian tried to kill his commanding officer by firing on his own troops as they attacked. A Volga German was thought to have gone over to the enemy as soon as he could slip away. But the real renegades made their escape with more style. Two senior officers ran twenty miles at dawn to get away from the front line, while the commander who had ordered the first antiaircraft attack "got in his car and left" as soon as the operation began. The report of the day noted that no one had been punished because the local military judge, reared in the hard school of purging and lies, refused to investigate anything unless he had sufficient papers on his desk.[80]

Even the Germans were surprised by the level of chaos. It was as if the entire population, soldiers and civilians, had run wild. Whenever the Wehrmacht captured a place where supplies of food and consumables were held, they could expect looting to start. In one town several women and children were crushed to death by the mob as it swept toward the army warehouse. "If a man could not carry a bag of sugar," the German army's observer reported, "he simply cut it apart and poured half its contents onto the floor, carrying home the rest." The citizens of Pukhovichi plundered half the military supplies in their town in a single day, taking, as their new masters observed, "an average per family of 200 kilos of sugar, 200 kilos of fats, almost 350 kilos of grits, and a quantity of fish, individual rations, and vegetable oils. . . . The population had not seen such opulence for a long time." The Red Army itself joined in at Bobruisk. "The only difference," wrote the German reporter, "was that while the inhabitants were plundering the shops, the soldiers were looting the homes of the inhabitants."[81]

The Stalinist regime of the late 1930s met its nemesis in Ukraine and Belorussia in those early months. Eventually, its near collapse led to a rethinking of policy and leadership, to changes in the way war would be waged and people ruled. But one tool in its armory would prove essential for the duration. On 15 July, Lev Mekhlis issued a directive to the army of political workers at the front. It was the prelude to an order, signed the following day, that reinstated the political commissars in all their pre-1940 authority. Morale, the report tacitly admitted, had collapsed entirely. The *politruks* had failed to convince their men that this war could be won or even, perhaps, that there was any point in fighting on at all. And yet, Mekhlis insisted, these were the soldiers whose task was "to decide by force of arms whether the Soviet people would be free or become the slaves of German princes and barons."

The bracing, epic formula behind these words might well have given heart to the people back at home and also to the new recruits still training in their camps. But at the front, they had a hollow, even an insulting ring. It was a mistake to tell soldiers, as Mekhlis did, that Hitler's blitzkrieg had failed and that the best divisions of his army were already defeated. And then came the depressing part on tactics, formulaic nonsense borrowed from the sloganeering days of civil war. "Teach all personnel how to rush into attack," the order instructed. "Teach them implacable hatred and rage against the enemy, ardently to crush the Fascist cur, to grind his face into the earth, to be prepared to fight to the last drop of their blood for every inch of Soviet soil. Tell them that tanks are not frightening for a brave and experienced soldier. Tell them that abandoning their posts without a direct order is a crime."[82] The words were empty that summer, but they pointed to one of the ways that this war was conceived and fought, the war in soldiers' minds and in the hopes of their civilian families. By saturating public discourse with simple, much-repeated formulas, the government forged new resolve to replace the lost innocence of 1938. It also helped to exclude all the other words, the panic-stricken, angry ones, that might have crowded into people's conversations. On 19 July, a further order called for the mass recruitment of political officers to replace the hundreds who had been lost since 22 June.[83]

The propaganda effort never flagged. Red Army troops were presented, effectively, with two wars simultaneously. The first, the one that they alone could know, was the war of the battlefield, the screaming war of shells and smoke, the shameful war of terror and retreat. But the other, whose shape was crafted by writers, was a war that propaganda created. Soldiers and civilians alike could learn about it in the newspapers, the most popular of which, *Red Star*, was read aloud to small groups at the front. Serving troops also saw film shows that included newsreels, some of which, because they were carefully staged, could seem more vivid than their own fragmented memories of combat. Fighting might seem to take place outside real time, in horrifying moments that later defied recall, but Stalin's official war unfolded with an epic certainty, in regular and well-planned episodes.

In all, over a thousand writers and artists joined the campaign to report the front, four hundred of whom would die in the fighting.[84] Their work was controlled by yet another new body, the Sovinform-buro, which monitored everything from *Pravda* to the news sheets that soldiers were given at the front. Each captured or disabled German tank or plane was recorded, often with a photograph, but the blank space where Soviet losses should have been, padded with slogans and even short verse, was noticed by newspaper readers everywhere.[85] The trouble was that no one could get to the censors' offices to find out more. Security was so tight that even full-time members of the Sovin-formburo's staff sometimes discovered that their passes were not valid for its central building.[86] Inside, trusted officials combed draft front-line reports for ideological mistakes, correcting even punctuation that might not conform to the official line. The famous correspondent Ilya Ehrenburg nearly resigned in protest at the pettifogging rules. When an editor changed the word *victories*, meaning real successes at the front, to *progress* in an article he saw, the future voice of Stalin's propaganda war declared that it was all a waste of time. "We spend so long on corrections," he complained, "that we lose the whole day, all our creative time."[87]

One victory, or maybe piece of progress, that the Sovinformburo chalked up for Red Army troops that summer was the Battle of Smolensk. The losses were devastating—300,000 prisoners captured and 3,000 more tanks lost—but the Soviet papers were silent about these. They focused on the fact that the Germans had been held up in their advance on Moscow.[88] It was at this moment, too, that a desperate

*Soldiers near Leningrad receiving a consignment of books
and paper, 1942*

Red Army deployed its most impressive weapon for the first time. So secret that it had no real name until the troops gave it the feminine
"Katyusha," the BM–13–16 multiple rocket launcher and its descendants proved that Soviet designers could produce hardware to rival any
in the world. "We first tried out this superb weapon at Rudnya, near
Smolensk," remembered Marshal Andrei Yeremenko. "On the afternoon of 15 July the earth shook with the unusual explosion of jet mines.
Like red-tailed comets, the mines were hurled into the air. . . . The effect of the simultaneous explosions of dozens of these mines was ter-

rific. The Germans fled in panic, and even our own troops, . . . who for reasons of secrecy had not been warned that this new weapon would be used, rushed back from the front line."[89] Katyushas were quite inefficient for their range, consuming prodigious quantities of propellant to hurl rocket mines less than ten miles at this stage in the war. But the gratifying sight of German soldiers running from the field gave Stalin's propagandists something they could really write about.

★

"The retreat has caused blind panic," the head of the Belorussian Communist Party, Ponomarenko, wrote to Stalin on 3 September. To make things worse, "the soldiers are tired to death, even sleeping under artillery fire. . . . At the first bombardment, the formations collapse, many just run away to the woods, the whole area of woodland in the front-line region is full of refugees like this. Many throw away their weapons and go home. They regard the possibility of being surrounded with extreme anxiety."[90] This frank report would translate for the secret police into a case of collective "betrayal of the motherland," but moralistic talk was wasted on the leaderless and lost. Millions of men that summer were simply encircled, trapped. Others, with little training and scant knowledge of their companions, let alone the foibles of their equipment, were thrown into battle against an enemy that was still, until the first snow fell, as confident as it had been when it marched into Paris thirteen months before. The ones who simply made for home were the most understandable of all. "In June 1941 our unit was surrounded by some German troops near the town of Belaya Tserkov," an ex-soldier explained. "The *politruk* mustered the remaining troops and ordered us to leave the encirclement in groups. I and two other soldiers from our unit . . . changed into civilian clothes and decided to go back where we used to live. We made this decision," he explained, "because, according to rumor, the German troops moving up toward us had advanced far away to the east."[91]

The Germans themselves were unprepared for the number of prisoners they took. By the end of 1941, they held at least two to three million Red Army troops. No thought had been given to these men's accommodation, for their lives, in Nazi thinking, had never been worth a plan. As the Wehrmacht swept eastward, many of its prisoners were herded into their own former barracks or prisons; others squatted in the open air, enclosed by nothing more protective than barbed wire. The shock that June was so severe that it took time for the atrocity tales to circulate, stories of Jews and Communists singled out for torture and illegal execution, tales of beatings, hunger, crude sadism, and collective slow death. In the first few days of the war Red Army soldiers simply gave up when they found themselves surrounded and outgunned.

On 22 June the Supreme Soviet granted the army power to punish deserters. That day, provision was also made for the establishment of three-man military tribunals that would operate at the front and in all other areas affected by the war. The tribunals had the right to order death sentences if they chose, although a clause in their regulations instructed them to inform Moscow by telegraph when they did. If they failed to receive a reply within seventy-two hours, the sentence could be carried out without appeal; any other punishments they ordered, some of which amounted to death sentences by other means, could be imposed directly.[92] These powers were comprehensive enough, but in practice commanders often acted on their own. On 14 July, Mekhlis received a note from his deputy on the southwestern front complaining of the excess use of the death penalty within an army desperately short of men. As always, lurid examples were cited. In one case, a lieutenant had shot two leaderless Red Army men and a woman who had come to his unit to beg for food.[93]

Reports like this changed nothing at the front. Few officers knew their men well, and none could have known all of them, so rapidly did whole units dissolve and new ones form. Pavlov's execution, and others like it, proved that the penalty for an officer's failure was either a Fascist bullet or one from NKVD troops. Foot soldiers were coerced because their commanders in turn feared for their skins. Cruelty became a way of life. In August 1941 the officers' vulnerability to punishment was emphasized again. Order no. 270, which Stalin himself signed, was not published at the time, but its contents were widely disseminated, read out at meetings that the front-line *politruks* were forced to call. It followed the surrender, on a single day, of a hundred thousand men near the Ukrainian town of Uman. These hapless troops had little choice, since, unlike Boldin, they were encircled on the open steppe, not in woods and marshes where they could hide. But with its customary moralism, Moscow judged them disgraceful and cowardly. Henceforth, its order stated, any officer or political officer who removed his distinguishing marks in battle, retreated to the rear, or gave himself up as a prisoner would count as a malicious deserter. Officers who tried to desert could be shot in the field by their superiors. Even reluctance to lead from the front could count as desertion if the authorities on the spot so deemed it.[94]

The order also declared that the families of malicious deserters would now be liable to arrest. This was a cruel notion, although in its essence it was not entirely new. For years, deserters' families had been punished through the withholding of pensions and other material rights. But the threat of prison was an awesome one in a system where everything, even a child's schooling, depended on a family's collective honor in official eyes. The order came to mean that anyone whose corpse was lost—which tens of thousands were, shot down over rivers and marshes, blown to pieces, or gnawed away by rats—counted as a deserter for the army's purposes. To go missing in action was a dishonorable fate. That first summer, however, there were plenty of men who shrugged off rules like these. As Nikolai Moskvin observed after his own thirteen troops disappeared, "I've talked to our commander. He's warned the rest about responsibility. He's told them that there is a list, we have a list, of all their relatives. But the truth is that lots of these boys come from places the Fascists have already taken. They don't care about addresses anymore."[95]

Moskvin shot his first deserter on 15 July. The soldier came from western Ukraine. Three weeks of shelling, marching, sleeplessness, and terror had brought the man to breaking point, and maybe it made little difference what pretext he chose at the time. His crime was to urge all his comrades to surrender or at least to hold their fire. He then confronted Moskvin. "He made a salute to, I suppose, Hitler, shouldered his rifle, and walked off toward the scrub," Moskvin wrote. It was too much for one of the other Ukrainians in the group. "Red Army private Shulyak brought him down with a bullet in the back," the *politruk* went on. The dying man swore at his former comrades from the dust. "They'll kill the lot of you," he said. "And you, you bloodstained commissar, they'll hang you first." Moskvin did not hesitate. He raised his Nagan revolver and shot the victim in front of the whole company. "The boys understood," he wrote. "A dog's death for a dog."

Whatever tales he had to tell his soldiers, however, Moskvin's own confidence was gone. At the end of July his unit was shattered in a German attack. Moskvin himself was injured. His companions could not transport him, so he and two other men were left to wait for rescue in the woods. No help arrived, and they convinced themselves that their mates had forgotten them. In fact, most of the regiment was dead, betrayed by a deserter in their ranks a few hours after they had left their wounded. "I am on the verge of a complete moral collapse," Moskvin wrote on 4 August. His wounds were painful and he was afraid of gangrene. "We got lost," he went on, "because we did not have maps. It seems we didn't have maps in this war any more than we had airplanes." The two men slept beside him, but he could not rest. "I feel guilty because I am helpless and because I know that I should pull myself together," the *politruk* despaired. Communist Party faith was supposed to make him a hero, but instead "I just don't have the strength."

The woods where Moskvin lay were not far from a village in the region of Smolensk. After three days, during which, as he slept, someone found the time to steal his small arms, a group of peasants rescued him. Moskvin would learn later that his saviors had also discussed the possibility of betraying the group to the German police. The decision to hide the three may have been clinched by the thought that reasonably healthy men could help at harvest time. Moskvin described the work he put in when the beets and potatoes had grown large enough to lift. He had to keep his mouth shut when the peasants told him that they had dissolved their collective farm and no longer worked to Soviet rules. He had to tolerate the hard work and the mud, the crude delight in Stalin's discomfort, the speculative hope for change. "Not everything works the way it was described in the books we had to study," the *politruk* scribbled one night. These villages, he wrote, were nothing like the buzzing, cultured towns that everyone had been so proud of in that other universe, the peacetime one. Perhaps, he pondered, even Soviet power could not have changed the village, the primeval world, that he was now coming to know. Moskvin had been at war less than two months. It was still summer, and the woods were green, but he had lost touch with the certainties of Soviet life.

FOUR

BLACK WAYS OF WAR

★

The summer lingered till the first week of October. It was an alien, an uncanny, treacherous season. Perfect weather ripened crops whose fate would be to mellow, color, choke, and rot. Across the steppe lands of Ukraine, fields that had teemed with cattle were now rank with weeds. Berries ripened in the woods untasted; few people were around to care. Those who passed by, heading east, were not traveling for pleasure. On Moscow's orders, entire industries were being crated up and moved to the deep hinterland; it seemed as if the whole world were bound for the rails. Families who had no special rights, no contacts, set off on foot along the roads. Columns of dust followed the people and the carts, the droves of livestock, children, and the long, thin lines of troops. After the refugees had gone, and after the last Soviet soldiers, the tanks came, and the trucks and horses, and the plague of gray-clad men.

The Baltic, Belorussia, and most of Ukraine were all in German hands by the end of August 1941. Kiev itself fell in the middle of September. By then, too, Leningrad had been cut off from its main sources of supply. The railway at Mga, the last transport route into the city, fell to the invaders in late August. Now German heavy guns and fighter planes closed in on Russia's second capital, their sights fixed on its industry, its wealth. The Wehrmacht was so sure of victory on this front that some troops were diverted south to seize an even greater prize. Hitler's orders were to capture Moscow and then to gouge it from the earth, to turn the city into a huge lake. That autumn, German troops looked set to carry out their task. On 2 October they captured Orel, and by midmonth they had taken both Kaluga, on the Oka River to the southwest of Moscow, and Kalinin, modern Tver', toward the north. They were within a hundred miles of the Kremlin.

Red Army soldiers faced the prospect of a complete rout. By contrast, their enemy seemed vigorous and optimistic. "The SS and the tank divisions went into attack with such enthusiasm that you would have thought that what they had just come from was not four months of heavy fighting but a long rest," Erich Hoepner, the commander of Panzer Group Four, wrote in an arrogant report.[1] His men had just motored south from the Leningrad Front to join Heinz Guderian's tanks in the campaign for Moscow. Killing appeared to feed their appetite for war. "The number of Soviet military deaths was even greater than the number of prisoners we took," Hoepner went on. "Each night the villages went on burning, coloring the low clouds with a blood-red light."[2]

The Germans blamed the weather for what happened next. Hoepner would claim that the capital's defensive trenches and mines were no barrier to his determined men. His losses, he wrote, were heavy, but those of Moscow's defenders were more catastrophic still. The snow, at first, seemed no deterrent, either. Hoepner was at Borodino, barely sixty miles from the Kremlin, when he brushed the first dry flakes from his greatcoat. But then the rain began, the Russian autumn rain that goes on falling day and night for weeks. It was this rain, so unexpected and prosaic, that "snatched from German hands the victory that we had almost won." The Wehrmacht was sunk axle, knee, and fetlock deep in heavy gray-brown mud. "It took two days and nights," Hoepner recalled, "to cover ten kilometers, if you could travel on at all." The wheels of trucks and carts spun uselessly, forcing the vehicles to sink deeper; men cursed and shivered in the all-pervading damp. "Our supplies were

completely cut off," Hoepner continued. "Ammunition, fuel for our vehicles, and bread soon came to be worth their weight in gold. We could
not even transport our wounded to safety." Somewhat grudgingly, as if
the Soviets were cheating in a fencing match, he added that the enemy
had used the time to bring forward its trained, experienced reserves.
The mud was no impediment to the railways that ran eastward across
the steppe.

The Red Army deserves more credit for stalling the Nazi advance
than Hoepner gave it. With nothing left but their pride and despair,
some soldiers fought with suicidal courage. But there was no denying
the depth of the Soviet crisis. In less than four months, the Red Army
had lost more than 3 million men, hundreds of thousands of whom had
been captured in the great encirclements at Kiev and Vyaz'ma that autumn. An army that had fielded nearly 5 million troops in June could
now muster just over 2.3 million.[3] Reserves and new conscripts were
drawn up behind the front line, but there could never be enough, even
in a country of Russia's size, to compensate for such a crippling loss. By
October, too, nearly ninety million people, 45 percent of the prewar
population, found themselves trapped in territory that the enemy controlled.[4]

The Red Army had the first call on manpower then and later in the
war, but the industries that supplied and maintained its troops needed resources, too. Labor would always be a problem, since the workforce was
now little more than half its prewar size.[5] But the most immediate economic crisis was the loss of plants. Roughly two-thirds of prewar manufacturing had taken place in territories that the Germans seized in 1941.
Anything that could be moved in time had been evacuated beyond the
Volga to the Urals, but serious losses could not be avoided. Not many
guns were made in August and September 1941. Four-fifths of Soviet war
production was "on wheels."[6] Moscow's defenders soon ran out of shells
that autumn. They ran out of cartridges. They even ran out of the guns
with which to fire them. The equipment to assemble more was still packed
up in crates. New factories were thrown together inside wooden shacks,
the workforce laboring around the clock, but even so, production would
not pick up for some months. In December 1941 an entire reserve army,
the Tenth, arrived for service without heavy artillery or a single tank.[7]

The German boast was that the Soviets were finished. It was a mistake, but an easy one to make. The same thought had crossed the minds of many Soviet civilians that autumn. In Moscow, the scene of June's naïve patriotism, embittered citizens prepared to flee. Hoepner was gratified by the panic that his tanks created. "A large part of the population fled," he wrote. "Valuable equipment in the factories was destroyed. The approach of the tanks and infantry units of the Fourth Panzer Group brought terror to the red capital. Looting began. The Soviet leaders made off to Kuibyshev on the Volga."[8] Stalin, in fact, remained in Moscow, rekindling many people's hope. But even his presence could not quell the panic that October. With enemy troops in its very suburbs, Moscow almost collapsed from within. "Those were dreadful days," a textile worker remembered. It started on 12 October, but the crisis came four days later. "My heart went cold," the woman recalled, "when I saw the factory had closed down. A lot of the directors had fled."[9] So had the managers of other plants, some party bosses from the city's local wards, and almost anyone who could squeeze into a car and head east.

The state's answer was to prepare a war on its own people. If they would not behave like epic heroes of their own accord, then NKVD guns would force them to. Special troops were stationed around the capital, their assignment to defend it from invaders outside and defeatists within. The most important of these secret bodies, the forerunner of the postwar Soviet Spetsnaz, was the Motorized Infantry Brigade of the NKVD Special Forces, OSMBON. Among its members was Mikhail Ivanovich, the son of peasants but one of the beneficiaries of Stalin's rule. Like Kirill, he had found promotion and adventure in the army. In his case, the initial attraction was the opportunity to prove himself at sports like boxing. More than eight hundred athletes would join OSMBON in 1941.[10] To be enrolled was to be part of a select and glamorous elite. Now that elite was asked to save the capital, and they felt honored by the task.

Mikhail Ivanovich's specific duty was to defend the Spassky Gates, keeping a vigil from the second floor of the GUM building. His sniper's rifle was ready to fire at anyone—civilian or soldier—who threatened the sector under his guard. But looting was more of a problem than enemy troops. Mikhail Ivanovich was unemotional. "It was necessary, absolutely necessary, to establish order," he recalled. And yes, we did shoot people who refused to leave the shops and offices where food and other goods were stored. Meanwhile, Mikhail Ivanovich's colleagues made sure that Moscow itself would not surrender. The people could die with their city if it fell. Strategic buildings—including the Bolshoi Theater—were mined. The Special Forces' own radio headquarters, which was housed in Moscow's Puppet Theater, was set to blow up with the rest.[11]

The Battle of Moscow, which resumed in mid-November when the gray mud froze, came to be counted among the Red Army's decisive victories. Hoepner's tanks took the riverside town of Istra, with its golden-domed cathedral of the New Jerusalem, on 26 November. But his men were exhausted, the veterans among them muttering that even in its bloodiest days the First World War had known no harder fighting. Their ordered blitzkrieg had dissolved into a hell of hand-to-hand combat; their rich new land had drained of pleasure in the vicious cold. Even their darkness, as Hoepner observed, was dissipated in chaotic light as tracers flashed and glittered on the snow.[12] Red Army troops, by now, were dressed in the camouflage suits they had adopted for winter campaigning since the Finnish war. Unlike their adversaries, they were also prepared for the cold. Looming out of the dark like phantoms, they unnerved their German conquerors. And then they fought, it seemed, with new determination and new stealth. By late November it was clear that the German tanks would get no farther before Christmas. Then, on 5 December, the Red Army attacked in its turn, driving the enemy back from the capital and breaking, link by link, the chain that threatened to encircle it.

Credit for Moscow's defense usually goes to Georgy Zhukov. Stalin's political entourage had failed as military strategists, and now the generals were fighting back. The other heroes were the reserve troops—twelve entire armies—that were brought to the front that October.[13] But the capital was also defended by conscripts from the hinterland, and even by intellectuals, old men, and students. This second group went into battle with the mindset and the preparation of civilians. Back in July, Stalin had called on people to join a *levée en masse*, and plans for Moscow's citizens' defense, the *opolchenie*, swung into operation immediately. Each district of the capital raised its companies of volun-

Soviet infantry in their trenches, winter 1941

teers. Anyone who wanted to, almost, could serve. Their ages ranged from seventeen to fifty-five. As one survivor put it, most volunteers believed that they were destined to celebrate the anniversary of the revolution that November in Berlin. "The newspapers, cinema, and radio had been telling our people for decades that the Red Army was invincible," recalled Abram Evseevich Gordon. Like everyone else, he believed that "under the leadership of the Communist Party and our Great Leader any enemy would be defeated on his own soil."

Male volunteers of Gordon's age soon graduated from digging trenches. By August, *opolchentsy* had joined the defense of the strategic highways leading into Moscow. Gordon himself was sent out to the old Kaluga road. He recalled the grim faces of his "most unmilitary" comrades as they set out to defend the capital, some on bicycles, others on foot. At their new base they received uniforms, drab black affairs that made them look, they thought, like Mussolini's Fascists, although in fact the worn garments had probably been captured in Poland in 1939. They also saw some Polish rifles, although not every volunteer was armed. And then their training started, which, to Gordon's horror as an urban dweller and an intellectual, involved mastering horsemanship. Their instructor, an old cavalryman called Kovalchenko, used training methods that recalled the days of Napoleon and Kutuzov. The recruits had to ride bareback for hours at a stretch, enduring unaccustomed pain until the bloodstains from their blisters began soaking through their pants. "The only escape from this torture," Gordon wrote, "was the medical tent." Meanwhile, the news coming from the front grew bleaker, "though we did not want to think the worst."[14]

Other cities went through the same procedures when the call to arms went out. In many places, militias showed courage, if not conspicuous success. Alexander Werth regarded the response of his native Leningrad as a model of local patriotism, but the use of *opolchentsy* there involved heartbreaking loss of life. Wherever they were made to fight, unprepared and unmilitary *opolchentsy* would die in the thousands. In Fatezh, a small town in Kursk province, the three thousand volunteers who stepped forward in July had received no training by September 1941. They did not know how to hold or aim a gun; many had never fired one in their lives. They had not even decided where to locate the main defensive positions around the town. Among collective farmers in the region the appeal for volunteers fell on unwilling and resentful ears, while in nearby Kursk itself, training sessions were poorly attended after the first heady week. Even Communists neglected blackout and no-smoking rules.

Some people still believed that their country's huge size would protect them. As late as the last week of September, the danger to Kursk province felt distant enough for locals to focus on other things, including their own private plans to get away.[15] They paid a high price six weeks later when the region was crushed by the tracks of German tanks.

But some had calculated that obsolete guns and homemade bombs were useless in the face of this invader, anyway. There were plenty of deserters in the villages with fatalistic tales to tell. Near Moscow, too, Gordon heard terrible stories from the lips of refugees. By day, the volunteers were buoyed by collective spirit; at night their private fears ran free.

Like many other *opolchenie* groups of its kind, Gordon's division was absorbed into the Red Army in August. In the presence of members of his local Communist Party branch, he and his friends took the Red Army oath and exchanged their black uniforms for the infantry's olive green. By then, he estimated, most of them had scarcely handled a real gun; he himself had fired a training rifle twice. These men became the refounded 113th Rifle Division that September—refounded because the first division with that number had been wiped out near the Soviet border several months before. This version, too, would be consumed and reborn in the coming weeks, first in October 1941 and again in the opening months of 1942. Gordon's incarnation of the division was destroyed in a single day.

The disaster took place in the skeletal woods of birch and pine that line the Warsaw highway leading to the capital. Gordon's division had the task of blocking the predicted German advance. But the men panicked at the first whiff of an enemy. Like greenhorn soldiers anywhere, they could not hold their fire. By the time the enemy was within range, they had almost no bullets left. The Molotov cocktails ran out next. Gordon watched young researchers he had known from Moscow University's geology and physics faculties hurling bottles of burning kerosene at looming German machines. The lucky ones died instantly. Others suffered terrible injuries, dying slow deaths in the woods after their friends had retreated or facing the mercy of the German SS detachment that went around the next day to clear debris from the battlefield.

Only three hundred members of Gordon's division survived till nightfall, and most of these would perish in the coming days as they tried to break out of the German ring that now surrounded them. Gordon himself was captured. He would have died in the camps, but the vast size of his column of prisoners saved him. The bemused German guards could not keep watch on everyone, and Gordon slipped away into a haystack, hiding overnight and through most of a second day. His own future would lie with the regular army. But he never forgot his first comrades in arms. In a final irony, he observed that they included many, patriotic to the last, whose names had not been entered correctly in the Red Army's rolls when they made the transition from *opolchentsy* to regular troops. Their papers were consequently not in order, and that meant that they counted as missing in action. The rules on this were unambiguous: the state regarded them as deserters. Instead of praise and much-needed financial help, their families carried the stigma for another fifty years.[16]

The slaughter of Gordon's 113th Rifle Division stalled a panzer unit for a day or so. The waste of life and talent for so little gain was heartbreaking. Whatever else Stalin's regime might lack, it did not begrudge human lives. The Germans put the carnage down to some trick of exotic guile, declaring the Red Army to be "the craftiest and most stubborn enemy that we have ever faced." If you want to resist a Russian-style attack, a captured report advised that winter, "you need strong nerves."[17] But German observers also noted the lines of special troops behind the riflemen, the men with machine guns who waited to cut the stragglers down. "As a rule," another report declared, "they do not fight out of some ideology or for their motherland but out of fear of their officers, especially their commissars."[18] "Fear and hate," agreed one observer, "leave Russian soldiers to fight with nothing but the courage of desperation."[19]

The soldiers were indeed afraid. Among Moscow's defenders were some, like the famous twenty-eight "Panfilov men," who fought to the last bullet, in part because retreat would mean tribunals and a death sentence.[20] But threats were not sufficient on their own. For one thing, there were those who still dreamed of simply giving up. The illusion that Fascism would turn out to be no worse for Slavs than Stalin's rule was a temptation to these hungry and exhausted men. "We should stop fighting," a soldier in the Sixteenth Army urged his friends that October. "It won't make any difference whether we beat the Germans or not." "Half of our collective farmers are against Soviet power," added another. "Our generals shouted on about how we were going to defeat the enemy on his own soil, but it's turned out the opposite. We Russian people have been betrayed by our generals." His friends seemed to agree. "They are trying to starve us to death now. They'll kill us all," another rifleman complained. "They treat the Red Army like dogs."[21] Secret police wrote all this down, not least because the bitterness so readily translated into action. That October, nearly 130,000 people were detained in Moscow for "breaches of military regulations." Nearly 5,000 of them were Red Army deserters and 12,000 more were charged with evading military service.[22]

Desertions on this scale were evidence that tyranny alone could not make heroes out of frightened men. It merely wasted yet more lives. The number of death sentences that military tribunals passed rose steadily between November 1941 and February 1942. The accused were mostly charged with desertion and fleeing the battlefield.[23] While all armies take measures of this sort to some extent, even this leadership was horrified by some tales of its own brutality. Investigators singled out the case of a lieutenant who shot a soldier for no reason (or none that they could see); in another case, a commissar shot his sergeant for smoking and a major for outspoken language. It was a cruel regime, but even so the desertions continued. The men feared battlefield death and mutilation more than their gun-toting commissars. "You won't need to be in the army long," a soldier wrote home, "perhaps a month or so, before, no doubt, you end up in the German meat grinder."[24]

Stalin, the expert, observed that terror was becoming ineffective. In October 1941, anticipating the army's total collapse, he ordered that "persuasion, not violence," should be used to motivate the men.[25] Obediently, the political administration and Sovinformburo took every measure to "persuade," maintaining a stream of distortions and lies about the army's courage and the enemy's distress. The strategy did not work. "Don't believe the newspapers," a soldier wrote. "Don't believe the papers or the radio; the things they say are lies. We've been through it all and seen it all, the way the Germans are driving us—our own people don't know where to run; we've nothing to fight with; and when the Germans catch up with us, our men have nothing to escape in. We've got no fuel, so the men abandon the cars and tanks and run for it." Another bleakly added that "they make us keep our mouths shut."[26]

The task of inspiring these wretched men should have fallen to their officers. Some of these would prove to be extraordinary men, but many, including some of the most efficient, were tyrants whose coarse language and rough discipline came straight from the primeval world of the village. The rest were often so inexperienced that seasoned troops despised them as mere boys or, worse, as bureaucrats. The gravest offenders here included men promoted in the atmosphere that followed Stalin's purge, the ones whose talents had appealed to politicians. It was absurd to think these people could inspire anyone. Konstantin Simonov described the type. At Kerch, in 1942, he met an officer he called Sorokin—"I can't quite recall his name"—who struck him as "unwarlike, knowing nothing about war. His only good quality," said Simonov, "was the fact that he knew he understood nothing, and so he did whatever he could not to interfere, or if he had to, he just made it look as if he were involved, although he was not really doing anything at all."[27]

"We never saw an officer," surviving *opolchentsy* complained as they limped home from the front. "The generals ran away. They changed their trousers and left us to fight."[28] Their story was repeated among divisions of experienced troops. In October 1941, the commander of the Fiftieth Rifle Division of the Fifth Army, Dorodnyi, reported that his men had received none of the artillery support they had been promised for the defense of Moscow's Mozhaisk highway. "We had to hold the tanks at bay with rifles and machine guns," he said. The commanding officer, General Kamera, listened for a few moments before barking that the artillery commander, Vasyukov, should be shot at once. The order was beside the point. Vasyukov and his big guns were needed for the next morning's campaign. "I'll look into it," Kamera replied, and climbed into his car. "I never saw him again," Dorodnyi wrote. "He seems to strengthen his authority by doing nothing, letting other people shed their blood."[29]

The officers who remained in the field, men like Dorodnyi, acted from a sense of duty and probably from military experience that dated from the civil war. Some were professionals, and some stiffened their trained resolve with Communist faith. The rank and file, however, had fewer incentives. If they stayed in the field that winter, it was out of inertia, out of loyalty to their friends, or out of the team spirit that the shared experiences of terror, hardship, and isolation from their former lives instilled.[30] Their worlds had shrunk, their desires attenuated. Instead of choosing a future, they had become the creatures of their fate. The world beyond the lines of trenches and the army's controlling routines was frightening in its own right, and the tales that were coming through from refugees and stragglers made it seem more terrible and uncanny still. But one emotion could be singled out among the confused impulses of almost every serviceman that winter, and it was the desire for revenge.

"At last after half a year I am on your trail," Misha Volkov wrote to his wife in February 1942. "My joy is without bounds today, though it will be complete only when I receive a letter from your hand." That consummation came soon after. "Today is the happiest day of my life," the artilleryman wrote. "At last, after all the searching, I have found you." Volkov had been tortured by his worries. The last time he had seen his wife she and their daughter had been settled in their home in Kiev. There had been no time for letters after that, for Volkov himself had been at the front line, and then, in September, Kiev had fallen. The rumor was that all its Jews were dead. Desperate for news, Volkov wrote to everyone he knew. Finally, in the new year, he made a public appeal on the radio. Three letters came from people he had scarcely met. His wife was safe. They told him how to find her new address.

"In the last eight months I've been through quite a lot," Volkov wrote. "But my troubles can't be compared in any way with all that you, no doubt, have been through. First that time in Kiev, then the evacuation and the uncertainty over me. I can imagine how difficult all that must have been for you, but at least you did not stay in Kiev to fall into the hands of the Fascist monsters." For once, he said, the papers were failing to blacken the enemy enough. He was beginning to understand what he was fighting for. "However much they write in the newspapers about their atrocities," he went on, "the reality is much worse. I've been in some of the places where the beasts have been. I've seen the burned-out towns and villages, the corpses of women and children, the unhappy, plundered residents, but also I've seen the tears of joy when these people encountered us. . . . The spirit of these places has affected me and it has grown in all our soldiers."[31]

Men like Volkov had no chance of returning home. They had to trust the army and the state to protect their families. If they had doubted Moscow and its ideology before, and even if they still doubted, the only way to sleep at night was to attempt to believe that Stalin, the government, and their own fellow soldiers would take care of the people they loved. And they were learning fast about this war. They might not have believed the rumors in the first few weeks—the propaganda machine had always generated lies—but before long they could see and touch the evidence for themselves. That winter, the first mutilated bodies—burned, butchered, bruised, and left to freeze in the thin snow—were found and photographed by front-line Soviet troops retaking villages near Moscow.

Their enemy seemed to rejoice in violence. Escaping refugees told of mass shootings, the torturing of partisans. The Fascists drank and laughed as the corpses of their victims burned on gasoline-drenched pyres. "According to the local people," wrote a man from Smolensk, "on 13 December 1941 the enemy locked captured Red Army men in a four-story building surrounded by barbed wire. At midnight the Germans set fire to it. When the Red Army soldiers started jumping from the windows the Germans fired at them. About seventy people were shot and many burned to death."[32] Some Wehrmacht soldiers treasured souvenirs of violence. A snapshot found in the breast pocket of a fallen German infantryman that winter showed the massacre of Kovno's Jews. Another showed a German soldier contemplating two hanged Russians swinging from a rope. Even the most hardened Red Army men could not ignore the gruesome truth these pictures showed. It was no longer wise to argue that any dictator would do if Russia could just have some peace.

Not every soldier reached this view at once—some never did—and few reached it with ease or lightly. It was as if each person's world, his prewar world, had to collapse, to fail him before he understood the purpose of his life. Volkov had nightmares about his wife and child; Moskvin, in his dark hut, had to rethink his Communism. Older men seemed to look back over their time, the dreamlike years of state-directed change, in something like bewilderment. The past now shimmered like a story-book paradise. Contrast alone made every image clearer. Those years of peace, years that had seemed so hard, had been accepting, easy, safe, a time of opportunities that each man valued only now, in retrospect. But strangely, when there could be no escape, the rush of wartime action brought a sense of renewed worth. "It's like the way that a healthy person is not aware of his body," a soldier wrote of this feeling. "It's only when something starts to hurt that you understand what health really is."[33]

The fear of death also gave some people—including grown men in their late thirties or older—their first real taste of life. At this stage, the effect was often bleak. Veterans fell prey to fatalism, a sense, based upon fact and not on premonition, that though they had just learned to value life they were as good as dead. Their hopes, if they had them, now focused on their families and children. "It's hard to know how long I will remain alive," a man wrote to his wife in January 1942. She was expecting their first child, but he knew he would never see it. He told her that he could not describe the things he had witnessed at the front. Instead, he wanted to think about her future and that of the child. "Deal with my things as you see fit," he wrote. "They are yours, as I am yours and you are mine. Simochka, whether it is a boy or a girl, please bring it up according to your own beliefs. Tell it about me, about your husband and its father."[34] "You couldn't say that I'm alive—no," another soldier wrote to his wife and daughter. "A dead person is a blind one, and for that reason the only thing that interests me is your life, my only concern is to remember you."[35]

The prewar sense of homeland dissolved just as quickly as the dream of easy victory. Gordon had been a naïve internationalist at school. The first Germans he met were prisoners, an officer and two infantrymen. One of the soldiers was a worker. "He didn't understand at first," Gordon recalled, "what the interpreter meant when he asked him how a proletarian could take up arms against the land of the Soviets, the first homeland of the proletariat of the whole world. He answered that most of the men in his unit were either peasants or workers and that for them the 'fatherland' was not Russia but Germany. That answer made us all reflect on the meaning of the phrase 'The Soviet Union—homeland of the world proletariat.' "[36] So did firsthand exposure to that homeland's cold realities: forced marches, blizzards, fog, hunger, and digging, endless digging in chill, clammy earth. "The party told us that

The massacre of Jews at Kovno (photograph found in the pocket of a German NCO captured later in the war, courtesy of the State Archive of the Russian Federation)

German soldiers with the bodies of their Russian victims (another photograph that its German owner had cherished, courtesy of the State Archive of the Russian Federation)

there was nothing dearer than motherland," a Belorussian veteran declared. But the way that motherland was imagined was changing for everyone. For some, like Moskvin, the notion enlarged to encompass a new landscape, villages, unlettered peasants, and dour local fighters whose toughness equaled his own. For others, the idea narrowed, shrinking away from universal brotherhood in a xenophobic tide of holy Russian chauvinism.

It was at this time, in the late autumn of 1941, that Stalin began to revise his own rhetoric of the motherland. His address at the Red Army's state parade on the twenty-fourth anniversary of Lenin's revolution that November spoke of Russia's heroic past. The bitter trials of the civil war, when Lenin's government nearly died, were recalled at length—nothing else was possible on this of all occasions—but older epics joined them in a catalog of struggle. Russian soldiers were called to emulate their ancestors: Alexander Nevsky, Dmitry Donskoi, Minin and Pozharsky, Alexander Suvorov, Mikhail Kutuzov.[37] "May you be blessed," the leader continued, "by Lenin's victorious banner!"[38] Russia's defending troops could also hope for blessings from the Orthodox Church. From the first day of the war, Metropolitan Sergii of Moscow and Kostroma had insisted that it should stand by the people in their struggle.[39] The state's prewar restrictions on worship were gently eased. But though the soldiers cherished totems—tin crosses or copies of poems—formal religion, so comforting to some civilians, was of little use at the front. Rage and hatred, which the state also nurtured, were more likely to inspire men on the brink of combat. In 1941, *Pravda* dropped its peacetime masthead, "Proletarians of all lands, unite!" The slogan that replaced it was "Death to the German invaders!"

"I never lost the feeling that this was a genuine People's War," wrote Alexander Werth. "The thought that this was *their* war was, in the main, as strong among civilians as among the soldiers."[40] It would have been hard to remain neutral after witnessing the effects of that year's German conquest. When Kursk fell in November, its able-bodied men were rounded up and interned wherever the barbed wire could be unrolled. The lucky ones were herded into the central movie theater; most others shivered in the open air. They were not fed at all. Then they were made to work, and those who failed to satisfy their captors were beaten with rubber truncheons and threatened with death. On the second day of the occupation, fifteen Communist activists, including four young women, were made to dig graves in the black loam near the central square, and then each one was shot. Rumor had it that about seven hundred other young women had been rounded up and forced to work as prostitutes in makeshift brothels for the German troops. "The streets are empty," Soviet intelligence reported. "The shops have been looted. There is no mains water and no electricity. Kursk has collapsed. Life there has frozen."[41]

Kursk had not been a city with a large community of Jews. If it had been, it would have seen larger mass graves, more killing, and even more fear as newly blooded executioners enjoyed the privilege of power. The mass shootings in any town began as soon as the Wehrmacht arrived. Some, such as the massacre at Kiev's Babi Yar, were carried out by special units, the Einsatzgruppen, but many, including the shooting of 650 Jews at Klintsy, 540 at Mglin, 350 at Kletna, and thousands more in the old Jewish Pale, were treated as routine military operations. The first killings terrified the local people. But, as a Soviet agent near Smolensk observed, eventually their effect was to harden them. "They laugh at the Germans now," affirmed a report in 1942. "People have become braver in the face of death. They know that they must fight the enemy with every ounce of their strength." There had been many willing collaborators in the early weeks, but by that first autumn the people's "hatred of the enemy" was "growing and growing."[42]

Moskvin observed the same shift in the peasants' mood. In late August 1941, the *politruk* came close to absolute despair. The shooting of Jews would not have troubled his peasant hosts, he realized, for they blamed them for most of the troubles Communism had brought. Their antisemitism went hand in hand with a "fanatical belief in God," a faith that the invading Germans wisely indulged everywhere. Some even volunteered to become Fascism's local agents—*politzei*—but at heart it was not politics but survival that impelled them. "After each battle," Moskvin noted, "they rush to the field to loot the corpses for whatever they can find." The dearest hope of these peasants was for an end to Soviet power. In September 1941, though, they learned that the Germans had ordered that the collective farms should stay. Like the prewar Soviet authorities, the conquerors cared only for the ease with which the peasants' grain could be collected and shipped off. It was an irreversible mistake. "The mood of the local population has changed sharply," Moskvin wrote on 30 September. His heart still sickened at the news that reached him from the front. Like everyone around him, he was desperate for advice.[43] But he was no longer in danger of cheap betrayal.

Moskvin was also lonely. The army of his memory glowed with the warmth of comradeship. But regular troops could have corrected his illusions. At this stage in the war, few referred to their fellow soldiers in their letters home. The primary groups, the "buddies," that mattered so much to American soldiers in Vietnam, seem hardly to have featured in the shadow of defeat. Units were butchered and entire divisions smashed. The survivors, shocked and exhausted, were redeployed piecemeal wherever men were needed. Tank and air crews, both of them types of soldier who form strong bonds through mutual dependence and shared risk, were not as evident at this stage in the war as they would be from 1943. And the army was in retreat, disordered, scattering across a giant space. Men still formed friendships in this extreme world, truer and stronger than their peacetime ones, but most were doomed to loss. Peer loyalties, indeed, could well be retrospective, grieving. The strongest sentimental ties, in 1941, were often with the dead, the strength of every soldier's resolve made holy by blood sacrifice.

The other missing character in the soldiers' imaginary worlds at this stage in the war was Stalin. Moskvin scarcely mentioned him. The leader was an irrelevance in his remote village. Only the memory of peace seemed still to conjure the great man. Older people would never forgive the betrayals of 1929, the pain of poverty and loss; now Stalin was failing them again. But the young, and the millions who rethought their universe as they watched comrades die, looked for solace as the winter drew on. This was the process by which the leader became a totem, the one constant that promised rescue, remained strong. The Stalin who fulfilled this role was not the same man, in imagination, as the leader of the 1930s. Or rather, he represented the lost paradise remembered from a vanished world. He was a talisman, a name, a hollow image that some privately abhorred. But it was better, in this darkness, to find something to believe in than to die in utter desolation.

According to patriotic myth, whole armies used the same slogan to raise their spirits on the brink of battle. Though German veterans mainly recall the Soviets' bloodcurdling "Hoorah!" the official war cry that millions of Red Army survivors remembered later was "For the motherland! For Stalin!" In recent years, some old soldiers—especially those who were never officers—have expressed doubts about the use of this phrase. "Did we shout that?" Ivan Gorin, a soldier and the son of peasants, asked, laughing. "I'm sure we shouted something when we went at the guns, but I don't think it was that polite." The officers and policemen were too far back behind the lines to hear. But those who used the slogan had good reason to chorus the familiar words. Whatever Gorin claimed later, or writers like the veteran Vasil Bykov, superstition forbade swearing on the eve of battle.[44] And it would have been hard for the men to have agreed on an alternative expression without alerting the secret police. Thus, though the men muttered lots of things and all used the drawn-out, terrible "Hoorah!," the famous words may also have been as common as survivors have claimed. The point was that it hardly mattered what the men shouted—they needed a war cry, a loud noise that united every pair of lungs and forced their muscles on. The sound, and not the meaning, was the point. The slogan became sacred in its own right. And then the real man slowly assumed the charisma surrounding it.[45]

At this early stage, however, the people who cared most about Stalin and his image were the propagandists. Despite the pressures of likely defeat, some officers considered that time should be spent, as it had always been, fostering myths and grooming spurious internal enemies. In February 1942, a recruit from Siberia was sent north to the Volkhov front near Leningrad. The ski battalion he had joined was broken up by German fire within a week, and he was redeployed to a regular infantry division, the 281st. This was a war of position, and he and his comrades spent their days digging new trenches, dodging shells, and wondering what they were fighting for. "All we knew," the old man later told his children, "was that we were fighting for the motherland." His surname, Khabibulin, suggests that the motherland for him had once been to the east of Russia itself, which probably explains why he was picked when the Special Section needed a scapegoat. The pretext was a casual remark he made to a Ukrainian soldier who had botched an attempt at shooting his own thumb off. "You could have done that better," Khabibulin observed. "They'd have demobilized you." The young man asked him sharply if he did not want to fight. "What can I say?" Khabibulin answered. "We're fighting." And then, less cautiously, and maybe out of pity for the boy, he added something about the sad loss of life.

Khabibulin was arrested three days later and accused of fomenting opposition to the popular struggle on behalf of the motherland and Stalin. The charges carried the death penalty, but Khabibulin escaped with a ten-year sentence, part of which, ironically, he served in a prison where Stalin himself had languished forty years before. So he survived, and much later, after the fall of Communism, he was able to see his files at the KGB. It was then that he learned how other men, his comrades, had agreed to testify against him and how the investigators had been obsessed, of all things, by his attitude to Stalin. The depositions would have been dictated by police; they tell us more about the state's propaganda needs than about real soldiers' thinking. So it is interesting that a man who scarcely seemed to have given the leader a thought until his arrest found testimonies that quoted him as saying "I won't fight for Stalin. If it's for Stalin, I won't fight."[46]

★

When the men were fighting, they rarely thought of food, but every other waking moment was tormented by incessant hunger. Their usual diet, according to a *politruk* who served in the defense of Moscow, was breakfast at six o'clock, including soup "so thick that a spoon could stand in it any way you liked," a lunch of buckwheat kasha, tea, and bread, and then more soup and tea at nightfall. A medical orderly supervised the preparation of all food, testing each dish before it could be served up to the men.[47] In 1941, the daily ration for front-line soldiers theoretically included nearly a kilo of bread, 150 grams of meat, buckwheat, dried fish, and a healthy lump of lard or fat.[48] But even the *politruk* conceded that "in battle, it was much harder with food."[49]

What that meant was that most combat soldiers received nothing but dry rations, and sometimes nothing at all, for days on end. "We're living in dugouts in the woods," a soldier wrote home. "We sleep on straw, like cattle. They feed us very badly—twice a day, and even then not what we need. We get five spoonfuls of soup in the morning. . . .

Artillerymen dining beside their weapons, 1941

We're hungry all day."[50] Mere discomfort, in those conditions, was the least serious consequence. That winter, temperatures dropped below minus twenty degrees Fahrenheit. "Seven of our boys have frostbite on their legs," a soldier wrote to his mother in February 1942. "They're in the hospital now. We had to go seven days without a crust, we were exhausted and starved. I've done nothing since I got back but eat. My legs have started swelling up a bit at night, I eat a lot, and my stomach aches all the time."[51] Even the bureaucrats became concerned. That winter saw a stream of orders about hot food and vital supplies for the front line.[52]

Men were also short of basic clothing. Russian people feel the cold

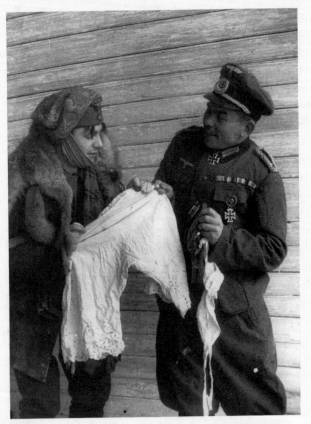

Humorous portrayal of the "Winter Fritz," from a Red Army
theatrical revue called The Thieving Army, *February 1942*

like every other European does; they have no magic inner warmth, whatever their shivering opponents thought as the October rain began to turn to sleet. After the Finnish war, the general staff had reviewed the question of cold-weather gear for Soviet troops, and there is no doubt that *valenki*, padded jackets and trousers, fur gloves, and warm hats saved thousands of lives in the Red Army through the war. One of the stock characters of Soviet wartime farce, by contrast, was the "Winter Fritz," the hapless German forced to clothe himself in stolen mitts, newspaper padding, and some babushka's outlandish drawers. But the

Red Army had problems, too. With manufacturing at a near standstill, new supplies could not be guaranteed. In 1942, for instance, the Soviet footwear industry would turn out enough boots to supply just 0.3 pairs for every person in the land.[53] Storage, repairs, and salvage were vital for mere survival. But habits learned through years of coexistence with state bureaucrats and planners could be difficult to break. In September 1941, inspectors found a forgotten shipment of 266,000 pairs of army trousers stacked without covers and already dripping with mildew.[54] Tens of thousands of winter boots awaited overdue repair while hundreds of recruits faced winter without footwear of any kind.[55] By the spring, the situation was so critical that officers and men who served behind the lines were barred from receiving greatcoats with their summer kit. Instead, they had to be content with cast-off padded jackets from the front.[56]

The black market flourished. All kinds of military property were diverted or filched, including boots and other clothing, fuel, food, and even kitchen pots.[57] Tobacco had become so scarce by 1942 that Muscovites would light a cigarette and offer passersby the chance, for two rubles, to take a puff.[58] Army supplies—wholesale, anonymous, and easy to steal—were treasure even honest patriots could not resist. Another thriving trade sprang to life in response to the introduction, on 25 August 1941, of a front-line ration of vodka. The idea was to issue every soldier on active duty a hundred grams a day. Special officers were charged with measuring the portions, and the unused surplus was supposed to be accounted for every ten days.[59] But vodka is too precious to be treated with such pedantry. Officers and men who were not entitled to a ration helped themselves from the stores. Hard-pressed quartermasters sold it off.[60] In Moscow, Simonov observed, people were drinking more vodka than tea by January 1942. Drunkenness remained a problem among front-line troops.[61] And everyone knew that the supply would increase after a battle. "It was always good to serve with the infantry," a survivor remembered. "The infantry or the artillery. The death rates among them were highest. And no one was checking how much vodka we sent back."

No one checked up on the dead, either. "Not rarely," ran one of Mekhlis's mealymouthed notes, "the corpses of soldiers . . . go uncollected from the battlefield for several days and no one cares, although it would be entirely possible to bury our comrades with full military honors." He mentioned a case where fourteen bodies had lain unburied for five days, a not-surprising occurrence in December, with the ground frozen and every soldier needing to conserve his strength. "Corpses on the field," Mekhlis observed, "have a political resonance that affects the political-moral condition of the soldiers and the authority of commissars and commanders."[62] More urgently, the dead had possessions that living soldiers desperately needed. New uniforms were reserved for each new army as it formed; front-line troops needing fresh supplies relied on recycled clothes and equipment. "After very severe battles," recalled a *politruk*, "we had to send our soldiers back into the field to gather the dead with their weapons so that we could use them again the next morning."[63] That December Mekhlis would order that all bodies should be buried promptly with the proper respect (and careful documentation).[64] Ten months later, the authorities complained that corpses were still being pitched into trenches and shell holes or, worse, that they were being left out for the rats. As for their possessions, a further order, dated 29 November 1942, listed the items that burial parties were expected to retrieve, including "greatcoats, tunics, hats, padded trousers and jackets, sweaters, gloves, boots, and *valenki*."[65] Burial teams were not considered to have recovered a corpse unless they also carried back a gun.

Death was probably a better fate—if it was swift—than capture for Red Army troops. "Our treatment of prisoners of war," a German intelligence officer observed in February 1942, "cannot continue without consequences. It is no longer because of lectures from the *politruks* but out of his own personal convictions that the Soviet soldier has come to expect an agonizing life or death if he falls captive."[66] The knowledge made Soviet troops fight bitterly and fueled deeper hatred. "If the Germans treated our prisoners well," a colonel told Werth in 1942, "it would soon be known. It's a horrible thing to say, but by ill-treating and starving our prisoners to death, the Germans are *helping* us."[67]

The tens of thousands of Red Army soldiers who surrendered in June and July 1941 never imagined the fate that awaited them at German hands. But by the late summer, terrible stories had begun to spread. In August, Moskvin met the first of the many escaped soldiers whom he would harbor in the coming months. The man's account chilled his blood. "They say there's no shelter, no water," Moskvin wrote, "that people are dying from hunger and disease, that many are without proper clothes or shoes. They are treated like slaves, shot for the slightest misdemeanor, or just out of mischief, for fun." Ukrainian captives, who already enjoyed, if they so chose, a kind of privilege within the camps, were encouraged to finger Communists and Jews. The victims suffered beatings, dug their graves, and died with bullets in their backs.

Moskvin sustained one of his frequent stabs of spiritual pain. "I realize how naïve our army training was," he wrote in his diary. "We excluded the idea of becoming prisoners entirely from our view of what was acceptable in war, but what we told the soldiers and ourselves was that the enemy would use prisoners to extract secrets, that he would torture people to persuade them to betray. All our examples were drawn from the last war, the imperialist war, and from notions of class war. But now we're dealing with the Gestapo and the SS, and as far as they're concerned we're nothing more than Reds."[68] It was a lesson others also slowly learned. This enemy was not fighting a cartoon battle with the Bolsheviks. Its sole aim was to wipe them out.

"In the town of Rzhev there is a concentration camp with fifteen thousand captured Red Army soldiers in it and five thousand civilians," noted a smuggled report of December 1941. "They are holding them in unheated huts, and they feed them one or two frozen potatoes each a day. The Germans threw rotten meat and some bones through the barbed wire at the prisoners. This has made them ill. Every day 20–30 people are dying. The ones who are too ill to work are shot."[69] It was a holocaust that devoured millions. Until the German rout at Stalingrad, most Soviet prisoners were held near the front line. "Many of them died on the bare ground," a German witness admitted at Nuremberg. "Epidemics broke out and cannibalism manifested itself." "It was not until well into 1942," Werth commented, "that the surviving Russian war prisoners began to be looked on as a source of slave labor."[70]

Among the minority of captured soldiers who survived, a disproportionate number belonged to non-Slavic ethnic groups. They owed their lives to German racist fantasies and to the handful of quixotic nationalists, based in Berlin, who had escaped from their own countries during the troubled founding years of Soviet power. These men now toured the camps in search of fellow countrymen. The rescue that they offered was conditional. Those they selected were considered to have volunteered for the so-called legions—Georgian, Cossack, Turkestan—whose sacred duty was to free their homelands from Bolshevism. But the men's choice could seldom be described as free. Their decisions say more about the torment they endured than about their real loyalties.

Ibrai Tulebaev escaped in just this way. In 1942, he was recruited for the Turkestan legion. But he defected back to the Soviet side in 1943. The police who interrogated him then filed every detail of his account of the camps that he survived between August 1941 and the spring of 1942. The first camp, on Polish soil, consisted of twelve blocks, each housing between fifteen hundred and two thousand inmates. The men were penned inside at dusk; any who stepped outside were shot. Each night ten or fifteen of them met this fate. By day, the German guards used prisoners for target practice and baited some of them with dogs. Sometimes they placed bets on the animals—not on the men—to see which would fight hardest. There was so little food that hungry prisoners ripped flesh from corpses. Disease killed those who survived German sport. But Tulebaev was spared; the Germans had noted his ethnicity and had already begun to segregate potential nationalist freedom fighters. They had a cruel way of breaking the men's hearts. In December 1941, Tulebaev calculated, there were about eighty thousand prisoners in his camp. Most were in the light uniforms they had been wearing back in June. By February, all but three thousand or so had died of cold, malnutrition, typhus, or dysentery. Twelve men were shot for cannibalism that December; too few survived for punishment to matter much when the snow melted in April.[71]

The same stories were repeated in camps across Poland, Belorussia, and Ukraine. In Dubno, they beat men to death. In Minsk they tortured naked victims with alternating jugs of icy and boiling water. Wherever prisoners were held, the *politruks* and Jews were shot as soon as they were recognized. And then the Germans started sifting out the non-Russians. It would be months before the new legions were fit to bear arms on the German side. Many recruits had first to spend weeks in special hospitals recovering from the purgatory of their imprisonment. They were not always fully conscious of the turn that events were about to take. "They did it for an extra crust of bread," the daughter of Georgia's wartime nationalist leader, Shalva Maglakelidze, told me. "They knew my father had saved their lives." Maglakelidze, who had not set foot on Soviet soil since 1921, believed that he was raising an army to liberate his people. The Georgians he rescued, by contrast, were clutching at a slender chance of life.

The threat of death was just as real for the people who found themselves on the wrong side of German lines. This was a war, they soon learned, of annihilation, a war of scorched earth, mass deportation, and easy, public slaughter. With little information and no faith in either the Soviet or the German state, each person had to weigh the options for his own survival. In July 1941 thousands of local people joined the German side as *politzei*, agents of Nazi power in the occupied zone. Some were willing enough. They were the ones who celebrated the coming defeat of the hated empire they saw as a Soviet, Bolshevik, or even Jewish monster. Others made their choice on impulse, to avoid imprisonment or a bullet. "During the retreat of the Red Army our agitation was very weak," a Soviet intelligence report conceded in September 1942. It insisted that many joined the *politzei*, and the thousand-strong paramilitary Ukrainian legion that had terrorized the partisans of the Smolensk region that summer, to escape death or torture in German prison camps, but the implication was that for others the Soviet dream (if it had ever held appeal) had soured.

In Soviet eyes, the problem was that far too many people in the occupied regions, finding themselves leaderless and stateless, had "listened to the Hitlerites and followed them."[72] Moscow's answer was to reach these people through a new group of combatants, the partisans. Scant planning had been made for guerrilla war in the months leading up to Barbarossa, but the potential of partisan detachments was soon understood in Moscow. "There must be diversionist groups for fighting enemy units," Stalin ordered in July 1941. "In the occupied areas intolerable conditions must be created for the enemy and his accomplices."[73] The wartime myth still celebrates these tough guerrilla fighters, the men and women who cut German supply lines by blowing up railways and bridges, the heroes who prepared the way for the Red Army's troops. That was indeed part of their work—a costly part—but it is doubtful that their true value was sabotage. As a 1942 report put it, "nature abhors a vacuum."[74] The partisans' main task was to maintain the grip of Soviet power.[75]

Mikhail Ivanovich's OSMBON unit was among the first to hazard the route back into country that the Germans held. His task was to round up Red Army stragglers, shoot provocateurs, and shape some kind of discipline behind the lines. The groups of partisans that he helped form became the face of Soviet power in the remote woods of Smolensk province. His men brought more than discipline. Their revolvers were backed up with the promise (not always kept) of supplies. Later, they would also help to establish the routes by which letters (carefully censored) could be exchanged across the front-line zone. News from the "big country" off to the east fostered new hope and loyalty in some beleaguered villages.[76] OSMBON troops even wooed the peasants by helping them in the fields. They carried out agitational work, collecting and disseminating Sovinformburo reports to counteract German propaganda. They organized party meetings to celebrate anniversaries, teach hygiene and basic survival tactics, and generally to remind people of the joys of Soviet life. Their efforts helped to form a new, parallel army in the woods. By November 1942, according to Soviet reports, there were about ninety-four thousand partisans behind the German lines from the Baltic to the Crimea. Just under 10 percent of these were in the Smolensk region.[77] It was to them that Nikolai Moskvin eventually turned.

The *politruk* had not been able to decide, at first, if he should join the partisans or make for the nearest Red Army base. Rumor reached him in October 1941 that there was fighting near Vyaz'ma, but then the trail went cold and he began to fear that the army had fled beyond his reach. What sustained him through the first snow was the news, brought by escaping prisoners, of Stalin's speech of 7 November, an address made to soldiers in Red Square. "Everyone is still at their posts," he wrote. "Soon there will be a celebration everywhere." But his relief was premature. It would be months before the fugitive could make a bid to break through to the Soviet zone. In March, when the winter began to lift, he headed east, his goal the Red Army beyond Kaluga. Moskvin was captured as he neared the German lines. German troops took him to the camp at Granki, a front-line holding station, little more than a large yard. There he met the survivors of the previous autumn's encirclement at Vyaz'ma. They had been in the camp for six long months. "If you haven't seen this," Moskvin wrote, "you won't be able to imagine the utter horror of this human tragedy. I saw it with my own eyes. People were dying of exhaustion, cold, and beatings."

Moskvin was not destined to die with them. Healthy and determined, he still had the will to evade guards who were themselves cold and depressed after the winter. Six days after his capture he was on the run again. But he had lost his papers. Loyal though he was, he knew that the Reds could easily shoot him as a deserter. It was this knowledge that impelled him to head west, not east. That June, he joined a partisan group made up of former soldiers like himself. "It's really satisfying to fight the Fascists this way," he wrote jauntily that month. "We can get them on the roads, from hiding, with almost no cost to our own men." On 29 July his battalion killed a group of German guards, taking a score of *politzei* as prisoners and seizing two new machine guns. "I'm really doing business," he reported. And then, in August, came the best news of the year. "A really great joy for me today," he wrote. "I've received three letters at once from the big country. My parents are alive. Mariya is alive. Hurrah!"[78]

If letters could get through and men escape, then many partisans, including skilled fighters, might also have gone back to strengthen the Red Army. But the state had use for them just where they were. As ever, the policy was callous, for though the men had orders to remain, they received neither food nor weapons. "We have instructions to stay in the triangle near Smolensk and keep on fighting," Moskvin noted in September 1942. His optimism had begun to ebb. "The winter will be hard. Half our men don't have the right shoes or clothes." Like the outlaws they had become, his troops began to desert. Moskvin himself would soon curse Moscow's indifference. "We're supposed to live by stealing from the enemy and appealing to the locals," he wrote. But there was nothing for it but to extort food if everyone was starving. "In many places groups of enemies masquerading as partisans are engaging in banditry," a party report from Smolensk alleged. But the looters were more likely to be Soviet men. "It's not surprising that local people run off and complain to the Germans," Moskvin confirmed. "A lot of the time we're just robbing them like bandits."[79]

Once again, the Germans' own atrocities were all that held the Soviets in place. "At present," a partisan leader stated, "the situation is this: we in the forest believe that Communism (which 70 or 80 percent of us hate) will at least let us live, but the Germans, with their National Socialism, will either shoot us or starve us to death."[80] "Are you alive? I don't know," a soldier called Vasily Slesarev wrote to his wife, three sons, and daughter in December 1941. It would be seven months before he heard from them. They, too, were trapped behind the German lines. A letter from his twelve-year-old daughter, Mariya, brought out by partisans, finally told him their news. "We had already started to think that no one was alive, but it looks as if you are and Shura, though we have not heard from Sergei," the child wrote. Near Smolensk, in her village, there had been deaths. "Papa," Mariya went on, "our Valik died and is in the graveyard at Sumarokovo. Papa, the German monsters set fire to us." The family home had been razed on 30 January 1942. Survivors and their animals had been driven away. The boy Valery had died of pneumonia in the damp shelter where his family was hiding. "Many people have been killed in the villages around here," Mariya told her father. "And all they think about is the bloodthirsty monsters, you can't even call them human, they're just robbers and drinkers of blood. Papa, kill the enemy!"[81]

Among the many secrets of this war was its true cost. On 23 February 1942, Red Army Day, Stalin announced that the Germans had lost the advantage. The Red Army was driving them toward the west, he said, and it had cleared them completely from the provinces of Moscow and Tula.[82] Fighting talk like this was one of the few resources that the leader still commanded.[83] In reality, those weeks in February were among the darkest of the war. Moscow had not fallen, but Leningrad was under siege, its citizens facing a "white death" by starvation. To the south, the Crimea, with its strategic command of the Black Sea coast and the gates of the Caucasus, was almost entirely in German hands. Only the port of Sevastopol, besieged and under constant fire, still held out through the winter. Tula, as Stalin said, was free, but almost every other town and city to the west had been destroyed. The Germans had certainly lost large numbers of men, and Stalin was also right to say that their reserves were stretched, but Soviet losses had been greater by far. In addition to nearly three million captured men, the Red Army had lost 2,663,000 killed in action by February 1942. For every German who was killed, twenty Soviet soldiers had died.[84]

These figures alone should have been enough to cause a collapse of morale, if not a revolution. But they were not released. No one could calculate the total human cost of the war they were living through. Civilians who witnessed fighting, like the soldiers who fought, knew plenty about individual battles. But their knowledge was anecdotal, and even they could scarcely have guessed the true scale of the carnage. The very magnitude of the Soviet people's loss put it beyond imagination. And no figure could ever represent the truth of so much pain, or even the enormous heaps of bodies, the rotting, semifrozen flesh. The dead were not yet skeletons, their graves not yet those solid monuments of black granite. Their faces still showed shock and agony, their fingers clutched at mud and snow. In some places, the bodies lay on other bodies, heaps of human corpses rising up as if to stem some bloody tide. The only places where images like this were known and shared, apart from front-line camps, were hospitals. It was not for nothing that cheerful komsomols were sent to sit with convalescing troops, to read them letters, poems, and selected extracts from the press. Only at night were the real stories whispered around the wards.

The most desperate, that spring, came from the south. The men caught up in campaigns there learned to expect and even welcome death. "We used to say that whoever survives this winter will live a long time," a soldier who fought near Feodosia, in eastern Crimea, told his diary. The road along the coast was strewn with bodies, but his comrades could not bury them because of German fire. "I'm ready now," he added, "for a death of any kind."[85] With Sevastopol still in Soviet hands, a major expedition had been launched in December 1941 to liberate eastern Crimea. Its aim was to take the Kerch peninsula and use it as a bridgehead to relieve the pressure on Sevastopol and recapture the entire region. The project was doomed. As one young conscript wrote in February, "Our troops have abandoned Feodosia. What was the point in taking it, if we had not made preparations for its defense? If we've got to take every city twice like this, then maybe in 1945 we'll get to the end of this war."[86] A Soviet force remained in the lowlands around Kerch, the easternmost point on the Crimea, but its prospects were bleak. In early May, the Germans attacked for a final time, driving the Soviets toward the narrow strait that separates Kerch and its ancient harbor from the Russian mainland.

Kerch saw several kinds of tragedy that spring. First came the fighting itself. Stalin's favorite, Lev Mekhlis, was put in charge. For him, the struggle was a matter of morale. What that meant in practice was that military preparation for the last defense was minimal. "Everyone had to go forward, forward!" Simonov, who witnessed some of it, recalled. Ten kilometers behind the lines, he observed, there was nothing—no support, no reserve, and no transport. Mekhlis believed that trenches sapped the spirit of aggression, so none was ever dug. But beyond the port itself, the landscape of the Kerch peninsula is gently rolling steppe, treeless and sometimes marshy, offering no shelter to men fighting for their lives. The infantry divisions of the Fifty-first Army, many of them Georgians recently arrived from an entirely different countryside and climate, had neither plan nor cover as they faced the guns. Simonov was horrified when an initial round of German shelling left the land strewn with more corpses than he had seen at any time in the whole war. "There were no officers anywhere," he said. "It all took place on an open, muddy, absolutely barren field."[87] The next day, more infantrymen were driven over the same ground, passing the bodies of their comrades in the fog as they rushed on toward their deaths. A hundred and seventy-six thousand men were slaughtered at Kerch in just twelve days.[88]

The outcome was as Simonov predicted. In mid-May the last remnants of Mekhlis's army boarded small boats and set off across the five-mile strait toward the mainland. But the German advance had been so swift that many—several thousand—remained trapped in limestone hills behind the town. These men and women looked down on the strait below—they must have dreamed of walking it—and knew there could be no escape. But what came next was anguish of a kind that even this war would see only once or twice. It was typical because it involved individual courage, shattered faith, and then a cruel waste of life. It was unique because the drama took place underground. The heroes of the story found their graves in a maze of tunnels deep within Crimea's rock.

The officers of the Special Section, hardened agents in the mold of Mikhail Ivanovich and the OSMBON, took charge at once. Barking their orders and fingering loaded guns, they gathered every straggler and mustered the men. Then they produced a group of local guides, people who knew the landscape and its secret caves. These men led the entire company into a quarry, an enormous labyrinth of pits and tunnels from which the stone to build a fortress for the port's defense had been taken eighty years before. This cave city would now become the soldiers' home. Three thousand people, including nurses and refugees from Kerch (these people had survived a brief episode of German rule already that summer and knew to fear a second even more), huddled away into the darkness. They dragged their horses and their guns, they carried bundles of supplies. If they had glanced behind them as they shuffled down into the earth, they would have glimpsed the grassy steppe, the blue spring light, burgeoning yellow tansy, and the crimson splashes of the first poppies. These colors would have been the last that they would see. Few would blink in daylight again or even feel a cool breeze on their skin.

The cave city was organized. That is, the men from the Special Section knew their work. They split their company into detachments and assigned clear tasks to each. Some were organized into sentry rotations, others sent off down dank tunnels to look for hidden exits, search for water, or scrape together any food or fuel. The men in charge made their headquarters in the largest, safest cave. The hospital was set up in the deepest one. It was soon needed. Without a regular supply of food, the refugees began to eat the flesh of horses that had died in the escape. Three months later this meat was still the only food they had. At first scouts from the quarry made raids to the surface, seizing whatever they could steal and harrassing the German guards who watched over the site, but in a few weeks all that stopped as well. The quarry people were trapped. As they waited for death, they lit their darkness with thin, stinking candles made from burning strips of rubber tire.

The Germans planted explosives around the exits from the site. Rocks and splinters rained down on the fugitives below. Then poison gas was released into the tunnels, killing all but a few score of the Soviet defenders. These last died hungry and despairing in the next few weeks, but they did not surrender. In Soviet myth, the quarry at Adzhimuskai became another Leningrad, a Brest fortress, a place where heroes held out to the last. But in fact these brave men and women had no choice. Although some of the officers, the Special Section men with their revolvers and their survival training, must have escaped and reported the tale, the others were forced to remain. They were kept in the pit at gunpoint, threatened with death by comrades from their own side. If they would not behave like heroes, choosing a noble end, they would die from a Soviet bullet in the neck.[89]

The fall of Kerch sealed Sevastopol's fate. Since the previous autumn, the city had been holding out, although it was a grim shadow of the Black Sea resort that Messerschmitts had bombed a year before. In late May 1942 the defenders heard that German troops were converging on the city. Some of its residents—women, the elderly, and children—were evacuated by sea from the port that week. Among the many who remained was the writer and humorist Evgeny Petrov, who died during the last days of the siege. The NKVD guards, meanwhile, disposed of their prisoners—allegedly in caves near Inkerman—and then made their escape into the night. The bombardment began. There were so many planes, naval officer Evseev wrote, that there was no space above the town for them to circle. The sound, "a hellish cacophony," was so constant and deafening that citizens found any silence troubling. "And the heavier the bombing," Evseev remarked, "the greater and stronger became our rage and hatred of the enemy."

It was a passionate but futile anger. By early July Junkers were flying as low as a hundred meters above the northern suburbs of the city. The pavements and boulevards where sailors had once strolled were strewn with corpses now, the lovely buildings gutted, thick with smoke. "Heat," Evseev wrote. "We were all desperately thirsty. But no one had any water in his flask." He and a group of other men had taken shelter in the caves and tunnels underneath the port. Someone was sent to find water, and the others passed the time by dreaming of the things they might have liked to drink: "Lemonade, kvass, seltzer water, beer, and, if you please, ice cream. But we agreed on one thing. We'd drink anything, even if it was not cold fresh water, even if it was polluted, even if it had been flowing through the corpses." They had, in fact, "been drinking water from under corpses for several days." The bodies had been thrown into the concrete tanks and reservoirs around the town. As Evseev commented, "We never managed to clear them out."

Evseev was among the many who escaped, shipped off the coast within a few days of the city's fall. Thousands of others, many of them military personnel like him, remained behind to face a pitiless enemy. "The city was unrecognizable," Evseev lamented, looking back from an army truck. "It was dead. The snow-white city of a little while ago, Sevastopol the beautiful, had turned into a ruin." As the men boarded their boat to cross a perilous Black Sea, they swore they would be back to take revenge.[90] Some eventually fulfilled that brave boast, but for the ninety thousand or so women and men of the Red Army and Fleet captured with the town, it offered little hope.[91]

The Soviet retreat continued. Kharkov had fallen to the enemy in May. With the Crimea securely under their control, the Germans now launched an attack on Rostov, a vital gateway to the Caucasus and to the Volga citadel of Stalingrad. By mid-July most of the Don basin was occupied. Only Voronezh, to the north, held out. Staryi Oskol was taken, the Don crossed. "The majority of our commanding officers are cowards," a young man called Gudzovskii wrote. "Surely we did not need to run away. We could have stood our ground and faced them. Give us an order to go west! To hell with retreating! I'm sick to death of pulling back from the places where I grew up."[92] It was the last thing he would write before his death. The army could not even save the local people it would leave behind. "They shared their last crusts with us," a front-line officer remembered. "I ate that bread and knew that in an hour I'd be leaving, retreating. But I said nothing! I didn't have the right! . . . If we had told them, they would have run away as well, and then there would have been bottlenecks along the road for us."[93]

The old man added that he felt ashamed. The army was failing in the rawest human terms. Many civilians in the threatened districts lost faith in Soviet troops that summer. "God knows what's going on," a woman from a village washhouse hissed at two soldiers one evening. "We work and work, and they are just abandoning our towns!" One of the men shot her a pained look and walked away. The other thought despairingly of his own home, Voronezh, which was under fire and which, because the road north was still blocked, he could not even dream of defending.[94] Worse news was to follow. On 28 July 1942 the Soviet people learned that Rostov and Novocherkassk had fallen. There was no stronghold now between the Germans and the Caucasus, and little to detain them on their way to Stalingrad.

FIVE

STONE BY STONE

★

The second summer of the war blew with an arid wind that offered neither victory nor hope. The campaign that was meant to end with triumph in Berlin now threatened stalemate, if not unthinkable defeat. "We never doubted that we would win," the veterans have claimed. But the delusion of invincibility, sustained through the first months of shock, could not survive the truth of constant failure. The police did their duty, demanding rigid cheerfulness from everyone. One soldier was arrested merely for observing that "we're retreating, and we won't be coming back."[1] But by August 1942 the men themselves were getting tired of the despair and shame, of the reproachful stares that followed them as they abandoned, one by one, the gaunt, semideserted townships of the steppe. They had been dragging back across the wheat fields of Ukraine, the Don, and the Kuban for months. Behind them, somewhere over the eastern horizon, flowed the Volga, the river that divides the European part of Russia from the gates of Asia. Eastward again stretched thousands of miles of dust, a landscape little changed since Tamurlane, and one that sons of Russia's gentler, settled heart found alien. Symbolically at least, the time was coming when the army would have nowhere left to go.

The mindset that Stalin's regime had fostered in its people—in public optimistic and naïve, in private wry and cynical—had failed the soldiers in these bitter months. For years, they had been incited to blame their misfortunes on others, the scapegoats that the state chose to call enemies and spies. Stalinism had shaped a culture that discouraged individuals from standing out. Buck passing—for which its mandarins would coin a special word, *obezlichka*—became during the purges after 1937 a matter, literally, of life and death. More than a year into the war, this pattern of behavior had brought the Red Army to the edge of defeat. Now it was clear that every soldier's effort, and perhaps his life, would be required. But months of humiliation had left the men edgy, prone to panic at the first rumor of German tanks.[2] Morale was at its lowest ebb. "We wept as we retreated," a veteran recalled. The tears flowed from exhaustion, but they also signaled shame. "We were running anywhere to get away from Kharkov—some to Stalingrad, others to Vladikavkaz. Where else would we end up—Turkey?"[3]

Years of habit drove each man to lay the blame on someone else. Troops from the Russian heartland pointed fingers at Ukrainians, especially the "westerners" from former Polish lands. "Whole companies were abandoning the front line, the Ukrainians were melting away," Lev Lvovich, now an officer, recalled. "They weren't going to the German side, but just back home." "Only the Russians are fighting these Germans," a young infantryman grumbled at the time. "Most of the Ukrainians have just stayed home." As he looked out across the Kalmyk steppe, he added that "my own home is a long way from here, too. Why should I lay my bones in foreign soil?"[4] The tens of thousands of Ukrainians at the front line, naturally, found other scapegoats for it all. "There were many, many cases . . . where people deliberately shot themselves in the hand or the shoulder, just in the flesh," recalled a Kiev-based infantryman. "Then they'd be in the hospital and wouldn't have to go to the front line." And there was always a new ethnic minority to blame. "All those men from Central Asia," he continued, "when it was their mealtime, or after a bit anyway, they'd throw themselves on the ground and start up with their 'O Allah!' They were praying, and they weren't going to rush at the enemy or get involved in combat at all."[5] Racism was so prevalent that even Moscow grew alarmed.[6] The armed forces, like the society from which they came, were shattering like bombed-out glass.

The tales of cities lost and farmland left to burn or rot arrived in the capital almost by the day. To the north, embattled Leningrad was holding, though the country's leaders knew that its survival was as fragile as a hair. But to the south the news was bleak. By late July, Stalin himself could stand no more. Interrupting a report that his chief of staff, Aleksandr Vasilevsky, was delivering, he ordered the general to draft a new command to the troops, a piece of paper that would come to symbolize that summer's crucial turning point.[7] The object was to change the mental habits of a generation. In fact, defeat itself was starting to break the old patterns, and there would be more changes in the coming months. Order no. 227 came at the army's lowest point. But war itself would be the crucible in which a new mentality was forged.

Order no. 227 was issued on 28 July. At Stalin's insistence, it was never printed for general distribution. Instead, its contents were conveyed by word of mouth to every man and woman in the army. "Your reports must be pithy, brief, clear, and concrete," the *politruks* were told. "There must not be a single person in the armed forces who is not familiar with Comrade Stalin's order."[8] In ragged lines, huddled against the sun and wind, the soldiers listened to a roll call of disgrace. "The enemy," they heard, "has already taken Voroshilovgrad, Starobel'sk, Rossosh', Kupyansk, Valuiki, Novocherkassk, Rostov-on-Don, and half of Voronezh. A section of the troops on the southern front, giving into panic, abandoned Rostov and Novocherkassk without offering any serious defense and without waiting for Moscow's orders. They covered their colors in shame." The leader then spelled out what every soldier knew, which was that the civilian population, their own people, had lost almost all faith in them. The time had come to stand their ground whatever the cost. As Stalin's order put it, "Every officer, every soldier and political worker must understand that our resources are not limitless. The territory of the Soviet state is not just desert, it is people—workers, peasants, intellectuals, our fathers, mothers, wives, brothers, and children." Even Stalin conceded that at least seventy million of these were now behind the German lines.[9]

Stalin's remedy was embodied in a new slogan. "Not a step back!" was to become the army's watchword. Every man was told to fight until his final drop of blood. "Are there any extenuating causes for withdrawing from a firing position?" soldiers would ask their *politruks*. In future, the reply that handbooks prescribed would be "The only extenuating cause is death."[10] "Panicmongers and cowards," Stalin decreed, "must be destroyed on the spot." An officer who permitted his men to retreat without explicit orders was now to be arrested on a capital charge. And all personnel were confronted with a new sanction. The guardhouse was too comfortable to be used for criminals; in future, laggards, cowards, defeatists, and other miscreants would be consigned to penal battalions. There, they would have an opportunity "to atone for their crimes against the motherland with their own blood." In other words, they would be assigned the most hazardous tasks, including suicidal assaults and missions deep behind the German lines. For this last chance, they were supposed to feel gratitude. Only through death (or certain specified kinds of life-threatening injury) could outcasts redeem their names, saving their families and restoring their honor before the Soviet people. Meanwhile, to help the others concentrate, the new rules called for units of regular troops to be stationed behind the front line. These "blocking units" were to supplement existing *zagradotryady*, the NKVD troops whose task had always been to guard the rear. Their orders were to kill anyone who lagged behind or attempted to run away.[11]

Order no. 227 was not made public until 1988, when it was printed as part of the policy of glasnost, or openness. More than forty years after the end of the war, the measure sounded cruel to people reared on the romantic epic of Soviet victory. A generation that had grown up in decades of peace balked at the old state's lack of pity. But in 1942 most soldiers would have recognized the decree as a restatement of current rules. Deserters and cowards had always been in line for a bullet, with or without benefit of tribunal. Since 1941, their families, too, had suffered their disgrace. Like a slap in the face, the new order was intended to remind the men, to call them to account. And their response was frequently relief. "It was a necessary and important step," Lev Lvovich told me. "We all knew where we stood after we had heard it. And we all—it's true—felt better. Yes, we felt better." "We have read Stalin's order no. 227," Moskvin wrote in his diary on 22 August. "He openly recognizes the catastrophic situation in the south. My head is full of one idea: who is guilty over this? Yesterday they told us about the fall of Maikop, today Krasnodar. The political information boys keep asking if there isn't some treachery at work in all this. I think so, too. But at least Stalin is on our side! . . . So, not a step back! It's timely and it's just."[12]

To the south, where the retreat Moskvin abhorred was taking place, news of the order chilled the blood of depressed, tired men. "As the divisional commander read it," a military correspondent wrote, "the people stood rigid. It made our skin crawl."[13] It was one thing to insist on sacrifice but quite another to be making it. But even then, all that the men were hearing was a repetition of familiar rules. Few soldiers, by this stage in the war, would not have heard about or seen at least one summary execution, the laggard or deserter drawn aside and shot without reflection or remorse. The numbers are hard to establish, since tribunals were seldom involved. It is estimated that about 158,000 men were formally sentenced to be executed during the war.[14] But the figure does not include the thousands whose lives ended in roadside dust, the stressed and shattered conscripts shot as "betrayers of the motherland"; nor does it include the thousands more shot for retreating—or even for seeming to retreat—as battle loomed. At Stalingrad, as many as 13,500 men are thought to have been shot in the space of a few weeks.[15]

"We shot the men who tried to mutilate themselves," a military lawyer said. "They weren't worth anything, and if we sent them to prison we were only giving them what they wanted."[16] It was helpful to have a better use for able-bodied men—that much was a real outcome of Stalin's order. Copied from German units that the Soviets observed in 1941, the first penal battalions were ready well in time for Stalingrad. Though most assignments in this war were dangerous, those in the *shtraf* units were wretched, one step removed from the dog's death that awaited deserters and common crooks. "We thought it would be better than a prison camp," Ivan Gorin, who survived a penal battalion, explained. "We didn't realize at the time that it was just a death sentence."[17] Penal battalions, in which at least 422,700 men eventually served, were forlorn, deadly, soul destroying.[18] But there could not have been a soldier anywhere who doubted that in this army, in any role, his life was cheap.

Though Stalin's order formalized existing regulations, the process of its implementation exposed a fundamental problem of mentalities. Indeed, its reception in many quarters was symptomatic of the very weakness that it was supposed to remedy. People brought up in a culture of denunciations and show trials were used to blaming others when disaster struck. It was natural for Soviet troops to hear Stalin's words as yet another move against identifiable—and other—anti-Soviet or unmanly minorities. The new slogan was treated, initially at least, like any other sinister attack on enemies within. Political officers read the order to their men but acted, as some inspectors observed, as if it "related solely to soldiers at the front. . . . Carelessness and complacency are the rule . . . and officers and political workers . . . take a liberal attitude to breaches of discipline such as drunkenness, desertion, and self-mutilation." The warm summer nights seemed to encourage laxity. In August, the month after Stalin's order, the number of breaches of discipline continued to increase.[19]

Obligatory repetition turned the leader's words to cliché. The new instructions, once ignored, could sound as stale, if not as benign, as orders to eat more carrots or be vigilant for lice. The message was drummed into every soldier's head for weeks. Some hack in Moscow composed pages of doggerel verse to ram it home. Inelegant in the first place, it loses nothing in translation. "Not a step back!" it rattles. "It's a matter of honor to fulfill the military order. For all who waver, death on the spot. There's no place for cowards among us."[20] Groups of soldiers, weary of government lies, were always quick to identify hypocrisy, and that autumn they watched their commanders evading the new rules. Few officers were keen to spare their best men for service in the blocking units. They had been in the field too long; they knew the value of a man who handled weapons well. So the new formations were stuffed with individuals who could not fight, including invalids, the simpleminded, and—of course—officers' special friends. Instead of aiming rifles at men's backs, these people's duties soon included valeting staff uniforms or cleaning the latrines.[21] In October 1942, the idea of regular blocking units at the front (as opposed to the autonomous forces of the NKVD) was quietly dropped.[22]

Meanwhile, the retreat that had provoked the order in July continued in the south. German troops took another eight hundred kilometers of Soviet soil on their way to the Caucasus. The defense of their Caspian oil that autumn cost the Red Army another 200,000 lives.[23] As late as September, army inspectors would observe that "military discipline is low, and order no. 227 is not being carried out by all soldiers and officers."[24] It was not mere coercion that changed the fortunes of the Red Army that autumn. Instead, even in the depth of their crisis, soldiers appeared to find a new resolve. It was as if despair itself—or rather, the effort of one final stand—could wake men from the torpor of defeat. Their new mood was connected to a dawning sense of professionalism, a consciousness of skill and competence, that the leaders had started to encourage. For years, Stalin's regime had herded people like sheep, despising individuality and punishing initiative. Now, slowly, even reluctantly, it found itself presiding over the emergence of a corps of able, self-reliant fighters. The process would take months, gathering pace in 1943. But rage and hatred were at last translating into clear, cold plans.

The first move was to clear the officer corps of its burden of incompetents. Voroshilov, the champion of the prewar dream of easy victory, was demoted to a desk job for failures on the Volkhov Front around Leningrad in April 1942.[25] In May, Mekhlis was relieved of his Crimean command, and eventually he was also removed from his positions as deputy defense commissar and head of the main political administration of the Red Army.[26] Semen Budennyi, the aging hero of the civil war, was placed in charge of the Red Cavalry. "He was a man with a past," Marshal Ivan Konev remarked, "but no future."[27] Their places were taken by younger, more professional officers with recent battlefield experience—leaders like Zhukov and Konev himself, and generals like Vasily Chuikov, the ambitious forty-two-year-old who led the sixty-second Army at Stalingrad.

Mekhlis's downfall signaled a change of fortune for the army's multitude of political officers. The first hint of reform was a campaign of whispering. "It is not unusual," a report ran, "for political workers in the units to fail to notice that there has been no salt in the men's food for three days in a row, although there is salt in the stores; or that the men have had to sit for thirty to forty minutes in the canteen without getting their food, for no other reason than that the quartermaster has failed to provide a ladle. And after all this, they claim that they have been engaged in political work."[28] Quite rightly, *politruks* were also said to be "complacent" about the men's attitude toward order no. 227.[29] With Mekhlis gone, there was no one in Moscow to protect them. One group of recruits to the army's political wing, men who had hoped to make their mark as high priests of the party line, discovered when they reached their training camp that it was their turn to eat the thin soup, go without boots, and shiver in unfinished, overcrowded huts.[30] The money seemed to dry up overnight. On 9 October 1942 their privilege within the structure of command ended.[31] *Politruks* still had a role. Their tasks would be to work on political consciousness and morale and also to keep everyone informed of the official news. But their approval was no longer needed for much else. Military decisions were henceforth to be taken by the generals alone.

Professional commanders would find that they had an increasing measure of autonomy. "The most important thing that I learned on the banks of the Volga," Chuikov would later write, "was to be impatient of blueprints."[32] He and his peers cherished the right to make decisions, and not only the spur-of-the-moment ones that any officer faces. A new pragmatism was apparent everywhere; the measure of a leader shifting from his political background to his competence and skill. The reports that Stalin heard from favored advisers now dealt with the demands and pressures of contemporary war. They noted the weak coordination between the Soviet Union's infantry, artillery, and tanks. They noted the poor state of military intelligence. They noted, above all, the lack of discipline that led to random fire, wastage of shells, and panic on the battlefield.[33] The conclusion they drew was that more emphasis should henceforth be placed on drill and less on comic-strip heroics.

Habits that dated from the civil war were abandoned. There would be no more suicidal leaping onto barricades, no more distracting competitions to see which unit could march fastest or form into the straightest line.[34] A new culture was slowly taking shape, whose key values were professionalism and merit. Where a man's class or social origin had defined him before, the army started emphasizing skill. Orders to improve training, and especially the tactical preparation of infantrymen, streamed from the general staff.[35] That autumn, the soldiers massing near Stalingrad heard about a new play by Aleksandr Korneichuk, the text of which was also serialized in *Pravda* in late August. *Front!*, which was staged by Moscow's prestigious Art Theater itself, was designed to "answer the questions of every Soviet patriot about the successes and failures of the Red Army." As the correspondent of the local soldiers' paper, *Red Army*, put it in his review, the play showed that "nothing in the Soviet land will sustain an ignorant or unskilled leader—not personal courage, not honors from the past." The time for "conservatism" was over. The war, it added, "would test them all."[36]

Hard economic fact would underscore the change of mood. That summer, the Soviets' capacity to turn out weapons, shells, and tanks recovered after months of dislocation. The revival of manufacturing seemed like a miracle. Tanks and airplanes soon came to symbolize the Soviet recovery, with Chelyabinsk, the new manufacturing center in the Urals, earning the nickname Tankograd. Mass production accelerated everything. Manufacture of the world-beating T–34 medium tank, for instance, was adapted so that the turrets could be stamped, rather than cast. Troops still dubbed it the "matchbox," partly because they expected it to catch fire as readily as its predecessors, which had been nicknamed *zazhigalki*, "lighters," but also because T–34s poured off production lines in such prolific numbers after 1942.[37] Meanwhile, lend-lease military aid, principally from the United States, began to make a crucial difference in the supply of weapons, airplanes, and food.[38] Studebaker trucks, 200,000 of which were to be shipped to the Red Army by 1945, began to rattle round encampments at the front, and soldiers learned to recognize the taste of Spam.[39] It was a small step—and the Allied aid package, crucially, did not include the promise of a second front—but for men who had seen raw despair and death the slightest improvement was like a turning of the tide.

The change was subtle, for the men still faced the shortages that left them without basic gear, but that autumn the leadership also began to take an interest in hierarchy and even in style. Defeat was written in the shabby uniforms and depressed gait of too many Red Army men. Complacency about the men's appearance had to end. On 30 August, a campaign began to get the soldiers' boots mended and polished, to inspect officers' uniforms, eliminate dirt, and drill the ranks in self-respect.[40] The

Red Army troops repair their boots, 1943

men themselves were set to cobbling leather soles and sewing seams. Armies of women scrubbed and laundered in makeshift washhouses near the front. "We used 'K' soap to get rid of the lice," one laundrywoman remembered. It stank, and it "was black, like earth. Many girls suffered hernias from picking up the heavy loads or developed eczema on their hands from the 'K' soap. Their nails broke and they thought they would never be able to grow them again."[41] Women workers might suffer, but the prize was a morale boost for elite soldiers. "Nina, don't worry about our uniforms," an officer wrote to his wife just before Stalingrad. "We dress better these days than any commander from the capitalist countries."[42]

Women launder soldiers' clothes on the First Ukrainian Front, 1943

With the new focus on looks came new features to distinguish a man's rank. On 11 November orders were promulgated to establish clear new rules for the award of military decorations. These would soon prove a wild success. In an army where there was no chance of leave, the medals, some of which had romantic names recalling Russia's military past, became a vital currency for reward. Eleven million decorations were awarded to members of the Soviet military between 1941 and 1945. By contrast, the United States awarded only 1,400,409.[43] The U.S. Army often took as long as six months to process individual awards. In Stalin's army the equivalent was frequently three days.[44] The message was conveyed that military professionalism would not go unnoted. While individuals wore stars and ribbons, the number of units and even of armies that were awarded the title and material privileges of "guards" increased from 1942. Individually or in groups, as guards or as the wearers of golden or scarlet ribbon, soldiers who made the grade could expect more substantial things than gratitude. Each honor carried specific rights, including increased payouts for men's families and benefits like free travel or extra meat. Officers were singled out still further. In mid-November they received the news that shoulder boards were going to be restored.[45] Rank and authority had not enjoyed such ostentation since the fall of the Romanovs.

"They'll bring the tsar back next," the older men complained. Shoulder boards had long symbolized the arbitrary cruelty of the imperial Russian army. In almost every film of Lenin's revolution angry soldiers crowded on the screen to rip the gold braid from the jacket of some army swell. A few veteran sergeants, remembering their own rage back then, refused to wear the new boards, risking a tribunal and a charge of insubordination.[46] But though the malcontents suspected that their revolution had just been betrayed, some of the younger men thought they perceived the dawning of new hope. According to an officer whom the Germans later captured, some soldiers held the reintroduction of epaulettes—along with the reopening of many churches—to be the first sign that the government was going to disband the hated collective farms.[47] The new insignia began to appear on officers' uniforms in January 1943 and became standard for the entire military that spring.[48] By then, the German invaders had been encircled and defeated in the city of Stalingrad, and the Red Army had redeemed its long record of shame. For the first time, soldiers could really think that the prewar order—bosses, prison camps, and all—was coming to an end. They could believe that they were fighting to create the promised, longed-for better world.

A change of mood, in other words, was evident before the battles at Stalingrad. For now, it was barely more than a shift of inflection, a fragile change of emphasis in letters and in some men's talk. New policies took months, not days, to influence a culture dating from the prewar years, while fourteen months of hardship took a heavy toll. Morale was still low. Defeat at Stalingrad would almost certainly have extinguished hope entirely, engulfing it in terror and despair. But even in August and September, a sense of individual responsibility, of a last chance, was emerging. There was a mood of expectation everywhere. As Alexander Werth wrote in his diary in mid-July, "Black as things are, I somehow feel that Stalingrad is going to provide something very big."[49]

★

As Stalin's generals prepared for the battle that would alter the whole balance of morale, another change was taking place within the army. It was a shift of generations. The Soviets entered the war with just under five million men in active service. Reserves and replacements flooded westward in preparation for the battles around Moscow in October 1941, but the carnage of the war's first fourteen months was indescribable. By the late summer of 1942, a man who had been in the field for six months was an old hand, a real veteran. Large numbers returned to the front after sustaining wounds. On average, almost three-quarters of injured men were patched up and sent back to fight during the war.[50] But this was still the era of defense to the death. The old army, the army that had seen surrender, mutiny, and defeat, was literally dying.

The ghosts of prewar infantry might well have shuddered to see what was coming next. The most conspicuous innovation, which began in earnest in the summer of 1942, was the recruitment of young women.[51] In the first weeks of the war women had been discouraged from applying for active service roles. But a labor shortage everywhere, at the front line and in the factories, changed everything. That summer, the military expressed itself keen to recruit "healthy young girls."[52] To some extent the idea was to shame the men into greater effort. The other goal was to make civilian women more effective, to shame them, too, into working long hours in armaments plants or on the farms. Either way, some 800,000 women would serve at the front during the war. Smirks and official condescension followed them. Unlike the men, they found it hard to fit their bodies into the heroic mold, to see themselves as warriors. There had been women at the front in Russia's other wars, but never on this scale.[53]

Old soldiers did not know whether to regard the women as feminine or comradely. New female recruits suffered agonies of embarrassment when faced with field latrines (or no latrines). Their uniforms, designed for men, would never fit. They did not know whether to welcome the muscles and dirt that changed their bodies into those of troops. They curled short haircuts, washed with moss, shared tiny scraps of soap. Equally confused, the authorities introduced, on an experimental basis, mobile front-line tea shops, forty-three of which, equipped with hairdressers, small cosmetics counters, and supplies of dominoes and checkers, had been deployed by August 1942.[54] The same month a decree was signed authorizing the issue of rations of chocolate, in place of the standard tobacco, to female soldiers who did not smoke.[55] One veteran recalled taking a suitcase full of chocolate when she went to the front. Another was disciplined for picking violets after target practice and tying them to her bayonet.[56]

Femininity turned out to be no obstacle to certain kinds of soldiering. Among the military specialties to which women would eventually be assigned—and at which, in the field, they could excel—was sniper training.[57] Accounts describe the level of expertise that new recruits of either sex might expect to acquire. "We learned to mount and demount a sniper's rifle with closed eyes," a female veteran remembered, "to determine wind velocity, to evaluate the movement of the target and the distance to it, to dig in and crawl. . . . I remember that the most difficult thing was to get up at the sound of alarm and to get ready in five minutes. We would take boots a size or so bigger so as not to lose much time putting them on."[58] Women like this, or like the aviators of Marina Raskova's all-female 588th Night Bomber Squadron, which flew its first missions in the summer of 1942, began to make the front pages of newspapers, setting a standard for self-sacrifice, professional pride, and patriotism.[59] But those who were not famous struggled with a confused, physically draining role, surviving, they report, only because youth and their comrades remained on their side.

New male blood also replenished the Red Army that season. Despite the losses of the war's first year, there were more than six million troops in the field at the end of 1942. Among the other population groups that the army now tapped were former kulaks and their families, for the law that banned them from front-line service was repealed in April 1942. But the majority were drawn from a new generation. These latest recruits had been teenagers, really children, when the war began. They had anticipated their call-up for over a year, but their expectations and mentality were unlike those of the old guard. For them, army service was not a chore imposed by circumstance; it was a sacred duty, mortal sentence, fate. Their culture, the idiom of their growing up, had been shaped by the war itself. The process was a brutal, shocking one, and not all were eager. Some evaded service, and new laws had to be passed to force youngsters to take the oath.[60] Few, if any, came to the front from secure, settled lives. But they had no time to mull over the discontents that had preoccupied their predecessors in the prewar years. "Just three months," one veteran told me, describing the training camp. "They taught us fast. And what was there for us to complain about? They taught us, they sent us, they killed us."[61]

The training these recruits received was brutal, quick, and very focused. "Army life is cruel, especially right now," nineteen-year-old Anatoly Viktorov wrote to his father. "In a short time you have to develop courage, boldness, resourcefulness, and, quite apart from that, the ability to hit the enemy accurately with a gun. You don't get any of these qualities as a free gift."[62] "We work for nine hours a day—and if you add the preparation we do by ourselves it's twelve," another young man told his father.[63] Thousands of miles to the west, newly recruited German infantrymen were training at the same accelerated pace.[64] The eastern front claimed more lives than all the other theaters of European war combined, and even Hitler's army had to change its rules and turn out soldiers fast. But for new recruits to the Red Army, it was no comfort to know that "Fritz" was suffering similar stress. For most young Soviets, the struggle to get through those first few weeks alive and fit was utterly preoccupying.

David Samoilov found himself in a camp for infantry officers. The man in charge of his training was a "bestial and innate scoundrel" called Serdyuk. This old hand used drill to torment the new recruits, forcing them to don their gas masks and run out across the steppe at the first hint of dawn. Samoilov had to carry a machine gun on these sorties, and he remembered its weight to the ounce: "base—32 kg, body—10kg, armor—14 kg." He also remembered the meaningless torture of reveille practice. He would be ordered to lie down, get up, dress, undress, and repeat the process over and over again. The idea was to reduce the time that each recruit needed, until the whole thing took mere seconds, but like all drill, the exercise was also intended to beat the wind out of a dilettante, to turn a man into a soldier. "Serdyuk," Samoilov recalled, "was the first personification of hatred in my life."[65] No one described their training camp with love. "We fall in for classes, we fall in for meals," another officer trainee wrote to his wife in April 1942. "You can't call a moment your own."[66]

Private Aleksandr Karp was assigned to the artillery, leaving to train as soon as he had finished school in the summer of 1942. "Reveille is at 5:00 o'clock," he wrote to his grandmother. "We wash and all that.

Breakfast at last, which usually consists of some kind of kasha with a hunk of sausage, butter, sweet tea, and bread, which is never quite enough. Immediately after breakfast, lessons, without going back to barracks. We work for eight hours until lunch." After a few weeks, he had graduated from basic square bashing to the more sophisticated study of weapon assembly and disassembly, target practice, geometry, and mathematics. Time was always reserved for political education, which included reports on the war. The classes ran without a break, so that by early afternoon the men were ravenous. "Lunch is usually something like soup with grits," Karp continued, "admittedly with fat, and then for seconds either that kasha again with that same sausage or else dumplings with gravy." The men were then shepherded off to spend their afternoon preparing for the next day's classes. Then came supper: "bread and butter (25g) and sweet tea (half a liter)." "All our lessons," Karp wrote, "are in the open air. We have to sit for eight hours in the scorching sun, which sometimes means that nothing sticks in our heads. . . . We're getting used to it a bit now, but we're all terribly tired."[67]

Karp had just left home. He was not interested in vodka or tobacco. Instead, like many others of his age, the young man craved milk, sweets, and bread. He was always hungry. He traded some of his rations for sugar and sneaked out of field exercises to buy milk and dried fish from the local peasants.[68] That autumn, he begged his grandmother to send more money. Men who had cash could quell their hunger with the berries and nuts that nearby children brought to sell at the barracks. Theft was a problem; new recruits soon learned to hide money and even food. They also had to dodge the bullies who threatened to beat their possessions out of them.[69] It was tempting to raid the supplies from local farms, and in Karp's unit men stole out at night to dig potatoes from outlying fields. They made small fires and boiled them on the spot, using their helmets as saucepans. More enterprising youths stole chickens or took shots at wild hares. Karp's own diet was so poor that within weeks he had come out in septic boils.[70]

As in peacetime, not all the farmwork that the men performed was unofficial. "They've sent us to the collective farm," Karp reported in October. "We have in fact been told to dig potatoes. The work is very hard. It was all made far worse this time by the fact that it was very cold and there was even rain with hail in it from time to time. The earth was cold and wet and it was terribly hard to dig in it, looking for spuds. . . . We were all black and filthy, exhausted. We worked without a break. They gave us half an hour for lunch. We ate it with the same dirty hands that we had been digging with. The mud poured down our hands and faces and into our mugs . . . but there was nothing much to eat anyway." When Karp was given time off to recover from another bout of boils, he noted that he would be excused from "the building work, my lessons, and mucking the horses out."

It was not what they had signed up to do, but at least the digging was good practice for their real work. In November, Karp experienced "the toughest day of my training." He and the others were dumped on the cold steppe and left to make an earth dugout in which they had to spend the night. These shelters, *zemlyanki*, were a core part of the Red Army's survival plan. They could be quite elaborate, with curtained-off rooms, an iron stove, and even a window. But all were dug into the earth, concealed with turf or branches, stuffy, cramped, and thick with the cheap tobacco, the *makhorka*, that almost everybody smoked. The description that an infantryman sent back to his wife that spring was typical. "We live like moles, in the earth," he wrote. "The walls are made of planks, and so is the roof, although there is no floor or ceiling. We sleep on planks as well, two-story bunks. . . . It's a bit uncomfortable when there is a lot of noise, because up to four hundred people have to live in here."[71]

The digging, then, was not a trivial task, and Karp's team had yet to learn the knack. "We were saved by the fact that they gave us warm things," he wrote. "Padded clothes and *valenki*. But all the same we froze to our bones." Sentry duty was particularly bad. As each man came back inside, he realized "what a great thing a campfire is. That night, we took turns freezing."[72] The trainees grumbled, but so, unfortunately, did the inspectors who reviewed their work. That autumn, a report written with new standards of training in mind found infantry and gunner recruits wanting in almost every area. It also noted that their discipline was weak, that they were too fond of slipping away without permission and of sleeping at their posts, and that their manner toward superior officers was rude.[73] "We studied for ten years in school," wrote

Sappers from the 193rd Dnepr Rifle Division building a shelter, 10 December 1943

Karp sulkily. "And now we have to start all over again, working without a break. I'm sick of it. On the other hand, we can't expect that what's ahead will be any better."[74]

The irony was that most did expect something better. Recruits climbed patiently onto the trains that took them to the Volga or the north because they could see no future except through war. The humiliation of the training camp would end, the waiting would be over, they would begin to do a real job. They would also get their revenge, and not just on the invader. The prospect of combat and death loosened the hold of duty, party, and the whole Communist state. Samoilov remembered his own journey to the front. He and his comrades traveled with the hated Serdyuk. As they put miles of track between their company and the old camp, their tormentor seemed to withdraw into his thoughts. "The tragedy of the tyrant," Samoilov noted, "lies in the fact that his power is never limitless." On the train, the balance would shift. It was a story that would be repeated elsewhere as beleaguered men be-

gan to weigh their value. The hope—or fear, depending on your rank—
was that the battlefield would level former differences out. A group of
Uzbeks gathered around Serdyuk one evening. Their teeth flashed in
the semi-dark, their bodies, muscled from years on the steppe, crowded
their victim like the walls of a cell. "We're going to the front, aren't
we?" asked one of them. Serdyuk looked up into a fixed, confident
smile, the "slant-eyed glance of Tamurlane." As soon as he arrived at the
unit's reserve base, he asked to be transferred to another group.[75]

★

"Without exception, we are all worried about Stalingrad," a junior officer called Ageev wrote to his wife in October 1942. "If the enemy succeeds in taking it, we will all suffer, including the people in our unit."[76]
The city that bore Stalin's name acquired a mythic significance that autumn. "I am writing to you from this historic place at a historic time,"
Viktor Barsov wrote to his parents in August.[77] His mother guessed correctly where he was. The Moscow press was full of tales from the embattled town; the whole country waited for news. As Barsov put it in
another letter that October, "I am defending the histor[ic]. t[own].
form[erly]. Ts[aritsyn]. now St[alingrad]." His boots were soaked
through and his fingers stiffened through his thin gloves as he wrote. He
was no more a superman than young Karp and just as preoccupied with
hunger, cold, and lack of sleep. Instead of steppe, the city that surrounded him for miles was no more than a wilderness of rubble, twisted
steel, and mud. But his letter suggests a certain pride in his position. Already everybody knew that the fighting here was likely to decide the war.

Stalingrad stands on the west bank of the Volga River, the mightiest
in Europe. The city, originally named for the Tsaritsa, a tributary of the
Volga that cuts it in half, came to bear Stalin's name in honor of a civil
war campaign in which the future leader had played a conspicuous role.
Partly because of its association with the leader, Stalingrad had been developed as a model city for the region, with open spaces, parks, and
pristine-looking white apartment blocks that reflected the river and the
summer glare. Even had it not borne a famous name, the city would still
have been important for its engineering and manufacturing, its university
and technical schools, and its extensive network of supply and storage

facilities for the armies fighting nearby on the river Don. In 1942, Hitler regarded Stalingrad as a critical bridgehead on the Volga River and as a vital staging area for armies heading south toward the oil fields of the Caspian. He also savored the prospect of capturing the city bearing Stalin's name.

The battle to take Stalingrad began in the heat of the southern Russian summer as Red Army units stationed on the river Don fought to hold off an enemy advance from both the south and west. On 4 August, the German Sixth Army reached the southern bank of the Don, which bends east at this point in a great arc toward the Volga. By midmonth they held almost the entire stretch of territory within this Don bend to the west and northwest of Stalingrad. The Soviet defense was more determined than of late, but conditions did not help to raise morale. On more than one occasion, whole armies gave way to panic, rushing headlong for the barren gullies on the far side of the Don. "I am taking part in a very large operation," Volkov wrote to his wife in August 1942. "For the past few days and still right now I am in the front line. I don't have time to describe what's going on, but I can tell you that what's around me is a very hell. There's wailing and roaring all around, the sky is splitting with the din, but my eardrums are already used to it. One shell burst just three meters from me, and I was spattered with mud, but I'm still in one piece. But as to what will happen, I can give you no guarantees."[78]

In fact, the fighting in the Don country helped to delay the German advance, which mattered later in the campaign when the ice and darkness finally set in. At the time, however, the breathing space seemed made for working on the great city's defense. As in Moscow a year earlier, citizens were pressed into militia gangs and given shovels, carts, and lumps of wood. Tank traps and trenches were prepared, defensive drills rehearsed. None of these preparations would prevent the cataclysm when it came, and local people seemed to sense as much. While some exhausted Stalingraders dug, their neighbors, no less frightened, were streaming eastward to the Volga, pulling carts, carrying bundles, driving stock.[79] They were rushing to escape from a trap. Many of the bridges across the river had been mined, while the roads were already exposed to sporadic aerial machine-gun fire. Thousands of refugees would never make it to the sallow hills of Asia.

The attack came on Sunday, 23 August. That day, six hundred German planes circled over Stalingrad, flying in low and carpet bombing in relays. By nightfall there was little left above the ground but rubble, searing flame, and smoke. "The streets of the city are dead," Chuikov would write as he toured his new battleground a few days after the catastrophe. "There is not a single green twig on the trees: everything has perished in the flames. All that is left of the wooden houses is a pile of ashes and stove chimneys sticking up out of them. The many stone houses are burnt out, their windows and doors missing and their roofs caved in. Now and then a building collapses. People are rummaging about in the ruins, pulling out bundles, samovars, and crockery, and carrying everything to the landing stage."[80] Tens of thousands of civilians would never manage to escape. In that first day and night, an estimated forty thousand people died.[81]

The bitterest and most appalling phase of Stalingrad's defense also began that August. For a few weeks, the Soviet Sixty-second and Sixty-fourth armies retreated from the city's western suburbs to strongholds in the center and the north. By mid-September, the Sixty-second Army was holding the city on its own. Its orders were to destroy the enemy—the Sixth Army of General Paulus—in the city itself. Soldiers holding the narrow strip of ruined earth along the Volga's western bank were told to fight as if there were no land across the water on the eastern shore. What that would mean soon became clear. Chuikov's men, reinforced by any troops who could be shipped across to join them, clung to their bridgehead by contesting every house. Inside the ruins, sometimes in the dark, men fought with bayonets and their bare hands to hold each stairwell and each bullet-pitted room.

From October, Chuikov's soldiers in the city would be supported by well-organized artillery, this time sensibly sited on the Volga's eastern bank. But the enemy maintained complete superiority in the air. All troops in the city, German and Soviet—and the few civilians who had not succeeded in escaping after the first fatal days—were subject to unrelenting bombardment. So were the boats that brought supplies and men across the river from the Soviet side. The food ran out, bullets ran out, the cooling water in machine guns boiled. The men lived and died amid a litter of corpses and rubble, the bodies blending with the dust. As Chuikov himself recalled, "The heavy casualties, the constant retreat, the shortage of food and munitions, the difficulty of receiving reinforcements . . . all this had a very bad effect on morale. Many longed to get across the Volga, to escape the hell of Stalingrad."[82] His men were close to absolute despair. "It is all so hard that I do not see a way out," a soldier wrote home that October. "We can consider Stalingrad as good as surrendered."[83]

For tens of thousands, there could be no escape. True, some of the top brass, as well as some police, shipped out to safer ground, leaving the men to face the wreckage and the flames alone.[84] Chuikov himself is said to have requested several times to remove his headquarters to the safety of the other bank.[85] But the general had little choice. His orders were to lead the soldiers by example. He had a relatively free hand about tactics, and the promise of daily replacements of men, but there would be no going back. The troops who disembarked at Stalingrad could do nothing but fight. One sanction, which Chuikov was never ashamed to use, was the threat of a bullet in the back. The discipline he maintained was savage even by the standards of Zhukov's Red Army. But the Volga River, steaming from the heat of German shells, was a barrier more deadly than any secret police line. Just over half a million troops were massed for Stalingrad's defense in July 1942. Well over 300,000 of these would die.[86]

The physical toll defies imagination. The day-to-day conditions on their own wore the men down. It was not just the bombing, the unrelenting noise, the dust, flames, cold, and darkness. The city's defenders relied entirely on the river boats to deliver supplies. As these began to fail, soldiers turned into scavengers, taking the boots, the guns, and even writing paper from corpses. The reek of decayed flesh mingled with the smell of hot metal and sweat. There was little clean water in the shelters where soldiers huddled at night, so washing was out of the question. Lice, always a problem at the front, infested clothing, gloves, bedding, and the men's matted hair. Unlike the rats and birds that also moved among the ruins, these vermin were not even good to eat. The men had their own way of describing siege rations. "You'll live," they would say, "but you won't be able to fuck."[87] The bitter words ignored the fact that they still had to fight. Only the injured, proven in combat, stood a chance of a place on the boats that slipped back to the east bank every night. The hospitals filled up. Their staffs worked to exhaustion.

The men's view was that ten days were as much as anyone could take. Even the toughest said that after the eighth or ninth day they were certain to be wounded, if they did not die.[88] Most had grown used to the sounds and smells of war, and old hands felt that they could judge, even predict, what lay ahead. It was the closest they might ever come to controlling the chaos at the front. "We knew by the flight of a shell if it would hit you or not," a survivor remembered. "We could also tell where a mine would land by the noise it produced."[89] But the endless struggle to remain alert destroyed a person's concentration in the end. The archives do not talk about stress much—the Soviet army operated with less sensitive measures of the soldiers' health and fitness—but, as one survivor put it, the men became "a little less than human" as they strained to hear the shadows in the dark.[90] "At least I can say that I saw a lot of heroic things," an officer wrote later to his wife, "but I also saw a lot of things that the Red Army ought to be ashamed of. I never thought that I'd be capable of the kind of ruthlessness that really borders on cruelty. I thought I was a good-hearted person, but it seems that a human being can hide within himself for a long time the qualities that surface only at a time like this."[91]

Men also learned that there were worse outcomes than death. "Whether we like it or not," the same officer wrote, "we all end up thinking, What if I become a cripple? How will my wife react? You absolutely don't want to think about the possibility of being crippled. Of course, it's a real possibility, but you want to think of other things—of a full, healthy life."[92] A healthy life, perhaps, or else the catharsis of death. Soldiers began to find a kind of ecstasy in action, even in suicide. Against the blackness of their daily lives, the strangest things glowed with an unexpected light. Some accounts read like scenes from a macabre ballet. That is, the witnesses—all soldiers—had come to imagine action in cinematic terms, while the dead, the principals in these dramas, could not correct the script. Chuikov, who was no sentimentalist, described the death of a marine called Pankaiko in just this way. As the doomed man prepared to lob a gasoline-filled bottle at a line of German tanks, a bullet ignited the fuel, turning him into a pillar of flame. But the marine was still alive, and somehow, with some last reserve of rage or maybe from some grim reflex, he managed to reach for a second missile. "Everyone saw a man in flames leap out of the trench," Chuikov later wrote, "run right up to the German tank, and smash the bottle against the grille of the engine hatch. A second later an enormous sheet of flame and smoke engulfed both the tank and the hero who had destroyed it."[93]

A story like this was soon turned into fable. Amid the violence and death, the guilty pleasure of survival wove strong bonds of brotherhood. The brute simplicity of life pared down to its sinews produced a sense of freedom, while battle itself often seemed like release.[94] The party was quick to claim the soldiers' valor for its own, calling them loyal komsomols and faithful patriots, but though its bureaucrats supplied a rhetoric, the emotion that fired the men was beyond words. Sheer rage combined with something very close to love. The emotion is echoed, at a distance, in the comments of those who clung to Stalingrad in memory, regarding the city as the scene of their most vivid life. Vasily Grossman, the novelist and war correspondent, was one who did not want to leave. As he wrote to his father, "I still want to stay in a place where I witnessed the worst times."[95] Once victory was certain, others claimed to share this view. "It was pretty terrifying," a survivor told Alexander Werth, "to cross over to Stalingrad, but once we got there we felt better. We knew that beyond the Volga there was nothing, and that if we were to remain alive, we had to destroy the invaders."[96]

"I cannot understand how men can survive such a hell," a pilot in the Luftwaffe wrote home. "Yet the Russians sit tight in the ruins, and holes and cellars, and a chaos of steel skeletons which used to be factories."[97] "The Russians are not men, but some kind of cast-iron creatures," another German concluded.[98] This was outrage speaking, the voice of shock when victory was neither swift nor cheap. But until November Paulus's men could still believe that they would beat the Slavic devils, crushing them as they had been doing for seventeen months. Their German rear guard would support them, their planes deliver vital food, rescue the wounded. As the thermometer dropped and the nights grew longer, however, it was the Red Army and not the invader that would take the initiative.

The ruins of Stalingrad were the icon of Red Army stoicism, but the outcome of that winter's long campaign would not be decided within the city. Chuikov's Sixty-second Army surely earned the title of guards; nevertheless, it was planning, not just endurance, that would save the Soviet cause. In November 1942, a massive operation, led by Rokossovsky and code-named Uranus, was set in train, its aim to encircle Paulus's trapped Sixth Army, cutting off its retreat from the city. As Soviet and German troops duelled over rust and rotting bricks, more than a million Red Army soldiers were gathering beyond the horizon. Armies were brought into position on three fronts, forming a giant trap round Stalingrad. They waited only for the signal to move across the steppe.[99]

It would not have consoled the city's defenders, but life was hardly easy for the divisions that converged on the city from bases to the north and east. Supply problems would dog them, too, including shortages of winter clothing. Men died of frostbite and hypothermia before they ever reached the front.[100] But the operation, which began on 19 November, was a swift and complete success. Three days later, the Sixth Army had been surrounded, trapped in the city that their Führer would not allow them to abandon. The mood among Red Army troops in Stalingrad would lift, though there were months of suffering to come. General Paulus held out till the end of January, and the battle to secure the region as a whole continued for weeks after that. But action and a glimpse of victory raised Soviet morale despite November's fog. Survivors of the great encirclement campaign would later remember the day the order finally came to strike the enemy as the happiest of their war.[101] As Rokossovsky's trap closed around the city, it was even possible for wounded veterans to complain, as one did to his wife, that they were lying in the hospital and "missing all this."[102]

For months, Red Army men had nursed envy for the invader, for Fritz, with his well-nourished body and his modern guns. There was even, among the better-educated troops, a kind of cultural awe, for these were the people whose civilization had produced Bach, Goethe, and Heine (no one, I found, referred to Marx). There had been signs that German morale was cracking elsewhere on the eastern front by October. Soldiers based near Smolensk were said to be depressed as winter closed in yet again, and those returning from the Don to rest in occupied Ukraine were already anxious about the possibility of a Soviet recovery.[103] But from November, trapped in Stalingrad and on the frozen steppe around it, Wehrmacht soldiers tasted their first despair. "Snow, wind, cold, and all around us sleet and rain. . . . Since my leave I have never undressed. Lice. Mice at night," Kurt Reuber, a thirty-six-year-old German from Kassel wrote to his family in December. "There is just enough food to keep us from dying of hunger."[104]

While Paulus struggled to resist surrender, the two sides starved in a twilight fog. "Clay and mud," Reuber explained. Like the Russians, the Germans lived in dugouts. There was hardly any wood left to reinforce the walls or roofs after the bombing and the fires. Nor was there much vegetation growing amid the rubble. In late December Reuber observed a scrawny Russian pony that had wandered over to his dugout and was nibbling a piece of broken timber. The shivering creature was so hungry that even this would do for food. "Today it will be our dinner," Reuber remarked.[105] When the last Germans were captured a month later, their wretched shelters impressed the Russian troops.[106] Soviet dugouts had been even more primitive and cramped. Their commanders, writing from well behind the lines, were concerned about the darkness, the lack of air and space.[107] A woman veteran put it more vividly. "Let's just say," she told me, "that with those people sleeping there, and all their clothes, and a fire—well, it wasn't a place where you went to breathe."

Those last weeks were a calvary for soldiers of both sides. A near equality of misery prevailed. The adversaries locked together, contesting spaces that passed between them, back and forth, each time costing dozens, hundreds of lives. After Stalingrad fell, Alexander Werth toured the ruins and was struck by the battle relics that close combat had left. "Trenches ran through factory yards and through the workshops themselves," he wrote. "And now at the bottom of the trenches there still lay frozen green Germans and frozen grey Russians and frozen fragments of human shapes; and there were helmets, Russian and

German, lying among the brick debris, and now half-filled with snow."[108] When the thaw came that spring, another witness saw a chunk of ice floating along the Volga with two frozen bodies, a Russian and a German, fixed to it just as they had died, clasped in a simultaneous assault.

Described like this, the city might have seemed to be the same nightmare for everyone, but from November there was a crucial difference between the experience of Soviet and German troops. For the invaders, suddenly besieged, Stalingrad was a terrible shock, a catastrophe after the victories of 1941. "We have not received any Christmas packages yet," a soldier in Paulus's Sixth Army wrote home on 10 January. "They've promised us that they're keeping them behind the lines and that when we come back they'll give them to us. . . . We have absolutely nothing to eat, our strength is ebbing away in front of our eyes, we've turned into wrecks. . . . I've reached the point where I no longer thank the Lord that he has spared my life thus far. I see death every hour."[109] Soviet troops had always had lower expectations. They were not dreaming of their Christmas trees or of the sweets and cakes that they had never known. If they thought about home, it was about the life their enemy had destroyed. But now, backed up by their spectacular Katyushas and by the first friendly aircraft that they had seen since 1941, they seized a chance to take revenge. The Germans, in other words, were facing a kind of antiprogress, losing one by one the things that made them feel human. Red Army men, by contrast, were getting their first scent of real success. Exhausted, filthy, battle-hardened troops prepared to celebrate. "The prestige value of having fought at Stalingrad," Werth wrote, "was enormous."[110]

★

The party took the credit for the spirit that emerged at Stalingrad. The brotherhood and selflessness to which that battlefield gave birth were rapidly adopted as the offspring of its ideology, its wise guidance. "Thousands of patriots are proving themselves to be models of fearlessness, courage, and selfless dedication to the motherland," the soldiers' front-line paper crowed. "After the war, our people will not forget the ones who honorably served their homeland. The hero's children will be proud of their father. But the names of the coward, the panicmonger, and the traitor will be pronounced with hatred."[111] On the anniversary of the revolution that November, a Stalingrad oath appeared in the press, allegedly penned by the city's defenders. "In sending you this letter from the trenches," the men declared to Stalin, "we swear to you, dear Joseph Vissarionovich, that to the last drop of blood, to the last breath, to the last heart-beat, we shall defend Stalingrad."[112]

The message was drummed home at mass rallies and repeated in the printed orders of the day. Newly arrived men, anxiously waiting to know if fate would send them across the Volga, were made to sit through lectures on the epic heroes of the past. In small groups led by their *politruks*, freshly recruited soldiers discussed courage although none of them had ever have seen a German, let alone a corpse.[113] Films also worked on the men's consciousness. That autumn, soldiers in camps along the Volga might have seen *The Defense of Tsaritsyn*, *The Great Citizen*, or—especially for the Ukrainians—a re-creation of the life of the Cossack Bohdan Khmelnitsky.[114] Epics like these could roll out every few weeks now that the film industry had been mobilized entirely for the service of the front.[115] Soldiers were also shown newsreels of Soviet successes, while documentaries, such as the famous *Defeat of the German Armies near Moscow* reminded them how bedraggled and beaten the invader had looked only months before.[116] "You look at our own captured Fascist beasts," a man remarked, "and you know there just aren't enough ways to punish them for all the atrocities, betrayals, and crimes they've committed."[117]

It helped that some of the reserves were well trained, well prepared, and fit. The army had begun to look the part. Siberians were valued most of all. They seemed to be professional, not least because many had learned to shoot; they also knew how to take cover and to dig the deep, narrow trenches that provided shelter from tank tracks and airborne shells alike. "The most important thing," Ageev wrote home at this time, "is that there is no more of the 'tank fright' that we saw so much of at the beginning of the war. Every soldier . . . knowingly digs deeper into the earth."[118] Those who still panicked at the sight of these eyeless, sinister machines were trained out of their fear by an exercise (called "ironing") that forced them to lie in a trench while Soviet tanks drove over their heads. "After this," a German intelligence report noted of Red Army troops, "they all fought with exceptional courage."[119] The men, meanwhile, dismissed their terrors with black humor. "The deeper you dig," they quipped, "the longer you'll lie."[120]

For all the pretense, the real culture of the front could not be hidden from the men. Whatever the party might say, stories of cruelty, deceit, and wasted life flooded back from the front. Military hospitals were not sealed off from the civilian world. Local people could smell the blood and gangrene; they often helped to dig mass graves near battle sites. As ever, they also participated in the parallel economy that flourished when the NKVD's grip was weak. Wounded soldiers traded in guns, watches, pens, and even Zeiss cameras.[121] The German trenches were full of attractive loot. Meanwhile, a new class of outlaws—deserters—dealt in every trade from cash and weapons to the trafficking of human lives. The NKVD detained more than eleven thousand military personnel near the Stalingrad front between October and December 1942, more than a thousand of whom turned out to be deserters or former Red Army men now working for the enemy.[122] A favorite ruse was to dress in women's clothes, though one man, who had been hiding for eleven months, was found buried at the bottom of a grain bin.[123]

The police could not keep up with the crime wave. Instead, they tried to make examples of any men they caught. Desertion was the infraction that most offended them. "Comrade commissar," an NKVD man told his boss as he escorted ten new miscreants. "We should carry out Comrade Stalin's order 227 with these deserters and shoot them on the spot. They're saving not the motherland, but their own skins."[124] Overall, though, the number of deserters, as opposed to criminals, was falling. The weather must have played a part. As the thermometer dropped to twenty below, there was not much hope for anyone who chose to strike out on his own. But there were other reasons for compliance in the ranks.

Some soldiers on the Volga steppe did not revolt because their lives, paradoxically, were improving. Ilya Nemanov explained how the process worked in his own case. As the son of a so-called enemy of the people, he had not been allowed, at first, to hold a gun. Instead, he had been assigned, back in 1941, to a labor battalion. The assignment was a version of conscription, since he had no choice, but it involved backbreaking work, not battlefields. The government sent him to a construction site for evacuated industry in the Siberian town of Zlatoust. The men, a mixture of convicts, conscripts, and supposed political misfits like himself, felt that they had been exiled to the middle of nowhere. "We worked in Asia," Nemanov joked, "and came back to shit in Europe." Like front-line soldiers, they lived in dugouts, and like the soldiers, too, they worked until they collapsed. Nemanov relied on help from a couple of Kazakh herdsmen, who finished his work for him every day so that the group's norms would be met. The foreman could be rough, the criminals were violent. "It is not at the front that war is frightening," Nemanov told me. "It's when you're destroyed, when you have exhausting work to do, when people are dropping around you for no reason, when there's hunger, when there's no way you can help yourself—except by risking your life—when they give you frozen potatoes to eat, when you'll eat even carrion, when you'll take the rations off a dead comrade. That's what's frightening, not bullets!"

At the end of 1942 a group of men from Nemanov's labor unit were taken off and trained to handle mortars. When they boarded a train heading south, they knew that they were going to Stalingrad. It was bitterly cold. They were apprehensive, exhausted, and hungry. One man tried to run away and was taken aside and shot. For several nights they slept in all their clothes and used their boots for pillows. When they arrived at the front, their first order was to go to the baths and wash. Obediently, the men rubbed themselves with noxious medicated soap, only to find that there was no water left to rinse it off. Gritty and itching, they dressed again, hauled the mortars across their backs, and headed out, as Nemanov explained, "to where the lives were needed." Lives, it seemed, but not mortars. "We'll get you some rifles, you're infantrymen now," the men were told. By luck they were spared. "We froze, but they never sent us into battle."

It was a grim version of progress, but for Nemanov the front line was a better place than Zlatoust. Like thousands of other suspect citizens, he knew that war service was likely to clear his name. He was working his way back into Soviet society as he aimed his unwieldy gun, not serving time like a convict.[125] What's more, he had learned skills in the camp that made survival easier now. "We were rogues," he told me.

The men soon made the front a sort of home, managing daily life until they felt they had some individual control of it. Like soldiers everywhere, they improvised, and failing that, they stole. Local people were often kind, too, although they had little enough to share. "They all loved us," Nemanov said, "and we used that. One of my mates found a house, walked in, and crossed himself. The old lady immediately started up with all that stuff—'You lovely, darling man, my darling'—and sat him down at the table." Mistaking the youth for a devout Christian soul, she ladled out the tea and cabbage and a crust of bread. "Naturally," Nemanov added, "lots of us had affairs. War's about that—it's a time of death and love." His account squares with others of its kind, with those of men who found the front line—even this one—better than the camps.[126] Life was not easy anywhere, but at least near the front there was a chance that soldiers could carve niches, make connections, for themselves.

The chance to kill Germans was also a source of joy.[127] Soldiers had good reasons, specific ones, to hate these foreigners. The men who had seen combat were exhausted, and their dreams would be forever haunted by the stink of war. Others already knew that they would never see their families again, and everyone, including new conscripts, had lost comrades and close friends. It did not take much effort to foment their hatred, but even so the Soviet wartime press encouraged it. Few writers were more popular at this point in the war than Ilya Ehrenburg, the publicist who called on every Soviet citizen to "kill the German. If you have killed one German," he wrote simply, "kill another. There is nothing jollier than German corpses."[128] His language, violent and bitter, so caught the soldiers' mood that the newspaper pages where his column appeared were deemed too sacred to be used for rolling cigarettes. But Ehrenburg, whose prose was at its most lurid in 1942, was not the only creator of hate propaganda. Simonov, the soldiers' poet, joined in with "Kill Him!," a lyric exhortation to revenge.[129] Cartoonists sketched the enemy in every kind of trouble: Romanians panicking, Italians sneaking under cooking pots, Germans dying. A pun on the Russian word for snowdrop, *podsnezhnik*, whose literal meaning is "under the snow," showed the thaw that spring yielding new "snowdrops" in the form of German corpses.[130] When a Soviet commander died in

Stalingrad that winter, the order was to fire a salvo in his honor "not in the air but at the Germans."[131]

Strangely, soldiers in other theaters often envied the action their comrades on the Volga saw. Even men who knew exactly what combat involved yearned for a chance to get moving, to reenter the war. "When the devil are we going to attack?" an officer called Nikolai Belov wrote in his diary in January 1943. The twenty-seven-year-old was stationed near Lipetsk, well to the north of Stalingrad. His unit was within range of the German army near Voronezh, but its orders were to sit and wait. Belov was not writing out of ignorance, the romance of a man who has not seen battle. He had joined up as soon as the fighting began. Wounded that first summer, he had been evacuated for treatment, which meant that he had escaped the capture and death that awaited his comrades. He had returned to active service in the grim summer of 1942, retreating before an enemy that now controlled the entire Russian south.

That Christmas, as Rokossovsky's armies swept across the snowfields of the Volga steppe, Belov was sitting tight. He found himself digging in, drilling the men, and waiting. The routine was less tiring than the previous July's long marches, less dangerous than fighting hand to hand in Stalingrad. But it was hardly pleasant. The weather was cold, and the occasional slight thaws brought freezing rain and fog. Every few days there was some German shelling, and then there were the suicides, the desertions, the self-inflicted injuries, and brawls. "I've become terribly irritable," Belov wrote, "and I've developed this awful apathy toward everything. I feel as if the whole thing is making me tired as hell. If we could only attack, I'd probably come to my senses again."[132] His chance to test that thought would not come until the following July. Stuck in his snowbound dugout, meanwhile, he grew painfully depressed.

It would have been a different tale for everyone if Stalingrad had fallen. Victory was the greatest inspiration of all. Red Army men began to believe that their efforts might one day bear fruit. Though many knew that they were still likely to die, it mattered that there was some chance of victory. The news from Stalingrad flew round the entire Soviet world. "I long to leave and go and live permanently at the front," Belov told his diary one night. At the beginning of November he had been cheered by the story of Allied activity in Africa. "It's a long way away, but it also seems quite close. What a comfort." But nothing matched his delight at the triumph nearer home. "Our soldiers are having nothing but success at Stalingrad," he wrote on 27 November. "According to the news this morning they have taken 70,000 prisoners since the beginning of the attack. The figures for seized goods are astronomical. Our joy for the soldiers at Stalingrad knows no bounds."[133]

Far to the west, Nikolai Moskvin, whose information came from covert agents operating well behind the German lines, was also overjoyed. "There's been a great victory at the front!" he wrote on 19 January 1943. The tide had turned at last. "Every one of us wants to cry with all his might 'Hoorah!' Stalingrad has turned into a huge trap for the Hitlerites." For weeks now, he and his fellow partisans had been hiding out in dark *zemlyanki* waiting for instructions from Moscow. There had been skirmishes that autumn and Moskvin at last felt that he had a real job, but boredom and physical hardship had taken their toll as a second winter closed in. Now there was something to rejoice about. As ever, Moskvin turned his pen on himself. "I want to tear out the pages of my diary where I wrote about the collapse of my will," he wrote. "But let them stay there as a lesson in life that it's wrong to jump to conclusions just because things aren't going well."[134]

The victory even helped soldiers overlook the hardship of their daily lives. It was as if triumph itself could alter consciousness. Frostbitten Russian soldiers, hungry, injured, desperate, gloated when German troops appeared to suffer more. They seized on every scrap of compensation, every sign that life might change. Their enemy abandoned weapons, trucks, and food in his retreat, an unimaginable hoard of loot for half-starved Soviet troops. Some gorged themselves on German stores, others fell on the Sixth Army's supplies of spirits, occasionally discovering too late that what the attractive-looking bottles contained was antifreeze.[135] "At the moment there are colossal battles going on and terrible things are happening all the time," a forty-seven-year-old Red Army man wrote to his wife. "But all the same, don't worry about me. . . . The Germans are on the run, we're taking loads of prisoners and supplies. These days we eat only meat and tinned stuff, honey and all that rubbish, though there isn't any bread."[136]

Most amazing of all were the new prisoners of war. The Red Army captured 91,545 men in January 1943. They were in such poor physical condition that they might have perished anyway, but the state of the NKVD's prison camps made sure of it. Fewer than a fifth received hot food. Among the minority who did, death often followed when they ate too fast. Others dropped dead on the journey to the camps or died of their old wounds or of the typhus and dysentery that consumed their bodies within hours. Poor diet and hunger accounted for two-thirds of the deaths in Soviet POW camps in 1943. Those who survived faced a growing threat from the tuberculosis that thrived in their cramped, unhealthy quarters.[137] Things would become so bad that even the NKVD took steps to reform the system, though its motive was to preserve a potential labor force, not to spare human lives. But every haggard, frightened prisoner brought the war's end closer. That was the main thought in most people's minds. The victory at Stalingrad felt like a turning point.

"The Germans are throwing everything away as they run," that forty-seven-year-old wrote in his last letter home. He now believed the propaganda about Soviet strength. "We're feeding ourselves with their supplies. The Germans are running, and the Hungarians and Italians are giving themselves up. Just now fifty of our guys took five hundred prisoners. They freeze like flies, they can't stand the cold at all. . . . There are loads of dead ones on the roads and streets, but the more the better."[138] Less than a month after he wrote these lines, this man also would die. He was no less a victim of the cold than the invaders whom he scorned. But his discovery that Fascist troops could be beaten had made the winter bright. Ageev would have understood. "I'm in an exceptional mood," he wrote to his wife. "If you only knew, you'd be just as happy as I am. Imagine it—the Fritzes are running away from us!"[139]

SIX

A LAND LAID WASTE

★

A t last there was a kernel of real hope amid the dreary mass of promises. A year before, when the German army had turned back from Moscow, there had been relief, even modest celebration. But the crisis had been too deep, and the shock of invasion too recent, for anyone to sense a turning of the tide. Now, like February's first false hint of spring, the Soviet army's westward progress appeared to signal the approach of peace. On 26 January 1943, Voronezh fell to General Golikov's advancing troops. On 8 February, the Red Army marched into Kursk. Just six days later, it had reentered Rostov, and on 16 February it liberated Kharkov, the largest and most important city in the region. The places it retook were depopulated husks of cities, nests of fear and hunger, crime and mutual suspicion. Apartment buildings had been mined or shelled, windows blown out, power and water systems wrecked. Uneven soil beneath the melting snow hinted at vast mass graves. The people who had seen it all could find no words for their distress. But Stalin's propagandists supplied images of triumph. The enemy was on the run, and when he had been driven back to his lair, when he had been defeated and the dead avenged, the Soviet people would rebuild an even better world.

The politicians rushed to make the victory their own. The Red Army, "the army that defends peace and friendship between the peoples of every land," as Stalin called it on its twenty-fifth anniversary that February, came in for plenty of loud praise. It had "carried out a historic struggle without precedent in history," its "valiant soldiers, commanders, and political workers" had "covered its military colors in unfading glory."[1] But soldiers had not done this alone. Stalin's own role assumed a greater prominence now that there was something glorious to claim. His wise leadership, his "military genius," was now regularly invoked to explain successes for which tens of thousands of people had given their lives. The party, too, now came to feature as the guide and teacher of the masses. The people might regard this as their war, their epic struggle for freedom and dignity, but their leaders were already getting down to the work of memorializing themselves. The first Museum of the Great Patriotic War was established in March 1943.[2] The version of the war that it began to generate would soon become the template for official truth.

The birth of the glorious wartime myth was managed all the way along. The censors ensured that words like *retreat* and *surrender* would never feature in the annals of Red Army operations, but more cruelly they also suppressed evidence of the war's human cost. The victory at Stalingrad had been won at the expense of just under half a million Soviet soldiers' and airmen's lives, but this truth would remain concealed. All the way through, and even at Berlin, more men and women in the Red Army would die than soldiers of the side that they were supposed to be defeating. On average, Soviet losses outnumbered those of the enemy by at least three to one.[3] But multiple pressures conspired to hide this statistic. Red Army deaths might go entirely unrecorded at moments when there was no time to mark mass graves, let alone to count the bodies that had been pitched into them.[4] The pressure would relent a little after 1943, but even so, it was a common practice for the army to report fewer losses, and even fewer bodies to bury, than it in fact sustained. Graves that contained hundreds of men were marked with the names of thirty.[5] Meanwhile, official reports understated casualty rates—and the loss of Soviet military hardware—but carefully enumerated scores of German deaths. Emotions, too, were censored. Grief was allowed—as long as it stirred soldiers to revenge—but other reactions to danger and pain remained unspoken. The Sovinformburo made sure that nothing that was published referred to men's fear or doubt. By 1943, even the first year of the war had been rewritten for the public as a tale of grand heroic feats.[6]

Censorship worked. Sixty years on, many of the enforced silences hold. Government policy was effective in this case because it keyed into much deeper instincts and desires; people seldom enjoy revisiting the memory of pain. The bland version, the glorious one, suited the soldiers and the state alike. It kept things simple, after all, and allowed a ration of dignity—on Stalin's terms—to veterans. Personal anecdotes, the real ones, began to look as odd as fragments of color glued to a black-and-white picture, and some still do. In 2002, Ilya Nemanov struggled to recall his own response to the grave wound that he sustained in 1943. Part of his right side was blown off by a German bomb, and his first thought was "That's it." But then other ideas jumbled across his mind. "I remembered that before the war even began my mother had said that they wouldn't kill me, but my hand would be cut off," he said. "And then someone in one of the shelters along the way explained that if your hand was injured you should try to get them to sew the fingers on again, because if it worked, and there were still nerves there, you might save the hand itself."[7] These thoughts sustained him as he bled into the dust, waiting for rescue or for death. But superstition was not part of the official story of the Soviet war, and memories like this, personal ones, became increasingly difficult to recover as the long campaign progressed, let alone when it was over.

The wartime censors' ambitions were staggering. Nemanov reminded me of another instance, more graphic even than his own story. In January 1943, the siege of Leningrad was lifted. The city was still exposed to German shelling, still encircled, but now convoys of medicine, fuel, and flour could cut through by rail, where previously they had relied on a fragile—and seasonal—track across the ice of Lake Ladoga. Another year would pass before Leningrad was entirely free, but relief for the desperate remnant of its population had arrived at last. The moment called for reflection, for mourning and muted celebration, but for

Stalin's men it was a propaganda minefield. They did not like to draw attention to the fact that Soviet people had been left to starve to death, and the ban on discussion extended to the army. In the spring of 1943, when a soldier who was assigned to Nemanov's unit from the Volkhov Front near Leningrad tried to describe the siege to his new comrades, he disappeared, arrested. "He had mentioned starvation," Nemanov remembered. "That wasn't something we were supposed to hear about."

Ol'ga Berggolts, the poet of the Leningrad blockade, discovered the same thing when she visited Moscow at the end of 1942 to broadcast her reflections on the siege. "I have become convinced that they know nothing about Leningrad here," she wrote to her family. "No one seems to have the remotest idea what the city is going through. They say that the Leningraders are heroes, but they don't know what that heroism consists of. They don't know that we starved, they don't know that people were dying of hunger. . . . I couldn't open my mouth on the radio, because they told me, 'You can talk about anything, but no recollections of the starvation. None, none. On the courage, on the heroism of the Leningraders, that's what we need. . . . But not a word about hunger.' "[8]

As ever in the surreal Soviet world, people were being asked to say one thing, to subscribe in public to one version, while knowing something else, at least with some part of their minds. The Red Army, the people's savior, was prime territory for the myths. A set of stereotypical propaganda images—the noble warrior, the courageous Russian son, the defiant partisan—was being struck somewhere inside the Sovinformburo. Real people were picked to represent each type, for there was no shortage of personal heroism from which to choose. But Zoya Kosmodemyanskaya, the famous martyred partisan, or Vasily Zaitsev, the iconic Stalingrad sniper, were ideals, as inspiring and popular—and also as typical of the masses—as sports personalities or saints. Among Red Army men, the hero types were almost always snipers, gunners, or members of doomed tank crews. They were relatively literate, in other words, they were likely to be sympathetic to the Communist Party, and if they were not dead when stardom came, they could at least be certain to behave themselves in public. Although the press selected dozens of lowly privates for star treatment, the style and values that these men displayed resembled those of officers, and certainly of Communists. The culture of the rank and file, the dark world of real men, was jostled out of view.

Soldiers themselves adapted to this double standard. They seemed to have at least two cultures, an official one, which included everything they were allowed to do in front of officers and journalists, and a concealed, almost tribal one, the culture of vodka, *makhorka*, the lilting sayings—spontaneous verses—that they called *chastushki*, and crude peasant jokes. David Samoilov, who observed the men with a poet's eye for the unexpected, summed up this flexibility. In the presence of an officer, he wrote, a Russian soldier would be "subdued and tongue-tied." Perhaps there was no common language to unite commander and man across the divide of ideology and rank, perhaps there was not a great deal to say. There was certainly no time for any words in battle, when, Samoilov said, the tongue-tied private would turn out to be "a hero." The manner of his dying would be remarkable, too. "He will not abandon a comrade in trouble," Samoilov wrote. "He dies in a manly and workmanlike way, as if it were his accustomed craft." But the price of the subservience and stress had to be paid somewhere. When the officers were off the scene, the same soldier, Samoilov wrote, became "querulous and abusive. He boasts and threatens. He's ready to take a swipe at anything and to come to blows over nothing at all." This was not merely boorishness. "This touchiness," added Samoilov, "shows that his existence as a soldier is a burden to him."[9]

By the spring of 1943, the army had been at war for two years, and at almost every level below that of the high command its ranks were dominated by recruits whose military careers had started since the invasion. The gap between officers and men was closing. No one could doubt the basic cause for which they were all working, and a sense of common interest was vital for morale. The better young officers, including Samoilov himself, worked with the men, attempting to meet them halfway rather than taking cover in privilege. Although entitled to food of his own, and also to private quarters, Lev Lvovich insisted on eating with the soldiers in his regiment, sharing the thin soup and the buckwheat porridge that they all called shrapnel.

It was becoming easier for a junior officer to befriend the men because the gulf in experience between the ranks had narrowed so much.

The Red Army of 1941 had almost disappeared. The twenty-six-year-old lieutenant Lev Lvovich, his head full of advice from an uncle who had served under Nicholas II, set out to encourage and cajole young men and aging reservists, not disaffected veterans. Remembering names was not hard, either, because he didn't have to manage a full complement of troops. Though he should have commanded 120 infantrymen, he seldom had to get to know more than 60. There never were enough recruits and reserves to keep Red Army units up to strength. What this meant was that the young officer could talk to a frightened first-timer personally, although "a bit of swearing was often the best thing for the rest of them." Good relations paid off. As he recalled, the men thought it mere child's play, during operations, to get rid of an officer they hated, just as Samoilov's comrades had planned to do. "It happened," Lev Lvovich assured me. "Of course it happened quite a lot."[10]

Even the best officers could not entirely close the gulf between the semiliterate and men who could read, between townsmen and all the rest. "This was the last Russian war," Samoilov wrote, "in which most of the soldiers were peasants."[11] True, they were now collective farmers, Soviets, not Tolstoy's archetypal sons of earth. But all the same they were not fond of taking notes. As the party wrote itself into the war, the voices of the mass of troops were edited out or lost. Political officers occasionally reported their talk, but only where soldiers' comments concerned their own preoccupations—Communism, Stalin's orders, the digest of most recent news. The men's culture, the bedrock of the soldiers' fighting spirit and morale, of their survival and perhaps of Russia's own, would vanish with the settling wartime dust. There are a few survivors still, but even they look back across a fog of time, and they, too, have been influenced by postwar newspapers and films. To reach back to the infantrymen's world is to explore beyond the range of memory, beyond the scope of the archival mountains of buff-covered files. Even their contemporaries, Moscow-based staff officers and bureaucrats, had trouble understanding soldiers' real lives. The peasant village was exotic, almost foreign to Stalin's officials, a site for ethnographers and folklore expeditions. By 1943, the army, with its closed ranks, its male intimacies, and its violence, was like another universe.

This universe was ruled by fate, just as the quality of men's daily lives depended on the weather. If they stuck to the regulations, as soldiers, the men would have no say in their own existence, no right to run away from danger, no way of telling where they would be sent to die or even what they would eat every night. Their response was to develop a cosmology of their own, a system for predicting, and thus taming, the madness that threatened to engulf them. Parts of that cosmology were very old, inherited through their fathers and uncles from the armies that had defeated Napoleon. There were taboos about sex—a wounded, even an unconscious, man would die if he touched his own genitals—about swearing, and about the advisability of wearing clean linen before battle. There were many predictions based on vagaries of the weather. Some men believed it was unlucky to swear while loading a gun, others that a man should never swear before a battle. It was also unlucky to give anything to a comrade before going into combat, and soldiers all had tales of borrowed greatcoats that brought death.[12] They also favored talismans. Many carried a photograph in their tunic pockets. Others kept a copy of Konstantin Simonov's love poem "Wait for Me" folded against their hearts. The veterans explained that they did this for good luck. It was also safe. Officers from the Special Section searched men's pockets on the eve of any operation, and if they discovered personal, let alone incriminating, information, the owner might well end up in trouble with the military police. A scrap of paper that was just like all the rest was reassuring but it was also beyond reproach.

Religion was a controversial matter for the men. Prayer had always been a woman's job. Since 1917, the party had taught everyone that faith in God was an outmoded relic. The *politruks* and many komsomols within the ranks agreed. As one explained to me, "When you see the atrocities that are taking place minute by minute, you just think, God, if you're so omnipotent and just, how can you let so many innocent souls suffer this torment and die? I'm a Communist, an atheist, a materialist. To the marrow of my bones." The Red Army would give the lie to the old saying that there are no atheists in a foxhole.[13] But though this was a generation that had seldom visited a church, everyone observed the men who wore small silver crosses around their necks, hiding them under their shirts and explaining, if they were challenged, that the trinkets were gifts from their grandmothers. Some made their own crosses by cutting shapes out of old tins.[14] "They burned their party cards if they were going to die," a veteran remembered. "But they did not throw away the crosses." Very large numbers—perhaps a majority of rank and filers—crossed themselves in the old Russian way before they faced the guns. The gestures and the words were totemic—echoes, rather than formal evidence, of faith. "They said things like 'God save me,' but what they believed I couldn't say," a veteran explained. "I'm an atheist myself, but not very strongly. I came back alive. I suppose I live under a lucky star." "I had a guardian angel," Ivan Gorin explained. "I could feel her beside me all the time." The angel, he told me, was in fact the spirit of his mother.

Faith might have turned into superstition, but one passion that did not falter was the men's love for their songs. They sang while they marched and they sang for festivals and parades. They also sang, more mutedly, in hospitals, which is where they swapped lyrics and developed new rhymes.[15] The songs that have survived are poignant and lyrical, maudlin rather than tragic. Many were adapted from the patriotic ballads of 1812.[16] Others were written at the time by Stalin's favorite hacks, including Lebedev-Kumach and Demyan Bednyi. Songs about women naturally multiplied, many of them based on a prewar classic, "The Blue Scarf," whose words promised one of the things men wanted most: a happy ending, a tender reunion between the soldier and his girl. In the same vein, Simonov's "Wait for Me," with its recurrent promise, "Wait for me, and I'll come back," offered a protective totem, a sort of individual spell. The soldier who sang the words—for they were quickly set to music—was thinking of his own survival, for, as the poem concludes, "Only you and I will know / how I survived. / It's just that you knew how to wait / as no other person."[17]

New ballads of a different kind dealt with the soldier himself, the simple, stout-hearted, and earthy conscript who fought for his motherland. Poets like Lebedev-Kumach wrote Stalin into the lyrics of some of these, but veterans claim to have preferred more traditional material, and the leader does not feature when they sing their wartime favorites today. The most popular song of all, a folksong with its origins in tsarist times, was about a Russian girl, Katyusha. This classic developed hun-

A soldiers' choir on the Kalinin front, May 1942

dreds of variations in the course of the war, many of them playing on
Katyusha's new role as a rocket launcher. Technological versions of
Katyusha end up killing Hitler and his cronies, and her unearthly music
deafens and defeats the generic Fritz. What she does not do, on the
record at least, is stoop to obscenity. Even subversive irony does not figure in her repertoire. Whatever the men may have sung in private, and
political reports describe their "crude eroticism," no one allowed a
folklorist to collect disrespectful versions of the army's songs.[18] Singing
was a public act. It was forbidden except at designated times.[19]

Everyone knew that songs were vital for morale. "You can't have a
war without songs," a former partisan remembered. "It's easier to die or
go hungry if you have a song."[20] Belorussian journalist Svetlana Alexiyevich found the same when she talked to women who had fought in the
war. "When I asked them what they remembered best about their departure for the front," she wrote, "the answer was unanimous. They had
sung their favorite songs!"[21] Songs were even used to teach the men
commands. In 1941, two sergeants wrote a ballad, which they sang in
off-key male voices to the new recruits. It was a love story, and each line

included one of the commands that every man needed to know—left, right, down, attention, fire![22] The song caught on in other companies, and eventually soldiers sang it as a kind of joke, imitating the voices of their sergeants and commanding officers in the roles of a young woman and her naïve lover.

Music like this worked better than the rote learning of the *politruks*. Wartime tunes were lilting, easily learned and hummed. They were so attractive, in fact, that even the Germans could fall under their spell. Later in the war, members of a Soviet artillery regiment were surprised to hear a German accordion player on the other side of no-man's-land playing the song they had been singing since they pitched their camp. A few days later, a piece of paper was found in a shell case near their lines asking—in broken Russian—for the words to go with the tune.[23]

Poetry was just as vital to morale as song, and the two often overlapped. Verse came naturally to Russian speakers, even peasants, for whom it recalled the oral culture of the recent past, and they listened eagerly to recitations of their favorite ballads. The most famous, Aleksandr Tvardovsky's "Vasily Tyorkin," describes a brave but fallible soul who endures shelling and forced marches with stoical good humor and an unflinching sense of duty. Crucially, Tyorkin always survives, although his comrades often come close to despairing of his life. "Boys— it's him!" they shout as he emerges from yet another close call. This time, he has crossed an icy river where "even fishes must be cold." The men stand peering on the bank when, "large as life, Vasily Tyorkin / Rose alive—and in he swam. / Smooth and naked, as from bathing, / Out he staggered to the shore." The rhythms recall Tennyson or Longfellow, and so, in their cartoonlike narrative, do the words, but Tyorkin is a Russian through and through. As the doctor massages him with alcohol in the recovery hut, he sits up and blearily asks to drink the stuff: " 'Pity on my skin to waste it!" / Had a glass—and came alive."[24]

Verse was easy to learn, pleasant to recite, and valuable because it compressed emotion to an intensity that seemed normal in war. As well as memorizing other people's work, the men themselves wrote rhymes and aphorisms. Their letters home were full of poems—sentimental vignettes of love and homesickness, stirring patriotic odes. Caught in the spirit of the times, some wrote about the red flag or the Communist

Party. The more romantic took their cue from famous published work. Simonov's "Wait for Me" fathered hundreds of wartime love poems, while the Russian landscape and heroic deeds provided inspiration for countless other verses. Those who could not write memorized, and developed variations on, the short folk poems, *chastushki*, that peasants had been composing for generations. The *politruks* wrote some of these, adapting the folk themes of fate and motherland to the current world of Stalin and the party. *Chastushki* were as catchy as limericks. The men composed thousands of them, with themes that ranged from grief and thwarted love to the irregularity of field post. "Tell me / in God's name / if my dear is alive / in Stalingrad," ran one. The news was often bad. "From far away a brother writes, / dear little sister, / they killed before my eyes / your own beloved." "I've had a little letter," sang another, "that the censor has gone over. / He died heroically / but it doesn't say any more."[25]

Chastushki were the nearest folklorists would get to the coarse humor that soldiers loved. In her old age, Vera Krupyanskaya, the famous wartime ethnographer, told one of her colleagues that the censors had forbidden her to record erotic, satiric, subversive, or criminal lyrics. She was not permitted to write down words that denigrated national minorities, including Jews, and the songs she collected would not be published if they lacked a patriotic theme.[26] This strict political correctness guaranteed that she would overlook a large part of reality. The songs and aphorisms that have made their way into Soviet textbooks about soldiers' lore are prim, polite, and Stalinist. Their sentiments are truly part of wartime idiom—people really believed, with part of their brains, in the ultimate triumph of virtuous Communism—but they offer little clue about the way men coped with their tough, dangerous lives. And they bear no trace of the humor, much of it obscene and very dark, that was so central to the front-line way of life.

One problem for outsiders wanting to know more—whether wartime ethnographers or historians writing today—is that the men's language was meant to exclude strangers from their close groups. Among themselves, the men larded their sentences with expressions that were so profane that few are willing to repeat them to this day. In its developed form, obscenity amounted to a parallel language on the scale of cockney rhyming slang. The word for it—and the object of many of the crude sexual gibes—was *mat* (mother). No outsider could follow *mat*'s staggering twists. A real man not only swore, he used "three-story mother," piling the profanities in stacks. It was crude, creative, visual, and exclusive—strictly for the boys. Little, if any, of it has made its way into the histories of Stalin's war.

It is the same with soldiers' other diversions. Lev Pushkarev was embarking on a research degree in ethnography when the war broke out, and he decided to use his time in the army to collect material for a dissertation about the soldiers' culture. The NKVD quickly found his notes. At first, they wanted to suppress them all, but when they had established, by writing to his university department in Moscow, that he was a genuine scholar, they agreed to let him keep a record of some of the words, the decent ones, to the men's songs. He came home with a briefcase stuffed with polite ballads and rhymes. Laughter, however, was a different matter. Pushkarev had also been collecting jokes. The NKVD seized his notebooks of these at the outset, and he was forbidden to collect any more. Humor, which sustained so many people and which reflected their authentic, spontaneous voice, was deemed to be too dangerous to record. There must be a file somewhere in the bowels of the Ministry of Defense that contains examples of the men's uncensored talk. Till that is opened, there is only memory or, failing that, the screeds of poisonous antisemitism that German intelligence officers collected from captive soldiers and filed for future propaganda use.

Today, the veterans find it hard to remember the things that used to make them laugh. So much was instantaneous, based on the foibles of an officer, a non-Russian, or a newcomer to the unit. Sometimes, too, there is a hint of shame. Some soldiers hesitate to recollect the way they used to mock specific ethnic groups. Jokes based on bodily functions, too, might have seemed funny once, but now these men are old. "I'm not sure I can tell you those," people would say to me. It was easy, however, to laugh at the enemy. By 1943, the Germans were alleged to be so desperate for conscripts that they would take men with almost any disability. "But I can't be fit for service," a soldier tells the Berlin medical board. "In Russia they shot off both my legs and both my arms, destroyed my lungs, and even gave me a bad back." "In that case," the doctors reply, "nothing can happen now that hasn't happened to you already."[27] This kind of thing was suitable for satirical newspapers, but the warped landscape of the Soviet state was fertile ground for humor of a more subversive kind. If the military police got hold of you, the men knew all too well, the charges would be absurd and the procedures byzantine. "You have to prove," the wags explained, "that you are not a camel."[28] Another story comes straight from the world of *politruks* and spies. One evening, an officer is telling a joke to his men. They are all laughing except for one, whose glum expression does not change. The officer calls a *politruk* over to find out if the man is all right. "Have you had bad news from home?" the *politruk* asks. The man has not. No one in his unit has died recently, either, and he is not feeling frightened or unwell. "So why aren't you laughing?" the *politruk* inquires. "I'm from another regiment," the glum man says. "That's not my commanding officer."[29]

Laughter could lighten the heavy atmosphere of propaganda. At times, it also helped to dissipate the cloud of fear. But its other effect was to bind groups of soldiers together, cementing the front-line friendships that sustained each man in this world of extremes. Stalin's regime was suspicious of groups. All through the war, spies from the Special Section were detailed to pry whenever unsanctioned new friendships formed. But trust was crucial for team building. Effective tactics demanded that men knew and relied on their mates. Reluctantly, for they despised most sentiment, the country's leaders began to mimic their enemy.[30] From March 1942, units in need of new blood were withdrawn from front-line service before they received reserves and replacements. Ideally, the new formations were supposed to train together for some weeks before they faced real danger as a group.[31] This was not always possible, but it was known to work. Team building was a trick the U.S. Army would not learn till after 1945, when it looked back on the mistakes and lessons of the war's campaigns.[32]

Red Army friendships might not last long, but they certainly were fierce. At this stage, an infantryman was unlikely to serve with his friends for more than three months before a wound, death, or even a promotion removed him from the group. "It's enough for a person to be with you two to seven days," soldiers would explain, "for you to know his qualities, all his feelings, the things it takes a year to know in civilian life."[33] It is a testimony to the power of soldiers' loyalties that many petitioned time and time again, even after each discharge from the hospital, to be allowed to get back to their mates.[34] "We were like a boy and girl," a veteran remembered. "Like lovers, you'd have said. We couldn't bear to be apart." He was not talking about homosexuality. No one ever broke that taboo; sex, in any case, was the last thing on a soldier's mind when he was hungry, tired, and frightened. This was a difference between the front line and the rear, between the trenches and the officers' mess. Friendships were close, but the pleasures that men shared, and talked about, at the front line centered on food, drink, warmth, and smoking. When David Samoilov's unit was at the front, the men sat up for hours, "tormented without tobacco." They talked endlessly, and a favorite subject was each man's wedding. What interested them, however, was not the wedding night and sex, or even thoughts of love and home, but the scale and contents of the feast that had been set for each celebration.[35]

Subversive and passionate, brutal or dark, this was a world that the Sovinformburo did its best to keep well out of sight. "Our soldiers" portrayed in the Soviet press were no more realistic than the brave boys of adventure comics. Survivors had a lot to gain, after the war, by endorsing the myth. But there was one group whose members had nothing left to lose. These were the *shtrafniki*, the members of the punishment units. Not many are alive to tell their tales. Ivan Gorin, for instance, was the only survivor in a group of 330 men. All the rest died in a single morning when they were sent, armed with rifles and rushing over open ground, to storm a battery of entrenched German guns. When this man remembers the war, his starting point is a prison.

Gorin's father had disappeared when the police drove the kulaks away in 1930. That is, he deserted his wife and children and made for the south. Gorin himself was sent to a foster family who despised him for his supposed bourgeois roots. It was an inauspicious start. The boy lived on the edge of the illegal world, and when the war broke out he turned to forging ration cards. When he was caught, the judge gave him a choice: the Gulag or the front. He had already decided to fight, for when he was in prison, pending sentence, he had imbibed the patriotic mood. "Lots of people asked to go," he said. "There was enthusiasm for the front even among prisoners." At least it felt a bit like tasting life. Soon everyone would learn that it was merely execution by another means.

The *shtrafniki* discovered that their lives counted for less than those of Budennyi's beloved horses. The only food they ever saw was thin gray soup. "The old hands told us that we got a tenth of the normal army ration," another survivor remembered. "Whether that was right or not, our menu consisted of four spoonfuls of food a day . . . and unlimited quantities of the best-quality profanities." Convicts were herded into camps to await military orders. These barracks were as murderous as the Gulag, and much of their atmosphere derived from it. A man could be skinned alive for losing in a game of cards, he could be murdered in his bed for his boots or a crust of hoarded bread.[36] Everyone lived in fear of the *starshiny*, the older convicts who ran everything. Reaching the front, even without a scrap of professional training, came as a relief for the inexperienced Gorin. "We wanted to get to the front as fast as possible," he said, "so as to escape from the torment of that reserve base."[37]

Once there, with a gun in his hand, Gorin realized that he was someone officers respected. They could not know, after all, which way he was planning to shoot. "We went into battle," another man remembered, "and we never shouted for the motherland and Stalin. We were all swearing and cursing. That was the 'Hoorah!' of the *shtrafniki*." Gorin agreed but added that the men regarded their leader with a fatalistic respect. "If Stalin dies," they muttered, "another will come in his place of the same kind." They were not alienated nihilists, either. Russians fought on because they believed in a real cause, and even surviving *shtrafniki* remember their love of the motherland. "We all wanted to defend it," Gorin said. "I think that the criminals felt more devotion, more love for their native soil than the higher-ups in the leadership, the bosses." And there was pride even in death. "He doesn't run away, the *shtrafnik*," another survivor told journalists. "Ordinary soldiers are more likely to do that."[38]

The convicts' life expectancy was short, but their culture, raw and vivid, distinct from that of the party cell and officers' mess, infused the whole atmosphere of the front. The same was often true of the criminals who were shipped to the front from the Gulag after April 1943.[39] Cast into this most murderous war, they depended on skills they had first learned in the hungry villages of the 1930s and then in the hard school of Kolyma. They had the peasant *muzhik*'s eye for a deal, the convict's for self-preservation. Brutal conditions made survivors of them all. And yet most of them cared about the outcome of the war. "This war was a war of extermination," a rank-and-file soldier later recalled. "It stirred up hatred, the thirst for revenge, finally ripening into a cause, which would inspire the Red Army into furious battles over a four-year period." It was the bosses, however, ever ready with their slogans, who gave that cause its official name. "This cause was named 'patriotism.' "[40]

★

The celebrations had been premature. The victory at Stalingrad had wounded the enemy severely, but it had not permanently broken him. Even the gains of February 1943 proved ephemeral. The Soviets held on to Kharkov for barely a month. In March, they were driven back, leaving the city to the Fascists once again. It was a bitter moment for the army and a catastrophe for Kharkov's citizens, who now faced the redoubled anger of their conquerors as well as the privations of another hungry spring. Far away, in the unimaginable light of the Tunisian desert, Montgomery's troops were driving Rommel and his men toward the sea. The outcome of the Soviet Union's war was still unclear.

That spring, the Soviet leadership gathered to consider the coming year's campaign. On 8 April, Georgy Zhukov, newly created Marshal of the Soviet Union and decorated with the first ever Order of Suvorov, First Class, delivered his assessment of the enemy's plans.[41] Grave and businesslike, he told the general staff that Germany lacked the resources for a new push in the Caucasus or along the Volga. But the Fascists were far from beaten. Winter was never their best time of year; nor were the sodden weeks of spring, when melting snow dissolved into thigh-high mud. But for two summers already, their tanks and horses had raced eastward over sun-baked ground, driving the Soviet army back, encircling whole divisions at a time, instilling panic in many of the rest. As the days lengthened and the mornings warmed, they would attack again. Zhukov believed that they would choose a narrow front and muster concentrated forces for a direct strike, whose ultimate objective would probably be Moscow. The blow would come from the places where German forces were strongest, namely the open wheat fields between Orel and Belgorod. Its likely focus would be the region around Kursk, a city in the black-earth zone near the border with Ukraine. The Soviet front line bulged westward at this point, exposing the Red Army's flanks from the northwest to the southwest. In Zhukov's view, the onslaught, when it came, would be designed to devastate. The Wehrmacht was running short of men. This was a battle that would be decided by aircraft, artillery, and tanks.[42]

Zhukov's assessment, which drew on detailed intelligence from British sources, was correct, although the timing of the blow was difficult to calculate. For once, too, Stalin accepted the military analysis, including the advice to prepare, in the first instance, for resolute defense. It was not what prewar propaganda had prescribed, with its images of bold strikes at the Fascist barricades, but the strategy that summer would be to take the German blow, absorbing it with line after line of defense. Only then, when the extravagant advance had been stalled, would the Soviets go into the attack. The preparations would begin at once. Training programs in all types of specialties would be intensified, and preference would be given to men with secondary-school education.[43] Even front-line troops would face new drills and classes, and tank crews would receive special attention. Once ready, hundreds of thousands of men would march toward the south and west, traveling at night. In anticipation of heavy casualties—a prediction that would prove entirely correct—450 hospitals and field treatment stations would be refurbished, rebuilt, or equipped. Two hundred of these were planned for the Voronezh Front alone.[44] Meanwhile, around Kursk itself and for over a hundred miles behind the front, militia groups and soldiers were set to shifting dirt. By July, when the bombardment finally began, a total of three thousand miles of trenches had been prepared behind the front, crisscrossing in an angular geometry.[45] The rich black earth was also sown with metal in unnumbered tons. On average, by July, there were over five thousand antitank or antipersonnel mines for every mile of fortification.[46]

The military plan was brilliant, but obstacles remained. Battlefields are not pieces of bland green baize. The future front-line zone was home to thousands of civilians. The next four months would see the army interacting all too closely with the local population. At their best, such relationships were warm and appreciative. Some men found friends who would share their last crust with a soldier from their own side. The local people had suffered—some had survived a German occupation—and almost everyone had a son or husband or father at the front. Soldiers could count on the support of patriots. "The directors of the collective farm and its farmers treated me really well," an engineer called Vitaly Taranichev wrote to his wife at the end of 1942. "They sent me on my way like a member of the family, they baked pies and biscuits for me to take, cooked some mutton, got hold of some *makhorka* and all that. I agreed to stay in touch with the *kolkhoz* chairman, an old guy of seventy who has four sons at the front."[47] Taranichev was in fact some distance behind the lines at this point, still in the reserves. His hosts had not seen the war as the peasants of the Kursk region had come to know it. In the spring and summer of 1943, parts of the black-earth zone were far from welcoming to anyone.

"Our conditions are very good," Aleksandr Slesarev wrote to his father, who was also in the Red Army. The young man had been on the road for several weeks, but now he and his comrades had dug in. "We are living not far from a forest, in *zemlyanki*, of course. Our food is first-class—and apart from that we get an extra ration because we're at the front. My work is interesting, and I get to travel about." His only complaint, which others heartily endorsed that spring, was that "there isn't much free time."[48] Slesarev, who came from Smolensk, was in the newly formed First Guards Tank Army. He was supposed to spend his spring on exercises, improving the coordination and field tactics that tank units had so badly lacked in previous years. There were indeed many classes, especially in his own elite formation, but military work was once again neglected, on occasion, in favor of other tasks. That spring, even tank men's duties would include helping on collective farms and working with the engineers whose job was to rebuild the region's communications, stores, and hospitals.

Nikolai Belov was still with his rifle division. Based just outside Maloarkhangel'sk in the Orel region, he, too, was working very hard. "We've got to do some tough training," he wrote in his diary. "We'll have to work in earnest again now, and you can't protect yourself from the intensity of it." He was exhausted, but activity agreed with him. By 22 May, after a fortnight in his front-line camp, he had "got used to the work a bit." Practical problems, not depression, would disturb him most that spring. "The regiment hasn't really come together," he observed. The training would soon see to that. But nothing he could do would remedy the shortage of guns and other supplies.[49]

The men in Belov's regiment did not enjoy the waiting or the drill. Belov himself noted a steady drip of desertions. On 27 May, five infantrymen slipped away from his unit to join the German side. "It's hard to understand," he wrote, "what brought that on. Evidently the general tiredness." The Germans were also dropping leaflets, encouraging the men to believe that changing sides would save their lives. On 30 May, two more men would disappear—"it's a real nightmare." One of them, Belov observed, was a candidate member of the Communist Party.[50] The total number of Red Army troops deserting to the German side seemed to be growing by the month. Just over a thousand were recorded by German intelligence in February. In April, the figure would rise to 1,964, in May 2,424, and in June 2,555.[51] But these figures do not reflect the real picture. For one thing, fugitives did not always make for the German lines. As the Red Army moved west, the NKVD searched the bombed-out towns for truant soldiers masquerading as civilians. Kursk and its province turned out to be full of them. Many were lifelong criminals; others would now begin careers in crime. In March 1943, for instance, the Kursk NKVD reported on a deserter called Ozerov, an ex-convict who had escaped to the occupied zone in 1942. His violence surfaced again when he battered and killed the woman who was hiding him as well as her elderly mother. He was captured and shot.[52]

Kursk itself was little more than ruins. In fourteen months, the German occupiers had plundered its factories and stores, destroyed its official buildings, and murdered hundreds of its citizens. The residents they did not murder or deport they left to starve or at least to sicken with the diseases of poverty and filth—typhus, dysentery, tuberculosis, and syphilis. Those who were still alive to greet the Red Army that spring had witnessed scenes they could never forget; they had also learned that survival depended on unusual kinds of skill. As the city had emptied late in 1941, in advance of the Germans' arrival, the marooned residents had looted anything that they could carry. Early in 1943, they had also taken supplies that the Germans left as they hurried away. Now, with the city full of troops again, the locals sought to feed themselves by selling their eccentric hoards. A woman was apprehended by police in March for peddling sheets. When her flat was searched, she was also fined for the possession of a stockpile consisting of two mattresses, three blankets, forty electric light bulbs, and eighteen kilos of soap. This last was a kind of currency. One man was found with sixty-seven bars of it, all taken from the German army's stores, together with eight pairs of trousers, four pairs of German army boots, three woollen blankets, and a sewing machine. Another had ten bars of household soap, eighty-seven tins of meat, and five hundred German cigarettes. Among the other trophy goods were German bicycles and cartloads of their fine white flour.[53]

The penalty for hoarding groceries was seldom more than a stiff fine. Weapons were another matter. Violent crime, including robbery and rape, was now a daily problem. Guns were easy to acquire, and gangs formed readily among the orphaned teenagers and army fugitives. Deserters lived by picking pockets in the city streets or stealing pigs and cattle in the villages. Meanwhile, children were injured almost every day as they played with or near unexploded mines and shells. Most desperate of all were the women who gave birth to children as a result of rape or informal relations with German soldiers. The babies had no fathers now, and the women no means to support them. Everyone was hungry, so there was no sense in keeping bastard mouths to feed. All through that spring, police and passersby found the depressing bundles in ditches, shallow graves, and even piles of rubble. The reinstated city officers wrote one another anxious notes, but they knew that the military effort took priority. There were no resources to police, let alone support, civilians in the region.[54] Instead, these same exhausted local people, however unfit for the job, were now ordered to help with physically demanding tasks that ranged from reconstructing roads to digging mud and clearing mines. That May, too, their leaders issued an appeal for them to start donating blood.[55]

The hardship in the countryside was indescribable. By the spring of 1943, 200,000 people in the region were deemed to be invalids, orphans, or other dependents requiring support from state funds of food and fuel.[56] The areas of enemy occupation had been plundered, the people's livestock slaughtered or driven away, their crops destroyed or looted. Suspected partisans had been hanged, and then their neighbors—entire communities—had been punished for good measure. Nearly forty thousand houses, over half the region's entire stock, had been burned to the ground.[57] Many able-bodied adults had been dragged off to work for the Reich as forced laborers. There was no one left to rebuild houses, dig the fields, or gather what was left of the previous year's crop. Terrified householders, many of them widows or lone women with children, had often failed to sow their fields as the snow melted and the ground warmed up in 1942. The collectives were moonscapes of scorched scrub and thorn, nettle, and tough wild grass. But the Red Army had played its part in all this devastation, too. The Kursk region had been its front line since September 1942. To prepare for the campaign of 1942–43, the army set out to evacuate civilians who lived within twelve (sometimes fifteen or twenty) kilometers of the front. What followed sometimes looked like civil war. This was not western Ukraine or the Baltic, where the Red Army would encounter resistance as it attempted to reimpose Soviet power the following year. It was not a region of nationalist banditry. But Kursk would prove that soldiers were not always welcome even among ethnic Russians.

The problems began in the autumn of 1942. When soldiers of the Thirteenth and Thirty-eighth armies arrived in the front-line zone that September to evacuate the villages, the population resisted en masse. Later reports suggested that the operation had been botched, allowing the peasants a chance to get together and foment a storm of rage. But the real problem, as even the authorities understood, was that the locals feared a trick. This was the army that was losing battles by the day, the army that had yet to prove itself at Stalingrad, and now it wanted to take people's cows and pigs and drive whole families from their homes. The campaign looked like nothing so much as a repeat of the hated process of collectivization. Troops had been used then, too, in some places, and animals and people had been driven from their homes in the same violent way. Now the soldiers were back to steal everything again. Villagers were told that they would be given tokens for the animals they lost, they were assured that there were lodgings waiting for them far away behind the lines, but—not unwisely—they did not believe a word.

Hunger and fear made the peasants' anger worse. The crowds that gathered to resist the soldiers were large and organized, two hundred people in one district, three hundred, "armed with pitchforks, spades, and axes," in another, while in a third "a hundred and fifty women and youths took part, most of whom were armed with staffs and bricks and the like." These desperate mobs hurled missiles at the troops, the women taunting them with cries of "deserter" and "jailbird." "If you try to evacuate me," an old man told a local official, "I'll kill you. I've sharpened my axe and I can kill at least six people with it. And my wife and daughter can kill two each, and there surely won't be ten of you. And if each household kills ten people, then there just won't be an evacuation, will there?"[58]

The threats were real. The Thirteenth Army held back from evacuating its allocated zones. But the Thirty-eighth proceeded with the evacuations. When they returned to the villages where the first crowds had gathered, they met an armed, furious mob. On 13 October they were driven back by the entire population of one village, by women brandishing pitchforks and shovels. The next day, neighboring villagers attacked soldiers again, knocking out one man's teeth and cracking another's skull. But the soldiers had new orders by then. With the help of NKVD troops, they arrested the most active members of the resistance. They also shot some of the others in the legs, a measure that soon terrified the crowd. None of this was good for military public relations. The region's leaders, working with the generals themselves, now faced the task of restoring local people's faith in their defenders. Henceforth the NKVD would be used for evacuating citizens. The Red Army itself would no longer be sent to confront Russian peasants.[59] Its reputation as the people's vanguard would need some careful nurturing in the coming weeks.

Fortunately, a string of real victories, beginning with Stalingrad, would soon reinforce the army's image as a liberator. The first appearance of Soviet troops in a town or village that the Germans had abandoned was often greeted with tears of exhausted, desperate relief, whatever followed when the NKVD set to work. But it would be a long time, if ever, before some of the villagers around Kursk would trust authority again. Their fears were grounded in cold fact. In May and June 1943, just weeks before the epic confrontation of the war, General Rokossovsky himself would set his battle plans aside to consider the unsolved disappearance of two cows. It was not the first such case. Three had vanished less than a week before. They had gone missing from farms near soldiers' billets. And then there were all the official irregularities. "In recent days," he read, "eighty cows have been taken from the population [in the twenty-five-kilometer front-line zone], but only thirty receipts for these have been issued. The collective farms have also lost a hundred and fifty horses and almost all their transport equipment. All this," the general would be informed, "disrupts the agricultural work of our collectives."[60]

Fighting was clearly only one aspect of the war effort. Food was a real problem everywhere. The army took the lion's share, and soldiers often ate better than they had eaten back in their homes, but civilians faced serious want. In 1943 the government printed ten thousand copies of a leaflet instructing people how to cook nettles. Two scientists produced another that discussed the caloric possibilities of feral meat. "When they kill animals for fur," it began, "hunters often forget that there is useful meat on the carcasses." The scientists pointed out that squirrel meat contained more calories than any other kind save that of the polecat, and certainly far more than pork. Admittedly, a typical squirrel yielded just 200 grams of meat (or so they claimed), but the flesh was palatable, unlike that of wolves, whose pungent carcasses were fit only for pigs. To test this last contention, a commission had gathered at the Academy of Sciences that spring to approve the flavor and nutritional value of a range of creatures from foxes to gophers and mice.[61] While the academicians dined, civilians were going hungry. "We have had to sell a lot of our things," Vitaly Taranichev's wife, Natalya, wrote to him that March, "because everything has become very expensive. It's enough to say that we spend twenty rubles a day on half a liter of milk for Kolya." Their infant son needed the food. "If we took that milk away from him, we'd be condemning him to complete emaciation."[62]

In front-line regions, the hunger was greater still. There were no men left to rebuild the ruined buildings and barns, restore the roads, or sow that year's new crop. At the start of the agricultural season in 1943, average sowings in individual districts in the Kursk area looked set to fall to less than 10 percent of their 1941 levels. But the region needed grain to feed its people, and the army would need food to keep men on their feet. Women worked like animals, sometimes harnessing themselves to ploughs. The land itself was wrecked, and it would not recover quickly in the years to come.

Once again, the soldiers had to roll up their olive-green sleeves and dig. On 12 April, an order to troops on the Central Front required them to help farmers sow the spring crops, do the ploughing, deal with lambing, and transport seed grain to the farms. They were to do this, the order added, "without detriment to their military duties."[63] Meanwhile, presumably without detriment to food production, civilians were formed into militia squads and sent to dig trenches and clear abandoned German mines. "It is a shame, when you travel around the liberated villages," a Red Army soldier wrote to his family that June, "to see the cold attitude of the population."[64] The whole region was plunged in a struggle for survival. The armies that would fight near Kursk trained and prepared in scenes of medieval brutishness.

★

The battles that they were about to fight would turn the air itself to flame. If tanks represent a certain kind of modernist dream, then Kursk would see its revelation as apocalypse. The fighting around the salient was set to involve more armor, more machines, than any other in the entire war. That summer, the black-earth steppe of Kursk province would bristle with seventy thousand guns and mortars, twelve thousand war planes, and an epic thirteen thousand tanks and mobile artillery pieces.[65] Vast numbers of troops, including tens of thousands of riflemen, were also gathered in the zone. To guarantee the success of this most vital blow, the Germans brought fifty divisions to the region, including handpicked SS troops of certified Aryan stock and (more importantly) proven military skill. In all, there were 900,000 German officers and men around the salient by midsummer. But the Soviets were

Soviet refugees, a mother and son, rest on their journey, April 1942 (courtesy of the State Archive of the Russian Federation)

ready to meet them. By late May, they had 1.3 million troops in readiness behind the maze of crisscrossed lines.

By the time these adversaries engaged each other in July, they had been at war for two entire years. The contest had been ugly and violent, but like any other it had forced the two sides to learn from and even to mimic each other. For the Germans, what this meant was a new focus on the technology of armor. In 1941, they had possessed no tank that could match the maneuverability of the Soviet T–34. They also had nothing to compete with the mighty KV heavy tank, whose armor was almost impervious to their antitank guns. The Wehrmacht's success against these machines owed more to the poor training of Soviet tank crews, and to the Red Army's general unpreparedness, than to any German technological sophistication. Berlin's answer was to develop two machines, the Panther and the Tiger I, respectively the most advanced medium tank in the field and the most invincible heavy tank of its time. The Panther was less prone to catch fire than the T–34, it offered crews much better visibility, and the radio that was designed for it stood a real chance of working. The Tiger I, meanwhile, was fitted with the fearsome German 88 mm antiaircraft gun. It threatened to be deadly, not just difficult to destroy. In addition to these metal giants, German factories were now producing a self-propelled gun, the Ferdinand, as well as stockpiles of field-tested types of mortar, rocket, and flamethrower.[66]

The Wehrmacht could demand creative new designs, the best of German engineering, but what it could not wring out of its leader was more time. In the entire war, German industry would produce only 1,354 Tiger I and 5,976 Panther machines.[67] By 1943, the Soviets were turning out T–34s at a rate of over 1,200 a month.[68] One of the Red Army's advantages that summer was that it had a greater number of field-worthy, modern tanks. The Germans might possess a limited stock of truly fearsome machines, but for numbers they would still have to rely on obsolete, much older models. The calculation was deliberate on the Soviet side. In 1941, the Red Army had lost nine-tenths of its tanks in a matter of weeks, and it had also lost its main production centers in Kharkov and Leningrad. As the tank factories were reconstructed to the east, it was decided to focus on existing models and to turn them out in bulk, a prudent move in view of the disastrous rates of loss that Soviet crews continued to sustain. With a few modifications, the T–34 would continue as the Soviet mainstay through the war.

Refinements, let alone entirely new designs, would have meant delays in the factories and new training challenges for the men. So only a limited amount of innovation was permitted, even after the defeats of 1942. The T–34 was adapted to improve visibility, though tank drivers remember seeing only dust and smoke. A small number of new weapons improved the Soviet arsenal of armored vehicles and artillery. The most important of these was the SU–152 mobile assault unit, which was designed to carry a 152 mm howitzer. Nicknamed the *zverboi*, or "beast basher," it was the only Soviet armored vehicle that could defeat the Panther and the Tiger I in the field.[69] This was important, since these newest German tanks were deadly even for heavy KVs. The technological balance between the adversaries had shifted, and the Soviets no longer led the field. But they would not run short of armor again. In this case as in almost every other, the Red Army's approach to technology was to churn it out and keep it simple.

Still there was more to Soviet preparation than mere numbers. Indeed, in individual confrontations around Kursk, including the decisive battle near Prokhorovka, the two sides had roughly equal numbers of machines within range of the fighting.[70] It was the human, not the technological, factor that weighed heaviest that July. Self-sacrificial, almost suicidal courage was crucial for the victory at Kursk, as the many Soviet casualties—seventy thousand dead in the defensive phase alone—would testify. Equally important, however, was the Red Army troops' increasing mastery of war. Coordination between tank crews had been improved by intensive training, while military thinking about the deployment of armor had also progressed. The tank was now a weapon in its own right, not a gas-guzzling substitute for a horse. Five new tank armies, of which Slesarev's was one, were created in the early months of 1943.[71] The skills of the tank crews in these new formations were also improving. Slesarev had begun his military service as an artilleryman. Selected for promotion in 1942, he trained for nearly a year before receiving his first tank command as a lieutenant. A fellow tank lieutenant, twenty-two-year-old Ivan Gusev, described the pressure of his work that summer. "Every hour is taken up with fussing over the machines," he wrote to his family in June 1943. "Sometimes you forget the time and date. You forget everything."[72]

The crews that men like Gusev and Slesarev commanded had trained with record speed. But they had also been forced to focus more narrowly and thoroughly than any of their predecessors. Since the evacuation and restructuring of production, the main tank schools were now located near the factories that made the tanks. The instruction they offered, like the nearby production lines, was economical and specialized. Individual men were taught only to work in the specific model— the T–34, for instance—to which they were to be assigned. Each man, whether gunner or mechanic, was also trained for one speciality within the crew.[73] The entire round of preparation took less than three months. It turned out fresh tank men, in other words, as fast as the Germans could slaughter them.

The job attracted some of the best recruits, especially young men from the towns. In part, they were drawn by the glamour of the huge machine. If farm boys had been brought up to imagine themselves driving tractors, youths from the towns might well have dreamed of dashing over open country in an armored giant, controlling its movements with wheels and levers and monitoring the outside world through a bank of dials. Even the Germans would eventually learn to respect these soldiers. "The Russian townsman," wrote the SS general Max Simon, "who is highly interested in technical matters, is just as well suited for the modern tank arm as the Russian peasant is for the infantry. . . . It was amazing to see the primitive technical means with which the Russian crews kept their tanks ready for action and how they overcame all difficulties."[74]

The tank men's skill was not just a matter of knowing where to put the spanner. The other quality that Max Simon observed among these sons of the factory was their determination. "An added factor," he wrote, "is that the Russian worker usually is a convinced communist, who, having enjoyed the blessings of 'his' revolution for decades, will fight fanatically as a class-conscious proletarian. Just as the Red Infantryman is ready to die in his foxhole, the Soviet tank soldier will die in his tank, firing at the enemy to the last, even if he is alone in or behind enemy lines."[75] Gusev, who certainly was a Communist, put it more personally. At the end of a long day, he told his family, "you lie down to sleep late in the evening, you feel a terrible exhaustion in your whole body, you know that you have carried out a great and difficult task, but your heart is full of gladness, a special kind of sensation, a sort of pride or internal satisfaction. These are the best moments of all."[76]

A man like Gusev fought for the family and land he loved, he fought for broadly Communist principles, but he also fought because he was beside his dearest friends. Friendships among tank men were often very strong. They would spend hours together in a confined space. They shared responsibility for their machine. They often made a tank their own by painting it with slogans. Uplifting and uncontroversial messages included "Where there is courage—there is victory!"[77] More seriously, crews also had to keep the monster in good working order. Gusev's best friend was another tank lieutenant who had shared a rough fortnight with him that spring when they and three other men had been assigned to a captured German tank. "We didn't know a thing about the machine," Gusev wrote. Battered and worn, she was "capricious" anyway, and on their first day the Soviet crew managed to travel only twenty-five kilometers in twelve hours. "We tinkered with her all day, dirty, hungry, and cross." They had no rations with them, "not even a crust of bread." The weather outside was filthy, the roads almost impassable on foot, and Gusev expected that the other lieutenant, who was in charge, would order everyone to leave the moribund machine and march. Instead, he worked with them for twelve days to repair the tank. "In those twelve days," Gusev wrote, "we would have turned gray if we could have. There's no way of writing what we went through." The friends were more like brothers by the time he wrote.[78]

Tank crews were also bound together by the threat of a shared death. After the infantry, where service was almost guaranteed to end in invalidism or death—or, as they quipped, in "the Department of Health (*zdravotdel*) or the Department of the Earth (*zemotdel*)"—armored and mechanized troops faced the most certain danger.[79] Of the 403,272 tank soldiers (including a small number of women) who were trained by the Red Army in the war, 310,000 would die.[80] Even the most optimistic troops knew what would happen when a tank was shelled. The white-hot flash of the explosion would almost certainly ignite the tank crew's fuel and ammunition. At best, the crew—or those at least who had not been decapitated or dismembered by the shell itself—would have no more than ninety seconds to climb out of their cabin. Much of that time would be swallowed up as they struggled to open the heavy, sometimes red-hot, hatch, which might have jammed after the impact anyway. The battlefield was no haven, but it was safer than the armored coffin that would now begin to blaze, its metal components to melt. This was not simply "boiling up." The tank would also torch the atmosphere around it. By then, there could be no hope for the men inside. Not unusually, their bodies were so badly burned that the remains were inseparable.[81] "Have you burned yet?" was a question tank men often asked each other when they met for the first time. A dark joke from this stage in the war has a *politruk* informing a young man that almost every tank man in his group has died that day. "I'm sorry," the young man replies. "I'll make sure that I burn tomorrow."

The troops that waited on the steppe near Kursk were rightly anxious as the weeks went by. On 8 May, commanders on the four main fronts were ordered to prepare for an attack within four days.[82] Less than two weeks later, on 20 May, they were put on the alert again.[83] No one doubted that the enemy was planning to attack, but nervous men and officers struggled to predict the exact time. By day, the Soviet encampments hummed with diligent activity, but at night the steppe was treacherously still. "Every day there's something new," Belov told his diary on 13 June. "Today another two have gone over to the enemy side. That's eleven people already. Most of them are pricks. On 11 June our neighbors did some battle reconnaissance. They didn't find a thing. We're all sitting in this ravine, it will be a month soon, and there's just silence at the front." The next day brought news of the job they were to do. Within a month, his men would be helping to mount an offensive toward Orel. "A big operation is being prepared," he wrote. "Our division is going to attack in three echelons, and our regiment will be in the second. There will be thirty-five artillery batteries working in the division, not including two Katyusha regiments. It's going to be pretty interesting."[84] But though he had his orders, Belov would see no action for several weeks. "I've been in this place longer," he wrote, "than I've been in any one spot the entire war."[85]

The attack came in the first week of July. On the night of the fourth, a German prisoner told his Soviet captors that it would begin early that morning. At about two o'clock, another prisoner told Soviet interrogators that the onslaught was timed to begin within an hour.[86] Even along the vast horizon of the steppe, the sky had yet to fade into predawn. Zhukov ordered an immediate artillery and air attack, a spoiling action that ripped through the night, as he admitted, like "a symphony from hell."[87] But it was no more than an overture. Undeterred by the Soviet barrage, the Germans launched their own attack, the onslaught that was meant to win the war, from both faces of the salient. To the north of Kursk, not far from Belov's base at Maloarkhangel'sk, the Ninth Panzer Army, commanded by Walter Model, struck at the Soviet lines, concentrating its main thrust in a narrow ten-mile stretch with the aim of breaking through and moving south into the salient. More than a hundred miles to the south, nine panzer divisions, commanded by Hermann Hoth, pushed northward toward the small town of Oboyan. The troops were the best available in Germany and included the handpicked SS "Death's Head" and "Adolf Hitler Guards" units. Their first objective was the highway that connected Oboyan, Kursk, and Belgorod to the Crimea and all of southeastern Ukraine.[88] By 7 July, they had almost reached it.

This was the campaign that Belov had been preparing for. The bombardment of 5 July was audible from his own base, although some distance to the south. "In the area of Belgorod and along the Kursk-Orel part of our front, to the south of us, there are fierce tank battles going on," he wrote on 8 July. "The sound of distant artillery cannonades can be heard here." So could the music of Katyushas, which gladdened every Soviet who listened. "The forces are very concentrated," Belov noted on the ninth. "Every valley is bursting with artillery and infantry. The nights are just an endless roar. Our aviation is working near the limit of the first defense lines. There's a mass of tanks."[89] The young officer's optimism was justified. Red Army units on the Central Front, under Rokossovsky's command, withstood the German onslaught from the north with a resilience that their enemy could never have anticipated. On the first day, Model's panzers advanced just four miles. They would make little headway in the week to come, although the defense effort cost the Soviets more than fifteen thousand lives.[90]

To the south, however, along the Voronezh Front, a smaller number of Soviet divisions under Nikolai Vatutin were facing one of the deadliest struggles of the war.

The fighting would involve the First Guards Tank Army, including Slesarev and his friends, the Fifth Guards Tank Army under Pavel Rotmistrov, and the gunners and riflemen of the Fifth Guards Army, the one in which Lev Lvovich, the mild-mannered geologist turned lieutenant, was serving. On 5 July, when the onslaught began, the Fifth Guards Army was more than two hundred miles behind the front. Rotmistrov's tank army was at a base not far beyond. Two days later, both would receive the order to cover the distance, on the march and under German bombardment, within three days. The scorching summer heat, the flies, and the great clouds of dust were exhausting enough. But after all that, the men would still need to be fit to fight successive eight-hour battles amid yet more shelling and machine-gun fire.[91] Meanwhile, Slesarev and his comrades were already in the direct path of an onslaught whose ferocity exceeded even Soviet fears. Recovering from the unexpected setback of their first day under fire, Hoth's men, spearheaded by more than five hundred tanks, pushed forward toward Oboyan. As Soviet infantry units shattered under the intense bombardment, the First Guards Tank Army was almost the only barrier that held—or tried to hold—on 7 July.[92] Slesarev had no time to write home. He was lucky to have survived. But the courage and tenacity of men like him forced Hoth to change his plans. Instead of driving straight for Oboyan, the Germans shifted their objective to a piece of relatively high ground near the small steppe town of Prokhorovka.

The fiercest tank battle in history took place in open fields near settlements with names like October and Komsomol. To have lost here, to have allowed the Germans to push through to Kursk, would almost certainly have meant losing the entire defensive campaign. Six hundred German tanks were poised for this great strike. Concealed in scrub, orchards, and the rank grassland of a wet July, 850 Soviet ones prepared to halt them. At dawn, as the first light filtered through the mist, the future battlefield was silent, "as if there were no war."[93] The first blackbirds began to call across the valley. "I watched my friend spreading fat on a chunk of bread," a veteran remembered. "He was doing it slowly, taking his time. I kept telling him to get a move on because the Germans were coming." But he smiled. "Don't rush me," he said, with a prescience his friend would later find uncanny. "I'm going to enjoy this. It's the last meal I'll eat in this world."[94] He had finished eating just before 6:30, when the calm was shattered by the first of hundreds of Junkers swooping to dive-bomb the Soviet lines.[95] But the attack was not to be a repeat of the summer of 1941. This time, there were hundreds of Soviet planes to answer with equal determination. The tank battle began with an aerial dogfight that would fill the air with smoke and burning metal well before the great machines began their duel.

Prokhorovka was destined to be remembered for those tanks. The German and Soviet machines advanced to meet through a fog of smoke and driving rain. By midmorning, the rolling fields were strewn with lumps of twisted metal and the charred bodies of men. Survivors talk about the summer heat, but in fact the weather that day was cool. What the veterans are probably remembering is the inferno of burning metal, burning fuel and rubber, burning air. Faced with the superior Panther and Tiger tanks, Soviet crews refused to yield. If they could do no more, they rammed their enemy, locking metal onto metal. This was the way that Gusev and his crew died. "The lieutenant's tank was moving forward," friends from his regiment would tell his parents, "maintaining fire from every kind of gun. But an enemy shell set fire to the machine. The firing from the burning tank did not cease. The mechanic, selecting the machine's highest gear, contrived to drive it at one of the enemy's advancing tanks. The fire from Lt. Gusev's tank continued. They were firing, so they must still have been alive. Our tank and Lt. Gusev's tank drove forward at full throttle straight toward the enemy tank. The Tiger wanted to turn around and get out, but it succeeded only in turning sideways. Our burning tank rammed into the Tiger and both tanks exploded. The crew of heroes perished."[96]

Tank crews were not the only men who died. Brigades of riflemen and artillery, including Lev Lvovich's unit, were also sent to stop the German tanks. When all else failed, infantrymen would hurl grenades and flaming bottles at the monsters, in the spirit of the old war films.

They also tackled German infantry, sometimes in hand-to-hand combat. They found the foot soldiers less awe-inspiring than elite tank men and SS. Some of the German men (and probably some Russians, too) were drunk, their courage stoked with quantities of schnapps.[97] But that did not make the fighting less deadly. "The sky thunders, the earth thunders, and you think your heart will explode and the skin on your back is about to burst," a woman combatant told Svetlana Alexiyevich. "I hadn't thought that the earth could crack. Everything cracked, everything roared. The whole world seemed to be swaying." But this was just the setting for what followed. Hand-to-hand fighting, she remembered, "isn't for human beings. ... Men strike, thrust their bayonets into stomachs, eyes, strangle one another. Howling, shouts, groans. It's something terrible even for war."[98] What kept Lev Lvovich going was not his abstract sense of duty but the concrete, the specific hourly goals. Orders would come, he said, "to aim for this bank or trench, to focus on this oak tree, aim three fingers' width toward the left. ... That sort of thing helps a lot." It also helped that he was too proud to allow his men to understand that he, too, was afraid.

At least seven hundred tanks lay charred and twisted on the battlefield by nightfall. The fighting would continue for two more days, but it was the first that decided the outcome of the battle and also of the whole campaign. Prokhorovka would come to rank in Russian myth beside Kulikovo Pole, the field where Dmitry Donskoi defeated the Golden Horde in 1380, and Borodino, the site of the great battle against Napoleon. Like them, it was regarded as a place where Russia's sacred destiny was saved. But as then, too, the human casualties were huge. For weeks to come the air for several miles around would reek of bloated corpses, decomposing human flesh. Parties of sanitary workers and local volunteers helped to remove the wounded from the area. High tech gave way to the old world as the heavy bodies were piled onto waiting horse-drawn carts. Local teams would also help to dig soldiers' mass graves. There is no village in the district that does not maintain such a site today. Unless the Germans retrieved them in time, their own dead would be buried later, piled into massive pits not for the sake of dignity, but to prevent infectious disease. Meanwhile, it would be decades, not years, before the area was cleared of mines, discarded weapons, and

A medical orderly loads a soldier's body onto a horse-drawn stretcher, 1943

metal debris. To this day, children are warned not to explore the woods. The fields were turned to desert, but they bore a bitter crop.

There was not one but several battles of Kursk, arrayed across at least two fronts. But the campaign was regarded as a single struggle by both sides. On the same day as the defense of Prokhorovka, 12 July, the Soviets launched a counterattack in the north, striking westward at Orel. In anticipation, and to the Red Army's relief, a portion of Hoth's assigned tanks had been diverted north before the Prokhorovka battle.[99] But the Germans had not prepared for the storm that was to come. At midnight on 11 July, Belov wrote a hasty, excited entry in his diary: "We're going to attack . . . at Shchelyabug." It would be two more weeks before he managed to record another word. As he would put it on the twenty-fifth, "There has been absolutely no possibility of making notes these past days." The Red Army had fought its way across the heavily defended German lines, its aim to disrupt the German Central Front.[100] Belov's regiment suffered extremely heavy losses, more than a thousand men, in fourteen days. The compensation was that they were now within twelve kilometers of German-occupied Orel. They had also

Dog teams transporting the injured, August 1943

"killed a lot of Fritzes, which is really great."[101] The battle for the old city was yet to come, but the enemy had been pushed back far behind the lines it held before the campaign had begun.

To the south, meanwhile, Slesarev also found a moment to scribble a note home. "You will know from the newspapers," he wrote to his father on 18 July, "that stubborn and fierce battles are taking place here. We're beating the Fritzes good and proper, the battles don't stop day or night. You can hear the 'music of war' twenty-four hours a day." On the twenty-seventh, he was even more sanguine, his tone an echo of the party's own victorious mood. Indeed, his letter of that day reflects his newfound status as a real Communist. Like hundreds of other tank men, Slesarev applied to join the party on the field at Kursk, marrying his own perception of progress, social justice, and victory to the ideological message of the *politruks*. "Hundreds of planes, thousands of enemy tanks, including Tigers and Panthers, have found their grave on the fields of battle," he wrote. "Tens of thousands of Fritzes have fertilized the Ukrainian earth. The Germans are retreating. The moment to settle our account with them has come."[102]

Behind the brave words, there were plenty of exhausted, frightened, even disaffected people. German sources suggest that the rate of Soviet defections increased sharply when battle was joined—from 2,555 in June to 6,574 in July and 4,047 in August.[103] But the hemorrhage was no longer one-sided.[104] As the Red Army sensed its approaching triumph, morale among the German ranks was crumbling fast. The process had begun among the nonelite troops well before the campaign's launch. "The SS officers are surprised by the levels of pessimism in our division," a lieutenant, Karl-Friedrich Brandt, wrote in his diary on 6 July. If the SS frightened the Soviets, its arrogance and privilege offended German soldiers in the Wehrmacht's ranks. "The very sight of them stirs in our troops, exhausted and strained as they are, a sense of utter class hatred," Brandt went on. "Our soldiers have been drawn from whatever pitiful dregs can still be scraped together in Germany. They [the SS] are drawn from the finest human material in Europe."[105]

That summer saw the first large-scale humiliation of those "dregs." As the Soviets pushed forward, Brandt and his men fled so fast that they could not even pray over their dead. "We are not even in a condition to establish where each of our men lies anymore," Brandt wrote on 1 August, "because we haven't been able to snatch away their papers or their soldier's tags. We have not even had the water with which to wash the poison of the corpses from our skin. . . . How fortunate were the men who died in France and Poland. They could still believe in victory."[106] Now that belief was growing on the Soviet side.

On 2 August Belov went into action for a second time. Three days later he was in the vanguard that would liberate Orel. "Last night the Germans withdrew altogether," he wrote on 5 August. "This morning

Infantry and tanks near Kharkov, 1943

we arrived on the western outskirts of the city. The whole of Orel is in flames. The population is greeting us with exceptional joy. The women are weeping with joy." The next day his regiment, like all the others in the division, was renamed an "Orel Regiment" in honor of the great campaign.[107] That night, too, far away in Moscow, the first 120-gun salute of the war was ordered to mark the triumph. "I express my thanks to all the troops that took part in the offensive," Stalin's telegram declared. "Eternal glory to the heroes who fell in the struggle for the freedom of our country. Death to the German invaders."[108]

To the south, on the road to Kharkov, Slesarev was also on the move. Belgorod had fallen to Red Army troops on the same day as Orel. Now the formations on the Voronezh and Steppe Fronts were racing southward in pursuit of even larger goals. Slesarev's mood was bittersweet. On 10 August, his dearest friend was killed, a man with whom he had fought closely from the very first. But the cause he died for was no longer vain. "We're crossing liberated territory," Slesarev wrote to his father, "land that was occupied by the Germans for more than two years. The population is coming out to greet us with joy, bringing us apples, pears, tomatoes, cucumbers, and so on. In the past, I knew Ukraine only from books, now I can see it with my own eyes: the picturesque nature, lots of gardens."[109] Just for an instant, the Red Army could revel in its hard-won success. On 25 August, it recaptured Kharkov.

SEVEN

MAY BROTHERHOOD BE BLESSED

★

Stalin's regime waged war in the same spirit as it prosecuted peace. The first rule was that human life counted for little in the scale of history, which meant compared with interests of state; the second, that insiders, the citizens in whose name everything was done, should band together against enemies. By 1943, the first of these rules was causing strain. The supply of healthy troops was running out. The campaigns that winter would be constrained in practice because manpower was scarce.[1] The second rule, however, seemed to be going strong. Kulaks, spies, Trotskyists, and members of the civil war White Guard had been admirable scapegoats in the decade leading up to war. But Fascists—"Hitlerites"—were real foes. Soviet citizens answered the call to arms in epic style. The collective clarity of purpose that inspired millions was unprecedented. But it was not true that the entire people stood together. The war created hierarchies, winners and losers, millions of dead. And physical separation, hunger, and violence do not unite communities. The mythic wartime solidarity that everyone remembers was another sleight of Stalin's hand. It was possible to believe in it because of the third rule of this regime, which was to control the things that people were allowed to know.

Among the winners in the midst of war, at least compared with soldiers at the front, were the officials who stayed well behind the lines. On 6 November 1943, an invited crowd of them gathered in Moscow to hear Stalin speak. The occasion was the eve of the twenty-sixth anniversary of the Bolshevik revolution. Outside, the early-winter capital was gray, subdued by blackout drapes and power cuts. Inside, beneath the chandeliers, the audience basked in self-congratulation. In the twelve months since their last anniversary meeting, the prospects for these people's world had changed completely. First there had been Stalingrad, with all those German prisoners and dead. But that had been a winter victory. What Kursk had proved was that the Red Army could beat the Fascists in the summer, too. Since then, the news had told a story of unbroken success. Smolensk was recaptured on 25 September; the Taman peninsula—gateway to the Crimea—on 7 October. In a feat of remarkable daring (and at shattering human cost), the Red Army had forced the river Dnepr on 7 October, breaching the Fascists' most secure defensive line. And on 6 November, the elite would learn what everybody else heard the following day, which was that Kiev, the capital of Ukraine, had fallen to the Soviets at last.

The Red Army was the country's undoubted savior. But Stalin used his speech to emphasize that it had not been working on its own. It was time to celebrate the party and the government, the men and women who had stayed at home. He began with some real heroes, those of wartime labor. If the army no longer lacked for weapons and supplies, Stalin explained, it had to thank "our working class [stormy and prolonged applause]." It also owed a great deal to "the patriotism of the collective farm peasants," to "our transport workers," and even, for their initiatives in design and engineering, to "our intelligentsia [prolonged applause]." Stalin's message was unmistakable. He was declaring revolution vindicated. "The lessons of the war," he announced, "teach us that Soviet power is not only the best form of organization for the economic and cultural development of a country in years of peace but also the best form for mobilizing all the resources of the people for repelling an enemy in time of war. . . . The Soviet power that was established twenty-six years ago has turned our country—in a brief historical period—into an inviolable fortress."[2]

The men and women at the front—or those, at least, who had survived to join in that November's celebration—were just as proud of victory, although they tended to assume most credit for themselves. Vitaly Taranichev, the engineer, found a few moments to write home to his wife. "It's one o'clock in the morning," he explained, "the night of 7 November 1943. I've been at my military post since the eve of the twenty-sixth anniversary of the Great October revolution. . . . At 1600 hours today we heard the order of our Supreme Commander Comrade Stalin about the capture of the capital of our Ukraine, the city of Kiev, by our valiant troops. Natalochka! I can imagine how delighted you must be by this news! The time has passed when the Fascists controlled the skies—today they made a pathetic effort to disrupt the work at our station, but it didn't come to anything—everything is working like clockwork, and everything is moving forward, toward the west, toward the destruction of Fascism!"[3]

Thousands of front-line soldiers shared this view. They knew that they were on the road to victory. Like many other successful armies, they found themselves embracing some of the values of their nation and culture with new confidence and zeal. They also began to imagine that their sacrifice could build a better world. Many believed that they were laying new foundations for the peace, perhaps burning away the hatreds and confusion of the prewar years. Soldiers' friendships with front-line comrades felt like a foretaste of the brotherhood to come. And then there was the thrill of new machines. The tank battle at Kursk, the evidence of Soviet air superiority that summer, the deadly music of the Katyushas—all this seemed like a vindication of the five-year plans, a promise of a happier, mass-producing future. Zhukov, not Stalin, was probably the army's real hero (and each veteran will happily describe the wartime general he admired most, like sports fans arguing over star players), but even Stalin, because he lived mainly in men's imaginations, seemed to embody the qualities that success now guaranteed: progress, unity, heroism, deliverance. In word at least, it looked as if soldiers and leadership subscribed to the same goals.

The starkest ideological messages were drawn by looking at the

legacy of Fascism. "I've had to drive around a good many of the settlements that the Germans have abandoned in the recent past,"
Taranichev wrote home. "You cannot imagine what these places, which
used so recently to be blossoming centers of population, look like: not
one dwelling without damage, everything burned, and what they didn't
manage to burn has been destroyed by aerial bombing."[4] "I've been
marching day and night," a twenty-year-old machine gunner wrote
home in October 1943. He had traveled on from Orel to the river
Desnya and beyond, crossing country the retreating German army had
torched. "The population meets us warmly. I didn't even think that our
welcome would be like this. They weep, they hug us, everyone brings us
whatever they can." The reason for the people's joy was obvious. "I've
seen how the German burns villages, the bitch. I've seen the victims of
his violence."[5]

For soldiers, the Red Army was now the instrument of collective re-
demption, the arm of vengeance and of liberation. The greeting that
soldiers received from the people of western Russia and eastern
Ukraine was often overwhelming. But though many were proud of their
collective power, it was also possible, for large numbers of men, to catch
a sense of individual progress. The army furthered thousands of careers.
Vasily Ermolenko was at school in Kharkov when the war broke out.
The first year of the invasion saw his home overrun, his mother trapped,
and his father enlisted into the Red Army. But young Vasily, now a
refugee, received a training. When the Red Army liberated his native
city in 1943, he was already working elsewhere on the front as a radio
operator and communications engineer. Technology became his life, the
more so because every other landmark in it had been wrecked. He
joined the party in the spring of 1944. As he noted in his diary at the
time, the war had taught him to love his motherland, but it had also
confirmed his belief in socialism, "which will lead people to a happy
life." In his mind, all the Red Army's successes had become linked to
the party and its leader.[6]

The party spirit (the Soviets had a word for it, *partiinost'*) that soldiers like Ermolenko evinced was far removed from the careful
sophistry of Stalin's ideologues. The soldiers' brand of Communism was
also distinct from that of their political officers, many of whom had

joined the party well before the war. Rank-and-file belief arose from experience as much as from preaching, and it often coexisted with an impatience of paperwork, dislike of propaganda. "Considerable empirical evidence exists that indoctrination affects troops in much the same way as rain affects a duck," a specialist on combat motivation has observed. "It glances off their backs."[7] The men's beliefs, though shaped by everything they had been told (and limited because there was so much that they would never be allowed to say or hear), felt like their own philosophy. "If the *politruks* had let us," the nationalist writer Viktor Astaf'ev remarked, "we'd have lost the war in six weeks. . . . Our first victories started when we stopped listening to them."[8] Front-line ideology was strong and deeply rooted. But it was also so distinct from that of the civilian elite that it might have been evolving in another universe.

The nation tried to make the soldiers its own, especially as most were conscripts, everybody's sons. The press cultivated the image of the bereaved mother listening to stories told by soldiers of her son's age, of local people supporting the troops as if they were their own. In return, many soldiers learned to love Russia and its people with a new warmth. "It was war," the soldier in one of Simonov's famous poems remembers, "that brought me together for the first time / With longing for travel from village to village, / With the tear of a widow, with a woman's song."[9] While the soldiers explored a new and larger motherland, however, they struggled to hold on to the lives that they had left behind, to wives and children, and also to the memory of their younger selves. Combat had estranged them utterly. Front-line troops had long despised the "rats" who followed in the rear, the supply teams, staff officers, and caravans of reservists. But as time passed, soldiers were also becoming alienated from the civilians they were trying to save, and even from the families they loved.

Red Army men might have imagined that the bonds that united them had replaced these old loyalties, and to some extent this was true. Life at the front even fostered nostalgia for lost homelands—or for imagined ones—and soldiers who learned that someone from their own province had arrived within traveling distance of their camp would often rush to greet them, hungry for home news. War was so strange, and Soviet territory so unthinkably vast, that such people were deemed to be instant "neighbors." Women veterans told Alexiyevich that whenever newcomers from home arrived at the front their fellow soldiers pressed around hoping to catch a whiff of the familiar smells that might cling to their clothes.

For all the rhetoric of unity, however, close friendships still aroused suspicion in police circles. The NKVD monitored soldiers' conversations at the front, while the Special Section and its successor, SMERSh, whose name was an acronym for the Russian expression "death to spies," pursued each rumor of dissension.[10] SMERSh, or some form of it, was a necessary evil. The army was moving west, retaking territory that the enemy had held. In every town there would have been collaborators, men and women who had fed and sheltered Nazis, denounced partisans, or, worse, executed orders to imprison or shoot their own neighbors. There were also German agents in the liberated zone, some of them *Hiwis*, defectors from the Red Army, whose Russian voices and Soviet style concealed their real allegiances.[11] The threat of SMERSh helped to deter all forms of treachery, as well as terrorizing anyone whose labor was needed for the front.[12] But while they struck at real enemies, the informers of Stalinist counterintelligence also betrayed the spirit of the front. If they could find no real spies, the agents would not hesitate to fabricate a plot, making scapegoats of their own comrades. Soldiers constantly had to watch their tongues. "We knew that we could talk about our victories," Samoilov wrote, "but not about defeats. We knew that our junior officers also walked in this shadow. The fear of SMERSh . . . corrupted the lofty notion of a people struggling against the invader. . . . We seldom knew," he added, "which people in our midst were informers." Although comrades in arms still felt solidarity, the quality of human relations was marred by "the Stalinist bacillus of mistrust."[13]

These tensions preyed on soldiers' minds as the campaigning season dragged into the winter. The closing months of 1943 were a time of continuous movement. Tanks and motorized infantry contested the steep banks of the Dnepr. Whole armies slithered through the fields of sugar beet. Day after day, the heavy rain of the southwest soaked through greatcoats and leather boots. And then the shelling started, and precarious advances across saturated ground. Tanks sank through treacherous mats of sedge, losing entire crews. Infantrymen from Central Asia drowned in the Dnepr because they had never learned to swim. *Shtrafniki*, the members of the punishment battalions, were sent to defuse mines, storm banks of guns, or locate hidden foxholes. Soviet death rates were falling, but this was now a campaign of attack. Red Army losses after each engagement ran as high as 25 percent.[14] For men exhausted after the battles of the late summer, the challenges must have seemed intolerable. In other years both armies had found some moments in the cold months to regroup and make repairs. This time the mild winter of the south allowed for no respite.

Movement meant retaking Soviet towns and villages. The men were often driving through the places where they had grown up, but this was no homecoming. The Wehrmacht had orders to burn the countryside as it retreated west. Whatever had been left after two years of Nazi rule was torched, including livestock and harvested grain. The ruined landscape was made more macabre by the flotsam of battle. "There are heaps of German corpses by the roads," Belov observed in January 1944. The rotting bodies did not bother anyone, still less excite pity. Local civilian authorities would become concerned only when the weather warmed. Typhus had claimed too many lives already.[15] For now, as Belov knew, "No one's clearing them away. . . . They won't move them till the spring."[16] It took the unexpected, incongruities, to surprise soldiers now. As he marched west in the spring of 1944, Ermolenko, a native of Ukraine, watched the migratory birds that he had always welcomed as a boy returning to their nesting sites. The creatures seemed confused. They could not settle. The landscape they were looking for had vanished, and the trees where they had nested just a year before had disappeared.[17]

Nothing would set the troops apart more than the shared experience of combat. Even the men who tried to talk, to tell their wives or friends, found that they could not bridge the gulf between those who had seen battle and all the rest. David Samoilov, who considered his own wartime poetry to be "hopelessly bad," thought that the problem lay in war itself. When people sat down to write after surviving carnage, he observed later, their goal was not to reexperience the hell but to escape it.[18] "I can't write much to you—it's not allowed," a tank mechanic

wrote to his mother in September 1943. It was convenient to hide behind the censor's broad shoulders. "When we meet, I'll tell you about
the terrible battles that I've had to get through."[19] Ageev tried to explain why he could not write more about the fighting itself. "I got back
from operations only tonight," he wrote to his wife. "In these situations
the same well-known reaction always sets in. The strain of effort is replaced by inertia. When you're under stress, you don't think about anything, and all your efforts are directed toward a single goal. But when
the stress is replaced by inertia, which is explained by tiredness, then
you really need a bit of a shaking, because for a moment nothing seems
to matter."[20]

Civilians would never understand about battle. "I cannot describe
all my feelings and all my experiences," another man wrote to his wife.
He felt he could not reach her with words, nor she him. "The question
of our meeting after the victory," he continued, "that's what is worrying
a lot of us right now."[21] "Many of my friends have died," an officer
called Martov wrote to his family in February 1944. "The truth is that
we fight together, and the death of each is our own. Sometimes there are
moments of such strain that the living envy the dead. Death is not as terrible as we used to think."[22] Grief held the men together as much as
shared hardship. But battle marked them out from everybody else.
Whatever Stalin said about the whole nation's collective work, by 1943
most front-line soldiers valued only combat and the comradeship of
risk. By setting soldier against civilian, by raising fears of spies and stool
pigeons, by setting the *frontovik* against the whole community of military "rats" who did not fight, the war had shattered, not united, the Soviet people. Worst of all, combat had exiled front-line soldiers from
themselves.

★

"What's the definition of effrontery?" Ageev wrote one evening. "Effrontery means being somewhere far behind the lines, sleeping with the
wives of *frontoviki*, beating one's breast and crying 'Death to the Fascist
occupiers' and looking for one's name in the lists of people who have
been decorated for valor."[23] The men had been away for months. The
Red Army made scant provision for home leave.[24] As the fear of defeat

faded, terrors of a more intimate variety began to haunt the soldiers' nights. They were crossing Soviet territory now. They knew about the hardship and the crime, the people's desperation after two winters of total war. The married soldiers saw how local women often acted when they found a willing man, someone with food or cash, perhaps, or even just a guitar and some vodka. They all began to wonder what was going on at home.

Some of their fears were natural to soldiers on any long campaign, but Red Army troops faced more depressing terrors than the prospect of a "Dear John" letter. "Write me something about Mama," a young lieutenant asked his godmother in February 1944. "There's been no news from her since September 1941." The last time he had heard from her, his mother had been in her flat in Leningrad.[25] In this case, as in so many others, there would be no more news again. The Fascist occupation had torn families apart. Aleksandr Slesarev, the tank lieutenant from Smolensk province, at least knew that some of his relatives were alive. The partisans had brought one letter out in 1942, a note from his young sister, Mariya.[26] It was a catalog of death and violation under Nazi rule. As the Germans retreated, more letters came, and now—with agonizing gaps—the family's story began to take shape. As Slesarev fought south and west across Ukraine, he had to wait for weeks to receive news. Mariya wrote to their father first, and then the old man passed the news on to his soldier sons. The fourteen-year-old girl, working from dawn to dusk on the collective farm, could not find time to write to everyone at once.

The family had fled their village before the invaders came. For two winters they had been living in an earth dugout. It was cold and damp and the children were constantly ill, but at least they were alive. "They burned Danilkin's family," Mariya wrote, "and the Germans took Yashka away. They burned the whole Liseyev family and the Gavrikovs too, and another fourteen girls who were on their way back from work in Yartsevo. . . . At the same time we also lost Uncle Petya, he was coming from Ruchkovo, and the Germans caught him and burned him, too." Then news came that the Red Army was close. The Germans started seizing cattle and sheep, leaving the local villagers to starve. Winter brought typhus, then pneumonia. There was another string of deaths. "At the time of the [Germans'] last retreat, Mama, Yura, and I took cover with Uncle Mitya in a trench," Mariya finished. "Kolya, Uncle Egor, and Shura all ran off to the woods at the same time, they were there for four days and nights. They liberated us on 18 March, and [the three of them] came out of the woods the next day."[27]

Lieutenant Slesarev must have been relieved to read that his mother, sister, and two little brothers had survived. He sent them money when he could. But inflation, shortages, and a severe housing crisis had made their lives desperate. "It's not great for food at the moment," Mariya wrote in January 1944, "and clothes are really a problem, especially shoes."[28] It was the same in Kursk, the same wherever either of the great armies had been. "It's hard now that we don't have cows," a peasant woman wrote from Kursk province. "They took them from us two months ago. . . . We're ready to eat each other. . . . There isn't a single young man at home now that they're fighting."[29] "Everything was destroyed by the front," another woman told her soldier son. She had lost her home, her cow, and her land. She was living, as many did, in a corridor outside her sister's one-room flat. "We have not had bread for two months now," wrote another. "It's already time for Lidiya to go to school, but we don't have a coat for her or anything to put on her feet. I think Lidiya and I will die of hunger in the end. We haven't got anything. . . . Misha, even if you stay alive, we won't be here."[30]

Soldiers felt betrayed by their wives' hardship stories. The least they had expected, while they risked their lives, was that the state would provide for their families. The begging letters read like accusations. In January 1943, the Central Committee of the Communist Party responded with a secret resolution on the families of serving troops. Aleksei Kosygin, a rising star, was put in charge of welfare. His job was to make sure that flour, potatoes, and fuel were provided on the usual sliding scale of privilege from officers to men. But officials in the provinces could not turn rubble into houses overnight or conjure flour from ash. In May 1944, a survey in the Kursk region found 17,740 orphans and nearly half a million soldiers' families in need of urgent help. Of the families, just 32,025 were in receipt of pensions and supplies of food.[31] The same story was repeated across European Russia. There were over a quarter of a million soldiers' families on the register in Smolensk region by

A scene of destruction in the village of Kuyani (courtesy of the State Archive of the Russian Federation)

1944. More than 12,000 of these were living in earth dugouts. Nearly 11,000 soldiers' children in the region could not attend the newly opened local schools because they had no shoes.[32]

The families of decorated soldiers, including Heroes of the Soviet Union, were supposed to get extra help. It was an incentive with genuine appeal. The promise of privileged access to food and heating fuel for their wives and mothers was all it took to convince some soldiers that they were valued more than their comrades. But when the promise was not kept, such men's indignation was also proportionately greater. Letters of protest, angry demands from combatants who felt entitled to an audience, piled up on bureaucratic desks, but all the outrage in the world could not ease this crisis. In the spring of 1944, rural soviets in some regions were warning that the hunger in their villages would soon lead to fatalities. Hero of the Soviet Union P. L. Pashin went home to one of the affected districts to visit his family. He found them in a desperate condition. He appealed to the local collective farm to issue them bread or potatoes, but the committee was unable to meet his request. Another Hero's family was found to be in "severe need" of clothes, shoes, and dry accommodation.[33] Mariya Slesarev continued to write to her father. "It's a really bad situation for bread," she wrote in July 1944, "and with potatoes also." Prices were impossible. Her brother was sending her fifty rubles a month, occasionally more. But a liter of milk cost fifteen rubles, a cup of salt as much as twenty-four, and flour eight hundred rubles a pood.[34]

Prices were forced up by wartime black marketeers, but the army—sometimes illicitly—also sucked local farmers dry. Much as they feared for their own families, some men showed little qualm for other people's. "Everything for the front" was a slogan that was easily abused. If there was nowhere for soldiers to sleep, they drove the locals from their huts. When they needed horses, they helped themselves from the collective farms. Sometimes they used their new transport to seize and market peasants' grain. Illegal trading flourished with the army's unofficial help.[35] No rank or type of soldier was blameless. In February 1944, a member of the NKVD's own border troops was heard asserting that "we go round barefoot and half dressed, and if we didn't do some looting we wouldn't be able to survive."[36]

One of the most prized commodities was home brew, *samogon*. The rough spirit could be distilled wherever sugar and grain or potatoes could be obtained. Troops on patrol noted the barns that held illegal stills and timed their raids for the moment when the stuff was ready. It brought a good price from their comrades. Accidents and fights, even murders, were common results of its excessive use, but fighting was not all that spirit provoked. *Samogon* was currency. Networks of crime supported its production. Grain was stolen to make it, goods were looted to finance it.[37] The Nazis had gone, Soviet power was not yet established, and in the chaos that followed as the front moved westward a primitive barter economy emerged with raw spirit at its center and a variety of other goods as change. In October 1943, a group of men stationed near Belyi Kholm in Smolensk province commandeered four tons of potatoes from local collective farms. But they also stole on a more individual scale, helping themselves to flour, sugar, honey, and even the peasants' boots.[38] The guilty parties in this case were in the midst of a training course for junior lieutenants.

Among the most prestigious items of black market trade were German goods. They were, everyone knew, well made, advanced, and hard to get in normal times. The law on "trophies," the spoils of war, was redefined and tightened repeatedly in 1942 and 1943. Special teams, made up mainly of women and teenage boys, were sent around abandoned battlefields and other military sites to retrieve whatever debris they might find—bodies, weapons, or personal effects.[39] The state claimed it all for the war. But there was a pathetic pecking order around this carrion. Front-line soldiers were the first, although their opportunity was usually brief. "I came across a German corpse in the corner of one of their field cemeteries," Anatoly Shevelev told me. "They'd buried all the rest but they missed him. I took his wallet—I was curious, really. There was a photograph in it, his *Frau*. A photograph and a condom—we didn't have those. No safe sex in the Red Army. But what I wanted were his boots. I tried to pull them off. I pulled, I pulled hard, and the man's leg was so decomposed that it came off with the boot. I left him after that."

Behind the combat soldiers came the support troops, the "rats," as well as any local people who could find their way. The boot Shevelev wanted would have been no problem for experts like these. Frozen or decomposing limbs merely required the right technique. In the winter of 1941, Vasily Grossman met a peasant with a sack of frozen human legs, each one severed as if for harvest. His plan was to thaw them on the stove to make the leather boots easier to remove.[40] Meanwhile, discarded helmets and insignia were turned into children's toys, although the children themselves seemed to prefer grenades and knives.[41] Officials collected toys of a more sophisticated kind. Orest Kuznetsov was a military lawyer. One of his perks was to inspect the trophies that the German army had left behind before they were packed up for dispatch to the rear. In February 1944, he helped himself to "a very pretty radio set, which currently does not work, because it needs an electricity supply."[42]

The basic norms of peacetime life had long ago dissolved. Among the patterns that emerged was a new attitude toward sex. The front line, though not quite a club exclusively for males, was pungent with misogyny. "In the army they regard women like gramophone records," a young man wrote in 1943. "You play it and play it and then throw it away."[43] It was a prejudice that would erupt with vicious force a year later, when the army crossed into Prussia. But attitudes toward sex, among both men and women, were already changing. The least offensive of the new arrangements was a matter of short-term, and often mutual, convenience. Male officers were notorious for "adopting" attractive women. Sometimes they added them to the company list, creating a fictitious staff role somewhere so that they could bring a mistress with them on campaign.[44] The army slang for the women involved was "marching field wives," *pokhodno-polevye zheny*, or PPZh, a pun on the mobile field guns, PPSh. It was not uncommon for a man to have five or more such "wives" at once. And there were always more in line. Ageev knew a lieutenant who reacted to a farewell letter from his prewar wife by sending a card to the main post office in Moscow and addressing it to "the first girl who gets her hands on this." As Ageev added, "this correspondence has been carrying on for some months in the most active manner."[45]

"Wives" at the front were usually a perk of rank. "There was a bit of a tale," Ilya Nemanov remembered. "My commanding officer was fifty, a teacher by profession, the father of soldiers, fierce, though everyone loved him. And he had a twenty-year-old lover, Nina. She was already pregnant. And she liked me. I didn't get the message and just carried on without paying her any attention. She invited me to listen to the gramophone, and we stood there together, leaning close to each other. Someone saw us and reported it to the commander, although there was nothing in it. He flew into a rage. He held a pistol at me and said, 'If the Germans don't kill you, I'll shoot!' But he didn't shoot me, he just moved me away from her. He made me work as a telephone operator, and he gave me the heaviest equipment to carry in addition to my rifle." "You must think I have affairs with the girls, Polya," a private soldier wrote in 1944. "No, my dear, I'll never go for that bait. When we meet, I'll tell you a lot of things about military life. But my character hasn't changed, and for another thing, if you . . . have girlfriends you can end up in a punishment unit pretty fast."[46]

As long as the men were on Soviet soil, vodka, not sex, was the mainstay of their leisure time. But women who lived near their billets knew that trouble started if they could slip out in search of both. Rates of venereal disease were set to soar. The Wehrmacht had done its bit to spread infection wherever it camped. Now it was the Soviet army's turn. Reports at the time affected surprise, but syphilis infected officers—and even Communist Party members—as readily as the men.[47] In Smolensk province alone, the reported (and therefore underestimated) rate of syphilis infection increased by a factor of twelve between 1934 and 1945.[48] To some extent, the double impact of invasion and then reconquest explained the scale of the epidemic, but the Soviet attitude toward sex was also much to blame. The men received no education and, as Shevelev observed, they got no condoms, either. Soldiers who contracted venereal disease were treated like varieties of traitor. Medical treatment was sometimes deliberately withheld in punishment for what was seen as immorality.[49] For some soldiers, the shame—or even the fear—of venereal disease was one anxiety too many. Reports of men who shot themselves after contracting one began to accumulate from 1943.[50] Meanwhile, the civilian authorities considered deporting local women if they were known to frequent troops. They also dreamed (although they had no resources to run the scheme) of forcing them to undergo medical examinations and hospital treatment.[51]

Women would always find the culture punitive. Soviet morality judged them by a double standard, condemning behavior that would be admired, or at least condoned, in men. Some of the field "wives" hoped to marry their military patrons. But most were looking, as everyone was, for comfort and intimacy. It was male prejudice that painted them as whores. "I've had four letters from you," Ageev wrote to his wife, Nina, in the early spring of 1944. "At least I have some basis for believing that my family has been preserved intact. Nina! It's the biggest question for all of us *frontoviki*. What's going to happen when the war ends? There's madness on both the men's side and the women's with just one difference, that the women—with the aim of making sure they'll be set up for the future—forget the norms and go in for ten times more madness than the men do."[52]

Veterans often mentioned that the war was cruel to women. It aged them even faster than the men, especially if they chose combat roles.

Nurses and telegraph operators were more prestigious, as girlfriends, than female soldiers. "We did not look on them as women," veterans told Svetlana Alexiyevich in the 1980s. "We looked on them as friends."[53] This was the kindly version, anyway. In fact, the front-line women, wrecked or not, faced prejudice based on their wild reputation. One described what happened after she married her wartime sweetheart. Her new husband's parents were furious, convinced that he had cheapened their good name. "An army girl," they barked. "Why, you have two younger sisters. Who will marry them now?"[54] It was assumed that women slept with officers as a way of getting on. At the very least, a pregnancy would guarantee their escape from the front. Women veterans with medals were treated with suspicion for years after the war. When the coveted medal "for military service" (*za boevye zaslugi*) was worn by a woman, it was jokingly said to be "for sexual service" (*za polevye zaslugi*).[55]

Cruel humor was a mask for insecurities. Laughter—the shared male laughter of soldiers at rest—was like a kind of whistling in the dark. As long as they joked as a group, men did not have to face their private fears. The boys, recruited straight from school, laughed to conceal virginity. And it had been a long time since the older, married men had seen their wives. The problem was not just a matter of the passing months. It was that wartime moved at an accelerated pace. Soldiers in their thirties, who might have looked forward, in peacetime, to a last decade of youth, turned into old men overnight. A single day in a trench could age a man like a small death. His hair turned gray, his skin dried out, the lightness (and numbers of teeth) vanished from his smile. And then there were the injuries, truncated limbs and scars. "There are lots of stories of this kind on both sides," Ageev wrote home in 1943. "When officers are wounded and lying in the hospital, they get a letter from their wives, who have found out about the injury and write to tell them that they are ending the marriage on the grounds of the men's incapacity."[56]

Soldiers imagined that their wives remained the women they had left, still youthful while their husbands aged. If they did not start fretting that these sirens were deceiving them, they feared rejection, knowing what they had become themselves. The faithful Taranichev was afraid that his gray hair would drive his wife, Natalya, away. It was a metaphor for all the change he had endured, the violence that fascinated and appalled him. Ageev was frank about war's impact on his body. "You may ask—what about me?" he wrote to Nina. "I can tell you that the desire . . . is more than enough, but the fear of catastrophe after two head injuries has forced me to give up the whole idea." He had been worried for some months about his gray hair and the premature lines of aging on his face. Now he was telling Nina he was impotent.[57]

★

The Soviet wartime myth skirts around divorce, promiscuity, and venereal disease. Instead, it focuses on the pathos of waiting, drawing inspiration from Simonov's famous love poem. The images are still, reflective, but real life behind the lines was fraught with change and hardship. Simonov's poem evokes a woman at home, patiently counting out the days, but in fact soldiers' wives were obliged to learn new skills, to master techniques for survival, and to work exceptionally long and arduous hours. Few had time to sit and count the days as they stared longingly toward the west. Few, indeed, spent much time on their own. Housing was scarce, refugees were constantly at the gate, and by 1943 the family that waited back at home was likely to consist of cousins, sisters, neighbors, and several generations.

Vitaly Taranichev's family lived well behind the lines, in Ashkhabad, a city not far from the border with Iran. He had brought his wife there from her native Kiev before the war. Such an upheaval was the lot of thousands of other engineers, who were moved to the steppe—or in the Taranichevs' case, to Turkestan—because the railways or the mines needed their skills. Natalya was installed in a house with Vitaly's mother. If the arrangement had ever suited the two women, the war made sure that they would feud. First of all, their household lacked Vitaly, the one person they both loved and trusted. And in his place had come a string of refugees. By 1943, the house was home to Taranichev's mother, wife, and two children; to her mother, newly arrived from Ukraine; to his wife's sister and her children; and from time to time to a range of "wives" associated with Natalya's errant brother, Fedor.

The women squabbled over everything from money to the children's diet. They also competed for Vitaly's material support. The officer assigned parts of his pay to them by sending money orders, payable each month. "I've sent you two money certificates for this year," he wrote to Natalya in April 1944. "One for 350 rubles a month in your name and the other for Mama for 100 rubles. I think you won't have any objection to this arrangement, since you told me that Mama is always complaining that she has to pay all the taxes and so on. . . . By doing this I'm giving my mother some happiness in her old age—of course, not because of 100 rubles a month but because I'm taking care of her; you must understand me on this question."[58]

The women went on falling out. Each summer, the orchard produced a valuable crop of apricots. Vitaly's mother claimed them for herself. The children played truant from school. Vitaly's mother accused the hard-pressed Natalya of negligence. In 1943, Natalya and her mother were reduced to selling some of Vitaly's old clothes to raise cash; Vitaly's mother flew into hysterical tears and swore that they wanted to see him dead. "I beg you," Vitaly asked Natalya, "not to pay attention to words that were spoken in the heat of the moment. I could never believe that my mother would wish you and our children ill. . . . Read these words of mine to her and you will see that I'm right." Meanwhile, there was the question of the clothes. Vitaly told his wife to sell his trousers, coat, and summer things—he would come home, he said, in uniform. "Just keep my shoes, because it will be hard to find size 45 shoes when the war is over."[59] He also told her to keep their handgun. They would be grateful for that piece of foresight when the war ended.

Despite his help, and despite her own wages and the income from selling apricots, Natalya and the children suffered. "I've lost a lot of weight," she wrote to Vitaly in the summer of 1943. "I weigh 48 kilograms. We all manage with food, my love, however we can." It was a story any wife could have written at this time, a tale of hunger, not just of making do.[60] "The canteen at work doesn't really feed us much," Natalya continued. "The local administration sees fit to use some kind of blended oil that gleams with all the colors of the rainbow."[61] As for the children, they were going barefoot, running wild. School had become an intermittent event, and discipline at home, with everyone preoccupied, was lax. In the Taranichev household, only the baby, Kolya, still made everybody smile. Natalya had found him some colored bricks for his third birthday.

"He can sit at the table and build for hours," she wrote to his father. "He says, 'The Germans knocked it down, and Kolya's going to build it.'" The little boy was not yet three when he learned to shout, "For the motherland and Stalin!"[62]

Their regular letters were all the contact that Natalya and Vitaly would have for several more years. The mail had not improved since 1942, when letters disappeared or turned up after months of inexplicable delay. "It's such a shame that I'm getting your letters so irregularly," Natalya wrote in June 1943. "I'm getting the ones from March at the moment. But the state of our morale depends on them, doesn't it?" She

Field post arriving for soldiers in the Kaluga region, 1942

was also concerned about the money—650 or 750 rubles—that still had not arrived.[63] Taranichev himself was suffering as well. That June, he had received the first bundle of letters from home that he had seen in six entire months. "At last," he wrote. "I knew that you were alive and well. You can't imagine how pleased I was when they handed over these letters to me, and for three whole days I've been carrying them around in my pocket and rereading them whenever I have a spare minute!"[64] This time he did not mention that the long wait had sown wretched doubt in his imagination. But other letters that he wrote, including sharp rebukes to her, showed that it often did.

Sometimes, a soldier hungry for news of his wife found that he was stationed within miles of his old home. "There are some commanders among us, and even more of the soldiers, whose houses are 20–50 kilometers from the front line," Ageev wrote to his wife in 1943. "But they don't have the right to go there. Some women have contrived to work their way to the front (which is absolutely forbidden) to be with their husbands, but it's rare, and usually they intercept them and escort them back in convoys to face an inquiry."[65] It would be three more years, well after the victory, before Vitaly and Natalya would meet, and longer than that before they would live together again. Their children had been fatherless, effectively, for six years. It was a miracle that prewar marriages survived at all.

The people who adapted best, as ever, were the young. "Those who got married at the front," an old couple told Alexiyevich, "are the happiest people and the happiest couples."[66] The remark sounds sweet, like a happy ending, but real stories were usually grounded in loss. Kirill Kirillovich met his wife in Leningrad during the darkest months of the blockade. It was 1942, and Kirill and an older, married friend were on point duty near the Kirov theater. A young woman caught their eye, a teenager in military uniform who carried a Nagan revolver and a gas mask. "I've lived thirty years," the older man said, "and I've never seen such a pretty police officer." Eighteen-year-old Nina was a survivor. That winter, only weeks before, her family had starved to death. Her father had lain dead inside their flat for three weeks before anyone strong enough could be found to move him. Only her youth, the instinct for life, had saved the teenager, but she thought of the choice between life and death in terms of duty. When she had made her decision, she volunteered to donate blood, which meant that she received a guaranteed ration of bread.[67] The tiny quantities of food restored her strength.

What motivated Nina to volunteer for night patrol was the desire for revenge. By her own account, narrated through tears sixty years later, she was determined to see the lovely city rise again, determined to avenge her parents. She was also careless of her safety, willing to try anything. When the older man asked, she gave him her telephone number and address. Kirill, still shy at twenty-three, hung back. It was only later, back at the barracks, that he asked for the piece of paper. The couple began to meet in the city's bombed-out streets and ruins. Both had lost parents since the war began, and neither knew where home would ever be again. In 1944, Nina gave birth to their daughter. That was also the moment when the couple decided to register their marriage. "I was a deputy commander," Kirill said, laughing as he told the story. "And even then I was ashamed because we had an illegitimate daughter."

More tenuous were the affairs that sprang up around correspondence. From the earliest days of the war, civilians had been invited to adopt battalions of troops, to write them cheering letters and send packages and pictures. The morale-boosting work was organized as part of everybody's contribution to the war. But the letters were escapist on both sides, based on the private hopes that seemed so similar but in fact related to entirely different worlds. Vladimir Anfilov was another victim of the Leningrad blockade. While he was at the front, his wife, children, and two sisters died somewhere in the siege. In March 1944, he announced that he was ready to look for another confidante and friend. His letters to the new woman, the peacetime neighbor of one of the men who served with him, were full of cultural gossip, snippets about the latest film or poem. But they offered no clue about his real life. "Tonya," he wrote, "it's all so gloomy and it's best not to think about it." A month after their first exchange of letters, Vladimir wanted Tonya's photograph.[68] The letters grew more intimate. Tonya would be heartbroken, months later, when the friend who had introduced them told her that she was just one in a whole string of "wives."

Samoilov helped a young man called Anis'ko to write replies to the women who sent letters to him. "You're literate," Anis'ko said. "You'll know what to write." Samoilov ended up composing versions of the same letter to several young women at a time. It always explained that Anis'ko was alone, that his family had been killed, and that he was ready to give his heart to any woman who could love him enough to trust him with her photograph. When the replies arrived, Anis'ko would pass them around for the other men to read aloud. He gave it up after the joke backfired. "My son," he heard one of his comrades reading, "you're writing to me about love, but I'm already well into my seventh decade."[69]

The state was always ready with a project. The Sovinformburo and party organs were not bothered by the lack of comprehension between front-line soldiers and the people at home. They knew that they could foster an imaginary collectivity, not least because so many millions truly were working to support the front. This patriotic impulse was constantly stoked. In campaign after campaign, the state assembled packages for the front. In February 1942, one of the grimmest months in a hard wartime winter, the citizens of Omsk dispatched an entire train to the soldiers around Leningrad. Its cargo included 12,760 patriotic letters, but the twenty-four wagons were also crammed with 18,631 parcels, each of which contained meat, bacon, salami, smoked cheese, honey, fish, and tobacco. The train was also well supplied with vodka and other spirits, and someone had added 183 watches, stationery, a toilet, and 1,500 copies of a special edition of *Omskaya Pravda*.[70]

"Gifts" for the armed forces did not stop with consumables. Everyone, even the soldiers themselves, was under pressure to subscribe to state war loans. But some enthusiasts went further and bought weapons for the front. In 1943, a hero-beekeeper stepped forward in Kursk province. His first gift to the armed forces was 750 kilos of honey, but grander ambitions filled his heart. Throughout the summer of 1943, he saved the proceeds of his honey sales until he had raised the 150,000 rubles needed to buy a Yak–9 airplane. The new machine would bear his name, Bessmertnyi, which in Russian means "immortal," and the pilot who flew it swore that it was a lucky plane.[71] A similarly patriotic couple donated 50,000 rubles to buy a heavy tank, trained side by side at Chelyabinsk, and then served in their own machine, fighting all the way to Germany. When the husband of a woman called Mariya Oktyabrskaya died, she donated her life savings for the purchase of a T–34.

She, too, became a tank driver, and was killed near Vitebsk in 1944.[72] As Bessmertnyi put it, "The more I work, the more food the Red Army gets and the closer it comes to victory over the enemy."[73]

While civilians were busily adopting troops, the soldiers were taking on a few strays of their own. The simple kinds of affection were best. Among the veterans I met at Kursk was a comparatively young man—still in his early seventies—called Vasily Andreevich. He told me how he had joined a regiment when he was just thirteen. It was after the Germans had left, taking his mother and leaving their hut to burn. The boy, an orphan now, had run away to hide in the woods. He was there alone for three days, he remembers, maybe more. He tried to eat pine needles and rough grass. All he could think of was his hunger. And then he stumbled on a Red Army encampment. Sixty years on, his eyes grew wider as he remembered that kitchen. "There was an enormous cauldron," he told me, "and the men were lining up to get a ladleful of the soup from it." The boy joined the line. Realizing that the men all had tin bowls, he took off his cap and held it out. By then, the cook was trying not to laugh, and all the men had realized that they had picked up a new "son." The regiment "adopted" him, providing a uniform and food in exchange for his work—which, naturally, involved cleaning that cauldron every day. "All through the war I stayed with them," he said. Even when he was injured in the leg he traveled on, refusing to retire to a field hospital. As he recalled, "I could not bear to be separated from that kitchen."

The adoption of "sons of the regiment" was so haphazard that no one can say how many children were involved. One estimate suggests that as many as 25,000 children between the ages of six and sixteen marched with the army at some point during the war.[74] Some were mere infants. The men took pity on them and treated them as substitutes for the families they missed, if not as mascots. Not all were sheltered from real combat. Some rode in tanks, others hefted rifles or learned to fire field guns.[75] It was the only schooling they would get. There were no classes, no other children to join them in reading or learning to write. Their bedtime stories were the men's own tales of heroes and magical knights. Many were already hardened fighters when the army took them on. David Samoilov met a fifteen-year-old called Vanka who joined his regiment from a group of partisans. When Samoilov's men captured a

The cook arrives with the soldiers' soup

German prisoner, Vanka asked to escort the man to the compound where some other prisoners were being held. "He led him away for a few steps," Samoilov wrote, "and then he shot him. Vanka could not bear to see a living Fritz. He was avenging his murdered family. Let God judge him, not people."[76]

The children almost certainly helped to sustain the men. It was a relief to take care of someone after months of military harshness and routine. If not a child, there might well be a horse or cow—this army marched with a whole range of barnyard stock.[77] Samoilov's unit developed a craze for puppies. While they were camped in Poland in 1944,

their commanding officer was called away for two weeks. He returned
to find the regiment boiling with dogs. Samoilov, too, had his own mutt.
When it slept beside him, he wrote, his feeling was "almost paternal."
During the soldiers' working day, the dogs ran wild, barking at anyone
who wandered near the camp. The commanding officer, Captain Bogo-
molov, was appalled. He gave the men twenty-four hours to dispose of
every canine in the camp. That afternoon, a makeshift dog show took
place in the woods. The price was a liter of vodka for each puppy, and
every one was sold.[78] Perhaps the locals knew that other regiments
would buy them back. A photograph from 1944 shows a tank crew
smiling from their cockpit as their mascot, a young dog, grins out as
broadly as the men.

★

The era of front-line counterinsurgency truly arrived as the Red Army
thundered west. The Soviets were now deep in territory that the enemy

Tank drivers pose with their mascot, 1944

had ruled. Almost every able-bodied male in these regions was suspect. The public, the people in Moscow, thought of these as liberated populations, and it was certainly the case that millions saw the return of Soviet power, after the Nazis, as a true deliverance. Pictures showed smiling children greeting tough Red Army men, while ruined streets in places like Smolensk and Kiev thronged with adults in hungry, grateful crowds. But on the ground the agents of dictatorship nurtured their doubts. From 1942, a network of camps was established near the front where anyone the NKVD deemed to be suspect could be detained, even former soldiers whose skills were sorely needed in the ranks.[79]

There were two basic policies toward suspected enemies of Soviet power. The first was armed repression. From 1943 NKVD border troops, backed up by units like OSMBON, hunted and killed known Fascist agents and guerrillas in the borderlands. The conventions on prisoners of war seldom applied.[80] Meanwhile, operatives employed by SMERSh gave themselves the task of "filtering" remaining suspect adults in the captured zones. The whey-faced policemen held court in ramshackle front-line camps, sifting through information that included tales that local people told. Suspects had to prove themselves innocent; in this appalling theater the burden of suspicion fell on anyone who was not dead. Ex-soldiers, for instance, customarily had to provide three witnesses to attest that they were neither deserters, collaborators, nor cowards.[81] But, though its operatives were indeed looking for spies and enemies, the most important—if unstated—task for SMERSh and its allies was to create a new order. Filtration, like terror, sent a message to the lawless populations of the battlefields. Soviet habits of discipline and fear were set to be rebuilt. Whatever they had thought or done in the anarchic summers after 1941, the people's loyalty was now owed to one leader and one system of thought.

The collapse of all forms of government in the front-line regions had been total. For months, the Nazis had been fighting for their lives. Even before the catastrophe of probable defeat, too, they had always been an occupying army, not to mention one whose goal was genocide. As they retreated, burning buildings and supplies, they left a wasteland in their wake. The Red Army, as it advanced, moved too fast and was too engaged with military affairs to care about the law. A vast belt of liberated territory on both banks of the Dnepr became the domain of armed gangs. In some places, the partisans had been the only effective government for months. In others, bandits or guerrillas ruled, sometimes under the leadership of former officers of the Red Army.[82] The security organs set themselves the task of sifting the true patriots from all the rest. Demobilized partisans, the people best equipped to assess local stories from the party's point of view, played a prominent role in the purging process. As one of these, a weary, soft-voiced survivor called "Uncle Mitya" remarked to Alexander Werth, "We shall be merciless with traitors now. It's no use crying in wartime."[83]

Dictatorship was reimposed—slowly—using the bullet or the punishment battalion. In each region's chaotic network of government offices, a new structure of party rule was hammered into place. Here, counterintelligence worked beside Communist Party officials, since the party always assessed its members' records for itself. Communist survivors who were deemed suspect or even negligent were purged. Some were drafted at once into the Red Army. The rest were transferred to the Gulag. Later in the war, they would be joined by the thousands of Communist troops who had grown tired or critical as the Red Army crossed into the capitalist world.[84]

The group at the top of SMERSh's wanted list, for now, was the Russian Liberation Army (ROA), a Fascist-sponsored force composed mainly of ethnic Russians and identified with General Andrei Vlasov. The general, a former star in the Red Army, had turned traitor when he was captured on the Volkhov Front in July 1942. He came to symbolize the ragtag of desperate prisoners and disgruntled anti-Communists who hoped to save themselves by working for the Germans. In 1943, partisans near Smolensk reported that leaflets bearing Vlasov's portrait and that of his deputy, Malyshkin, had been dropped in the area, and there were rumors that Vlasov himself had visited Smolensk.[85] Moskvin encountered "Vlasovites" when his group was surrounded and attacked in April 1943.[86] But the phrase was a catchall for the armed bands that the Germans liked to use when they destroyed partisan groups. By labeling local collaborators, including anyone who was fed up with partisan extortion, as Vlasovites, SMERSh fostered rumors of a larger and more sinister conspiracy. It was a technique that had always served the secret police well.

The real Vlasov army, forlorn and poorly equipped, was sent off to France and southern Europe in the late summer of 1943.[87] Vlasov's German paymasters no longer trusted his troops on Soviet soil. And even before that, the general had not been responsible for every leaflet that called on Soviet citizens to resist Stalin's rule. With or without him, a string of shadowy "liberation armies" had been at work in Ukraine and the western provinces of Russia throughout 1943. There were "Russian committees" and "People's Parties of Russia" in many occupied cities, each working, under German supervision, to undermine Soviet habits of thought. They revived long-forgotten flags and colors, promised (tardily and desperately) to dissolve collective farms, and swore that Communism would end. One group even used the letters SSSR, the initials of the Soviet Union, for its own masthead. But in this case they stood for a different slogan: "Smert' Stalina spaset Rossiyu"—Stalin's death will save Russia.[88] The whole thing was convenient for SMERSh. Wherever there were real traitors, there could be convincing arrests.

Genuine Vlasovites, in fact, were thinner on the ground than collaborators and *Hiwis*, and none were as numerous as the rabble of small-time opportunists, local bosses, deserters, and crooks. Ideology, as Stalin and Hitler defined it, was less of a priority for wartime populations than the fight for life. Given the choice, large numbers of people might have preferred to escape from dictatorship altogether, and this impulse found reflection in the appeal of nationalist bands. These had been active in some regions since the war began. Some were large and even, for a time, successful, imposing a kind of frontier law in the districts they controlled. In 1944, the most powerful guerrilla group in Ukraine was the UPA, the Ukrainian Insurgent Army.[89] This movement, thought to number twenty thousand members by the end of the war, scored a notable coup in February 1944, when one of its detachments shot and fatally wounded the talented Soviet general Nikolai Vatutin.[90] But the UPA's support would be strongest in the western, recently annexed regions of Ukraine. The history of intermarriage on the Soviet side of the Dnepr, together with a tradition of loyalty to Moscow, ensured that nationalism in this region posed little threat.[91] It was anarchy, not organized disloyalty, that disrupted the Red Army's supply lines and support troops at this stage. Apart from arrests, the best remedy for that was forced conscription. People who served under the red flag, too, could not be recruited so easily by other gangs.

In October 1943, a former soldier named Andreev experienced this form of liberation at firsthand. The letter that he wrote to his mother, five pages in length, has the quality of a last testament. It was also the first news he had sent home since he was taken prisoner in August 1941. Back then, Andreev's unit had been surrounded by tanks. But in the general chaos of the time, he had escaped from the escorting German guards and hidden in a village called Annovka. There he married Oksana, the daughter of the woman who was hiding him. A daughter, Nina, was born in 1943. What prompted him to write and tell his mother all this news was the approach of the Red Army. "There was a huge battle here today," he explained, "and I, Oksana, and Ninochka had to cower in a hut with all the old people. They say that a military commission is coming here and that it will examine all the former prisoners of war. The fit ones will be taken for the front, which means that instead of going home I may end up in the front line."[92] Andreev passed the tests that SMERSh set up. But he was unfit, untrained, and without equipment. He died a few weeks later on the banks of the Dnepr.

Detachments of partisans posed different problems. Many were working as adjuncts of the Red Army. It was they who disrupted German supply lines before the campaigns at Kursk, Orel, and Kharkov. They also helped regular troops to capture the potential informers— "tongues"—who might betray the enemy's planned maneuvers. Partisans could send reports from deep behind German lines, informing Moscow about training bases, repair shops, and even German pigeon coops.[93] Moskvin's diary for 1943 reads like a list of military engagements, each with its own objective. "Every day we have carried out some kind of action against the enemy," he wrote in April. The usual targets were the railways and roads. It was like army life again. The men were formed into battalions, each including about ten explosives groups. They were becoming expert in laying and in clearing mines. At the end of a "month of uninterrupted battle," Moskvin felt "the same creative sense that I had when we destroyed the Vitebsk airfield in 1941, except that then our tragedy was about to begin."[94]

The problem was that renewed battle meant increased numbers of casualties. "I am writing for posterity," Moskvin noted on 25 March, "that partisans undergo inhuman suffering."[95] The losses could be made up only by recruiting new people. That spring and summer, and especially after Kursk, the task became easier as "1943 partisans"—peasants who saw which way the war was going and resolved to save themselves—made their way to the dugouts and the camps. The Grishin regiment, which included Moskvin's own battalion, grew from about six hundred to over two thousand members by the late summer of 1943.[96] All these people had to be retrained. There was the usual rough military drill, including target practice using captured guns. Recruits also needed to learn "equanimity in the face of death" and to combat "cowardice, panic, and whining."[97] But there were other types of lesson to be learned as well. A cultural gulf separated these young village toughs from the older generation of partisans, many of whom had once belonged, before 1941, to the elite of working-class soldiers and officers.[98] "We have to strengthen the discipline of the whole group," Moskvin wrote. "We have to improve their relations with the local population, not allowing cases of coarseness and shameful behavior by Soviet citizens."

The answer was an arid, brutal discipline. In preparation for the tank battle at Kursk, Moskvin's battalion was ordered to make a raid on the station at Chaus. When it was over, Moskvin cataloged the dead and injured. Three people had been killed outright and eighteen suffered wounds, among whom three would later die, including the battalion commander, Makarov, and Moskvin's friend Ivan Rakhin. One of the women who went on the raid, a medical officer called Pasha, was critically wounded in the arm. The only way to save her was to amputate the limb, an operation that was carried out with vicious home-brewed spirit for an anesthetic. They poured it neat into her throat. "The woman's fortitude is striking," Moskvin observed. But "we took 140 rifles and four machine guns . . . as well as a new radio." It was a strange economy of war. Strangest of all, the raid also produced a quantity of French champagne and cognac, tobacco and Havana cigars.[99] These would have been outrageous prizes for a band of outlaws in an earth dugout, but they were not the ones who got to taste the wine. Moskvin's battalion was under strict command. The bosses claimed all trophies for the state.

As the Red Army crashed on to Orel, conditions in the woods of western Russia worsened. The mood in Moskvin's regiment was tense, but its leader, Grishin, seemed to withdraw into a dream world of his own. "Only my deep respect for his talent makes me so tolerant," Moskvin observed. The retreating German army posed new threats to partisans whose territory had up till then been deep behind the front. Grishin's instructions were to travel east and join the Red Army as it approached Smolensk, but within days of setting out, he and his men were encircled. They had not reached their own front line. Instead, they faced the vengeful hatred of an enemy that was itself in flight. By 16 October 1943, Moskvin was sure that he would die. "I have one main desire," he wrote miserably. "If it is going to be death, then let it be quick, not with a serious injury, which would be the most frightening of all."[100] By then, as he added, the men had already eaten all their horses. As winter approached, and despite all the triumph to the east, they were starving to death.

The blockade lasted for about three weeks. It was Grishin who enforced Stalinist order. "We are encircled," he wrote on 11 October. "The exits from the forest are blocked. You can hear for yourself that the front is approaching. . . . Therefore, we must hold our positions. Retreat would mean extinction. There must be no cowards or panicmongers among us. Every honest patriot of our fatherland must shoot such people on the spot."[101] "In the last few days life has lost its meaning," Moskvin wrote on 17 October. He was coming close to breakdown. "My instinct for self-preservation isn't working the way it used to. It's not gone altogether, but it's become really dull, like a headache after a good dose of aspirin."[102] These thoughts remained private, for he was a political officer and it was his job to maintain morale. The feelings of less motivated men are clear enough. "For leaving his post without orders," runs an order dated 13 October 1943, "for cowardice, for being panicky, and for nonfulfillment of orders, Squad Leader Bacharov is to be shot."[103]

Moskvin was destined to escape. On 18 October, just after his most desolate diary entry, he and his men received orders to break the enemy blockade. It was an almost suicidal act. As they rushed at the German lines they were defenseless targets. Fifteen people were killed within a few seconds—one for each meter, Moskvin noted, that they ran. The losses were enormous, but the regiment was free. Its orders were to move southwest, not east, to evade German fire. The maneuver was conducted under military discipline, but the group received no help from the Red Army. Moskvin observed, without comment, that it was but a dozen miles away.

The Red Army's advance provided many opportunities for Stalin to demonstrate his policy on unity and brotherhood. By the end of 1943, almost the entire region of Ukraine was in Soviet hands. But one prize still eluded recapture. Hitler himself was determined to hold on to the Crimea. It was not simply that the peninsula represented a strategic gateway to the oil fields of Romania. It was also a place of striking beauty. The Germans had declared it a Black Sea version of Britain's Gibraltar, a kind of second homeland, as soon as they had captured it. During their two-year occupation of the peninsula, they had even planned a direct highway from Berlin to Yalta, and there were rumors that Hitler had chosen the seaside palace at Livadiya as his eventual retirement home.[104] With both sides set on taking it, the Crimea witnessed fighting as bitter as any in the entire war. But the aftermath, for thousands of the peninsula's inhabitants, would be crueler still. When Stalin talked about the Soviet people and their great collective epic, there were already tens of thousands who would never share in the rewards.

The liberation of the Crimea was accomplished in the space of a few weeks beginning in April 1944. The Soviet military operation, a coordinated strike from both the north and east, was bold, effective, and prodigal of human life. It was also physically grueling. As Alexander Werth observed, the men who headed the invasion from the north, across the grim and fog-bound Sivash marshes, had to "spend hours waist-deep or shoulder-deep in the icy and very salt water of the Sivash—the salt eating into every pore and causing almost unbearable pain" as they laid the first pontoons across the inlet.[105] But once they reached the firm Crimean soil, their progress was faster. Within two days the first Red Army troops had reached the capital, Simferopol, which lies at the heart of Crimea's inland steppe. Meanwhile, a second group, starting near Kerch, began its rapid westward drive along the coast road to the south, securing Kerch itself and then the port of Feodosia. From there, the soldiers' way lay around the pointed crags that shelter the resort of Koktebel, and beyond that, passing terraces of vineyards and sunlit forests of beech, they would speed through the Tatar fishing village of Gurzuf, through Yalta, Livadiya, Alubka, and—eventually—to the outskirts of Sevastopol itself.

It was spring in the Crimea. The place was an exotic paradise after a winter rotting on the steppe. "I spent the May Day holiday in a wonderful way," Vitaly Taranichev's brother-in-law, Fedor, wrote home. "In the first place, for fulfilling the military duties that my commanders assigned me I have been awarded the Order of the Red Star, and secondly it was jolly because of all the wine we drank and the great company." He was writing a full week after the party, but he added that "I will only be in a sober enough condition to work and to continue with the rout of our enemies tomorrow."[106] The wine was not just local stuff. Since 1941, high-ranking German officers had often spent their leave in the Crimea. To help them to relax, their staff had imported the best products from Alsace, Champagne, and the Rhine. No one had time, in the emergency, to pack it up. When they arrived in places that the Germans had vacated days before, Red Army officers like young Fedor could drown in vintage Riesling if they chose. Like many other Soviet troops on this campaign, the young man vowed to make Crimea his future home.

But this was not a holiday. The port of Sevastopol remained in the enemy's hands. As each mile of hinterland fell to the Red Army, more refugee detachments of the Wehrmacht and its Romanian allies arrived in the port city. At the beginning of May, the commander of the German Seventeenth Army in Sevastopol, Jaenicke, expressed doubts that his troops were in a condition to withstand the predicted Soviet blow. He was replaced by a more loyal Nazi, Allmedinger. Hitler had ordered that there was to be no question of surrendering the port. It had held out for 250 days at the beginning of the war and now it was commanded to sustain a second siege. The city's readiness for this would be tested at once. On 5 May, two days after Jaenicke's removal, the Soviets attacked.

The first onslaught came from the north. On 7 May, a second wave advanced toward the famous Sapun ridge, whose name evokes the foaming sweat of horses galloping to reach the higher ground.[107] Less than a hundred years before, when British and French forces had faced Todleben's Russians in the Crimean War, the valley all around had echoed to the sound of cannon fire, the smoke and dust of battle breaking for a second now and then to show a glint of gold braid or a flash of steel. This time the landscape trembled to the shudder of Katyushas and the drone of planes. After the mortars came the men. Some were professionals and some mere boys, some Communists and some the blighted *shtrafniki*. But for the most part they were nothing like the ill-equipped, half-trained conscripts of 1941. The troops of 1944 knew their business, and for this campaign they were well supplied. Soviet industry had filled their ammunition belts; American lend-lease provided them with transport and tinned food. Among the corpses, when the scavengers came by, there would be pickings of watches, knives, pens, and Gillette razor blades. Even their boots, these days, were often better than the German ones.[108]

The port of Sevastopol held less than a week. A more realistic leadership might have evacuated the remaining German troops well in advance of the collapse, but Hitler still refused to cede his prize. Now the frightened, injured, and leaderless men who remained in the city panicked before the Soviet advance. Some managed to cram into the few ships that were putting out toward the west, while others surrendered with their backs to the burning harbor. The rest fled down the coast toward the ancient settlement of Kherson, whose cliff-top ruins would become a killing field. The Soviets trapped the survivors on the limestone rocks and blasted them with every kind of fire. Those who were not cut down in the gray dust drowned when they leapt into the sea. Werth, who arrived within days of the last battle, described the place as "gruesome." "All the area in front of the Earth Wall and beyond was ploughed up by thousands of shells," he wrote, "and scorched by the fire of *katyusha* mortars. . . . The ground was littered with hundreds of

German rifles, bayonets, and other arms and ammunition." It was also "scattered with thousands of pieces of paper—photographs, snapshots, passports, maps, private letters—and even a volume of Nietzsche carried to the end by some Nazi superman."[109] Estimates vary, but it is likely that at least twenty-five thousand people perished or were captured in this one defeat.[110]

The liberation of Crimea was complete by 13 May. But there was one group of Soviet citizens who would not celebrate for long. The Tatars, a people who could claim the Scythians, Goths, and Greeks among their ancestors, had lived and farmed in the Crimea for at least six hundred years.[111] Russian settlement, which dated from the eighteenth century, had never brought them luck. Their loyalties, like their language, their architecture, and their easygoing Muslim faith, were more inclined toward the Turks of the Black Sea's opposite shore. Like peasants everywhere, the farmers among them also hated the collectives, and in 1941, some of them saw the invasion as a chance to throw off the unwanted yoke of Soviet rule. Though many thousands of ethnic Tatars fought in the Red Army, a number of those who remained behind welcomed the Germans as liberators, or at least as an alternative to Stalinist dictatorship. Meanwhile, a small number of the Tatar soldiers held as prisoners of war in German camps had taken the only route to survival, as they saw it, and joined the anti-Soviet Tatar legion.[112] Just one week after the rout at Kherson, the entire Tatar population of the Crimea would pay the price.

That night, 18 May 1944, thousands of Tatar families were woken in the small hours before sunrise by a knock on the door. When they answered, they found that their visitors were armed. While the Red Army had been clearing the last Fascists from Crimea, tens of thousands of NKVD soldiers had been brought into the rural settlements and coastal villages where Tatars lived. Now these police were giving orders to pack quickly, to collect the children, and to be ready outside, on the road, in fifteen minutes. Many Tatars had seen the Nazis doing much the same in 1941, when local Jews were rounded up, each carrying a precious cardboard case of clothes and food. "We all thought we were going to die," survivors recall. The irony was that this time the men with the guns were Soviet fellow citizens.

Just under 200,000 people, or 47,000 families, most of them headed by women or older men, were herded to the stations and locked into cattle trucks that night.[113] The process was efficient, quick. Indeed, the NKVD troops already had experience. The railway cars that were used to take the Tatars east had just returned from other human transport missions—most recently, the deportation of the mountain peoples of Chechnya, Ingushetiya, and the autonomous republic of Kabardino-Balkariya.[114] The process, organized by NKVD chief Levrenti Beria, amounted to a smooth routine. The cars, as witnesses observed, were still smeared with the feces and dried blood of the last consignments of deportees.[115] There would be stops along the way—if the passengers were lucky—to bundle out the bodies of those who died from heat, from thirst, or from the typhus that soon raged within the crowded cars. About eight thousand deportees are thought to have perished in the airless, stinking wagons. The rest would have to build new lives from nothing when they arrived in Central Asia. They would find little welcome there. Their new hosts, fellow Muslims as well as fellow Soviets, would accept, for a while, the tale that all Tatars, as a people, were traitors.

Some of the deportees were genuine collaborators. Some had indeed helped to support the new Nazi regime.[116] But many had been dedicated to the Soviet cause. Among the latter were a number of partisans, including the political officers Ahmetov and Isaev, both of whom, as members of the Fifth Partisan Brigade, had been helping the Red Army as recently as April 1944. At least four Heroes of the Soviet Union, all of them decorated for their part in the Soviet landings at Kerch in November 1943, were also in the trucks.[117] So were the wives, parents, and children of soldiers who were still serving at the front, to say nothing of the families of combatants who had died. While Russian soldiers, including Vitaly Taranichev's brother-in-law, Fedor Kuznetsov, looked forward to new lives in the Crimea, delighted to have found through army life a place where they could thrive after the war, the Tatars in the same army would soon find that they had no home.

"There were thirty-four different nationalities in the forest," a partisan who spent the war in the Crimea remembered. "Most of them were Russians, of course, but there were Ukrainians, Belorussians, Crimean Tatars, Greeks, Armenians, Georgians, Slovaks, Czechs, and Spanish veterans of the civil war. We made absolutely no distinction between them." The citizenship that she assigned to herself, and that she still honors, was "Soviet." It was the label that made greatest sense in the political universe in which she lived, the name that conjured dreams of brotherhood, equality, and proletarian justice for all. It also matched the government's official line, the propaganda of the Sovinformburo. But by the war's end, 1.6 million Soviet members of minority ethnic groups had been singled out, tarred with a racist brush, and deported—in the Soviet Union's name—from the lands in which their ancestors had lived. Within a few years—just after the peace—about a third were dead.

EIGHT

EXULTING, GRIEVING, AND SWEATING BLOOD

★

April and May are often warm in the Crimea, but in Belarus, more than five hundred landlocked miles off to the north, the wind across the marshes is still cold and sour. In 1944, the state that was called Belorussia was a desert—bleak, snow-covered, wasted by two armies and three years of war. Nikolai Belov had been trapped for nearly six months in its landscape of ice and mud. As an officer, he could not complain about his lodgings. He had a cabin lined with local logs, not an oozing dugout. Unlike his men, too, Belov was well supplied with food and heating fuel. But the monotony of the Belorussian winter depressed him, the endless pine and fetid swamp suggesting shipwreck. He was bored, apathetic, and restive. To pass the time, he tried to read biography, starting with a life of Napoleon. In April 1944, he finished the second book of his war. Its hero was a Georgian general who had fought and died at Borodino. The general's name was Bagration. If Belov had known what Moscow was planning next for him, he might have smiled at the irony.

Operation Bagration, which he was just about to join, was one of the largest military campaigns of the entire war. Far to the west, the Allied forces under Eisenhower were preparing to launch their own great attack, Overlord, the forcing of the English Channel and the start of a long push through France. But the Soviet campaign to drive the German army out of Belorussia was no less ambitious than the D-Day landings. It was also more costly and, ultimately, more momentous. Planned for the early summer, it would be delayed by endless wrangles over supply and logistics. In the end, with a symmetry that was unintended, it was launched on 22 June, the third anniversary of Hitler's Barbarossa.[1] Like Barbarossa, too, it would tear through the country like a storm. If it had not been for Stalingrad, and then for Kursk, Bagration—which Stalin named for his Georgian fellow countryman—might well have looked like the war's greatest turning point.

In fact, the operation on the Soviet Union's western marches virtually escaped the kind of epic treatment that historians would later accord to Stalingrad and Kursk. For one thing, it was overshadowed, in western Europe and the English-speaking world, by the drama taking place in northern France. Bagration was also swallowed by the triumphs that came after it, as if, in some way, it was no more than a grand prelude. But above all, the army that would fight it, though still the Red Army, could no longer pretend to be the gallant underdog. Before Bagration, Soviet troops were still working to liberate their own country. When it was over, they were poised for conquest, facing westward across Europe in a manner that—in Central European minds at least—raised specters of an alien horde. The story of the Soviet Union's patriotic war would be much easier to tell if it could have a happy ending. But what came after Bagration, in keeping with the brutal nature of the times, was not the shapely stuff of fairy tales.

Zhukov and his colleagues had learned a great deal since 1941. The planning of Bagration showed just how much they could achieve on a grand scale, and also how far they had moved ahead on issues like coordination, secrecy, deception, and detailed tactical preparation. The Red Army was also by this stage the best-armed ground-based force in Europe. Among the tons of weaponry that it deployed that spring, there was an average of 320 artillery pieces for every mile of the front line.[2] But the background to Operation Bagration was no less tense, no less demanding on a human scale, than the months leading up to Kursk. The miracle was that soldiers who had been in action for months, if not for years, were able to galvanize their minds and bodies to fight on at all.

That winter, most of the men were bewildered, tired, and shocked. "The patriotic wave of the summer and autumn is receding," the hopeful German spies wrote to their masters in Berlin in January 1944. Within the ranks, consensus favored rapid peace. The soldiers seemed to want no more than just to drive the Fascists off their soil. Taking the war abroad, fighting for other lands, was not worth months of hardship or another winter in a trench.[3] The older men now longed for home, while new recruits, many of whom were not Russians, tended to lack the sense of purpose of the patriots of 1941. Almost all had reason to complain. Many now marched with injuries that would bedevil them forever, shortening their lives. The war had changed more than their bodies, too. By this stage it had swamped their thoughts, altered their language, distorted their tastes. It left each of them so exhausted that they could sleep at their guns, in clammy trenches, on the backs of tanks. They could sleep anywhere, in fact, but few were given chance enough. Most front-line troops had scarcely rested since the whirlwind of the previous autumn.

For those who survived it, Kursk had been intoxicating, and the onward march to Orel and Kharkov the progress of heroes. There was a pause in September, and sometimes even a few days when front-line divisions were in the same place for long enough to write letters or mend their boots. "I'm giving my lice a chance to sleep," Belov wrote on 9 September. For the first time in weeks, he sat for an entire afternoon. The fighting had not stopped, but now, as a staff officer, it was Belov's job to organize it all. He hated the work, longed for an active role, and pined for the men's company and for the next jolt of adrenaline.[4] He was addicted to war, just as he was also repelled and wrecked by it. But he would find plenty of action in the next few months. By early October, Belov's division had reached the river Sozh, which flows south into the Dnepr through the city of Gomel. "We are making war on Belorussian territory," he noted. By late November, they were almost on the Dnepr itself. It was progress, it was another step toward triumph, and yet it was still wretched, grinding, hard. "We'll have to spend the

Red Army soldiers on the Central Front sleeping after battle, 1943

winter in the woods and marshes," he wrote on 28 November. "We began our attack at ten o'clock. In twenty-four hours we've covered about
six kilometers. We've got no ammunition or shells. There isn't enough
food. The rear units have fallen behind. A lot of people have absolutely
no footwear at all."[5]

Belov's staccato notes sketch the bare outlines of collective misery.
The Red Army was preparing to deliver the last blow that it would need
to strike on its own soil, but many troops were in a poor state for campaigning. The host of men that seemed so alien when it reached Europe,
whose vanguard excited such terror, was indeed filthy, stinking, and un-
kempt. But few soldiers would choose to be that way. They did not
dwell on their wretchedness, perhaps, because it was by now so much a
part of life. By the end of 1943, daily realities like lice, rheumatic aches,
and unhealed sores were too familiar to mention. Few soldiers saw a
dentist at the front, though many city-bred young men regretted—for a
week or two—that toothpaste was so hard to find. Eventually, like
everyone else, they got used to a different kind of mouth. Toothache
joined hemorrhoids and conjunctivitis on the list of irritations that sol-

diers just lived with, as they lived with rats. In March and April, unhealed wounds and bleeding gums announced the first scurvy. No orders from Moscow could produce cabbage when the stores were down
to tea and dry buckwheat. The early spring was the worst time, after the
long winter and well before the first green crops had grown. And early
spring—late March in the Crimea, May in Belarus—was also the season
of the mud.

That April, as always, migrating geese skimmed east across the
Pripet Marshes to their nesting sites. Belov heard his first lark. For three
months, he and his men had been stuck fast, waiting for orders, digging
in "like moles."[6] It was a pause, but not a rest. For one thing, they were
still obliged to move from time to time, though each location was as uninviting as the last. For another, there were still plenty of enemy shells.
"Fritz does not let us poke our noses out," Belov complained. "Everything is shot up. Even at night it's dangerous to move from one building
to another." It was also wet. "Everything is melting," he wrote. "There
will be a terrible amount of mud here, and it won't clear up till June."[7]
He was right about that. "Time is going slowly again," he commented in
April. "The days drag endlessly. There's nothing worse than defense."[8]

That spring's inaction—or rather, the dull round of lectures, drill,
and training—simply cleared space for the sour thoughts to surface.
Whatever followed in the next few months, that late winter and spring
were bleak for almost everyone. "Enthusiasm for a military advance," a
German report claimed, "is still out of the question." Among the men, resentment found its expression in demands for home leave, brawling, and
a rash of self-inflicted wounds.[9] Belov indulged his depression, a lassitude
mixed with resentment at his wasted life. "In the last while I've been feeling an acute tiredness from the war," he wrote in mid-December. "It
must be because of that, I suppose, that I dream of my family and of my
peacetime situation every night. But it's all useless, of course. The war
isn't going to end this winter. My head aches." A month later, his letters
home were "sour, scrappy." He had never, he wrote, experienced such
apathy.[10] Even the news—the liberation of Novgorod and the final relief
of Leningrad—evoked no real joy. Vasily Ermolenko, stationed in
Ukraine to the south, felt much the same. "After three years of war," he
wrote in May, "the Soviet soldier is tired, physically and morally."[11]

Fatigue like this was too common to excite medical concern. Belov fell ill with a severe cold that spring, but the doctors discharged him after three days in a field clinic. They had to treat too many cases of tuberculosis to waste time on anyone whose lungs were sound. The medical attitude toward tribulations of the mind was similarly brisk. Stress, let alone a complicated diagnosis like post-traumatic stress disorder, was as foreign to the Red Army's medical orderlies as the hysterical indispositions of the bourgeoisie. A generation before, Russia had led the world in its understanding of battle stress, drawing conclusions based on conflict in the Balkans and Far East. But individual trauma, like individual desire, was a concept alien to Stalinism.[12] Soldiers were part of a collective; good morale was their duty, not their right. Those who complained, malingered, or showed signs of cowardice were likely to face punishment—a bullet or the *shtraf* battalion.

The Red Army's dismissal of psychiatry in this war—or rather, its obliviousness to it in the field—means that few records have survived about this aspect of morale. Without them, it is easy to forget that these soldiers were prey to the same emotions as their allies. It was the men's attitude toward such feelings, not the stress response itself, that varied between armies. Belov would not have thought to call his apathy a sign of battle strain. He would never have dreamed of attributing the suicides and "accidents" that proliferated as the war dragged on to its traumatic burden.[13] Unlike their British and American counterparts, the only kind of mental disorder that wartime authorities in the Soviet Union would always recognize was one that had a clear organic cause. The rest were weaknesses, personal failings, something to cover with shame. Unnumbered thousands of soldiers, weak with exhaustion and repeated stress, were executed for desertion in the field.[14] Other emotional casualties vanished from the records when they were killed, too tired, perhaps, or too confused to survive yet another round of shells. Psychiatric wounds were real enough, but only extreme cases, including instances where men developed schizophrenia after their call-up, were acknowledged.[15] Estimates vary, but it seems likely that only a hundred thousand of the Red Army's twenty million active service troops would eventually be counted as permanent casualties of the mind.[16]

For doctors operating in this war, trauma meant physical damage, concussion or contusion to the brain. In interviews in 1996, I was unable to persuade groups of veteran medical staff that any other kind of battle shock existed, beyond the fear and exhaustion that all soldiers can feel. "Contusion," implying shell damage, was an acceptable term, but they had never heard of trauma in the current Western sense. Mishearing me, they asked me to explain what I meant by this new thing, this "postdramatic [*sic*] stress."[17] Their surprise is not difficult to explain. Textbooks from their days at the front did not refer to mental trauma, and nor did the memoirs of their fellow doctors or even of the combatants themselves. Panic was weakness, it was shame, and shame was written out of this war's history along with drunkenness and crime.

The ignorance of medical orderlies in the field, most of whom were trained in the 1930s or even, with some haste, during the war itself, reflected a deliberate policy choice. Behind the lines, there were still specialists with all the necessary expertise, as well informed as any in the United States or Britain. Some of the older ones had led the European debate on stress during the First World War. As late as 1942, there had been some high-level discussion of shock, a conference or two.[18] But the ideas never reached the front-line teams. Indeed, there were no psychiatric staff below the level of entire fronts and armies.[19] Resources were one problem. Another was that military psychology, if not the treatment of the sick, had taken a different turn since Stalin's rise. A good deal of experimentation was devoted to a kind of Taylorism, the mental preparation of each soldier to fit the machine or weapon that he would have to use. Warfare was deemed to be susceptible to the same rules as mass production.[20] Men and machines would work in harmony. No allowance was made for hysteria.

Some symptoms could not be ignored. Men suffering from mutism, convulsions, and fugue states could not stand in straight lines, let alone clean and assemble guns or handle delicate equipment. They were generally treated close to the front line, not least because the larger hospitals were overflowing with wounded and dying men. The treatment was basic. Injections always seemed to help—they had a sort of mystic potency to peasants who had no idea of medicine. Let the men sleep, the idea went, and they would soon recover or at least be well enough to fight. Very often, this was true. Rapid attention to the problem—which was only possible at the front line—was also beneficial.

Some patients still refused to heal. Those needing long stretches of rest could be assigned to jobs in the warren of camps and transport depots just behind the lines. They worked as store men, stretcher bearers, cleaners, cooks. But only a very few of them would ever see a psychiatric ward. To get there, they would have to sustain their symptoms through weeks of tests and "treatments," including the administration of electric shocks (allegedly to stimulate the nerves) or the use of wet cloths and rubber masks to induce a sense of drowning (to test whether their symptoms were really under voluntary control).[21] The brutality of these initial steps presaged the grim world of the psychiatric ward. For those whose diagnosis held, life would be wretched: hungry, loveless, submerged under drugs.[22]

Along the front, a problem that was not a problem in official terms soon seemed to disappear. In that sense, the Soviet approach to trauma was effective. American troops, whose symptoms were taken very seriously, dropped out of active service at four to six times the Red Army's rate in this war.[23] Stalin's soldiers learned that battle stress was not the best way to demonstrate exhaustion, panic, and the inability to sleep. Physical injuries, which soon followed the mental ones, provided a more effective ticket home or, failing that, to a field station and a bed. "There was only one thought," a veteran later suggested. "To be wounded quickly, to get it over with, to get to a hospital, at least for a convalescence, for a rest."[24] The lucky ones would escape long-term invalidism, but even the tens of thousands of supposedly healthy men who were camped along the Belorussian Front in the spring of 1944 could scarcely be considered whole.

Front-line culture had to evolve to make room for exhausted, frightened, and aggressive men. At the same time, it also took on consignments of criminals. Trainloads of murderers and small-time crooks had long been running west out of the Gulag to restock the army. But now almost all felons convicted of banditry, robbery, and what were vaguely referred to as "counterrevolutionary crimes" were held close to the front, assessed, and, in almost every case, made to serve out their terms in *shtraf* units.[25] Originally, these had fought in formations that remained separate from the mass of serving troops. But now, the criminals and *shtrafniki* could find themselves assigned to regular units, their task to carry out the dangerous work, especially sorties behind the German lines.[26] More than ever, the culture and the language of the *shtrafniki* prevailed within the ranks. The press might call the men heroes, but when they gathered at the front, their idiom was that of slaves, or else of convicts.[27] It was not just the patriotic rage of 1941 that was fading. A kind of buttoned-up Communist morality was disappearing as well.

Violence was everywhere, whatever the men's current military orders. When they were not in combat, they could quarrel over booty, drink, status, or women. Most often the result was a brawl, but sometimes the authorities were left to deal with corpses. The victims might be found at first light with their heads blown off, or else they might be beaten up with rifle butts.[28] Sometimes the violence was a side effect of euphoria. Where the Germans had a practice of setting fire to villages as a calculated act of terror, the Red Army was capable of doing so—even on its own soil—by firing at dry straw in an orgy of celebration.[29] Drink—which scarcely anyone consumed for the pleasure of the taste— was often involved. Its purpose now, as the Tommies of the First World War would have entirely understood, was just to kill the mind, to escape from the war without leaving one's post.[30] Some units would pool their vodka ration so that each man in turn could have the chance to drink it all and lose himself entirely for one night.[31]

It was the proof strength, not the quality, of the liquor that counted. Vasily Chuikov took the precaution of sealing the cellars of fine wine that his men discovered when they overran Nazi quarters in Poland. But sometimes he arrived too late. When he visited one cellar, he found the driver from an artillery regiment already rummaging through the piles of crates. "I can't find any strong spirits like ours," the man muttered. He had been working his way through a succession of bottles of fine champagne. "This is the sixth case I've opened," he complained, "and all they've got is fizzy stuff."[32] Disgusted, the soldier let the thin liquid spill onto the floor. But though they spurned imported wine, men of his tastes would drink anything that smelled like spirit, including *samogon* and antifreeze. "When our soldiers find alcohol," a Soviet lieutenant confided, "they take leave of their senses. You can't expect anything from them until they have finished the last drop." In his view, expressed in 1945, "if we hadn't had drunkenness like this we would have beaten the Germans two years ago."[33]

Crime was also increasing with the soldiers' growing confidence. By this point in the war its scale was nothing short of heroic. The recent improvement in supplies, too, was an invitation to potential crooks. The business began at the top. Indeed, as the army's inspectors observed, a "significant proportion of officers" in front-line regions had been tried for large-scale theft and speculation between January 1943 and July 1944. The figures, which were based on "incomplete data" and covered only the first six months of 1944, told their own vivid story. This was an army that was billeted on Soviet territory; the glory days of German plunder were still months away. And yet, in that half year, detected thefts by officers alone included 4.5 million rubles in cash, 70 tons of flour and bread products, 22 tons of meat and fish, 5 tons of sugar, 4,872 items of equipment, 33 tons of petrol, 7 cars, and "other military property to the value of two million rubles."[34]

The total figures were impressive, but a string of individual cases suggested that they were wild underestimates. This was a time when food was currency in every hungry village on the steppe. "Back home," Lev Kopelev, now serving as a Soviet officer, would muse, "there were villages where the war had passed like a column of fire, or where, invisibly from afar, it had sucked out the bread and blood; where a piece of sugar was a thing of wonder, and the children, with their enormous eyes and bluish-white faces, choked and chewed on some kind of mud-black, bitter bread made of the devil only knew what."[35] With stores to spare, a group of officers in the 203rd Reserve Army put their minds to wartime profit. In two months in the autumn of 1943 they diverted 34 tons of bread, 6.3 tons of sugar, 2.6 tons of fats, 15 tons of grits, and 2 tons of meat from the soldiers' supplies. The trade was used to fund the luxuries that made life better in an army camp. As the report on the criminals' activities commented, this was a barracks where "drinking, carousing, and theft were a normal part of life."[36]

The following June, an even more ambitious racket came to light among tank officers serving on the First Ukrainian Front. Mere theft was only part of it. The other side was corruption. Officers in the field, it seemed, were eager to secure favors from their military bosses in the capital. The major general in this case had smoothed his path with a stream of generous bribes to Moscow, including—in just one consignment—267 kilos of pork, 125 kilos of mutton, and 114 kilos of butter. On another occasion, his munificence included five live goats. Meanwhile, among the items that had gone missing from army stores on this one front that June were 15,123 kilos of meat, 1,959 kilos of sausage, 3,000 kilos of butter, 2,100 kilos of biscuits, 890 kilos of boiled sweets, 563 kilos of soap, a hundred winter coats, a hundred greatcoats, eighty fur *gilets*, a hundred pairs of *valenki*, and a hundred pairs of boots.[37] Reports of this kind were a weekly, if not daily, event for the military courts. They testify to the presence of large-scale, organized, and well-established networks. But this was an army in which there was at least one spy in almost every company. What the reports also demonstrate, therefore, is that corruption extended to the security police, who no doubt enjoyed their live goats and butter, too.

No veteran, of course, remembered any of this later. Thieving was another dark truth that time and collective memory would bury. The consequent shortages were also a source of grievance, an insult that could rankle, and as such they had no place in the bright memory of war. But the losers, naturally, were the men whose stores were being skimmed. On a daily basis, they put up with watery soup, sugarless tea, and the lumps of gristle that could not be sold for cash. Even when the food turned up, they might find that there were no bowls or spoons to eat it with.[38] Everyone understood that reserve troops should suffer, but even at the front there were whole days when soldiers went without hot meals or tea.[39] Complaining could subject a man to a charge of anti-Soviet agitation. "On verifying the food," NKVD officers primly noted, "it was found to be of the required standard, and the portions were all in line with current norms."[40] The men had to choke down their fury with the cabbage soup. Statistics for recorded crime concealed the facts.[41] According to the overall figures in monthly reports, less than 10 percent of troops were disciplined for any crime, including theft.[42] There could be no truth, then, in soldiers' complaints, or so their officers alleged. But that was partly because high figures for crime reflected most of all upon the *politruks* and their bosses. The temptation to hold the statistics down was as hard to resist as the promise of a crate of contraband sardines.

Meanwhile, ordinary men and women found numerous ways to keep the hunger and the cold at bay. Pilfering, which was a sort of compensation for indignity, was one recourse. Another was extorting sheep and pigs from local people. Self-help, which could take many forms, was commonplace. As Zhukov was preparing for the great assault, soldiers in Belorussia were putting in their usual hours on the farms, digging the fields and shifting truckloads of young pigs for fattening.[43] As ever, despite the demands of the war, farmwork was deemed to be a part of army service. Now it was also profitable. Farms kept grain stores and chickens, not to mention larger animals for butchering. Beyond the cow sheds, too, there was more free food in the open country. Hunting accidents became so common on the Belorussian Front in the summer of 1944 that soldiers in the Eleventh Guards Army were banned from shooting deer and other wild game.[44]

Those worn-out boots and greatcoats also had to be replaced. "My boots have fallen to bits," lamented Ermolenko in July 1944. He was a long way from a depot that supplied American lend-lease. But he was in Belorussia, and he was on campaign. Trade was one option, the hunt for a well-shod corpse or prisoner another. As he put it, "I'll have to find some 'trophy footwear' somewhere."[45] Boots were resoled with leather from the seats of German tanks, coats mended with shreds of tarpaulin. If the Red Army looked bizarre by the spring of 1944, it could at least take comfort from the fact that the enemy, for the most part, looked worse.

This was the juggernaut, then, that was preparing to strike west that summer. The orders to its staff and officers suggest precision and planning. Forward and rear supply bases were established with fuel and ammunition stocks and generous quantities of food. The heavy guns, at least, arrived intact, since they were usually too large to steal. The rest depended on the vigilance of loyal staff officers. But everyone was working at full stretch. The preparations for Bagration, whatever the problems and leaks, were formidable.[46] Because so much depended on surprise, almost all aspects of supply had to be carried out in duplicate. The idea was to deceive the German army, to make it think that the attack—if it came at all—would come from anywhere but the so-called Minsk balcony, the bulge that pointed straight toward Berlin. A massive charade followed: the mustering of troops whose sole purpose was to appear to gather, the clearing of dummy airfields in the forest, the drawing up of precious heavy guns whose destiny was not to fire. The real army moved only at night, its tracks swept clear behind it so that the wide trails of tanks and guns had disappeared by dawn. All radio communications ceased. Even bathing at open points along the route was forbidden.[47] The operation was about to prove a huge success. But for the soldiers on the ground, it was, as Belov wrote one weary night, just "the old song beginning once again."[48]

One of the final entries in Belov's journal was written on 18 June. Apart from frantic planning, he had seen little movement for several months. But when Zhukov appeared with two of his most senior aides, Belov knew that the long wait was over. The night maneuvers started, the tension increased. His men were tired, quarrelsome. "There are grounds for thinking that we'll go into the attack on 21 or 22 June," Belov wrote, "which happens to be the third anniversary of the war. It's interesting that 21 June is also four months since we crossed the Dnepr. For some reason I have been feeling physically poor lately, and my nerves are utterly shattered. . . . There are no letters from home, the devil take them. In that regard, I can be very tolerant, because we'll soon be in battle, and then I'll forget everything. The whole thing is unpleasant and pretty strange."[49] These were not the last words that Belov would write. But from that day he never had the time to keep a diary again.

Bagration involved five separate but coordinated strikes along the Soviet western front. Although the most important was to be the drive on Minsk and westward through the whole of Belarus, the first attack came in the north, breaking the last resistance of the Finns. To the south, later, Lvov would also be encircled as a separate group of armies struck west over the Carpathian Mountains. The progress on each of these fronts was breathtaking. Minsk, the strategic prize, was captured by 3 July. Within three weeks the troops of Rokossovsky's First Belorussian Front had crossed the border into Poland.

To get there, they had thrown roads made of logs across the swamps. They had forded, swum, and sworn their way across the many rivers in their path. Each line of trenches that they took was mined, collapsing, fetid with the stink of rats and shit and death. But they would face and shatter the most redoubtable enemy formation still on Soviet soil. In just twelve days, the German Army Group Center lost twenty-five divisions and more than 300,000 men.[50] The cost to the Red Army also ran to tens of thousands of lives. "When we come to a minefield," Zhukov would tell Eisenhower later in the war, "our infantry attacks exactly as if it were not there. The losses we get from personnel mines we consider equal to those we would have gotten from machine guns and artillery if the Germans had chosen to defend that particular area with strong bodies of troops instead of with mine fields."[51] Some divisions, including those that fought near Mogilev, were so broken that they were forced to withdraw and regroup in late July.[52] But Belorussia had been almost cleared of German troops.

Most of the men in this great storm had little time to write. An exception was Ermolenko. His diary notes were typically brief, but they were true to the Communist idiom that he now espoused. "At last we have started to attack on our part of the front," he wrote on 22 June. The Soviet air force—supported, now, by a fleet of American planes based in Ukraine—had been bombing the German lines for two weeks.

Machine gunners of the Second Baltic Front fording a river, 1944

In the skies above the Pripet Marshes, the red star now enjoyed the absolute dominion that the swastika had exercised exactly three years earlier. But on the ground, the men waited for orders of their own. The drive on Minsk, the central campaign of Bagration, began in a barrage of artillery fire. "At 16:00 hundreds of weapons opened fire with hurricane force," Ermolenko went on. "Thousands of tons of murderous metal flew over the German positions." Within two hours, "the German positions were hidden by a veritable wall of smoke and dust." The enemy was so far away that this smoke was the only clue to the locations of the dugouts, trenches, and the lines of guns. Those guns now began firing in their turn, and the entire front was swallowed up in a hot yellow fog. The casualties would be enormous. But the shaking earth and smell of flame felt like the Red Army's reply—long overdue—to the insult of 1941. "Everyone's mood," Ermolenko noted, "immediately lifted." German intelligence reports that month confirmed his observation.[53] In contrast to some of the defensive operations of the previous three years, this was a campaign that made Soviet soldiers glad.

In Belorussia, the army's swift progress was helped by the coordinated work of partisans. Nikolai Moskvin, however, was nursing a neck wound that would plague him for the rest of his life. His war was coming to an end, though it would have an awe-inspiring finale. Camped in the woods near Mogilev, the *politruk* had seen no Soviet troops in combat since 1941. Now he could hear the pounding of the heavy guns and see the red stars on the swooping planes. Everything was new, everything spectacular. The Red Army of his memory, defeated and shamed, had been transformed into a technological marvel. To witness it, after so long, was electrifying. "And now," he scribbled on 4 July, "we are in the Soviet rear! The Red Army passed by like a typhoon. The enemy has scuttled off in disarray. Four days ago we were on occupied territory, and today the front is two hundred kilometers away from us." The pace of it all, after such a long wait, was breathtaking. "Even the Germans did not manage this in 1941."[54]

The chance of action on this scale was one thing that helped the soldiers to fight. It was better to get out and kill some Fritzes than to sit around burning off lice. The men longed for an opportunity to do the job, to put away the books and boot polish and get on with it. But officials ascribed the success of the troops to talk and comradeship. For weeks before the great assault, the political officers were detailed to discuss aspects of it in small groups with soldiers of every rank. They also listened to the men, hearing out their worries about home and their growing concerns for the future. The success of these conversations depended on the individuals, both soldier and *politruk*. Sometimes the whole thing was an insult or a waste of time. But that was less true of the pep talks that experienced veterans gave to the new recruits. "These personal talks," Chuikov insisted, "meant a great deal."[55] More tangibly, the men were offered cash and even leave incentives to take German prisoners or shoot down planes. The prices varied, but a German plane could be worth a week's pay, while the capture of a German officer at the front might (in theory) promise a man an extra two weeks' leave.[56] Even a rumor of reward could be inspiring, the prospect of some extra cash more enticing than chatting with the *politruk*.

The Germans themselves came as a surprise. By now, large numbers of Wehrmacht soldiers were laying down their guns. One of the largest groups included the survivors of July's Soviet encirclement of Minsk and Bobruisk. Almost half the area's Fascist defenders, some forty thousand troops, were killed. Their bodies lay in the streets and ditches like fallen apples, split and rotting. But that left fifty-seven thousand men, including several senior officers. Their captors, the Soviets, had learned how to keep prisoners alive since Stalingrad, but there was no prospect of comfort. Most prisoners were taken to interrogation camps— abandoned German ones often served very well—before they were deployed to the forced labor projects that were springing up across the Soviet Union.[57] But the men from Minsk were treated differently. They were herded into trains as usual—those NKVD wagons worked without a break that summer—but then they were transported straight to Moscow. A unique demonstration had been organized.

Stalin wanted the world to know that there were still real enemies along the eastern front, that D-Day had not eased the pressure on his men. Fifty thousand captured soldiers from a single battle were brought on to make the point. The prisoners, like captives in some ancient Roman triumph, were paraded beneath the Kremlin walls. They marched briskly, sometimes twenty abreast, but still it took three hours for the entire host to cross. "Some were smiling," *Pravda*'s correspondent told readers. They were glad to be alive, and possibly, like tourists, glad to see Russia's historic heart—or so the patriots assumed. But the audience could not fail to conclude that Germany was broken, Russia the victorious power.[58] Prompted by the political officers, whose lectures now included information about Germany's manpower crisis and its mobilization of teenagers and the sick, Red Army soldiers had begun to notice that their prisoners were not storm troopers anymore. Many were semi-invalids, malnourished and covered in sores. Some were teenagers, others weary shopkeepers or clerks. "They all looked pitiful," Ermolenko wrote in late June when he had prisoners of his own. "They are like bank clerks. Many of them wear glasses. This, no doubt, is the result of total mobilization in Germany."[59]

Like Ermolenko, most soldiers concluded that the Germans were as good as defeated. The moment of triumph was intense, heartbreaking, and bittersweet. The threat to the motherland was past. Even the territories that the enemy had occupied lay open for the Soviets to take. Like most Ukrainians, Ermolenko had never seen the villages of Belarus. "Most people speak the Belorussian language," he wrote in some surprise. The evidence of German destruction was everywhere, from ruined buildings to fresh-turned mass graves. Whatever joy the men felt at their victory, it would always be colored by their rage, their hatred of the invaders. But other feelings now surfaced as well. Ermolenko was convinced that the local people welcomed him. Their red flags fluttered from the ruined buildings in his path. "The girls in the villages are very pretty," the soldier decided. "Many of them dress in national costume. I should come here after the war and marry one of them."[60]

Away to the south, another soldier, the tank officer Aleksandr Slesarev, was also falling for a new country. "I am writing to let you know that I am alive and well," he wrote to his father. "I have not written to anyone for some time," he explained, "because I have been on the road for ages. We traveled day and night. For four whole days and nights we did not sleep. This summer I have been in a lot of places."[61] His favorite was western Ukraine, with all its little hills and orchards. "The nature there is wonderful, there are pretty towns and villages, abundant gardens, lots of sweet and sour cherries." In contrast with the cheerless winter steppe, the gardens around ruined Lvov, ablaze with lupins, marigolds, and roses, must have looked like a glimpse of Eden.

The problem was that these places were hardly Soviet lands. It was one thing to retake a Russian city like Orel or even a loyal provincial capital like Kharkov, but as the Red Army moved west it crossed into the territories that Stalin had annexed after 1939. Ermolenko might not have looked beyond the anxious smiles of the young women in the streets, but many villagers in western Belarus were mistrustful of their supposed liberators. To them, all that had occurred was the exchange of one imperial master for another. What's more, they knew already that the red flag was a harbinger of fear. Their farmsteads bore the recent scars of forced collectivization and the accompanying mass arrests. It was worse in western Ukraine. Lvov, the capital of Ukrainian nationalism, would never accept the authority of Moscow. The nationalists' prewar message, that supranational empires were bent on crushing Ukraine's noble culture, seemed proven by events of recent years. Lvov had seen violence on violence: the Soviets, the Wehrmacht, bandits, SS murder squads, and partisans. What mattered to the locals now was to avoid enslavement. They knew how Stalin treated nations that defied his rule.

The same story would be repeated later in the Baltic, where the Red Army symbolized all that was hated about Bolshevik dominion. At least, the fearful locals muttered, the Nazis had brought order, driven out the Reds. For that, many had welcomed them, and even applauded their racist, anti-internationalist, anti-Slav, and anti-Jewish policies. No one could forget the arrests and deportations of 1939, the swelling prisons and the echoing of shots. Significant numbers of Estonians, Lithuanians, and Latvians had helped the Germans, including the murder squads, because that seemed the way to build a decent, ordered, European life. Now they would have to watch in helpless apprehension as the war unfolded. Perhaps, just possibly, the Americans would reach the Baltic first. That was the dream in Tallinn and in Vilnius that summer. It was the gall within the Soviet triumph, the seed of greater bitterness to come. As they swept north and west, Soviet men and women, Russians and soldiers from farther east, would face successive populations who were either hostile to them or at best suspicious of their entire way of life.

★

Stalin had prepared the army for its new task earlier that year. His speech on 1 May 1944 had confirmed that German Fascist troops had been driven out of three-quarters of the Soviet territory that they had occupied. "But our tasks cannot end with the clearing of enemy troops from within the bounds of our motherland," he announced. "The German troops today are reminiscent of a wounded beast, which has to creep away to the border of its own lair, Germany, to lick its wounds. But a wounded beast that goes off to its lair does not stop being a dangerous beast. If we are to deliver our country and those of our allies from the danger of enslavement, we must pursue the wounded German beast and deliver the final blow to him in his own lair."[62] The Russian word for the beast's lair was *berlog*, and from this time some Soviet troops renamed Berlin accordingly. The slogan "To Berlog!" was written in red paint on the sides of many travel-worn T–34s. German intelligence reported that komsomols and officers especially were eager for the new challenge.[63]

The front-line press worked hard to convince soldiers that any westward advance would be an adventure. It was also sold as justifiable revenge. As soon as the first detachments crossed the border, newspapers started featuring pictures of tank men and gunners planting red flags on the foreign soil.[64] But all the propaganda was not idle. There was real resistance to be overcome. The truth was that not all Russian soldiers, and far from all recruits from other Soviet lands, were keen to step across the international border.[65] A young man like Slesarev could revel in the tourist aspect of his job because he was heart-free. But older men—the fathers and husbands, and the tired ones, the injured in body and mind—believed that their job would be completed when the last Fascist was driven from Soviet soil. They had no desire to fight on beyond that point. The rest of the world, which had left Russia on its own so long, could sort out Europe for itself. Behind that view lay fear, and not merely the fear of death. No one knew, among the mass of Russian troops, just what capitalism was, for none had seen it. For thirty years they had been told that it was dangerous, a monster (*Pravda*'s cartoon-ists were inventive) poised to undermine the workers' happiness. To cross the border would be little stranger than to step onto the moon.

Such misgivings were common among peasant soldiers from Russia and the countries to the east. But the greatest resentment was expressed by a group new to army life, ironically one whose knowledge of the cap-italist world came at first hand. Survivors of the darkest times, these re-cruits from the newly liberated zones, from western Ukraine and the western provinces of Belorussia—now found themselves swept into the Red Army and forced to take the Soviet oath. Large numbers of the new soldiers had been reared in nationalist traditions that were antipathetic to the Soviet, internationalist, cause.[66] Few felt any allegiance to Moscow. Many had to be drafted forcibly, even at gunpoint.[67] Others were pushed into the ranks when NKVD troops threatened reprisals on their families.[68] The conscripts knew that many of their Russian com-rades regarded the fact that they had survived Nazi rule as evidence of guilt, a dark stain to be washed away with their own blood.[69] Now they faced an indeterminate period of service in what, effectively, was a for-eign army. "They are treated as second-class soldiers," German intelli-gence reported. "They are branded '*zapadniki*' (westerners) and treated like prisoners, with mistrust."[70]

The first Soviet troops to cross into the capitalist world did so in the spring of 1944. Their journey to Romania began in the southwestern provinces of Ukraine. The crack troops in the advance guard were sea-soned professionals, but the reserves that followed to augment their ranks looked like a caravan of refugees. Few had received the correct papers, let alone a training, political or military. They did not march into Romania. Some sauntered, others limped along. In some units, up to 90 percent of the soldiers had no shoes, let alone the standard boots. In one group, fifteen had little but their shirts and underclothes. Their discipline was weak when they arrived. Indeed, large numbers of them never did arrive, since it was so easy to slip away.[71] Those who remained resented their exposure to danger, the fact that they were being sent to the front "so soon before the end of the war."[72] But they could at least hope for some compensation: loot was the ultimate reward for hard-ship, a temptation that many could not resist.[73] It had been little more than weeks since their own country had been recaptured by Moscow's troops. Now they were encamped in another one, but this time they were the occupiers.

Romania was not Prussia. This first incursion onto foreign soil was not an orgy of revenge. The shock to both sides was also mitigated by the fact that most Red Army troops were billeted in underpopulated country. Bucharest, with all its glittering temptations, was still several months of campaigning away. Meanwhile, there was a relaxed, almost blasé attitude toward ideology among the troops. The political officers had almost given up working on their Soviet consciousness.[74] The Sovinformburo urged that more be done to publicize Romanian atrocities, to instill hatred, but no one seemed inclined to work at this. Indeed, some units would not hear a lecture about ideology for months. Soldiers were either fighting—and the enemy, backed up at first by German officers, could be cruel—or they were encamped in the rear, where the danger of war seemed almost like a dream. In some areas, Romanian soldiers laid their weapons down and begged the Soviets not to shoot.[75] The only casualties in the 251st Rifle Regiment that May were victims of carelessness and horseplay in their own encampment.[76] It was in this context that some of the former victims of German rule in Ukraine would test the skills that they had learned from the Aryan supermen.

Moldavian wine would play its part. A group of Soviet engineers made themselves rapidly at home during their mission to rebuild the regions' roads and bridges. One officer was drunk for ten entire days. The alcohol removed whatever sexual inhibitions any of the men retained. As they watched officers leading their neighbors off at gunpoint, local women would soon learn to hide. Two sergeants who raided a village near their camp in search of women discovered that every hoped-for prostitute had fled. Their revenge was to shoot a local woman and her daughter and to try to rape their victims' neighbor. A particularly calculating soldier posed as an intelligence agent and demanded that the women in his district present themselves for inspection. The one he chose and raped was later found buried in a trench with a Soviet bullet through her skull. Checks were carried out one night in May in the town of Botoshani; one hundred soldiers, mainly officers, were found in bed with local women.[77] Thefts and extortion from civilians were daily occurrences, but there were also systematic schemes. One group of entrepreneurs ordered the villagers near their posting to bring them two hundred sheep. When these were delivered, they demanded another two hundred for the next morning.[78] No doubt, as any officer would do, they had already made sure of the transport and the market for their meat.

This kind of story caused alarm among political commissars. That June, a special resolution on the state of political education among the troops in Romania was passed in Moscow. The *politruks* were told to get their textbooks out.[79] The example of the Second Ukrainian Front in Romania was also used as a warning to others. Far to the north, near the Lithuanian city of Kaunas, Ermolenko heard a lecture about the Romanian "excesses" that August. "The Red Army is a just army," he wrote afterwards. "We are not robbers or marauders. Of course, if we meet armed resistance we will destroy it. But we will not allow illegal robbery and murder." The trouble was that it was just a few days since he and "the boys" had "gone for trophies" themselves.[80] Their orders seemed to be confused. The world around these men was already violated, wrecked; everyone had lost the things they treasured. Sometimes, the men received direct orders to live off the land. Property rights, which Soviet citizens always found perplexing, had little meaning in shattered, even deserted territory. And then there was the desire for revenge, to say nothing of the soldiers' simple, obvious material needs. The *politruks* could preach, but even they were unclear of the rules. And every day, the trucks would rattle past with crates of booty for staff officers at home.

In all, the late summer of 1944 was a disorienting, anxious time. The liberating army, the vanguard who had fought to free the soldiers' mothers and wives, was evolving into a rabble. New sorts of men were taking the places of the dead, but that was not the only change. Even the veterans, the heroes of Kursk and Orel, were facing unimagined challenges, temptations they could not resist. Exhausted men, freshly bereaved again by battle, surveyed the border through a web of emotion. This was epiphany, and there would be no going back. It was far better, as Lev Kopelev would learn, to turn a blind eye to some kinds of disorder and just get on with life. "I was saturated with French cognac," he remembered, and "my shoulder-bag was stuffed with Havana cigars. . . . They made you dizzy at first; then you got used to it. The constant inebriation from the cognacs, schnapps and liqueurs, and the biting smoke of those powerful cigars, seemed to steady us against the nastiness of what was going on all around."[81]

Though each would find the border at a different time, no one can forget what he felt. Every veteran has a tale to tell. "We wept when we saw the houses," one man told me. "Such pretty houses, small, and all of them painted white." A former peasant, Ivan Vasilevich, now living in Moscow province, remembered how he took a fancy to the cattle. The farm where he was billeted that summer was empty. The owners had fled, as thousands had, when they heard the first Soviet guns. The corn could take care of itself, but no one had attended to the cows for days. Ivan Vasilevich admired them, touched them, felt the solid flesh. More urgently, he set about milking them. Their lowing was the sound that he would remember most vividly from those first days.

Ivan Vasilevich would milk many other cows before the peace, and he would feed them, too. "The animals were hungry," he remembered. "There was a haystack nearby. So I fed the animals straightaway. They had to eat. And then I thought I'd leave their barn open. They could feed themselves when we had gone." The private farms were fascinating to this child of a collective, used to Communist neglect. "It was interesting to compare them," he began. "I mean, because I was brought up in this same thing, in agriculture." He stumbled, trying not to say something. Like thousands of others, he had discovered a truth that raised doubts about the entire war, about the revolution, and about the Soviet dream.[82] So far, the dawning understanding was still dim, uncertain. But it could never be forgotten. "The word for it is rich," he said. "The capitalist farms were richer."[83]

★

Soldiers had various ways of dealing with the real face of capitalism. Some were envious, some intrigued. Later, when they entered Germany, their main reaction would be rage. No one could understand why wealthy Germans had wanted to invade their neighbors to the east, why anyone who had this much would ever fight for more. "I'd just love to smash my fist into all those tins and bottles," was one soldier's response.[84] Wherever they went in Europe, Red Army men were repelled as well as fascinated by the *burzhui*, the bourgeoisie, with their ordered lives and strange views about property. But that summer, the *burzhui* that the armies in the south were meeting were Romanians—former enemies but scarcely storm troopers or millionaires. The sight of the better lives that these *burzhui* led inspired resentment and even anti-Soviet talk among the men. If Communism was so good, they argued, why did these peasants live so much better?[85] Instead of putting Romanian farms to the torch, the soldiers satisfied themselves with looting them.

The shock of relative plenty would be the same in Poland, except that there was less in that blighted countryside left to take. But as they crossed its sandy plains and pinewoods, Soviet troops were forced to confront a new, equally painful issue, a fresh betrayal of cherished belief. Internationalism had disappeared from Stalin's rhetoric when war broke out, but the myth that Soviet troops were on a liberating, fraternal, mission was revived as they crossed the border. In theory, Poles were supposed to see themselves as beneficiaries of Soviet power. As victims of Fascist aggression, their people awaited liberation. That, indeed, had been the original motive for the Allied declaration of war in September 1939. Back then, however, the Soviet Union had been Hitler's ally, and Poland had been dismembered by both dictatorships at once. Now that the Red Army was fighting beside the democracies of Europe and the United States, its arrival in Poland was supposed to be a cause for celebration. Fascist occupation, after all, had truly been a nightmare. But ethnic Poles had good reason to wonder what they might expect from Stalin's cynical embrace. There is a joke that some Poles still relate about a small bird that falls from the sky into a cowpat. A passing cat is kind enough to rescue it. "The moral," a Polish friend explained, "is that not everyone who gets you out of the shit is necessarily your friend." The cat, naturally, eats the bird.

In the short term, some Poles were willing to fight beside Red Army troops. The first Polish army on Soviet soil was formed in April 1943. Poles broke open the route to Lublin for Chuikov's Eighth Guards Army in July 1944, and they would go on fighting with these men until the fall of Berlin ten months later.[86] But Stalin's sympathies were never with the Polish nation, and most Polish soldiers knew it. They would complain that their uniforms and gear were substandard, that they were not issued with warm clothes as winter approached, and that they were given the most dangerous military tasks.[87] Their morale would plummet most of all when they heard news of the fate of their fellow countrymen in Warsaw.

In August 1944, encouraged by the prospect of liberation, Warsaw's nationalist underground staged an uprising of Polish citizens. Its aim was to destroy the German garrison. With Rokossovsky's troops camped nearby on the Vistula, the chances for concerted action appeared bright. But the Warsaw rising failed. The Polish capital's entire population paid in blood. As thousands of its citizens were slaughtered, Hitler ordered that the entire city should be razed. What most outraged the Polish troops was that the Soviets made no effort to intervene. Rokossovsky's men were probably in no condition to relieve Warsaw in August 1944, and it would have been difficult for Stalin to find fresh reserves.[88] The momentum of Operation Bagration had been used up in the great strike at Minsk. But the destruction of Polish nationalists in Warsaw suited Stalin's long-term goals. The tragedy, like the 1940 Katyn massacre, would poison Russo-Polish relations for decades.

In answer—or at least by way of self-justification—the Soviets would claim that they were fighting for a cause that transcended national interests. Internationalism had been downplayed since the war began—Russian troops themselves had found it redundant when they met their putative German brothers at the front in 1941—but the idea that the Soviet Union was a unique, pioneering, supranational state was never abandoned. Former Red Army troops and partisans still claim that their identity was "Soviet," a way of getting over the awkward divisions between the ethnic Russians at the front and all the rest. The Poles, like the *zapadniki*, could simply join the brotherhood. That way their future in the Soviet system, as opposed to under Fascist tyranny, was guaranteed.

This neat answer would never fit the facts. For one thing, Stalin himself had embarked on a campaign of ethnic cleansing. By the summer of 1944, the Gulag and the Central Asian labor camps were overflowing with Volga Germans, Chechens, Tatars, Kalmyks, and other so-called punished groups. Ukrainians and Poles began to join them in the last year of the war. Ethnicity had replaced economic or class status as a pretext for wholesale arrest.[89] Soviet rhetoric did not work among the people, either. Russians might claim that there were no distinctions between ethnic groups in uniform, but they were always, at every point, in the majority. "We were all the same" is an imperialist thought, dismissing the claims and perspectives of subaltern peoples. Large numbers—millions—of Poles, Ukrainians, Georgians, Jews, Kazakhs, and all the rest fought beside Russians, some of them explicitly for Soviet power, but minority groups were neither identical nor invisible within the army. There was even a slang, and usually derogatory, word to describe them. *Natsmen*, an ugly term formed from the Russian words for "ethnic minority," encompassed, amalgamated, and dismissed individuals whose homes might have been anywhere from Odessa and Tallinn to Ulan Bator.

Ironically, it was the Jews who seemed most readily at ease with the internationalist dream. The Soviet state, officially, deplored and punished antisemitism. In this respect, it marked an advance over tsarism and a stark contrast with the Third Reich. Its internationalist rhetoric, like its appeal to science and to the superiority of urban values, also attracted a people whose history had fixed them mainly in the towns. In 1941, Jews signed up in the thousands for the Soviet cause. Students from Moscow set their books aside, young Communists in government roles asked to be assigned to the front. Jews were among the keenest volunteers for every kind of army service. Not all the volunteers were Soviet-born. Refugees streamed east from Poland and from western Ukraine in the spring of 1941, finding their way into the Red Army by summer. As they would learn when their families perished in the old homelands, their loyalty to Stalin's cause was justified.

The Red Army itself boasted a set of regulations about antisemitism, including a stipulation that the insulting *zhid* (Yid) should not be used in reference to Jews. Soldiers were liable to punishment if they made antisemitic remarks or used offensive, racist language. Idealistic communists (many of whom were in fact Jews) believed that Soviets had truly overcome the hatreds of the tsarist past. But it would only have been in a burst of passionate idealism that a Jew could have seen the

Red Army as a benign environment. Official rhetoric was scrupulous, but among themselves the soldiers—and even many officers—were liberal with their racist gibes. The authorities' response, too, was generally feeble. The NKVD kept a record of the cases that it heard, together with the penalties imposed. A thirty-one-year-old got five days in the guardhouse for telling a Jewish comrade that "my father despised Yids, I despise them, and my children are going to despise them too."[90] Another soldier was expelled from the komsomol for spitting "What are you talking about, Jew face?" at another rifleman. It was better than Fascism, but there was a long way still to go.

The jokes, that humor that the NKVD controlled so closely, were worse. According to the vulgar story, Jews in the army had pulled off their usual trick. In other words, they had managed to dodge the front line and secure the safer office jobs. When tens of thousands fled their homes in the first months of war, they were christened "Tashkent partisans" after the city where so many had found refuge. "They have formed a battalion by themselves," a joke went among Russian troops, "and conquered Tashkent and Alma-Ata."[91] "The soul of a Jew is always at the front line," went another, "but his body stays behind the Urals." The context was contemporary, but the basic stereotypes were primeval. Jews were even said to favor crooked rifles. (The idea was that these shot around corners.)

Other rumors played on ancient themes of Passover blood sacrifice and cabalistic magic. Jewish doctors were accused of declaring wounded Russians fit for active service before they could even stand.[92] An anecdote from 1944 played on the theory of an international Zionist conspiracy. Rifleman Abram Abramovich keeps coming back from battle with trophies: a German gun, German maps, even the colors of a German regiment. When he is decorated for his deeds, someone asks him how he managed to do so much. "Ach," he replies, "I have a friend on the German side, Mark Markovich, and he brings me the German stuff and I take Red Army trophies around to him."[93] The story may have made some soldiers laugh, but if they had paused to look at their German enemies, they would have noticed that there were no Mark Markoviches left.

The persecution of Jews was the one Fascist atrocity consistently ignored by Soviet publicity. The core of the problem, from 1944, was an imagined hierarchy of suffering. This was a war in which Russia saw itself as the most important victim. It had been invaded, its land violated. It had stood alone while Europe slept; its people had bled themselves white in the defense of Stalingrad. The Soviet Union waged this war, but more Russians served in the Red Army than any other ethnic group, and soldiers frequently—and in their view, generously—overlooked distinctions among their comrades, calling them all "Russian" in their hearts.[94] Russian soldiers were also the largest single group among the multitude who starved and died as German prisoners of war, and Russian civilians suffered unimaginably in the years of invasion and struggle.[95] In almost any reckoning there could be no comparison between the price that Russia and the other Soviet peoples paid for war and that paid by their allies. But victimhood, at home as well as on the diplomatic stage, was a kind of capital. Internationally, it permitted the aggrieved party to claim substantial reparation, to say nothing of allowing a certain moral leverage. At home, it raised a storm of patriotism that was Soviet in name but generally Russian in nature. The epicenter of it all (his Georgian nationality notwithstanding) was Stalin himself. While the people had suffered, Stalin had labored and bled with them. He was identified with every moment of their pain.

The details were genuinely appalling. More than three million Soviet (principally Russian) prisoners of war were killed in Nazi camps, many as a result of direct acts of brutal—and illegal—violence. Even a German witness, a soldier writing about the Wehrmacht's successes in 1942, was surprised at the actions of his own regime. His prisoners, who were entitled to food and shelter (and even, arguably, to Red Cross parcels), had been reduced by fear and hunger to such a state that, as he wrote, "they whined and groveled before us. They were human beings in whom there was no longer a trace of anything human." Perhaps that judgment helped their captors to torture the men. The German guards amused themselves by throwing a dead dog into the prisoners' compound. "Yelling like mad," the witness wrote, "the Russians would fall on the animal and tear it to pieces with their bare hands. . . . The intestines they'd stuff in their pockets—a sort of iron ration." The very few who did not perish in these camps remember the terror, the humiliation, and the dark stories of *lyudoedstvo*, the dismemberment and eating of corpses.[96] No other army suffered on this scale, not even in Asia.

Civilians, too, would endure every kind of violence. From the first days of the invasion, in 1941, the Wehrmacht declared war on partisans. In reality, bystanders were shot or hanged alongside real guerrillas. Then came the requisitioning of food and other property. The famine that resulted was so desperate in some regions that local people would turn up at German camps "and ask for relief or beg to be shot."[97] Hardship resulted in epidemics among the civilian population of the occupied zones, the most serious of which, in 1943, was typhus. Nearly 7.5 million Soviet civilians are thought to have been killed under the Nazi occupation, the greatest numbers in Ukraine (3.2 million), Russia (1.8 million), and Belorussia (1.5 million).[98] But other victims did not even remain in their homes. The other major impact of Nazi control was the enslavement of civilians for forced labor. At least three million men and women (one famous Russian source gives a figure of over five million) were shipped off to the Reich to work as slaves. Many of these— probably more than two million—were worked so hard that they joined Europe's Jews in the death camps, discarded by the Reich for disposal like worn-out nags sent to the abattoir.[99]

Russia's long torment, then, was real, and like most cases of persecution it created in the sufferers a sense of outrage, of entitlement, of solidarity. No one had borne the weight of war more patiently, no one had fought or endured more. That was the story, and it became a political refrain. But Russia's access of outrage—and Stalin's preeminence within it—could not have been sustained if two specific truths had been considered. First, the group that faced the Nazis' most concentrated violence, a cruelty unparalleled even in this most vicious war, was not the Russian people but the Jews. Second, Soviet citizens in the occupied zones, including thousands of Ukrainians and Balts, had not only colluded in the genocide but welcomed and abetted it.

It was the army that made all the discoveries, soldiers who knew the most about the real fate of Jews. The first evidence of the mass killings was unearthed near Kerch in 1941, when Soviet troops began their abortive attempt to retake the Crimea.[100] Not until the great march west beginning in 1943, though, did the full picture began to take shape. A harrowing story emerged from Krasnodar, where seven thousand Jews had been gassed in an experiment involving special sealed wagons (the

Russian POW with his prisoner number (courtesy of the State Archive of the Russian Federation)

NKVD had already mastered a version of this technology in 1937, but it was a shock to see it used by someone else). When the mass grave was found, a group of corpses were ceremonially exhumed, dressed in fresh linen (as befits a Russian corpse), and buried with full honors before weeping crowds.[101]

The secret of Babi Yar, the ravine near Kiev that held the bodies of at least a hundred thousand Jews by the end of 1943, was printed in the Soviet press in tones of justifiable outrage. But it had been a real challenge for the Sovinformburo. Those Jewish corpses, gasoline-soaked and stained with ash, raised specters that Moscow could not confront. The Holocaust, as one account puts it, was "an indigestible lump in the belly of the Soviet triumph."[102] Moscow could never approve of the mass killing of Jews, but neither was it eager to accord them a special place in the myth of the war. For Russia to do so would have meant sharing its victimhood; its Communist leadership would also, by implication, have been forced to countenance the idea of a special closeness between Jews and Bolsheviks, a notion that Stalin had done his best to extirpate (not least by arresting Jewish comrades) for years. Those bodies, like those of Polish officers in the woods near Smolensk, threatened to pollute the fragile ecologies of Soviet righteousness and Russian certitude.

Equally dangerous was the fact that some Ukrainian nationalists had welcomed the genocide. The drive for ethnic purity that beset Central Europe in the 1930s and 1940s was not confined to Germany, and nor was loathing of the Bolsheviks. During the German occupation, the head of the wartime Ukrainian government himself had delivered the view, in 1941, that "Jews help Moscow to consolidate its hold on Ukraine. Therefore I am of the opinion that the Jews should be exterminated and [see] the expediency of carrying out in Ukraine the German methods for exterminating the Jews."[103] Sturdy, peasant-farming Ukrainians were encouraged to loathe all "Jewish-Muscovite proletarians." Some responded by joining the murder squads.[104] But to acknowledge all this now would be to shatter the brittle framework of Soviet brotherhood. It would certainly jeopardize Moscow's relations with the bulk of the Ukrainian population, including those who were currently fighting in its name across the western front.

The answer was to edit every report from the killing fields. Stories of genocide were presented as parts of a larger and appalling whole. Special care was taken to ensure that the burdens Russians had borne were emphasized. While the investigators were preparing the first report on the first death camp that the army discovered, readers of *Pravda* learned about a place in Ukraine where Red Army prisoners had starved, and even about a camp where Russians had been infected deliberately with typhus and allowed to die.[105] The policy of censorship was helped by the fact that the truth, as it emerged, was so horrific that it tended to overwhelm the imagination. When Alexander Werth filed his first report from a Nazi extermination camp, "The Death Factory," for the BBC, the corporation would not broadcast it. The story was so terrible, its directors argued, that it could only be another Soviet propaganda stunt.[106]

The truth began to surface in the summer of 1944. Lublin lies just beyond the Polish-Soviet border. When the Red Army freed it in July, they found a town scarred by the occupation and bombardment. Despite the damage, it remained the attractive mass of churches and whitewashed houses that it had been for centuries. Its secret, like a cold shadow, lay just two miles away. Maidanek was the first extermination camp that any army would discover. It was a vast and tightly organized facility, a group of prisons, gas chambers, and chimneys that covered twenty-five square kilometers. One and a half million people had been murdered there. The smell of corpses and of burning flesh forced Lubliners to shut their windows. They could not breathe, and even with the windows shut they could not sleep. The scale of the atrocity shocked every witness at the time.

Maidanek foreshadowed the genocide before the discoveries of Auschwitz and Bergen-Belsen. There was the forlorn little road, the barbed wire fence, the watchtowers. An entrance gateway arched above the track, and looming in the mist beyond were barrack huts and sinister-looking chimneys. There was a gallows, sturdily built and square, in every yard. There were concrete shower blocks, the units labeled "bath and disinfection." These were the chambers into which thousands of frightened, naked human beings had been herded, roughly, half guessing their fate. As he toured them, Werth found himself reflecting on those last moments, imagining the blue crystals of Zyklon tumbling through a ceiling grille and gently steaming into life. He was standing where the SS guards had stood, observing the room as they had observed it. Averting his gaze for a moment, he looked down at the concrete yard. At his feet was a blue mark, a scribble still intelligible as the word *vergast*. A skull and crossbones had been scrawled beside it. "I had never seen this word before," he wrote, "but it obviously meant 'gassed'—and not merely 'gassed,' but with that elegant little prefix *ver*, 'gassed out.' That's this job finished, and now for the next lot."[107]

Werth claims that *Pravda* covered everything, but this is not quite true. The reporting was vivid and its impact must have been immense, but Jews were not presented as the main victims. Conveniently, perhaps, Maidanek was a genuinely mixed-race camp, and its victims included large numbers of Europeans, Russians, and Poles as well as ethnic Jews. That catholicity made it easier to describe in the press. By contrast, the existence of the camp at Oświęcim (Auschwitz) was not reported to the Soviet public until 7 May 1945, just hours before the victory, although the Red Army had found it (and counted out each set of clothes, over a million of them) that January.

It is an open question what the soldiers thought about it all. At Maidanek, they were ordered to make a tour of the whole camp. At Auschwitz, too, they saw each horror for themselves. The images of atrocity helped to reinforce their hatred of Hitler, to make them pitiless and brave. So did the sight of Klooga, outside Tallinn, where murdered Jews had been piled among great pyres of logs, soaked in gasoline, and torched like stacks of kindling.[108] The pictures of the charred remains show Red Army troops standing in the snow nearby, viewing the ghastly shapes while plainclothes officials catalog them for history. But what these soldiers later read was not the same as what they knew. *Pravda* helped to form an alternative set of memories, to cover images so terrible that they could neither be considered nor forgotten. In place of the appalling reality of the Final Solution, the paper offered a simpler lesson to its readers: Soviet rage was justified; Russian revenge was just.

That lesson partly explains the violence that followed. The things that Fascists did, in soldiers' minds, had long been distinguished from anything that "we"—they—might ever do. Soviet propaganda had debased

Bonfire of logs and corpses photographed as evidence of German war crimes, Klooga, Estonia (courtesy of the State Archive of the Russian Federation)

the enemy to such an extent that he was scarcely human. There could be no comparison with "us." Meanwhile, the Russian people's victim status called for revenge and reparation. Within a few months, atrocities in East Prussia—Soviet killings, rapes, and thefts—would be perpetrated under the concealing cover of a double standard. The same inconsistency applied to the treatment of "our" Jews. When a Russian muttered that the Jews were better dead, it was not quite the same as when a Fascist did it. In 1944, the NKVD heard men muttering that "Hitler did a good job, beating up the Jews."[109]

The army, or rather some of its invalid veterans, brought its rough prejudices back to share with Soviet civilians. The stories were predictable enough. Jews did not fight, they said, but sat around in warm offices or anywhere that money might be found lying about. Then came the jokes, the judgments, the resentment. In the early summer of 1943, members of the editorial board of the army newspaper, *Red Star*, even discussed the need to find and publish some stories of Jews who were Heroes of the Soviet Union or front-line generals. Something needed to be done to avert racial violence. "There is a real agitation for pogrom," one of them wrote that May.[110] The predicted lynching followed years later. Kiev's pogrom of 1945 began after a fight between two drunken Ukrainians and a Jewish NKVD agent. The agent shot his assailants, whose funeral became the spark for anti-Jewish riots.[111] But postwar Russia, very soon, would target Jews with all the power of the state. From 1948, they were the objects of new arrests, denunciations, and public humiliation. They lost their jobs, they lost esteem, their children were denied the education that had been their right. Finally, Jews were the intended victims of the last great purge of Stalin's life.[112]

When I collected testimonies for this book, I found that Jews were disproportionately represented among the veterans who talked. This was not accidental, and nor was it some prejudice of mine. One reason is that veterans still believe that they should keep Soviet secrets. The state whose rules they promised to honor has gone, but many hold to it because it is the only stable entity in their political imagination. For Jews, so many of whom were marginalized in the postwar world, it may be easier than it is for ethnic Russians to see these old rules as absurd. Then there are questions of allegiance, for Jews suffered when Communism fell, and few have reason to welcome the new and chauvinistic Russian state. So it is easier for them to talk. The stories that I heard were vivid, terrible, humorous, and often sad. But they were never tales of office staff. Jews were indeed among the most determined combatants on every Soviet front. They had a great deal to avenge. Beyond that, members of this special generation tended to be loyal to the internationalist cause, to the utopian dream of communism, to just war, revolution, and new forms of brotherhood. Nemanov fought near Stalingrad and onward toward Kursk, Kirill survived the siege of Leningrad and led his men through Prussia. They both took part in some of the most dangerous operations of the war.

I remember a morning spent with another Jewish combatant. Boris Grigorevich was born in Kiev. His parents were both Jews, though he identified himself as Soviet. "Was there racism?" he repeated, smiling at my question. "Of course not. We were all Soviet citizens, all the same." His best friend, as he explained, was a Mingrelian from the Caucasus. "We were like brothers," he told me. The friend had died, but "I am still part of his family, they treat me like a son." That was not his last word on the subject, however. I asked him what his fears had been during the long nights before battle. "I was afraid of being thought a coward," he answered. "I knew that I was a Jew, and so I had to prove that I was not afraid." It would be years before he knew for certain that his father had been killed at Babi Yar.

NINE

DESPOIL THE CORPSE

★

The Red Army took more than three and a half years, from that first night in June 1941, to make good its threat to carry the war onto the Fascists' own soil. Stalin had argued for a drive against Berlin at the end of 1944, but the momentum of Bagration was exhausted by October. The troops involved spent the last months of that autumn in Polish villages or camped among the foothills of the Carpathian Mountains. As they drank to the new year, the armies that made up Zhukov's First Belorussian Front had yet to take Warsaw, or at least what was left of it. The Second and Third Belorussian Fronts, led respectively by Konstantin Rokossovsky, the charismatic hero of Kursk, and the brilliant thirty-eight-year-old Ivan Chernyakovsky, had still to close the ring around the Baltic citadel of Königsberg. But the sense of anticipation among their soldiers was palpable. The hour of revenge was at hand.

Yakov Zinovievich Aronov was swept into the army from his hometown of Vitebsk, in Belorussia, in May 1944. He would die near Königsberg just nine months later. In between, there had been little time to train him. His service began as it would end, in a storm of German fire. In June, as the battle to take Vitebsk was drawing to an end, he was assigned to an artillery unit, part of the Third Belorussian Front. Their path lay west, across mosquito-ridden woods and sour lowland farms. They moved so fast that they had reached Vilnius, the Lithuanian capital, by early July. It was a hard and not always rewarding journey. In Lithuania, the men encountered glum resistance more often than carnations and red flags. The roads into Prussia were littered with burned-out tanks, "like camels on their knees."[1] By winter, other shapes loomed from the snow, the huddled silhouettes of corpses, mercifully semi-frozen. "We are having to fight for every meter of Russian [he meant Lithuanian] soil," Aronov wrote to his sister. But his letters home contained no hint of fear. "You cannot defeat a people who are led by the Communist Party," he declared. "You will say that I am doing agitation on you again. But no, it's not agitation. I'm writing what I think now. If you knew how much of the German 'New Order' I had seen, you would clench your teeth in fury and the tears would well up in your eyes. But we just bear it. We're clenching our fists and moving unrelentingly toward the west."[2]

Aronov's westward progress would halt for some weeks between October and the new year. The strategists needed more time to prepare the coordinated campaign for Berlin, a set of operations that would draw in armies from the Gulf of Finland to southern Ukraine. But elsewhere the Red Army was storming ahead. By January, it had neutralized Romania, taking Bucharest on 30 August, and on 20 October a combined Soviet and Yugoslav force had recaptured Belgrade. Budapest, the capital of the only country, Hungary, that remained allied with the Reich, was under siege. Red Army troops were spilling into Europe in their millions. The border, that daunting barrier, had been breached comprehensively, and the exotic world of capitalism was scarcely a mystery in front-line culture now. But Germany was a different matter. The prospect of enacting vengeance on real German soil was prize enough to make even the darkest winter bearable. On 12 January the Red Army launched the campaign that would take it through Poland to Prussia and onward to the suburbs of Berlin.

It was rage that gave the troops their energy. Everything, from the deaths of beloved friends to the burning of cities, from the hunger of the children back at home to the fear of facing yet another hail of shells, everything—even the wealth of bourgeois homes—was blamed on the Germans. Consciously or not, too, Red Army soldiers would soon be venting anger that had built up through decades of state oppression and endemic violence. By the time they crossed into the enemy's territory at last, in the second half of January 1945, the men's fury could fix on almost any object. They were no deeper into Europe than East Prussia, a windswept enclave on the Baltic coast, but this was Germany, the land that had nurtured Russia's tormentors, and every detail that the soldiers saw was taken as a proof of greed, corruption, arrogance. "We are proud that we have made it to the [Fascist] beast's lair," a soldier called Bezuglov wrote to his friends back at the collective farm. "We will take revenge, revenge for all our sufferings. . . . It's obvious from everything we see that Hitler robbed the whole of Europe to please his blood-stained Fritzes. They took livestock from the best farms in Europe. Their sheep are the best Russian merinos, and their shops are piled with goods from all the shops and factories of Europe. In the near future, these goods will appear in Russian shops as our trophies."[3]

The men knew that their own conduct was turning brutal. "I have to say that the war has changed me a lot," Aronov wrote. "War does not make people tender. On the contrary, it makes them reserved, rather coarse, and very cruel. That's a fact."[4] But he was not really apologizing, and his comrades would also show little sense of shame. "Our soldiers have not dealt with East Prussia any worse than the Germans did with Smolensk," a Russian combatant wrote home from a town inside the Prussian border. "We hate Germany and the Germans deeply. In one house, for example, our boys found a murdered woman and her two children. You can often see civilians lying dead in the street, too. But the Germans deserve the atrocities that they unleashed. You only have to think about Maidanek. . . . It's certainly cruel to have killed those children, but the cold-bloodedness of the Germans at Maidanek was a thousand times worse."[5]

The organs of political education in the Red Army encouraged this kind of thinking. Until the spring of 1945, when Stalin's propaganda chief, G. F. Aleksandrov, finally reined him in, it was Ilya Ehrenburg, with his message of implacable hatred for the German nation, who shaped the army's thinking about vengeance. As the men approached Prussian soil, there was no diminution in the torrent of inflammatory venom that poured from his pen.[6] "Not only divisions and armies are advancing on Berlin," he wrote. "All the trenches, graves and ravines with the corpses of the innocents are advancing on Berlin. . . . As we advance through Pomerania, we have before our eyes the devastated, blood-drenched countryside of Belorussia. . . . Germany, you can whirl round in circles, and howl in your deathly agony. The hour of revenge has struck!"[7] Revenge was justified, revenge was almost holy. It was enough that a man's best friend had been killed, his sister abducted, a village on his route ransacked and burned. It was enough, too, to find a German kitchen hung with gleaming pots, a cupboard stacked with china. If there were no Germans to kill, machine-gun blasts could smash their antique glass, or the Red Army's fire consume their tidy cottages, their barns, even their stores of food.[8]

The anger of exhausted men, of frightened, anxious, supervigilant men stressed by the war and wrung with endlessly repeated grief, would have been easy to provoke. But in the early months of their incursion onto German soil, these men were also under orders. Their new task, said the *politruks*, was to take revenge on behalf of their people, to become the agents of natural justice. "The soldiers' rage in battle must be terrible," a slogan of the time declared. "He does not merely seek to fight; he must also be the embodiment of the court of his people's justice."[9] That last phrase turns up in hundreds of letters, proof that it struck a chord among the men. "We've met our first bunch of 'Fraus,'" a soldier from Vladimir wrote in February 1945. "What a pitiful and cowardly lot they are when they feel the blows on their own skin for a change. You can sense the crushing strength of the Red Army everywhere. The court has opened, and now it's here. We'll try them all on the spot, and our accusation will be the same everywhere—we will get our revenge."[10] "I've already written to you that I'm in Germany" Slesarev told his father that winter. "You said that we should do the same things in Germany as the Germans did to us. The court has begun already; they are going to remember this march by our army over German territory for a long, long time."[11]

Slesarev was a Communist, as was Aronov by the time he died, and tens of thousands of the other olive-clad Soviets who streamed into East Prussia from January 1945. The party they belonged to proclaimed strict morality, the virtue of the citizen who aligns himself with history, devoting his life to the creation of a better world. It portrayed human progress as a struggle between good and evil, although the epic that the soldiers understood owed more to Russian folktales or the psalmists than to Marx. Simple moral messages were woven across the dull warp of ideology like scarlet threads. Good Communists spent their whole lives fighting for self-improvement, for literacy and cleanliness, and then for the perfection of society itself. A soldier washed his neck to sluice the lice, but a Communist was on a cleansing mission that would end with the whole world. Party members in the army were to be "true leaders of the masses, aware of their responsibility to maintain iron discipline and the high political moral condition of the troops.[12]

"The ideological training of party members is now more necessary than ever," the soldiers' paper, *Red Star*, confirmed in September 1944. No one could forget the undoing of those armies in Romania. The troops who faced the border were in grave peril. "To find his way about in these new conditions, a Communist needs a sound ideological equipment more than ever."[13] In answer, the party tried to make its recruitment procedures more rigorous. It also established new courses for the *politruks*. But troops were too fond, by this stage, of thinking for themselves. *Frontoviki* would remain their own men, scornful of soft-fleshed propagandists from the rear. When it came to brotherhood and moral purpose, too, no preaching could improve on the front-line experience itself. For Aronov, the war, the boys, and the party were all bound up in one sacred idea. "We are from various parts of the Soviet Union," he wrote in November, describing his comrades in their dugout. "But we all have one aim: to defeat the enemy as fast as possible and get back home to the motherland. We have traveled from Vitebsk to East Prussia together. We remember all about our battles, but we try to talk of the good things, about our lives and dreams, about the good, bright future."[14]

The irony was heartbreaking then, and so it still remains. For that winter, large numbers of these heroes, the agents of the bright future, would embark on an orgy of war crimes. Historians have called them bestial and crude, as if they acted from some instinct, like animals. But their preparation for it all, the party's careful work, included a good deal of talking and persuasion, deliberate and sophisticated flooding of their minds. As if in reaction to that, too, the men who rampaged through Prussia were giving vent to the frustrations that had built up over years of suffering, not only in the war but through decades of humiliation, of disempowerment and fear. The party that had preached at them and re-proved their most human weaknesses now gave them license and they took it. The same party also offered them a cloak of indemnity. None of its speeches and reports, and none of the journalism that made it to the columns of *Pravda*, would ever mention Soviet atrocities. They simply did not exist in the official record. Accordingly, they did not intrude into the things that soldiers wrote. The brutal images may well have burned into the consciousness of thousands of front-line troops, but though many witnessed murder and rape, their letters home continued to describe the weather.

Lev Kopelev, a Soviet officer and ardent party member, was an ex-ception. He found the words to describe the horrors he saw, and he was brave enough to think about them for himself, to escape from the moral context of the times. He did not blame the men. He did not even blame the enemy, although it was the war itself that gave birth to the vi-olence. His anger was reserved for his own party, or at least for some of the people who controlled it. Whatever the appalling record of the Nazis, it was the Communist leadership, in his view, that had created the specific crisis, the humanitarian disaster, that would now unfold. "Millions of people had been brutalised and corrupted by the war," he wrote, "and by our propaganda—bellicose, jingoistic and false. I had believed such propaganda necessary on the eve of war, and all the more so for the war's duration. I still believed it, but I had also come to un-derstand that from seeds like these came poisoned fruit."[15] The bitter harvest began well before the troops crossed their own border, but it was in Prussia that it would be most abundant. The teaching that had helped to win the war now seemed to justify atrocity. "These young fel-lows," Kopelev added as he watched his fellow troops, "who had come to the front straight from school—what would they be like . . . having learned nothing except how to shoot, dig trenches, crawl through barbed wire, rush the enemy and toss grenades? They had become in-

ured to death, blood and cruelty, and each new day brought them fresh
evidence that the war they read about in their papers and heard about
on their radios and in their political meetings was not the war they saw
and experienced themselves."[16]

The first rumors of Red Army atrocities came out of Hungary. The
fall of Budapest was followed by a rampage of surviving Soviet troops.
As one visitor remembered, "It was impossible to spend a day or even an
hour in Budapest without hearing of the brutalities committed by [Russian] soldiers."[17] Hungarian women and girls were locked into Soviet
military quarters on the city's Buda side and repeatedly raped; houses
and cellars were ransacked for food and wine as a prelude to the multiple
rape of their female occupants. There was even a story that soldiers from
the Red Army had broken into the mental hospital at Nagy-Kallo and
raped and killed female patients ranging in age from sixteen to sixty.[18]

This was nothing like the marauding of soldiers in Romania. The
cruelty in Budapest was something new. The background was a prolonged battle for the city, the last stages of which recalled the blackest
days of Stalingrad.[19] Eighty thousand Soviet troops were killed in a frustrating, slow, and deadly campaign. When the civilians of the shattered
city emerged from their homes, some of them bearing bread, as well as
bacon, eggs, and bottles of the local wine, they found a conqueror
whom gifts would not appease.[20] It did not help, in Hungary as in Germany, that the two sides spoke different languages. From the earliest
days of the Hungarian campaign, incomprehension had added to the
Soviet wrath that brought catastrophe to local women. Survivors' depositions tell a graphic tale: "Malasz Maria, married, mother of four children, has been raped by three Russian soldiers one after another in the
presence of her husband. . . . Additionally, they were robbed of 1,700
pengo. . . . Berta Jolan, born 1923, Berta Ida, born 1925, and Berta
Ilona, born 1926. These three sisters were subjected to attempted rape
by three Russian soldiers after their parents had been locked up. The
soldiers decided to stop only after the girls' screams brought other civilians to the scene. . . ."[21] The testimonies could go on and on.

In East Prussia the story would be darker still. Here above all, three
years of hate (and of the propaganda of hate) were to be focused into
one cathartic act. As they approached the border the soldiers were

entering the beast's own lair. It was a move with overtones of violation in itself, the breaching of a boundary that no one had invited them to cross. Lev Kopelev had always admired German culture and he spoke German well, but even he called on his men to get out of their trucks and piss onto the hated soil. "This is Germany," he said. "Everyone out and relieve yourselves."[22] Another group crept to the border on an active mission near Goldap, a town just south of Königsberg. Their *politruks* crawled through the ranks as they advanced, telling each rifleman to look ahead. "There," they whispered, "there behind the trenches, behind the barbed wire obstacles, there is Germany." They added a reminder that this was not merely an invasion. The Red Army could still believe itself a liberator, this time of the tens of thousands of Soviets who had been forced to work in German camps. "Over there," the political officers hissed, "over there in Germany our sisters are suffering in slavery. . . . Onward to the destruction of the enemy in his own lair."[23]

At the border itself, Soviet troops would set small red flags into the earth. Often they gathered for another short political meeting. They heard again about the crimes that they had come to avenge, about the abduction and abuse of Russian women, the tears of bereaved mothers back at home. At Goldap, seventeen men took advantage of the occasion to apply for Communist Party membership.[24] This was the regiment that would go on to surround and capture Göring's castle. But like so many others, it was not the tough, seasoned formation that it might have been. Thousands of soldiers on the Prussian campaign, including Aronov himself, had been pressed into service from the occupied zones of Belorussia and Ukraine. Some had received no training, others lacked equipment, and few had combat experience. At Goldap, predictably, the conscripts panicked. Their mutiny had to be quelled at gunpoint. The heavy rate of casualties that followed was not surprising and nor, maybe, was the anger that exploded when the fighting was over. These men had been frightened beyond endurance, they had been forced to savor their own weakness, and most were in shock. But the party reassured them that the Germans were at fault. It positively urged them to take their revenge. "The nearer we get to victory," Stalin told everyone in February 1945, "the greater our vigilance must be and the fiercer our blows against the enemy."[25]

It must have been a dreamlike, a surreal, interlude. First came the

border and the lectures about vigilance and justified revenge. The troops were cautioned that German agents might have poisoned any food or wine they found, that women might conceal grenades, that everyone they met could be a spy. And then came the abandoned settlements, the ghost towns full of unattended loot. Goebbels had warned his people that the Soviets were an Asiatic horde, a barbarous rabble of savages bent on destruction and a primitive revenge. In answer, hundreds of thousands of Prussian civilians packed their bags and fled, braving the bitter winter cold and the threat of bombardment to form the greatest single tide of refugees that would be seen in Europe in the entire war. "There's not one civilian inhabitant left in the town," Ermolenko noted on 23 January when he arrived in a town called Insterburg. "So what. We wouldn't have eaten them."

The man was a master of self-deception. His army would prove capable of every kind of crime. But it was also poised to suffer yet more violence and strain. This was a time of extremes, of contrasts, and of the daily likelihood of injury or death. The town of Insterburg itself would soon be renamed Chernyakovsk in memory of the young general, who died in the battle for Königsberg. That January, the place was wreathed in flame. Its castle and elegant, spired churches loomed out of the layers of dusty, acrid smoke like sinister bones. Corpses, the bodies of humans and of horses, lay in the streets beside abandoned trucks and burned-out furniture. Smoke hung over the wrecks. The stores, however, had yet to be destroyed. "They have butter, honey, jam, wine, and various kinds of brandy," Ermolenko noted happily. "The civilians have left their houses in order. Our radio team has taken a room on the first floor. In the corner is a piano, two sofas, pretty chairs and armchairs, cupboards, flowers. In a German kitchen, on German crockery, we made a fantastic dinner."[26]

Aronov was in Insterburg that January as well. His last letter to his sister was a postcard, a German one, a picture of the cathedral and its delightful square. The NKVD would soon stop soldiers from making use of bourgeois images like this, but he would never need to care. "Hello, dear sister," he wrote. "Greetings from Insterburg. I am alive and well and send you this with best wishes. I kiss you."[27] Some time later, for these days the field post was getting held up on the railways by

A column of Soviet troops of the Third Belorussian Front arriving in an East Prussian city, 24 January 1945

all the crates of German plunder, his sister would receive another letter. "The person who is writing to you is an unknown soldier," she read. He was writing from a hospital, two days after receiving a grave wound, but he had made the effort to get paper and a pencil as soon as he was able to sit up. "Perhaps someone has already told you the sad news," he wrote, "but as Yasha's best friend I could not keep to myself, or from you, the news of his death. Your brother and I were together from 10 May 1944 until the end of his army life. How many sorrows and hardships we bore together! And now, right on the outskirts of Königsberg, we have been cut apart. I cannot write any more."[28]

★

The close relationships between the men (the soldier who wrote that letter to Aronov's sister would soon marry her, as if the bond with his best friend could never break) in part explain what happened next, for much of the Red Army's terrible revenge was enacted in gangs. The relations that mattered here were not between the men and their German victims but between the men and their mates, and even between the men and their shared memories of horror. The victims themselves scarcely seemed to feature in their minds as people. "They do not speak a word of Russian," a soldier wrote to a friend in February 1945, "but that makes it easier. You don't have to persuade them. You just point a Nagan and tell them to lie down. Then you do your stuff and go away."[29] The war had inured men like this to violence, but what was happening was far more than an outpouring of rage. The events in Prussia involved the soldiers' passions as well as their hatred. The passion in question was largely their love for each other, and also their grief—undrownable despite oceans of wine and schnapps—for all the people and the chances they had lost.[30] The objects of the hatred, whose corpses would soon litter the roads that led to the west, were German women and girls.

Among the Soviet troops who overtook the tide of Prussian refugees as it poured out of Insterburg and Goldap was a young officer called Leonid Rabichev. Decades later, this man would find the strength to write about the atrocity he witnessed. "Women, mothers and their children, lie to the right and left along the route," he wrote, "and in front of each of them stands a raucous armada of men with their trousers down." He might have added that the baying crowd included adolescent boys, for whom this gruesome ritual amounted to the first sexual experience of their lives. "The women who are bleeding or losing consciousness get shoved to one side," Rabichev continued, "and our men shoot the ones who try to save their children." Meanwhile, a group of "grinning" officers stood nearby, one of whom was "directing—no, he was regulating it all. This was to make sure that every soldier without exception took part."[31]

That night, Rabichev and his men were sent to sleep in an abandoned German shelter. Every room contained bodies—the corpses of children, of old men, and of women who had evidently suffered serial rape before their deaths. "We were so tired," Rabichev wrote, "that we lay down on the ground between them and fell asleep."[32] Mere corpses, after all, were barely shocking anymore. When they came upon another building and found the bodies of women who had been been raped and then mutilated one by one, each with an empty wine bottle in her vagina,

Rabichev's men were less composed.[33] The problem was that sympathy for enemy females was actively discouraged. Group pressures also worked to bind the men together in their crime. On another occasion, when Rabichev was invited to select a German girl from among a group of terrified captives, his first fear was that his own men might take him for a coward if he refused. Worse, perhaps, they might think that he was impotent.[34]

The first atrocity that Lev Kopelev would witness was the burning of a Prussian town. There was no military reason for it. Valuable food and other supplies—blankets, clothing, even medicines—were all consumed in the fire. It was this kind of profligacy, the waste of resources, that would eventually bring the great rampage across Prussia to an end. The interests of the war, as Rokossovsky would insist, called for more discipline. But military thinking seemed to have been suspended in those first wild hours—or rather, a new tactic had become widespread. The order of the day, Kopelev noted, was "smash, burn, have your revenge." Many of his fellow officers were shocked, especially at the wanton waste, but the political officer in charge dismissed the incident. "The Fritzes have plundered all over the world," he said. "That's why they've got so much. They burned down everything in our country, and now we're doing the same in theirs. We don't have to feel sorry for them."[35] Kopelev's own concern would soon be dubbed "bourgeois humanitarianism," and within a few weeks of his first complaint he was arrested for it.

There was nothing bourgeois or humanitarian about most Soviet troops in those cold days. "In the few German areas that have been occupied by the Red Army," German intelligence reported, "the behavior of the soldiers is exactly as predicted earlier in the war—in most cases it is horrifying. Brutish killings, rapes of young women and girls, as well as senseless destruction are taking place on a daily basis." A prisoner of war told his German captors that a specific order from Stalin had decreed all this by stating that revenge should be taken for German atrocities. "A confirmation of the Stalin order," the author observed, "is not available yet."[36] It would not be, for nothing as specific as an order to rape and destroy was ever issued. Indeed, all through these months the penalty for rape and looting, technically at least, was death on the spot.[37] But the men read license into every exhortation to revenge. "Red Army soldier!" a poster declared. "You are now on German soil. The hour of revenge has struck!"[38] A packet of the men's letters intercepted by German intelligence in February 1945 required no editing to make the point. "Happy is the heart as you drive through a burning German town," wrote one man to his parents. "We are taking revenge for everything, and our revenge is just. Fire for fire, blood for blood, death for death."[39]

"It was evening when we drove into Neidenburg," Kopelev wrote. It was a small town, meaner than Insterburg, and like all the others it was almost deserted. The Red Army had torched the place. Through the smoke, the officer made out the body of a dead old woman. "Her dress was ripped," he saw, and "a telephone receiver reposed between her scrawny thighs. They had apparently tried to ram it into her vagina." The pretext was that she could easily have been a spy. "They got her by the telephone booth," one of the men explained. "Why fool around?"[40] It was the first of several murders Kopelev would witness in that cursed place. Then came Allenstein, and more fire, more death. Near the post office, he met a woman with a bandaged head, clutching the hand of a young girl with blond pigtails. Both had been crying, and the child's legs were stained with blood. "The soldiers kicked us out of our house," she told the Russian officer. "They beat us, they raped us. My daughter is only thirteen. Two of them did it to her. And many of them to me." She wanted him to help her find her little boy. Another woman begged Kopelev to shoot her.[41]

The violence was on a scale that no one could have overlooked, and yet it disappeared from Soviet consciousness. Witnesses like Kopelev were soon cast out, the German victims dismissed or silenced. It would take foreign observers, historians especially, to rediscover it, collect the testimonies, and to describe how, in some East Prussian towns, almost all the women were raped. "The screams of help from the tortured," one witness remembered, "could be heard day and night."[42] It did not matter, in this polyglot transition zone, if the women were Germans or Poles, and thereby Russia's allies. It did not matter, either, if the women were young or old, for the women themselves were not the main object.[43] The victims of the gang rapes were just meat, embodiments of Germany, all-purpose *Frauen*, recipients for Soviet and individual revenge. Many soldiers, purportedly, found them "disgusting."[44]

Rape was not the only crime that Soviet soldiers would commit on their sweep through Prussia. Towns were burned, officials murdered, and columns of refugees were strafed and shelled as they fled west toward Berlin.[45] But of the violent crimes, rape was the most prevalent. One reason was that women far outnumbered men among German civilians, and probably in the entire surviving population, since so few soldiers were left. But other pressures were at work as well. Rape is a common instrument of war, a chillingly familiar accompaniment to conquest and military occupation.[46] The atrocities in East Prussia could be compared to others, such as those more recently in Bosnia or Bangladesh. And this was not just any war, nor Fascism just any system. Red Army soldiers on Prussian soil felt they were dealing with an enemy people, a people that would never rest until it had destroyed their world. "It's absolutely clear," Bezuglov's letter to his friends ended, "that if we don't really scare them now, there will be no way of avoiding another war in future."[47] In his own memoir, Rabichev speculates that Stalin might informally have encouraged Chernyakovsky to drive his men to commit what a later generation would describe as ethnic cleansing.[48] The murders around Königsberg, after all, would clear the way for future Soviet settlement, and rape ensured a generation of fresh Soviet stock.

It would certainly be convenient, now, to lay the blame for this war crime on Stalin and his leadership. Like postwar Germans before them, the Russian heirs of this atrocity will one day have to grapple with the question of individual responsibility in conditions of totalitarian rule.[49] There is no doubt that the men's actions were encouraged, if not orchestrated, by Moscow. Propaganda played an active part in shaping their perceptions of the enemy and in justifying vengeance. The Sovinformburo stoked the collective rage with manufactured images that could score themselves so deeply into a man's mind that he could think them a part of his own experience. The universality of the men's own tales is evidence of this. As Atina Grossman observes in her reflections on the rapes, "Again and again in German recollections of what Russian occupiers told them, the vengeful memory summoned was not a parallel violation by a German raping a Russian woman, but of a horror on a different order: it was the image of a German soldier swinging a baby, torn from its mother's arms, against a wall—the mother screams, the baby's brains splatter against the wall, the soldier laughs."[50]

That said, the men had motives of their own. They were not passive and, despite the power of their state, they were not helpless. If many acted in a kind of dream, it was in part because the majority, for understandable reasons, chose to use alcohol to numb their senses. "It is nearly impossible not to be drinking," a soldier wrote home in February. "What I am going through is indescribable; when I am drunk everything is easier."[51] "A drunken Russian is a wholly different person than the sober one," a German writer noted at the time. "He loses all perspective, falls into a completely wild mood, is covetous, brutal, bloodthirsty."[52] "Liquor greatly intensifies the sexual urge," an anonymous German woman observed in a diary of the fall of Berlin. "I'm convinced that if the Russians hadn't found so much alcohol all over, half as many rapes would have taken place. These men aren't natural Casanovas. They had to goad themselves on to such brazen acts, had to drown their inhibitions."[53] Sometimes the result was a binge that could leave scores of victims in its wake. Sometimes it was the alcohol that won. Gabriel Temkin was among the many troops who sampled the wines of Tokay in Hungary. The sweet liquor was greatly, and in this case fatally, to the Russian taste. "When I entered a huge wine cellar with rows of tall, black oak barrels I saw an incredible scene," the old soldier recalled. "The floor was knee-deep in wine, and floating in it lay three drowned soldiers. They had used their submachine guns to make holes in the barrels as 'the easiest way' to fill up their mess tins and then, having tasted it, evidently could not stop drinking and became so intoxicated that they drowned in it."[54]

Those who were not entirely drunk might well have explained their actions in terms of pent-up lust. Later, certainly, some Russian troops treated German women as legitimate spoils of war, selecting the prettiest ones whenever they had the chance to choose.[55] The anonymous author of the Berlin diary, watching from her basement shelter, noted that they preferred the plumper women. "Fat means beautiful; the more woman there is, the more her body differs from that of a man." It was a taste that she deemed "primitive," although she took some pleasure in the thought that Berliners who had stolen or hoarded food were now paying for their antisocial acts.[56] But whether the troops picked their prey or not, purely sexual desire hardly seems to have been their main motive, especially in Prussia. Here, above all, the rapes were both indiscriminate and extraordinarily savage.

There would have been reason enough for lust. Unlike the Germans (who made use of captured Soviet women for the purpose), the Soviets did not have field brothels near the front. Sex, in official terms, scarcely existed. Gabriel Temkin recalled how one regiment reacted when it found a cache of German condoms. "They blew them up," he wrote, "and the soldiers played with them like balloons."[57] The whole culture of party and motherland was dedicated to struggle and sacrifice. Women were chaste, waiting at home, while men—in theory, at least— thought only of their duty. If they fought bravely and kept up their leisure reading of Lenin and Marx, there would be no time left for soldiers' erotic selves.

This sterile blandness was not confined to the army and it began long before the war. Lenin himself had taken a dim view of lust, preferring healthy exercise and long sessions with piles of books. The flowering of sexual license that had accompanied the revolution, the silver age of the erotic, was crushed under the boots and hammers of Stalinist collectivism. Sexual passion was for the bourgeoisie (and, privately, for members of the Bolshevik elite). Good workers gave their energy to long shifts at the bench, and when they had finished turning out ball bearings, they went to a meeting or caught up with *Pravda*. "Dialogue in a Soviet picture," the satirist Ilya Ilf wrote in his diary. "Love is the most awful vice." Even the Venus de Milo was deemed "pornographic."[58] License gave way to ever stricter laws about divorce, abortion, and the family. Meanwhile, more and more people found themselves sharing their living space. Often they shared one room with children, who slept behind curtains or on wooden shelves, but sometimes they also shared with other adults, other entire families. If the good worker of Soviet iconography has a stern expression, his chiseled features lacking irony or humor, it may just be because he seldom got the chance to waste an afternoon in bed.[59]

Like almost every other human pleasure in the land of brotherhood, sex was something that went underground. The public emphasis on strict morality and sheer hard work pushed it into the darkness, to a twilight hazed by sweat, tobacco, and whatever vodka could be found. The gap between longing and reality was nowhere more apparent than among the soldiers at the front. It was a male world, a world of *makhorka*, cheap spirits, and decaying boots. The nearest many soldiers got to the women they cared about was in a letter, or perhaps in the stories that they sometimes told. "My army friend is telling us about his life," Aronov wrote one evening. "It's not the first time he's done that. Right now he's got to the bit where he falls in love for the first time."[60] His prewar life had faded into fantasy and, like all dreams, it could be better than the truth. "After the war," another man told his friends, "I'm going to go to the south somewhere, and I'm going to teach math and physics at a girls' boarding school, somewhere where the rules are that no girl can go out on the street. I'll use all my military experience."[61] The longing was there, and the desire for escape, for the feminine, but these feelings were miles away from gang rape and a bayonet in the belly.

Whatever lust they may have felt, large numbers of the men had stronger reasons for resenting and even hating representatives of the female sex. All through the war, they had been getting sad letters from home. Some were tales of hunger, others told of rape and death, but many were letters of farewell. Families were unraveling, new lives asserting themselves in separate worlds. The strain between soldier and family was part of the general gulf between combatants and civilians. It was also a symptom of the overpowering maleness of army life. Women were objects of suspicion, aliens, in a misogynistic universe. The soldiers' letters became more suspicious of women, and also more repressive, with the passing years. "We fought for our country from the very first days," a Red Army man wrote to Mikhail Kalinin, the Soviet president, in 1944. "Some of us have been wounded several times, but we did not begrudge our very lives for our motherland and families. And now our complaint is that some women are betraying us . . . and our children are losing their fathers. . . . We must take severe legal measures against these women betrayers for their treachery and the insult to their husbands."[62] The letter is one among hundreds.

Official policy was changing, too. In July 1944 the Soviet Union began its campaign to create iconic mothers, striking medals for the women who had given birth to large broods of healthy, surviving young. The ideal woman, if the photographs could be believed, was stern and provident, tough as a tank driver, the nurse and teacher of armies to come.[63] She was also sweet, innocent, and untroubled by hardship, let alone by war. Frivolity and sex (the many children notwithstanding) had no place in her life. Soldiers began to praise the type, to dream of faithful, moonfaced women and their healthy well-nourished sons. The gentleness, the sentimentality, of many Soviet troops toward small children in Prussia was noted at the time. A woman with a baby, local people learned, was practically immune to rape. But even sentimental troops, the men who kept their pockets full of sweets for hungry German kids, worried about their families back home. It was a long time since any had seen their children.

There were reasons to be concerned. Even the strongest marriages were showing signs of strain. The classic letter, received by thousands of men, contained an image of cold homecoming: "Our flame was not hot enough to last."[64] Each gap between his wife's letters prompted Belov to suspect that his own marriage was faltering. "I've had a note from my wife," he scribbled in March 1944. "I get the feeling that she and I are heading for a major fight. It's an unpleasant feeling, a kind of general inertia."[65] Perhaps she had been worrying, as Taranichev's Natalya had, about the cost of separation. "You won't know us at all if the war goes on much longer," Natalya wrote in October 1944. "It's a pity that you have become so remote from us."[66] "I try to write whenever I can," her husband replied in a brisk, reproving tone. "Even when I'm on the march. But I would remind you that there are moments when my mood is so lousy, because of the general situation, that I can't bring myself to write so much as a postcard, even if I have the time. I will remember Stalingrad for a long time!"[67]

The men whose marriages collapsed were angrier still, whatever infidelities they had committed for themselves. Part of the problem was the wartime idealization of the Soviet wife, the waiting girlfriend, the family for whom each soldier fought. Back home, where survival was a matter of humiliation, of exhausting struggle, real life was nothing like the image, and real women could not match up to the soldiers' dreams. At the front, too, a new morality prevailed. Kopelev was a father and a married man. He fully expected to return to his old life when the war ended. But at the front, he took a second "wife," as countless officers like him would do. "I told her that since we had to work together day and night, we couldn't avoid sleeping together, so why put it off?" The point was that "perhaps we would be killed together by the same shell."[68] Sauce for the front-line gander, however, was not supposed to be enjoyed by the geese back home. Among their petitions from these last months of war were soldiers' appeals for new laws to give them control over their children, to allow for postal divorces, and to punish the women who had shamed and betrayed them.[69]

But fighting men were powerless to change things back at home. The only world they could affect was here, in Germany, where the women who had brought on their ruin, the spoiled *Frauen*, still wrapped themselves in silk and fur—or so the soldiers fantasized— while Russian children starved. Where Russian women wore their peasant blouses and embroidered *sarafans* (in theory and in folklore, anyway), these German females dressed in provocative western styles, wore makeup, teetered on high heels.[70] The whole culture that had produced them seemed sick, disgusting—and wickedly seductive. Some German women were accused of deliberate whoring. "German ladies are . . . ready to begin payment of 'reparations' at once," a disgusted Soviet officer observed. "It won't work!"[71] "Europe is a dirty abyss," a soldier wrote home from Prussia that winter. "I have taken a look at German magazines, and they revolt me. . . . Even their music is indecent! Is this Europe? Give me Siberia anytime!"[72] Another discovered a cache of pornographic pictures (probably not, in this case, the Venus de Milo) in an abandoned German position near Königsberg. "What could be more disgusting?" he asked. "Our culture must be higher than that of the Germans, because you would never find such images among our ranks."[73]

Rape, then, combined the desire to avenge with the impulse to destroy, to smash German luxuries and waste the Fascists' wealth. It punished women and it reinforced the fragile manliness of the perpetrators. It also underscored the emotional ties between gangs of the men, and it was as a gang, not individuals, that the men usually acted, drawing an energy and anonymity from the momentum of the group. It was the collective triumph of these males, certainly, that rape purported to celebrate. And though women bore the brunt of the violence, German men were also victims of a kind. It was no accident that many rapes took place in view of husbands and fathers. The point was being made that they were now the creatures without power, that they would have to watch, to suffer this most intimate degradation.[74] One woman recounted the tale of a lawyer who had stood by his Jewish wife all through the Nazi years, refusing to divorce her in spite of the risks. When the Russians arrived, he protected her again, at least until a bullet from a Russian automatic hit him in the hip. As he lay bleeding to death, three men raped his wife.[75]

The anecdotes fill stacks of files, but the precise statistics will remain unknown. The violence was worst in East Prussia, but rape was a problem wherever the Red Army encountered its enemies. Tens of thousands of German women and girls undoubtedly suffered rape at the hands of Soviet troops; the figure may well have reached hundreds of thousands.[76] But numbers are dangerous tools, creating certainties on paper that have nothing much to do with life. This was a world of propaganda, a world colored, to the last, by Goebbels's pen. Numbers could make the Russians seem more terrible, turn Germans into victims, perhaps wipe out some dark stains from the Nazi past. They clearly helped to reinforce the image of the Red Army as an Asiatic horde.[77] But though the stories told by the rates of abortion and venereal disease infection after 1945 are evidence of a kind, some other numbers are less reliable.[78] When a Berlin newspaper reported that a seventy-year-old woman had been raped twenty-four times, the anonymous Berlin diarist wearily wondered, "Who was keeping count?"[79]

Estimating the number of perpetrators is equally problematic. The veterans themselves are unlikely to volunteer lists of names. Some officers I came to know would mention cases where they restored discipline, as Kirill did in East Prussia, by threatening two perpetrators ("not from my unit, of course") with his own pistol. But rank-and-file soldiers, who must at least have witnessed the atrocities, refused to talk of them. "They say there were rapes," one man told me. "I never saw any. The thing is, we never actually saw any Germans. They had always run away before we got to any town." For many, the silence suggested a kind of selective amnesia, no doubt the child of shame. But other pressures operated, too. No army trumpets its crimes, but the official Soviet silence about rape was numbing. It is enough to look at the records of the NKVD troops. Officials with responsibility for discipline, and for maintaining order among civilians in the front-line zones, were in a position to report cases of rape whenever they chose. Their records, after all, were marked "absolutely secret." But even these internal documents mention almost no incidents of gang rape and few individual crimes. It was as if the officers conspired to keep them out of their written accounts, filling the space with incidents of drunkenness or absence without leave instead.

The NKVD troops who served with the First Belorussian Front were in the eye of the Red Army storm. But the tone of their reports at the time remained cool. "In one house we found eight Germans," an officer observed, "an old man, five women, and two youths of twelve or thirteen." Like hundreds of others they had hanged themselves. The officers who reported the scene explained that local witnesses had suggested that "despite the fact that most of the women in the settlement are of a certain age" the victims had been afraid because "Russian soldiers are raping German women."[80] The allegation is reported with the skepticism usually reserved for sightings of the Virgin Mary, but this was January 1945. For six months already, the same army had been anxious about the rates of venereal disease among its troops in Poland, the Baltic, and Romania. Monthly examinations had been ordered for all soldiers of either sex.[81] But when it came to the reports on discipline, more space— many times more—was given to ideological wavering than to rape. It was only in April and May 1945, when Stalin himself intervened, that "relations with German civilians" began to feature in reports on discipline.[82]

Just as seriously, rape was seldom punished, especially at first. In the early months, up to the spring of 1945, the soldiers were still fighting under an order to take revenge. Thereafter, when even the Soviet leadership had begun to appreciate the cost, to discipline and to the army's combat capability, of the unmilitary violence, some officers took stricter control, and there were even executions for rape in the Red Army. In April 1945, when his army joined Konev's troops in Silesia, Rabichev recalled that forty men and officers were shot in front of their units to discourage further atrocities.[83] "Some commanders!" the soldiers would mutter. "They'll shoot their own men over a German bitch."[84] More usually, however, perpetrators whose crime was not condoned might be given relatively light punishments. Five years was a standard sentence, but it could be reduced to two or less on appeal, especially for soldiers with good war records.[85] In any event, these men were needed at the front. Their sentences were almost all deferred until the fighting stopped, and many, in the best Red Army style, had "redeemed their crime with their own blood"—died or been incapacitated—by that point. Rape, in other words, was treated more leniently than desertion, theft, or—as in Kopelev's case—a unilateral attempt to protect German civilians. A few instances were singled out (usually when other breaches of discipline were involved) but the majority simply disappeared from Soviet records.

It is unlikely that every one of the scores of veterans who agreed to talk to me was guiltless in this gruesome tale. But they have no incentive to discuss it now. Back then, they had a war to win. They fought, they suffered, and many would end up as victims, as invalids, themselves. What they remember after sixty years may not be a moment of rage but the long days in hospital, or else the boys, the night marches, the songs. Women—*baby* in Russian, a dismissive word that translates somewhere on the scale between bitches and old bags—would not be worth a thought compared with the regiment, the victory. *Baby* were not worth much at home in Russia. Why should they be so special in this other world? Why should they count against the crime of Maidanek, the tears of Russian children? "You want to hear about the war," the old men say. "Let's talk about that. Only journalists want to know about those scandals."

★

The men took more than memories from Prussia. This may have been a hard campaign, with tens of thousands of casualties, but it was also a time of strange abundance. Germany was rich. Hungary, too, and even Bucharest, were full of goods to loot. On paper, the last phase of the war marked the final triumph of Communism. In reality, it was like the first day of a great bazaar. The Soviets were not the only ones guilty of looting. Their allies in this war ransacked cellars and wealthy homes as well, as did the thousands of former prisoners and other displaced persons who now found themselves at liberty on German soil.[86] But the Red Army did everything on a monumental scale. It had suffered and lost more than anyone, and now it demanded the highest recompense. Stalin insisted that the Reich owed his people at least ten billion dollars' worth of reparations.[87] The army, more or less with government connivance, set about securing a portion of this as soon as it set foot on German territory.

A set of regulations was in place by 1944 to cover the capture and dispatch of "trophies." The list was comprehensive. Anything that was captured in battle or abandoned by the enemy—including weapons, supplies of ammunition, fuel, food, boots, livestock, rolling stock, railway track, automobiles, amber, and cases of vintage champagne—was deemed to be the property of the Red Army and Soviet state. Whole factories would be dismantled later in the war. Eighty percent of Berlin's industrial machinery had been hauled away by the Soviets before their allies entered the city in 1945. "They had dismantled the refrigeration plant at the abattoir," an American officer observed, "torn stoves and pipes out of restaurant kitchens, stripped machinery from mills and factories and were completing the theft of the American Singer Sewing Machine plant when we arrived."[88] The Soviets were retaliating for the utter devastation of the western regions of their own empire, but even so, the destruction was often pointless, at least as far as observers from the west could see. Meanwhile, back in the Soviet Union, the labor of German prisoners, ex-soldiers, was regarded as a war trophy as well. If anyone could reassemble the dismantled German plants, these were the men.

It was inescapable that troops faced with the chaos of a battle zone would help themselves to anything they found. Indeed, some looting was essential to the war effort. The supply lines for Zhukov's advancing armies were stretched to breaking point. When Aronov or Ermolenko sat down to German meals in Insterburg, they were getting the best rations that they had seen for weeks, not indulging mere gluttony. One officer wrote to his family about the meal he enjoyed with his exhausted and hungry men just after the fall of Königsberg. The unit was issued with passes to the local military store, a repository for all kinds of trophy food and other goods. They entered the premises at eleven and came out at five, having drunk beer, wine, and vodka, eaten sausages, and stuffed themselves with tongue, biscuits, chocolates, truffles, raisins, and dates.[89]

When their own stomachs had been filled, some men began to think about their families at home. They knew that there was nothing in Russia to buy. Their leaders were already packing crates with fine china, bed linens, and expensive German furs. Senior officers requisitioned cars to get the stuff home and even, later in the war, a fleet of special trains.[90] The men began to think along the same lines. On 26 December 1944, well in time for the Russian New Year, the Soviet Ministry of Defense confirmed a regulation that authorized all army personnel to send parcels back home from the front line.[91] It was, effectively, a license to loot. In fact, one officer who heard that his men were not sending much back home told them to "get better at grabbing."[92]

As ever, the looting was conducted according to privilege and rank. Only soldiers credited with good conduct were permitted to send their parcels back east, and even then they were supposed to send just one parcel a month. The permitted weight varied from five kilos for soldiers to sixteen kilos (a notional limit in practice) for generals.[93] Kopelev leafed through a library of exquisite rare books. His comrades in arms chose antique paintings, hunting rifles, and even a piano.[94] *Frontoviki* had the first pick, and often destroyed anything they did not take.[95] It could be a misfortune, suddenly, to be assigned to the second echelon. "I'm really miserable," Taranichev wrote to his Natalya. "They've just said that we can send ten kg of stuff a month [this was the allowance for officers], but I'm in a place where there is nothing, it's all been looted, and the prices are absolutely crazy."[96] He would soon overcome his disappointment, for even the least warlike of officers and "rear-guard rats" could fill their quotas when they learned to look. A favorite item, predictably, was food. "Eat for your health," an officer scribbled to his wife and daughter as he enclosed canned meat, sugar, and chocolate, "and don't have any pangs of conscience, and don't think of giving any of it away."[97] Other men sent packets of nails back home or even panes of glass, as well as more attractive gifts like china, tools, and piles of German shoes and clothes.[98] The jamboree involved no guilt. Even today, the veterans can talk of it without embarrassment, as if recounting a particularly fruitful rummage sale. Getting the best things was a sign of skill, of concern for one's family, of an ability to deal with the new beast, capitalism.

The men's choices were sometimes strange, or at least poignant. Soldiers took typewriters that they would never use, since the Cyrillic alphabet required completely different keys. Taranichev eventually picked out a radio ("made by an excellent German firm") but noted sadly that "for this, of course, we will need electricity. Wherever we decide to live after the war, we're not going to be in a place that has no electricity."[99] He did not say it, but a radio was a truly exclusive item back home. The Sovinformburo had seized every one in 1941. But other things were scarce as well, including those with more immediate utility. The engineer went on to send home parcels of food, an overcoat, a feather eiderdown with a silk cover, several sets of sheets, and padded trousers for those hunting expeditions of the future. He added a bolt of black silk for his wife, together with some yellow leather to make boots.[100] Like other Soviet wives in other provinces, Natalya was about to bring the fashions of 1940s Central Europe to the steppes of postwar Turkestan, not always with accessories to match.

More practically, Taranichev also sent shoes for each of his children, choosing sizes that they would grow into within a year or so. He also sent leather to use for extra shoes as well as the woollen cloth to make his family winter coats and white flannel for their underwear.[101] Again, he packed the parcels up with pride. So did Kirill. The young officer was based in Poland through the last winter of the war. He remembers his task there as a version of peacekeeping, a combination of strict governance, light engineering work, and crime prevention. Decent civilians, in his view, had reason to be grateful to him. When the time came to send something home, he folded up a quilt or two and packed a typewriter. But he also let it be known that he and his wife needed a baby carriage for their daughter. The next morning, two dozen models had

Infantrymen of a guards regiment stowing their bicycles for shipment, May 1945

been left outside his quarters. "I chose the best," he said with a smile. The local people's generosity seemed to confirm that he was a humane soldier, a Communist officer of the best kind.

The parcels helped to boost morale, but postal services were swamped. The soldiers' packages were pronounced to be "of exclusive political importance," which meant that pilfering, delays, and poor storage would count as crimes against the state. But the great dispatch began in January, in the depths of the Russian winter. In a few weeks, the railhead at Kursk—and anywhere that soldiers' families lived—looked like a giant warehouse. Three hundred parcels arrived in Kursk in January 1945. By early May, the monthly figure had jumped to fifty thousand, and the total for the five-month period was eighty-seven thousand parcels. Twenty thousand wagons of plunder were waiting to be unloaded by mid-May. A special tent was built beside the station to keep the rain off packages of printed cotton, canned meat and jam, typewriters and bicycles, bedding, hosiery, and china cups. But storage was only the start. Many of the recipients lived in remote villages. There were no cars. Soldiers' families had to rely instead on "German trophy horses," the worn-out nags that the Wehrmacht had abandoned, many of which were sick or injured. In the end, more staff (and more horses) had to be obtained. A special hostel was set up near Kursk station to accommodate a workforce specially brought in to sort and dispatch soldiers' loot.[102]

In Germany itself, the soldiers pilfered from one another. "I'm afraid to send things home at the moment," Ageev told his wife in May, "because there have been lots of cases of theft."[103] But some items were never meant to reach the post. Guns and ammunition, strictly forbidden for private use, were selling well on the Polish black market by the late summer of 1944.[104] Apart from alcohol and tobacco, the soldiers' other favorite items included bicycles and wristwatches. Some men were photographed with several watches on each arm, proof of their war record as well as future money in the bank. "The German makes always ran down," one survivor explained. "That's why we needed several at a time." It was the same with bicycles. The men had little grasp of riding, let alone repair. "They teach one another to ride," one witness wrote, "sit stiffly on the saddle like chimpanzees bicycling in the zoo, crash into trees, and giggle happily."[105] She could have added that the crashed bikes were left where they collapsed. There were always others to be had. A famous photograph of the time shows a Russian soldier pulling a bicycle out of its outraged female owner's hands. Others show the men stowing them away, preparing for the long journey back home. The idea of property had become as vague as privacy or peace. Amid the devastation, nothing seemed to belong to anyone much—unless, that is, the new owner was armed or wearing an official badge.

While the front line moved west toward Berlin, soldiers in the rear sections, and even the NKVD troops who were set to guard them, enjoyed a foretaste of the victory to come. There were orgies of looting, drunken binges, and haphazard relations with local women, including "marriages" as well as rape. Four years of fear and tension unraveled in weeks. Few soldiers feared the international border now. It was time to discover the entire world, to taste it, drink it, grab it, triumph over it. Reports from the late winter and early spring tell a story of chaos behind the lines, of soldiers getting drunk (of course), of soldiers stealing clothes and jewelery, dressing in civilian disguise, billeting themselves with local women, driving army vehicles around at breakneck speed. Relations with civilians in every "liberated" zone quickly reached the breaking point.[106] The very guardians of discipline, a detachment of NKVD troops, were discovered rolling around a Polish city singing their "uncensored songs." They even turned up drunk at their own party meeting and ranted on about the army's glory until someone could be found to take them out and make them sober up.[107]

The Germans knew they were defeated by the spring of 1945, but still the war was not over. Hitler refused to surrender, and the German army—the remains of it—fought on toward final collapse. This resistance mirrored the doggedness of which the Soviets had been so proud when they held out three years before, and it delayed the battle for Berlin, which Chuikov, the stoical defender of Stalingrad, had hoped to close in February 1945. Far from admiring German stubbornness, however, Soviet troops regarded it as yet another despicable trait. Ageev remained amazed at the sight of the Germans he was fighting. "Among the Fritzes whom we took prisoner," he wrote to his wife, "was a fifty-nine-year-old German, and he didn't have a tooth in his head, but this bastard was fighting like some kind of brainless automaton, even though he couldn't have chewed a piece of dry bread if he'd wanted to."[108] Ageev's outrage owed something to his apprehension that, for all its certainty, the coming victory against an enemy like this would not be cheap.

The battle for Berlin began in earnest in mid-April. By that stage, Königsberg had fallen at last, as had the Prussian city of Kustrin. These last campaigns—often described as "cleaning up"—were bitter, and they cost the Red Army thousands of men. But the prospect of Berlin itself seemed yet more daunting. Red Army troops could not have guessed how botched and ramshackle the final preparations for the city's defense had been.[109] As far as they could tell, the place was likely to have been fortified in advance by a maze of minefields, booby traps, entanglements. The dangers were drummed into them, as if the myth of easy victory, the dream of 1938, could be transformed into a tale of desperate odds to glorify the final chapter of the European war. But though they faced a broken, hungry, and demoralized enemy, Red Army soldiers knew that they had reached Hitler's own citadel. Whatever their superior strength—and the Soviets outnumbered Berlin's defenders by at least two to one—the coming battle was certain to be challenging.[110] Men who remembered Stalingrad, including Chuikov himself, began to train another generation in the art of house-to-house combat.[111]

The final chapter opened on 16 April. "There has not been a day at the front yet like today," an engineer called Petr Sebelev, who had been in the army since 1941, wrote to his family that evening. "At four o'clock in the morning thousands of Katyushas and machine guns opened fire, and the sky was as bright as day from horizon to horizon. On the German side, everything was covered with smoke and thick fountains of earth flying up in columns. There were huge flocks of frightened birds flying around, a constant humming, thunder, explosions. Then came the tanks. In front of the whole column floodlights shone, which was to dazzle the Germans. And then people everywhere started shouting, 'To Berlin! To Berlin!'"[112] "Flares soared into the sky," wrote Chuikov of the same scene, "and Lenin's face looked down as if alive from the scarlet banners on the soldier-liberators, as if summoning them to be resolute in the last fight with the hateful foe."[113] The thunder of the guns was so deafening that even experienced artillerists were awed. It was an effort to remember that they were supposed to keep their mouths open to equalize the pressure on their ears.[114]

The men's excitement was the thrill of action after a long wait, the joy of imagining the war almost won. "Today no one is thinking about death," wrote Sebelev. "Everyone is thinking only about how quickly they can roll into Berlin." The Soviets seemed poised to storm the Fascists' lair at last. But for a final time the optimism of Red Army soldiers played them false. Zhukov's assault on the Seelow Heights, the last formidable natural barrier on the way to Berlin, was destined to falter as a consequence of his own miscalculation. Instead of confusing the enemy, as he had pictured, the searchlight beams that he had ordered the advance guard to deploy merely reflected back into his own men's eyes, bouncing off the wall of smoke that their artillery had created.[115] Their bombardment, moreover, had made the ground ahead impassable. Worse, the trenches that the Soviets had been shelling with such energy turned out to have been deserted. A captured Red Army soldier had warned the Germans of the coming onslaught the previous day, and most had withdrawn well behind this forward line.[116] Far from moving triumphantly toward Berlin, the troops under Zhukov's command slowed down, unable to get past the second line of German defenders.

The delay was good news, oddly, for Zhukov's rival, Ivan Konev. The two commanders were supposed to work together in the campaign for Berlin, though it was Konev's task, in theory, to sweep around from the south, through Leipzig and Dresden, and cut the German front in two. But Stalin had encouraged a professional rivalry between the two marshals, a competition to reach Berlin first, and Zhukov's problems allowed Konev's leadership, briefly, to shine. It was a bizarre kind of race, and to the end of their lives the two marshals disagreed on the order of events. The most that can be said is that the contest secured Soviet priority over the Allies in the capture of Berlin. But in strategic terms it was disastrous. Zhukov's fury forced inexperienced men—some of whom were former prisoners of war, others forced laborers with no training—to battle on through deadly streets and mined emplacements so that Berlin would fall to them. Laggards, as ever, were promised a bullet or the *shtraf* battalion. Even experienced troops were overly tense, their terror heightened by warnings and threats. Chuikov, who also felt the lash of Zhukov's tongue, told his men to remain on their guard and advised them to use overwhelming force.[117] "The enemy is hidden in basements, inside buildings," he explained. "A battle in a city is a battle of fire-power, a battle at close quarters, in which close-range firing is carried out not by automatic weapons only, but by powerful artillery systems and tank armaments, all firing over a few score metres only."[118]

Red Army soldiers had no time, as they took their aim, to bother with the fates of the civilians who still lived in their way.

Berlin itself was poised on the brink of death. There had been no deliveries of food for days, and many of the water pipes were wrecked. "Children are dying," the Berlin diarist recalled. "Old people are eating grass like animals." Berliners crept into their basements, huddling in candlelit darkness while outside, in the street, the spring continued with uncanny, mocking clarity. The diarist crept out from her shelter one afternoon. Even the light was a surprise. "Clouds of lilac perfume drift over from untended gardens and waft through the charred ruins of apartment houses," she wrote. "Only the birds seem suspicious of this particular April: there's not a single sparrow nesting in the gutters of our roof."[119] Before the attack, she thought only of hunger, like the victim of a siege. Then came the bombardment, earthquakes of shelling and deafening noise, and in its wake soldiers, Ivans, advancing slowly, house to house and room to room, lobbing grenades into doorways and stairwells, firing first and asking all the questions later. Soon everything the diarist wrote would be about these strangers, Red Army soldiers with their booze and boorish tastes, their bandaged limbs, scarred faces, and their endless, unquenchable need.

As the outskirts of Berlin collapsed, cleared at the careful pace of men advancing through a maze of traps, more troops came to secure the liberated zones. There was not much to take in Berlin anymore, but they seized whatever food and other goods they still fancied. Almost casually, and without the intense hatred of three months earlier, they also wreaked their usual revenge on Berlin's women. The intimacy was not good for discipline, nor was it good for the men's health (not that most of them were without some form of infection already).[120] The looting and the drunkenness were disastrous for the army's reputation with its allies and among German civilians. In April, Stalin and Zhukov intervened, issuing a series of new orders concerning property, the violation of civilian living quarters, and what were euphemistically described as relations with civilian women. Confusingly, the most famous order deplored what it called liberal behavior toward the Germans in the same breath as it decried excessive brutality.[121] But the message was unmistakable. "Stalin's order," as the men soon called it, demanded restraint.

It was read to the troops at their political meetings, and German women learned to invoke it as a kind of spell to deter their Ivans. It does not seem to have made very much difference in Berlin. A lieutenant who briefed his men, the diarist claims, gave them "a roguish wink."[122] The only thing that was guaranteed to restrain them—apart from the barrel of an officer's Nagan—was the absolute priority of combat.

Zhukov's forces entered Berlin on 21 April. The following day, Konev's men crossed the Teltow Canal. It would be Zhukov's troops, including those under Chuikov's direct command, who surrounded and stormed the Tiergarten, a district eight kilometers long and two across. Though it was also the site of the Berlin zoo, this was the Nazi citadel. The bunkers at its heart, surrounded by antiaircraft guns, had walls two meters thick. One housed the Gestapo, another, on the edge of the zone, was Hitler's own bunker, a building that combined the functions of command post, bastion, and grand imperial reception room. To the north of it, beyond the Brandenburg Gate, was the Reichstag building, the symbol that the Soviets selected to embody Hitler's rule. The Tier-

The Soviets in Berlin, May 1945

garten itself was bisected by the Landwehr Canal, a pleasant landmark that would turn into a barrier and then a death trap when the SS blew up the underground tunnels deep beneath it. But that would be their last desperate throw. On 29 April, the whole area was a bomb site, the fires an ominous red glow that lit even the darkest sky above the rubble, dust, and smoke. There was no doubt at all what the outcome would be, but the last throes of this empire would not be gentle.

It took three days of intense fighting for the Red Army to capture the totemic buildings. The storming of the Reichstag was the emblematic moment. Stalin had wanted to publish the news of this (and, ideally, of Berlin's surrender) in time for the Soviet May Day holiday. In fact, the famous photograph of Sergeants Yegorov and Kantariya (the latter, like Stalin, a Georgian) waving their red flag from the Reichstag roof was posed, taken the next day when the real danger was past. On May Day itself, the troops were inching forward through a hail of machine-gun fire, risking grenades and booby traps. Three hundred defenders held them off for more than eight hours; two hundred of them were killed. The story was repeated at other sites, including the formidable zoo flak tower in the Tiergarten. Each time one of these bastions was captured, scores, if not hundreds, of Nazi troops surrendered. Many more, the wounded and the dying, lay in the basements waiting for the end.[123] Hitler himself was already dead. He and his closest aides committed suicide on 30 April. "The Wehrmacht fought on," notes one account, "like a chicken with its spinal cord severed."[124] It was not until six o'clock on 2 May that the commander of the Berlin garrison, General Helmuth Weidling, surrendered to the Red Army.[125]

One witness to it all was Nikolai Belov. "I wanted to write to you so much on the first of May," he wrote to his wife, Lidiya, on 3 May, "but the way it's worked out is that we've been in battle the whole time, and what's more they've been really hard and drawn-out battles, the kind where you don't have time to talk, let alone to think about writing." Four of her letters had arrived on 1 May, but he had been in the thick of the shelling in the Tiergarten, and when it was over he was too tired to open them. Then came the city's capitulation, a lull in the thunder of guns, and, finally, a chance to rest. "I haven't slept like I did just now for a long time—I was like a corpse," he wrote. But he knew the war was coming to an end. "I don't know if there'll be another round of fighting like we've just seen, but I doubt it. It's all finished in Berlin." When Weidling had signed the capitulation papers, Belov had been asleep.

The lieutenant had not witnessed the end of Operation Bagration. He had been wounded just weeks after writing the last entry in his diary, in the late summer of 1944. His reward had been the first home leave of his entire war, a second honeymoon with Lidiya. It was of home that he was thinking as he wrote on 3 May. A fellow officer had invited him to celebrate the first of May—belatedly—in his "baronial" quarters in Berlin, "where, as they say, you probably can unwind a bit," but the thought of luxury repelled the weary officer at that moment. "To hell with all this stuff," Belov declared. "I'd rather be in a hut somewhere—anywhere, as long as it's in Russia, so that I could relax and forget the whole nightmare of this war, including the bloodstained German race." The luxuries reproached his conscience, too, for he had not had time to send a parcel home, although he longed to help his family. He was exhausted and sick of the war, but his letter also contained a germ of real hope.

The point was that Lidiya was expecting their baby, a child conceived during his leave. He called the pregnant woman "fatty," affectionately telling her to eat well and get lots of rest. More seriously, he also contemplated the things his unborn children would think later on, when they asked what their father had done in the war. He had no reason to reproach himself, and the thought made him proud. They would, he believed, "not be ashamed, because we fulfilled our duty to the end." But all that was still in the future. In those first days of May the war was not quite over, and nor was the stress, the sense of endless combat, in his brain. "No doubt you are celebrating," he wrote. "I can imagine how delighted our whole nation must be, but for us, soldiers, it's difficult to grasp the true extent of our victory, our aim has been to take a city or to win a battle, and we're used to weighing the effect of a given battle, and we'll only start thinking about the victory when we have heard the last shot."

He knew that there would not be long to wait. "Perhaps," he concluded, "the war will have ended before you even get this letter." Five days later, Zhukov accepted Germany's unconditional surrender. The ceremony was as dignified, as final, as wartime conditions could make it. The cameras of the world's press flashed as Wilhelm Keitel, the German head of state, took off his glove to sign the act of capitulation just after midnight on 9 May. When the German delegation had left the hall, the Soviet and Allied delegations collapsed with relief, the wine and vodka appeared on the green baize tables, and Zhukov himself danced to the applause of his generals.[126] Outside, the men greeted their victory with salvos of heavy gunfire, rifle shots, and yet more drink. But Belov never heard the last shot of his war, nor did he ever see the daughter who was born a month later. He was sent west, to Burg on the Elbe, on 4 May. The next day, 5 May, he was killed there.[127]

More than 360,000 soldiers of the Red Army and of its Polish comrades perished in the campaigns for Berlin, perhaps a tenth of them in the battles around the capital itself.[128] Those men and women were the ghosts at the feast on 9 May. But for a few hours, most soldiers remembered life, not death. "We heard the joyful news on the radio at three o'clock this morning," Taranichev wrote home to his wife. "Anyone who was already asleep was woken up, and we organized a gathering straightaway: we fired volleys out of every kind of gun till morning, which means that right up till dawn the town was under such heavy fire that it looked as if a real battle were going on. My dears, you cannot imagine what joy there is among our officers and men because of the war's ending; it's true that you suffered very greatly back home behind the lines, and that our rear guard together with the valiant Red Army defeated the Fascist beast, but all the same for us at the front it was hardest of all, and you've got to understand us, *frontoviki*!"[129] Ageev spoke for many when he declared that "there has never in history been such happiness and pride as the Soviet people are experiencing today."[130] In Samoilov's base, the soldiers had been celebrating since the fall of Berlin on 2 May. On 7 May, they heard a rumor that the war was finally over, and some began to fire into the air. They fired again on 8 May, this time because the BBC had announced Germany's capitulation. But it was not until Keitel surrendered to Zhukov himself that they got really drunk.[131]

Elsewhere the men had not waited that long. On 5 May, a soldier in the NKVD's border guards happened to find a cannister of wood alcohol in the courtyard of one of SMERSh's Berlin stations. He drained an experimental portion into a teapot and shared it with two other troops in the security service. The single pot was not enough, and so they filled a three-liter container and shared that out, fetching yet more when the cook turned up and invited himself to the party. That night, another seven men joined in—or helped themselves, because the original drinkers had passed out by then, happily forgetting that the war was not yet won. They did not live to see the victory. The first three men died on the second day. The rest would die before Keitel had signed the final papers.[132] Such cases were repeated all along the front. Wood alcohol was frequently to blame, but so were antifreeze, white spirits, and even too much looted schnapps.[133] At least the victims never knew the disappointments of the peace.

On 10 May, Berlin was deserted, silent. The streets were empty, and the public squares, where the Wehrmacht had felled trees in preparation for its own artillery, felt blank, bereft even of songbirds. Most soldiers were sleeping off their hangovers. But not everyone had remained in the German capital to greet the end of the European war. Ermolenko was among the thousands of men already heading east. His company had received the news of victory as their train approached the Ural Mountains.[134] He did not know the details of his mission yet, but he was heading for Manchuria. The European war was over, but the Soviets would now join in the struggle to defeat Japan.

It was the first straw in the wind, the first hint, that Germany's defeat would not mean the end of military service for Red Army troops. They had fulfilled their duty, as Belov had said, not flinching even to the last. But now the first of many disappointments loomed. It would not be a few weeks, but some months, and even years, before most men would see their wives and families again. As for their hopes, the dreams that they had nurtured through long evenings of talk and writing, it would be a longer wait still. As Kopelev, watching the flames rising above Neidenburg understood, it was not clear what these people were now equipped to do. It would never be clear how they would deal with peace. The only thing that they could count on as they watched the spring unfold around the ruins of Berlin was the ruthless power of the state for which so many had died. They had saved it. Now they would learn the measure of its gratitude.

TEN

SHEATHE THE OLD SWORD

★

May 9 was a glorious day in Moscow. That night, just after one o'clock, the familiar voice of Yury Levitan, the Sovinformburo's wartime announcer, had confirmed that the war with Germany was over. The news flew around the city within minutes. People woke their neighbors, abandoning the caution that normally regulated social contact in the capital city. Whole families rushed out into the streets, the men clutching the bottles that they had been saving for this very hour, and a great party began that would roar into the coming evening. Dawn would bring yet more people to town, and as many as three million had crushed into the open spaces around the Kremlin by the afternoon. A day like this would have been unforgettable enough without the night to come. But then, well after nine o'clock, as the spring horizon began to fade, hundreds of searchlights were switched on. They flooded the famous ensemble of buildings—the art deco hotel facades, the crenellated walls and towers—with waves of purple, red, and gold. A fleet of planes flew low above Red Square, releasing colored flares into the darkness, and then the fireworks were lit, the best that even Russians could remember. "For once," wrote a delighted Werth, "Moscow had thrown all reserve and restraint to the winds. The people were so happy," he added, "that they did not even have to get drunk."[1]

The victory seemed to belong to everyone. There was no real distinction, for a moment, between factory workers and office staff, typesetters, engineers, collective farmers, and the designers of tanks; they had all paid a price, not least in prodigious effort, for the defeat of Fascism. But no one felt prouder, or more entitled to claim ownership of this victory, than the soldiers themselves. "On these joyful, happy days these lines are being written in Berlin by me!" Orest Kuznetsov wrote to his sister on 10 May. He was scribbling on a postcard of Unter den Linden, blotting out the German caption with his army pen. "There are no words," he wrote, "you can't choose them, to reflect the future joy of this victory, a participant in which you have been and saw it all with your own eyes, walking round the center of the 'den' as a conqueror, as the owner. The faces of every officer and soldier shine with the indescribable joy of our achievement! The Great Patriotic War is over—it is a golden book of history. I congratulate you on this great Festival!"[2]

Few people were in any mood to weigh the price that had been paid for this euphoric day, or even to forecast what peace might cost in future. A calculation like that might well have raised some doubt about the victory itself. Could a nation consider that it was triumphant when approximately twenty-seven million of its citizens were dead? What plaudits could the army really claim when twice as many civilians as soldiers had died? It was a strange species of victory that left twenty-five million people homeless, living in *zemlyanki*, or squeezed into windowless corridors. Only Poland could claim that it had lost proportionately more, and it was now a bitter, shattered semicolony.[3] The Germans, certainly, had paid a heavy price, and almost three-quarters of their military losses—human and material—were accounted for along the eastern front. The Red Army had truly punished and defeated the invader. But the toll was heavier for the Soviets than for their adversaries.[4] It is a testimony to the scale of wartime carnage that the estimates of military losses should vary by margins of millions. The nearest anyone has come to a consensus is to say that no fewer than 8.6 million Soviet military personnel were killed during the war, either in Nazi prison camps or on the battlefield. This is the "safe" figure—there are much higher estimates—but nonetheless it represents nearly a third of the total number of men and women who were mobilized into the armed forces.[5]

The Soviet dead included many of the country's best, fittest, and most productive citizens. Three-quarters of the men and women who died in military uniform were between nineteen and thirty-five years old. Of the generation of young men born in 1921, the conscripts who had been called up in time for the Battles of Kiev and Kharkov or for the calvary of Stalingrad, up to 90 percent were dead. The war left whole towns without young adults, and for some years into the future there would be fewer young couples and fewer children. In other words, besides the grief, a burden that Soviet women, in particular, would bear for decades, there was a long-term economic price, even for death. And in terms of strict profit and loss, the war had cost just under three and a half trillion rubles, an estimated one-third of the Soviet Union's national wealth.[6] For the exhausted and depleted labor force, the prospect of rebuilding must have seemed almost as daunting as another winter under fire.

But pessimism was in short supply that May. In Russia, and in large parts of the Soviet empire generally, civilians paused from their work in the fields or among ruined buildings to celebrate deliverance. The victory seemed to attest that this people could never be enslaved. The Soviet state, their Soviet system—and their now revered leader, Stalin—had secured a preeminent place in world affairs, the right to determine futures that stretched beyond the prewar borders. At the front, in Berlin, Prague, and across Central Europe, soldiers—and young officers especially—allowed themselves to dream of the utopia to come. The notion that a better life would be the people's just reward was commonplace. "When the war is over," a Soviet writer had remarked in 1944, "life in Russia will become very pleasant." His hope, like that of millions of others, was that the new friendship with America and Britain would bear lasting fruit, that the Soviet Union's prestige in the world would open doors that had been shut since 1917. "There will be much coming and going," he continued, "with a lot of contacts with the West. Everybody will be allowed to read anything he likes. There will be exchanges of students, and foreign travel will be made easy."[7]

Each person's hopes reflected his experience and interests. Officers, for the most part, favored reforms that maintained Soviet discipline and a conservative morality. But they still believed in the changes to come, and many felt that they had a right, even an obligation, to put their views about the peace to the government. Since 1942, military personnel had been learning how to think. In 1945, they brought their newfound skills and sense of individual responsibility to bear on postwar reconstruction. The task would be hard work at first, but these people were used to that. Real change, not promises of future happiness, was the priority now. "To search for friends in the future," a fictitious teacher tells a veteran in a story from this time, "is the doom of loneliness."[8] Konstantin Simonov captured the determined, hopeful, and reformist mood in the musings of another fictional character, Sintsov. "Something wasn't right even before the war," the veteran reflects. "I'm not the only one who thinks it; practically everyone does. Both the people who sometimes talk about it and the people who never do. . . . Sometimes, it is true, I think about the time after the war simply as a silence. . . . But then I remember again how the war started, and I already know that I don't want it to be the same after the war as it used to be."[9]

The question was exactly how to implement these changes, and even where to start. Again, Red Army officers were never at a loss for words. Still billeted wherever they had seen the victory salutes— forgetful, maybe, of the Soviet world that awaited to the east—they wrote to their advocate back in Moscow, to the Soviet president Mikhail Kalinin. "I have a series of considerations to put to the next meeting of the Presidium of the Supreme Soviet," a lieutenant wrote that July.[10] Like thousands of others, he had seen what a dictatorship, admittedly a Fascist one, looked like from the outside. He had also been to Maidanek, and the impression of its death camp lingered in his mind. The law on political prisoners, he wrote to Kalinin, should be reviewed. The Soviet state had Maidaneks of its own. If there had ever been a justification for these, the sacrifice that citizens had made had swept it away. It was a view whose echo could be heard in almost any army camp. Whatever guilt the people had incurred before the war for failing Lenin's great historic cause, for failing their own destiny, it had been expiated now. The shadows of the 1930s deserved to be exorcised.

The lieutenant's criticisms were not confined to arbitrary arrest and imprisonment. He also tackled the issue of the collective farms. "Give the land to the people themselves," he suggested. He had been listening to his men and knew their view on peasant life. With them, he had seen the condition of agriculture in Romania and Poland. Compared with the abundant world of fat Romanian cattle and well-stocked barns, the memory of Soviet collectives was like a miserable dream. And then there were the smaller things, the irritations that his men had asked him to convey. They wanted to receive their letters more promptly, he wrote, and they wanted the families of their dead comrades to receive parcels just as their own people did. They also wanted to be sure of a fair bread ration for everyone. Finally, like soldiers everywhere, they wanted to complain about the violence on ravaged, lawless Russian streets. "We need to fight all kinds of hooliganism."[11]

A similar list could have been compiled by almost any other officer that summer.[12] The idea that the sacrifices of the war had earned the Russian people something more than slavery was widespread, and the perception was made sharper and more urgent by the ghosts of the dead. A price so high, surely, could not be paid for nothing. The idea that so much blood bought only war, that it paid for the ambitions of dictators, and not for any of their people's dreams, was unthinkable. Officers' letters that summer asked for more freedom, more education, and a livelier cultural life. One man wanted a unified Ministry of Works to supervise the building of new homes, the provision of food, and the refitting of hospitals. Another, anxious about the neglect of education in the war, asked for a Ministry of Culture with powers to supervise all aspects of literary life from the provision of public libraries to the editing of newspapers.[13] But no one, not even the reformers, demanded democracy, let alone Stalin's scalp. The relative modesty of their claims against the Soviet state—especially in view of the sacrifice that had been made—makes the leader's reply even more callous. For there was never any chance. Not one request on these forgotten lists would ever be fulfilled.

It could be argued that the dreamers always wanted more than a devastated country could deliver. Even personal freedom, when there was so much work to do, was a luxury. To Stalin's mind, only forced labor and compulsory unpaid "voluntary" work could guarantee national recovery. By 1950, the Soviet economy was claimed to be twice the size it had been in 1945.[14] This growth was not achieved by fostering the people's leisure interests. And other postwar governments in Europe, including Britain's, were also obliged to call for austerity. The war impoverished Europe for some years. But the oppressiveness, the lack of trust, and the sheer violence of late Stalinism exceeded any economic or security requirement. There had to be some other reason for the darkness that closed in.

Veterans of a contemplative disposition were apt to blame themselves. They realized too late that they had spent their energy at the front line. Many were injured, even permanently disabled, and few escaped some kind of stress and shock. They were also haunted by disabling guilt. A cloud of collective depression stalled and then blocked such people's eagerness to call for change. "The dead are watching me," a soldier says in a poem of 1948, giving voice to a feeling all would have recognized. As Mikhail Gefter, himself a veteran and survivor, would recollect, the doubt that "tortures memory" is the thought that "I could, but did not, save them."[15] For some, the most absorbing peacetime project of the future would be the search for their comrades' graves.

All found it difficult to adapt to peace. In war, an officer gave orders and they were fulfilled, his life was organized around clear goals, and there were secret little pleasures—plundered cognac or a pretty frontline wife—to compensate for military rigors. Infantrymen also had narrow daily worlds, and as peace loomed the routines and close comradeships seemed curiously safe. With the war over, there were no absolute priorities, no rules. Some soldiers found that they could never make the change. To this day, many veterans continue getting up at five-thirty, a habit that retirement and the inertia of poverty still cannot break, but in 1945 the real diehards could hardly bear the very thought of peace. They listened hungrily to rumors of another war, this time with Britain and America.[16] Some even claimed to have seen the first lines of wounded men in Simferopol.[17] It was tempting to hold fast to old anxieties and patterns of familiar stress. War justified the only way of life most of these people could imagine, while peace meant facing the complicated worlds that they had left—and taking cognizance of all that they had lost.

Other postwar governments would work harder to help their veterans adapt.[18] Some did so despite the hardship and cost of war. It was difficult everywhere, but no other combatant nation emerged with quite the cold dictatorship that Stalin built. War alone was not to blame for it, and nor were veterans or memories of death. It was Stalin himself, the leader who took credit for the victory while Zhukov's ink was still wet on the page, who determined the postwar relationship between people and state—Stalin, that is, and the swarm of acolytes and bureaucrats who flourished in the system that his brand of government created. As the spontaneous joy of early May began to cool, the leaders of a dictatorial regime made plans for their own victory parade. The people's carnival was to be superseded by a ceremony along proper Soviet lines, something that put every person in his place.

It took several weeks to finalize the plan. By then, some people had begun to wonder whether grandeur was what they wanted. Some muttered about the expense, others about their private grief. "I won't be going to the parade," one Muscovite observed. "They killed my son. I'd rather go to a requiem."[19] Others of the same view began to call for a day of mourning, or even an annual week of it; no gesture could do justice to the loss that gaped in people's lives. For the next fifty years, real memories would infuse the annual victory holiday in early May with a solemnity that other socialist festivals, including the anniversary of Lenin's coup and Red Army Day, would lack. Wartime bereavement was a shadow that would never lift. For some, it meant the end of family happiness. "I have two children and no help from anywhere," a woman lamented. "That's why I don't see the point of celebrating, and I've got nothing to be pleased about."[20]

Anxiety, loneliness, and the fear of penury would grow more troubling for widows and orphans as winter approached. But still, that June, the consensus favored a state event, something to embody and contain the chaos of pride, victory, shock, and apprehension for the future. As usual, that meant a rehearsed ceremony and a handpicked crowd. The cost must have been staggering. Selected soldiers, sailors, and airmen were brought home from Germany and the Baltic. The cavalry got to shine its boots, the regimental bands tuned up, tanks, guns, and death-dealing Katyushas were lovingly oiled. Whole companies of cadets from

Moscow training schools, future artillerymen and engineers, took lessons in advanced parade-ground drill.[21] Each gesture and each step was choreographed, including those of Zhukov and the generals. The only thing that could not be controlled—apart from Zhukov's gray horse, which was known for its bad temper—was the Moscow weather. The grand parade, the culmination of four years of war, took place on 24 June in drenching rain.

The change of mood since 9 May could scarcely have been clearer, though thousands of Muscovites, still shocked and overjoyed by the war's end, may well have overlooked the shift. Instead of happy chaos, this was a day of geometrical precision. Red Square was filled with shapes, not individual people. Each rectangle in the parade was composed of scores of uniformed men. In the best traditions of authoritarian states (but for its massive scale, the event could have been a Nazi sports festival), they all moved to exact routines, none even looking in a direction that had not been agreed upon and rehearsed in advance. The parade was blatant with gold braid. This was an army with a sharp hierarchy and strong leaders, not a people's militia or even the sword of the world's proletariat. Zhukov himself reviewed the troops, perching on that tetchy gray and soaking in the endless rain. The themes that day were triumph and authority. The victory, it was made clear, was about Germany's defeat, not Russia's liberty. In a grand gesture of conquest, the captured German colors, each topped with a silver eagle, were hurled down in a pile before the Lenin mausoleum. They might have gleamed in the June light. Instead they made a sodden pile of red and black in the gray damp.

Stalin watched from the safety of his stand. He was, by all accounts, exhausted, and he had visibly aged. But he had lost none of his anxious jealousy. That night, at a banquet for twenty-five hundred Red Army officers and men, the leader would propose a toast to the Soviet people. It should have been the supreme moment of glory and gratitude. Instead, the words he used ought to have made an entire nation shudder. For though Stalin acknowledged that this had been a people's war, he was in no mood to elevate rivals. The time for homespun pride was past. While he could have hailed them as heroes, the people who had struggled, the millions whose efforts had kept the soldiers fed and bullets in their guns, became "the little screws and bolts" in the great engine of his state.[22] They were to be no more significant in the next decade than the replaceable parts of a machine. A peace on terms like this would be a disappointment to many civilians, but for *frontoviki*, with all their hopes and newfound strengths, it would turn out to be a kind of death, a loss of self. In many ways, it was also a betrayal.

"We've been living in peacetime conditions for about a week already," Taranichev wrote to Natalya on 15 May. "The cannons and machine guns aren't firing anymore, and the planes aren't flying; we don't have to observe a blackout any more—we work at night with the windows open and breathe the fresh air. But . . . there is still plenty of work to do. We will probably be here for a couple of months at least." The continued duty was no real hardship, as he went on to explain. He and a comrade had been billeted with a family near their base in Czechoslovakia. Their hosts were deferential, generous. "They offered us every convenience: we had a bath as soon as we arrived and we have been given a room of our own with wonderful beds and snow-white linen."[23] There was even a radio in the room—another excellent German one—that Taranichev (notwithstanding the kind hosts) already planned to take home when he left. Indeed, a good part of his letter was about the parcels that were on their way to Ashkhabad. His other main preoccupation was the future. Like his comrades, he yearned to know the date he would go home.

The bulk of front-line troops were now stationed in Central and Eastern Europe. Their demobilization was not just desirable in human terms. The Soviet state could not afford to keep an army several million strong in uniform. But what the older men dreamed of—a swift, joyful reunion with their families—would not be possible for most. No army simply dissolves overnight. And while it finalized its plans to debrief and transport over a million men, the Soviet state was content to use soldiers as cheap labor for some of the tougher jobs in construction and transport. As Taranichev hinted, these ranged from rebuilding the roads to securing the ruins of Berlin and dealing with the human columns of former prisoners and refugees. If soldiers in the European theater were bored, it was only because the peace would always be dull—thankfully—after the extreme world of the war. But some Red Army men still had some fighting left to do.

The war did not end on that much-celebrated evening in May. In August 1945, ninety divisions of the Red Army found themselves stationed in Manchuria. Some of these were drawn from the Far East, from Soviet Mongolia, but others, including the group that Ermolenko traveled with, were simply ordered east from stations in the Baltic and Central Europe. Ermolenko himself had been in uniform since 1942. The last action he had seen in Europe had been the battle for Königsberg, one of the bitterest of 1945. His surprise order to take the train east followed an argument with a superior officer in late April. Six weeks later, while his former comrades cracked open another crate of bottles in Berlin, he was setting up his radio station in the shadow of the Grand Khingan Mountains. "We heard with interest that there has just been a law on the demobilization of soldiers aged thirty and above," he told his diary on 28 June. "It's not for me. No one is leaving here for now."[24]

The fighting in Manchuria was short but savage. Ostensibly, the Red Army had been sent east to honor obligations to its allies. If human blood could buy goodwill, the Soviets would pay. In eleven days of fighting, 12,031 Soviet troops would die, the victims of a war that could have little meaning back at home.[25] What Stalin was really doing was attempting to secure the Soviet Far East, as well as backing up his claim to valuable territories such as the Kurile Islands and Sakhalin. Swift action became more important after 6 August, when the United States dropped its atomic bomb on Hiroshima, foreshadowing the war's end and making Soviet aid appear redundant. The very day that Soviet hostilites against Japan began, indeed, a second bomb would devastate Nagasaki. Washington's terrible demonstration of its power was a warning that Stalin was swift to heed. The Red Army went onto the offensive, mounting an attack over some of the remotest and least habitable land in Asia. Stalin's dream was to occupy a portion of the island of Hokkaido. A few more weeks of fighting could have realized that hope. What Ermolenko was witnessing, in other words, apart from hunger, fear, and personal confusion, was one of the first shots of the Cold War.

The shadow of this new conflict would haunt the Red Army in Germany as well. Ostensibly, the Allies—America, Britain, France, and the

Soviet Union—were still working in harness, assisting one another with supplies, the restoration of communications, and the all-important repatriation of displaced persons. But tensions were never far below the surface. The bomb, which crystallized relations between the two sides, was scarcely mentioned in the soldiers' writings in August. It may have seemed so appalling that it could be accommodated only after Molotov declared it safe, announcing to the world that Russia could make one of its own. But fear of America was not the main problem among Red Army veterans in Europe. From Moscow's point of view at least, the most dangerous development in their ranks was the soldiers' half-envious, half-naïve admiration for the lords of capitalism.

The superpowers were destined to be enemies for decades, but for a while their soldiers seemed to be making friends. The attraction was based on respect, gratitude, and complementary social skills. American troops enjoyed the Russians' spontaneity, their talent for impromptu drinks and music.[26] Red Army men were grateful for the razor blades, the cigarettes, the bright packets of gum. For Soviet utopians, too, Chicago was a prototype, these square-jawed, healthy men the models for their own children to come. America was starting to look danger-ously glamorous. The devil, they say, always has the best tunes, and it worried the *politruks* that blues and jitterbug were gaining ground on the Red Army's hymns. The longer they remained in Germany, the more uncertain—from an ideological and disciplinary point of view—the war heroes seemed likely to become.

It took a while for wartime discipline and the fear of the *shtraf* unit to crumble among victorious Soviet troops. The new mood developed in a setting of lawless devastation. The Red Army's own campaigns had destroyed Germany, but now—just like their former enemies—they had to make a life amid the dust and rubble that they had created. A stone's throw from Berlin itself, for instance, was the city of Potsdam. In July 1945, this once elegant suburb would become the setting for a summit meeting between Stalin, Churchill, and the new American president, Harry Truman. But it was no luxury spa. Scarcely a single large building remained intact. On 14 April, Allied bombers had destroyed the city's main industrial plants, as well as the power stations, railway depots, food warehouses, water treatment plants, and streetcar terminal. When the Red Army reached it on 27 April, it was already without supplies of medicine, clean water, electricity, or gas. Its civilian population had received no fresh food for two entire weeks. Without clean water or functioning sewers, they were living amid filth and rapidly spreading disease, including typhus and dysentery. Children were especially vulnerable, but the population as a whole was close to moral and physical collapse. To make matters worse, the city had become a staging post for refugees. Finally, in late April, it would become the site of a pitched battle, complete with all the devastation of the howitzers and mines.[27]

The reconstruction of this wasteland—and the scores of others like it—would have been a daunting task at any time. There were no resources to call upon, no food or fuel reserves to spare. Just as seriously, there was a shortage of experienced personnel. Typically, the Red Army placed its less able officers in charge of reconstruction after the front line had moved on. In Potsdam, the teams that helped to rebuild bridges and clear the streets were made up of individuals who were unfit for front-line service, former prisoners of war, and volunteers drawn from the thousands of expatriates the Soviets discovered as they liberated German soil. "Many of these . . . are extremely undisciplined," the military authorities lamented. They "take part in drinking sessions and in looting." Getting the locals to assist was essential, but most civilians feared to work. The women whose job was to cart away the rubble that blocked Potsdam's streets knew that they risked assault and rape. On one occasion, all six young women in a work brigade were raped at the end of their working day. The bodies of others would turn up like old timber in the piles of debris that littered the streets.[28]

After the peace, rape was sporadic, provoked by impulse or the arrival of new troops. Some German officials believed the Soviets tacitly sanctioned it, especially on public holidays, which were perilous times for women near the soldiers' bases.[29] *Frontoviki* now claim that the offenders were rear-guard rats and civilians, but there is evidence against all groups of men. Indeed, the mood that allowed for disciplinary infringements was often strongest among former front-line soldiers. Back home, staff officers and politicians were enforcing distinctions of rank, but in the field a cozy familiarity was developing between officers and men. Ironically, the effort of defeating Fascism had been a catalyst for breaking down the fear and mutual suspicion that Stalin's regime had worked so long to engineer. It was against regulations, for instance, but many officers habitually used the friendly and informal *ty*, for "you," in place of the more formal *vy* in conversations round the camp. Sergeants were the worst offenders, and old soldiers especially, but even lieutenants seemed to ignore the rules that detailed how to wear the correct uniform.[30] As they settled down, assigned the chores, and whitewashed the new barracks walls, the soldiers' lives, viewed from outside, had begun to look like versions of domestic bliss.[31]

During the war, good officers had learned to know their men, to lead them by building their trust as well as showing who was boss. Too often now—or too often as far as the NKVD's observers could see—these same officers were making themselves comfortable amid the men, condoning crimes if that helped everyone to thrive. Beyond their base, a whole country was in collapse, but inside the perimeter life could feel almost pleasant. At Potsdam that June an army village sprang up around the troops. The soldiers built it themselves, creating versions of bourgeois houses by seizing timber, glass, and even window frames from German ruins. Their main preoccupation after that could be called housekeeping. It was such a domestic business, such a matter of bed linen, eggs, and heating fuel that a report at the time referred to their activities as "self-service."[32] There were even gramophones—another piece of loot—on which the men could play American jazz and jitterbug. And self-service did not stop at the barracks fence. Elsewhere in Germany, soldiers were taking food from farms, demanding regular supplies of eggs and meat. One captain was caught with a haul of three horses and a pony trap, thirty kilos of butter, and twenty-one live geese. Another had demanded that the German population near his base deliver a daily tithe of a hundred eggs and twenty-five liters of milk.[33]

A good deal of this requisitioned food was then sold for stupendous sums of cash. The black market continued to thrive. Almost no item was deemed valueless. Even if the wires were down, a telephone receiver had a future somewhere in Europe. The trick was only to find a buyer. In one small town, Red Army troops corralled fifteen hundred bicycles within a few weeks of the peace. Fuel was also a valuable commodity, especially as soldiers themselves liked to screech through narrow streets in lend-lease trucks and on stolen motorbikes. And for the connoisseur, there was a chance of works of art. Many German treasures, including valuable paintings and other objects looted from Western Europe, were designated as reparations by the Soviets in 1945. But the warehouses in which the crates awaited shipment were no more secure than any other army base. The black market that dealt in art involved soldiers of every rank, including military police.[34] Later on, many of these people would embark on even more perilous deals. By 1946, the highest prices could be fetched for hard currency, tickets, and precious safe conducts to the West.[35]

As usual, the Soviet authorities monitored everything that locals said. "It is clear," one report read, "that apart from a few genuine anti-Fascists, the entire population is unhappy with the presence of the Red Army on German soil and hope and pray for the arrival of the Americans or English."[36] Germans expressed their views in a variety of ways. Bilingual signs appeared outside the few cafés and bars that still functioned, the Russian text inviting custom while the German "translation" proffered some form of disdainful abuse.[37] More seriously, soldiers who went out on their own at night, or even traveled in small groups, were likely to turn up at first light with their throats slit or a bullet in their skulls.[38] If the occupation was to last, and above all if the Soviet zone was not to be a drain on Stalin's resources, some kind of rapport needed to be built between the Red Army and its reluctant hosts. It was not just a case of taming former *frontoviki*. The core of professional soldiers and their officers was outnumbered by conscripts, ex-prisoners, and displaced Soviet civilians. All were in shock, uncertain that the war had really ended. That June, the political administration set out to build a new consensus for the peace.

The first step was to put a stop to the hatred. On 11 June, an order from the Red Army's political administration removed the words "Death to the German occupiers!" from the mastheads of all magazines and newspapers for military circulation. In their place appeared the blander slogan "To our Soviet homeland!"[39] Soldiers also heard lectures on the errors of their former idol, Ilya Ehrenburg. The idea was to turn their minds to other things than killing Germans. But violence had become something of a habit. It would take more than slogans to reverse the hatred that had consumed the men for years. Zhukov, fresh from his triumph in Moscow's Red Square, applied practical threats. "Many complaints continue about robbery, rape, and individual cases of banditry on the part of individuals wearing Red Army uniforms," he observed in an order dated 30 June. He gave his army just five days to put a stop to anti-German acts. Henceforth, he decreed, all troops would be confined to army premises unless they were engaged in official business and closely supervised. As to the growing problem of Red Army officers and men who took informal German "wives," the new order stipulated that anyone seen entering or leaving a private house was to be arrested and punished. Knowing that officers connived with men in every kind of crime, the marshal added that any officer deemed incapable of maintaining a strict disciplinary regime was to be named and recalled from service.[40]

The order had some effect in the weeks that followed. Each military base, at least, reported a drop in recorded crime. Later, investigations would suggest that officers were still colluding with their men, suppressing details of infringements to keep Zhukov's military police off everyone's backs. But there is a consistency to the figures that suggests a real change of mood.[41] Zhukov's prestige and the men's deep regard for him may well have played a part. So did the gradual effects of peace. Rape, for instance, became less common from late June, but one reason for this was that soldiers were striking up more stable friendships with the local women. Some would even form households of sorts, hoping to stay and make a life where chance had thrown them. The practice was so common that only the most brazen immorality was disciplined, such as the case of an officer who had left six "wives" pregnant from Poland to Berlin.[42] According to the mayor of Königsberg, the only Germans in his town who were adequately fed that winter were the women whom Soviet troops had made pregnant.[43] But the most frequent military crimes of the late summer would be drunkenness, failure to wear a proper uniform, and lack of respect for senior officers.[44] The thirst for vengeance had abated.

The other problem in the zone was to persuade the men that peacetime work was important. *Frontoviki*, including former members of punishment units, scoffed at the idea of discipline and regular working hours. "I've seen it all," one soldier remarked. "They'll never keep me here."[45] Men who had trained their bodies and their minds to kill must have found guard duties a bore, and many resented clearing debris from Germany's streets. It was widely felt, indeed, that German civilians should be given the dangerous task of mine clearance, and in many cities squads of volunteers did this work under military supervision in exchange for extra food.[46] But at least the disarming and demilitarization of the Soviet zone felt like a real job. The dismantling and shipping of the large factories that were to be seized as reparations must have been a stranger task. Wherever they saw evidence of German wealth, the men would wonder why the war had been started at all, what such rich people could have wanted with Soviet land. But through it all, whatever their demeanor, Red Army men had to believe that they were victors. Whatever tasks they undertook, they had to think that life was getting better from now on. *Frontoviki*, with all their problems, were an elite within the occupied zone.

It was a different matter for the other Soviet troops, the ones whose war had ended in their capture. Only a fraction of the millions of prisoners taken by Hitler's forces in the first years of the war were still living in 1945. But the total number of prisoners had been so great that there were still thousands of men in Central Europe waiting for rescue when the peace was signed. If they had hoped for swift release, let alone for reinstatement in their former homes, they were mistaken. On 11 May 1945, Stalin signed the order that provided for the establishment of another web of camps in Central Europe. There were to be forty-five on the First and Second Belorussian Fronts alone, each one designed to hold up to ten thousand men. By June, there were sixty-nine camps for special prisoners on Soviet territory and a further seventy-four in Europe.[47] Their purpose was to intern former Red Army soldiers who had been prisoners of war with the intention of "filtering" them, which meant looking for spies, fingering cowards, and assigning punishment to so-called betrayers of the motherland.

The fate of one, P. M. Gavrilov, who was among the very few survivors of the Battle of Brest in 1941, would prove the quality of Soviet justice. Gavrilov was a real hero. Although he had been wounded, and although certain that he would die, he fought to his last bullet, saving one grenade to hurl at the enemy as he passed out from loss of blood. His courage so impressed the Wehrmacht (which was seldom given to sentimental acts) that German soldiers carried his almost lifeless body to a dressing station, whence he was taken to a prisoner of war camp. It was for this act of "surrender" that he stood accused after the liberation of his German camp in May 1945. His next home was a camp again, this time a Soviet one. In all, about 1.8 million prisoners like him would end up in the hands of SMERSh.[48]

Building prisons to hold these "special" veterans was a challenge when resources were stretched. But Soviet secret policemen were always willing to adapt. "The camp is located well outside the town," an NKVD report on a possible facility commented that summer. "It is enclosed with secure fencing and has structures suitable for housing special contingent prisoners." Nazis had always known exactly how to build a jail. The site, just beyond the town of Oranienburg, was the extermination camp at Sachsenhausen. Thirty thousand people had been murdered there under the recently defeated Nazi regime. The Red Army had liberated it on 22 April, finding a few hundred survivors in conditions so desperate that many would die before doctors could save them. But though the gas chambers were empty and the guard posts abandoned, it was a well-built and convenient prison. For years to come, it would house consignments of expatriates waiting for the attentions of SMERSh, the cells and darkness, and the train ride to the east.[49]

The most miserable fate was reserved for the so-called Vlasovites, most of whom had also been prisoners of war at some stage in their lives. They included the men who had caved in and agreed to fight for the Reich rather than face starvation in the camps. A minority were also active anti-Soviets, especially the leaders of the "national legions" from the Caucasus, the Baltic, and Ukraine. Some of these ended their war in Western Europe, since they had been fighting in France and Belgium. Like tens of thousands of other Soviet citizens, they would be solemnly "repatriated" by Stalin's former European allies in the eighteen months that followed Berlin's fall. In all, about five and a half million Soviet citizens had been sent back to their former homeland by the end of 1946. Of these, something like a fifth were either executed at once or sentenced to twenty-five years of hard labor. Others took their own lives, and even those of their accompanying families, rather than face the mercy of Soviet military police.[50]

Detachments of Red Army guards whose job was to escort these men forgot about Soviet brotherhood. Their *politruks* told them that Vlasovites were the worst traitors, and soldiers treated their prisoners accordingly. Entire groups would be robbed, their cases opened and the soap, tobacco, razor blades, and socks removed for sale. "I took his shirt to clean my gun," a soldier told military police. It happened all the time.[51] "Specials" were treated as convicts while they awaited "filtration." The onus was always on them to prove their innocence. The process could take months, even years. SMERSh and its successors were still "filtering" displaced persons in the 1950s.[52] While they waited, the wretched prisoners faced insults and bullying, and the same treatment would continue when they were assigned to labor camps. By August 1945, just over half a million were already at work. Quotas of former prisoners and "traitors" were assigned to the coal-mining and power industries, to construction work, timber, steel, fisheries, engineering, chemicals—anywhere labor was needed and money was scarce. The condemned were supposed to be grateful to Stalin for sparing their lives.

The conditions of the disgraced men, as one survivor remarked, rivaled the hardships of a Nazi camp. Ex-combatants were sent to the Caucasus to work in timber yards with neither outer clothing nor footwear. With no solid housing and no means of bathing, they had no defense against the endless plagues of lice.[53] Many went hungry, and most worked without pay. "I won't pay you a penny," one labor organizer told his team. "You were sent to us as betrayers of the motherland, as self-seekers, and you're just here to work." The foreman of a Siberian mine assured a member of his work contingent that "a ton of coal is dearer to us than your life."[54] His hatred drew on bitter roots. Many of the toughs who managed former soldiers had originally been victims themselves. The camps and mines of Siberia were ruled by former kulaks, the peasants whom Communism had dispossessed in the early 1930s. Now they could vent their rage on disgraced soldiers. "As soon as your officers' backs are turned," one of them hissed, "we're going to kill you with hunger and hard labor. And you deserve it because in 1929–30 you were the ones who dekulakized us."[55]

The Soviet authorities pressed for the repatriation of the "specials" for several reasons. They wanted to make examples of some traitors, and they also feared, as historian Richard Overy puts it, that Vlasovites in Western Europe would prove to be "undesirable witnesses against communism."[56] But on their journey home, the prisoners would often turn out to be equally undesirable advocates of capitalism. There was always some contact between prisoners and their Red Army escorts. Thousands of these *frontoviki* had been impressed with the capitalist farms and private businesses they had seen, and they discussed it all with their new prisoners. "I haven't had enough to eat in my whole life," one young soldier declared. "So how come they live in such a civilized, orderly way in Poland, when we have none of that?"[57] The former Vlasovites laughed at such naïveté. Poland, they explained, was backward, war-ravaged, scarcely a place to envy. Some of them had seen France, Holland, even Belgium. An entire contingent of Georgian troops had been billeted on foggy Texel island; Ukrainians had been sent to fight in France. "Belgium is a country of high culture," one soldier told his audience. "It has a highly developed economy. You can live well there." When some smart komsomol snapped back that the Belgians had a high rate of unemployment—a common Soviet defense when faced with the glamour of capitalism—the soldier's reply was ready. "Oh yes," he agreed. "The women there have nothing to do, so they can exist exclusively for love."[58]

The party's answer was the usual combination of lectures and cold threats. Soldiers and prisoners alike were subjected to homilies with titles like "Comrade Stalin's Views on the Goals of the Red Army and Soviet People and on Relations with the Population of Germany," "The Fundamental Economic Tasks of the USSR," and "We Must Be More Watchful on Alien Soil."[59] Meanwhile, SMERSh listened for treacherous talk. "Filtration" was to be the fate of every former prisoner of war or deportee, and many buckled under the weight of suspicion. But even good *frontoviki* were watched for signs of weakness. The only sanction that Stalin's regime could use on a mass scale was the labor camp. During the war, the population of the Gulag had dropped sharply, mainly through hardship and death. By 1946, the camps were filling up again.

Red Army soldiers had not triumphed so that they could run a jail.

The longer Soviet troops remained in Germany, the less they cared for Moscow's homilies and threats. A culture developed among the old hands. Drink, women, secrets and hard currency were its main constituents. Eighteen months after the peace, it was clear to Stalin's officials that almost no veterans could be allowed to remain abroad. Their influence was too liberal, too damaging to the regime of discipline and ideological rigidity. Those who had worked with former prisoners of war and Vlasovites were deemed to be the worst. By the spring of 1947, the Soviet military authorities in Germany had come around to the view that all soldiers with two or more years of service on German soil (which meant all combat veterans), as well as anyone who had worked closely with candidates for repatriation, should be sent home without delay.[60] They were to be replaced by more reliable, younger, less capricious types. The *frontovik* was fine for winning wars, but authoritarian military rule demanded people with the souls of bureaucrats.

The first soldiers to be demobilized were told of their good fortune at the end of June. The military authorities began with selected categories of men aged thirty or over (these were deemed to be "in the older age groups") and also with women who did not have important specialties. It was assumed that older men would be the keenest to get home, and also that they might have family responsibilities to tend. "You should set up a committee and demobilize all soldiers thirty and over," a letter to Kalinin demanded, as if on cue, on 20 June. "We all agree about that. . . . What am I going to do with my wife if I'm over thirty and I still don't have a son? In five, ten years a man loses his chances with the female sex. The season for that doesn't go on after age thirty-five to forty, it's no secret to anyone." A law on demobilization followed three days later, although it was far from comprehensive, even for the older men. "What would you do," the same impatient veteran continued, "if every soldier demanded to go home on the same day? Our guards and officers wouldn't be able to do a thing, because they want to go home too. It's the power of the people."[61]

The reality was that the soldiers were trapped, at least in the short run. For one thing, the beleaguered, bomb-damaged transport system that stuttered between Berlin and Brest could not take them all home at once. But from the government's point of view the real problems were inside the soldiers' minds. To send them home without careful preparation was too much of a risk in ideological terms. The dismal, bloody victory needed its garland of heroes, which meant laying the ground for their reception, and that would take time and thought. Then there was the danger that the veterans might brag about capitalism or about life without collective farms. They might talk of brutality, of front-line executions, SMERSh, or even the horror of battlefield death. The free-thinking that had started to stalk the front would have to be suppressed before it could infect the civilian world.

Demobilization, then, began to be presented as a kind of privilege, not as the duty of a grateful state to every man and woman who had fought for it. The *politruks* called more of those earnest small-group meetings and explained what was wanted. Their duty, the soldiers were told, was "to keep military and state secrets as closely at home as at the front. Let the demobilized person preserve his warm recollections about the unit and about his wartime friends." But let him not discuss much else. "We had to sign something," the veterans admit. In fact, they were warned that their demobilization, and the material assistance that went with it, depended on their agreeing to keep most of their wartime experience and knowledge to themselves, from death rates and atrocities to missing rations and cold feet.[62] The veterans' discretion now, which often borders on a string of outright lies, dates back to the moment when they signed that document.

And sign they did, for it was only then that real life could begin. True, some soldiers would choose to stay and make their careers in the military—Kirill was one—but most were anxious to get home. The departing men and women were issued civilian clothes and a pair of shoes. They were given travel passes and the papers that would see them safely home. They also hefted packages of food and other small gifts from a grateful state. Their luggage would soon overflow the racks and boxes of their passenger trains, spilling into the corridors and contributing to the shared fug of tobacco, garlic, damp blankets, and diesel. Soldiers demobilized from Erfurt in 1946 could expect to be issued "a sports suit, sweater, underwear, leather, and slippers," as well as—if they were officers—"a pair of women's shoes." They also received five kilos of sugar, ten kilos of flour, a kettle, spoons, a carpetbag, a towel, and some biscuits for their journey.[63] Most also received money, the sum depending upon their rank and length of service.[64] But this largesse was offset by continual surveillance. The men were warned not to attempt to carry weapons. Their bags were searched before they left the base.[65] The ritual was futile, for anyone could help himself to weapons and explosives any time by digging in the scarred fields at home.

Eventually, with the inevitablity of a dream, the moment came to cross the boundary, to walk away from army life for good. Most veterans recall an aching loss. However much they yearned for home, it was a sudden wrench to leave the boys. The last few hours such men spent at a base were given up to speeches and to singing. "We sang our manly, stern soldiers' marching songs," Lev Pushkarev, the ethnographer, wrote. But these were the songs of victory. The real emotion surrounded the music of defeat, the songs of loss and homesickness from 1942— "Wait for Me," "Zemlyanka," "Oh, the Long Road," "Dark Night"— the songs that had sustained a generation as it struggled with despair.[66] The tunes would never sound the same again, nor evoke as much meaning. Many of the men would cry before their trains pulled out. As they said good-bye to the people who knew just what war was about, to the only people who could ever understand their stories, they were losing their true spiritual family. They would miss them—and most would keep in touch with almost all of them—for the rest of their lives.

It must have been a strange ride home. There was that inconveniently heavy bag to stow, and then the smaller one, the knapsack with the tobacco and the travel pass. Inside this was the salvage of a war, the material evidence of all that a man had seen and experienced. In almost every instance, that began with medals—for victory, for service, for valor, even a grand red star or red banner. Then came the photographs. During the war, press photographers earned petty cash by taking snapshots of the troops, portraits to send home to the wife, group pictures to remind them of their mates. Already, as the train rattled toward Brest and Smolensk, the men on board must have been thumbing these, wondering at the looming shapes of guns, the sunlight through last summer's trees, the smiles on young faces long dead. However long they lived, there would never be time to explain all this. And the gifts, the shoes and watches, these seemed to have a different meaning now. At the front, they had been easy booty, fragments of abundant victory. But now, as the world of triumph and comradeship began to fall away, they became totems, precious, rare, and at the same time tarnished by the secret guilt of having lived, not died.

The trains crossed the border again, this time heading eastward and home. They passed the familiar string of Belorussian and then Russian towns, the names that had been shouted in euphoric triumph as the Red Army stormed west. Now the men could actually look, and some would notice what the war had cost. Belorussia was a wasteland, Kiev blackened and destroyed. Whole swaths of farmland looked neglected, for there were fewer people living than five years ago, and scarcely any men or horses to take on the heavy work. The landscape was deadly as well, seeded with unexploded shells and mines. Bridges and tracks had been repaired, but the men who chose to hitch a truck ride for the last miles home would find the roads in chaos—broken, muddy, and still cluttered with the skeletons of tanks. It was one thing to glimpse all this in wartime, in a crowd, to know that all you had to do was fight. It was another to look at the pitted ruins of Leningrad, Pskov, or Stalingrad and understand that the whole landscape would have to be cleared, secured, and rebuilt. Berlin had looked little better, but it had never been these soldiers' own responsibility, their future.

There would be one more act in every soldier's odyssey before civilian reality took hold. As ever, Stalin's feral face presided. His portrait was emblazoned on the trains, his name written across the banners that fluttered above the local party halls. But the ceremonies of welcome for returning veterans were heartfelt. It had not been the party alone, but hundreds of families, who paid for the flowers that decked the trains as they pulled into Kharkov, Kursk, or Stalingrad. At every stop along the way, indeed, the red carpets had been unrolled, and the men had been offered gifts and food. There had been music, those Red Army hymns, and in some places there had been a real orchestra to play among the Stalins and the scarlet flags. Every platform had been a sea of red cloth, flowers, and cheering crowds. At its best, one of those early journeys was like an extended party.

Perhaps this festive mood carried the soldiers through the shock of coming home, but it was a tense and even terrifying time. They might

A train carrying demobilized soldiers arrives in Moscow, 1945

have longed for it, and even thought of little else, but the veterans' reunion with parents, children, wives, and friends was overcharged with
feeling. As the trains pulled into their final stops, the men would have
seen a crush of people surging forward, eager strangers, so many
women. They would have scanned the crowds, the printed summer
dresses, the children with their photographs of vanished, younger men.
And when they found their own people, they must have realized again,
in a second, what the war had meant. Caught in the flash of cameras
that July, the veterans look like members of a new species. Dusty and
sunburned, blinking in a long-forgotten light, they seem to bear no relation to the civilians who press around them. They certainly look older,
and their skin, as their own children reach to kiss it, looks tough and
dry as leather. And yet, as the pictures also show, the moment shone
with real joy.

The welcoming ceremonies had been planned in detail by the local
branches of the party. Attending to the former soldiers' needs was not
just a matter of proper gratitude—although it certainly was that. The
orchestrated welcome was also meant to flood men's minds. Where
politruks had influenced the soldiers' thinking at the front, the local

Demobilized troops arrive in the town of Ivanovo, 1945

party activists busied themselves providing education and approved kinds of entertainment. The men were kept supplied with newspapers and propaganda sheets. Their hostel rooms were provided with soft drinks, sweets, and tobacco. Married men whose families had traveled to meet them were sometimes put up in hotels until a horse and cart arrived to take them all back home. Single men, and especially the homeless, who faced long periods in transit, were given food parcels to supplement the ordinary ration cards civilians could use. They were also treated to lectures. In Kursk, which housed many transient ex-soldiers, that summer's program featured talks on the international situation, the heroic past of the Russian people, the life and times of Maxim Gorky, and "medical themes," presumably lice, drinking, and VD. Over two thousand people attended. They also showed up for the free movie shows and concerts that the town authorities laid on. Ex-soldiers could not be left to smolder on their own.[67]

More seriously, someone had to attend to housing, family life, and work. Some of the "hotels" where the men would stay were little more than tents. Wherever the Germans and then the Red Army had been, houses with solid walls were few. Men might go "home" to find their wives and children in a one-room flat with no kitchen, no water, and a leaking roof. They might find everyone in an earth dugout, worse even than the ones they remembered from Stalingrad or the Crimea. Local authorities scrambled to find homes for returning heroes. In Smolensk, though, a city that had suffered as much as any under the occupation, about a quarter of the veterans were still homeless in January 1946.[68] But that still made ex-soldiers an elite. In Kursk, even the shops where the men might have gotten their shoes patched or their worn-out prewar clothes repaired were in ruins.[69]

The initial waves of returning soldiers received the greatest applause. Later, in 1946, new groups of veterans would come home to silence or at best to a speech and a breadline. But everyone, even the first men back, would have trouble finding their feet. Most took a few days off, which the authorities approved. Some used the time to get to know their families. There was so much to talk about—or else so many silences, such doubts. But then came the question of work. At the top of the priority list for demobilization were teachers, especially those with experience in technical subjects, for the state needed its specialists more than ever. Next came students whose courses had been interrupted by war service; they would go to the head of the line for college places when the academic year began.[70] For those equipped to benefit, war service could be the start of a better life.

But the first groups to be demobilized also included veterans with seven or more years of service, the elderly (in army terms), and soldiers who had received three or more serious wounds. Typically, these men were destined for the farms. Well over half the troops came home to rural areas, to villages that they had left four years or more before. By

January 1946, nearly forty-four thousand soldiers had been demobilized to the Smolensk region alone. Of these, thirty-two thousand had found jobs in agriculture. A few had been made *kolkhoz* chairmen or the leaders of the many rural work brigades. A veteran commanded some respect, at least if his body was whole. But the majority, three-quarters of the total, had come back from the front to mud and cockroaches again.[71] In 1946 the harvest failed. In Ukraine and southern Russia the people starved, their bodies swelled, tales of strange murders, and even of cannibalism, began to circulate. Some returnees might well have wondered what it was that they had fought and suffered for.

★

They would have struggled, certainly, to find the promised better life. Their moment in the limelight was to be short-lived. It is probably never possible for postwar societies to cherish veterans enough: there are too many reasons to spurn the returning strangers, especially after the gaps that their departure left have closed. The Soviet state and many individual families made a genuine effort to welcome the veterans it chose to celebrate in 1945 and 1946. The ones selected for disgrace and exclusion, naturally, soon vanished from view. But it would not be long before even the most triumphant of returning soldiers became old news in a country struggling to forget. Stalin would set the new official tone. He was proud to take credit for the victory but reluctant to share it. He was also aware that stories of his own mistakes were waiting to be told, especially those that focused on the debacle and slaughter of 1941. His solution was typically simple. The rivals for his victor's crown, including Zhukov, were demoted, disgraced, or imprisoned, starting in the spring of 1946. By 1948, within three years of the peace, public remembrance of the war was all but banned.[72] There were still attempts to commemorate the dead, and commissions that worked to clean up and arrange clusters of military graves, but veterans of a reflective turn of mind could well have wondered if their state did not prefer dead heroes to the living kind.[73]

Initially, the easiest thing to offer to returning combatants was material help. Each meeting of Kalinin's Soviet seemed to propose a new pension or handout for the sick, the orphaned, the widowed and demobilized. The needy families of veterans were supposed to receive heating fuel—logs or turf—as the winter approached; they were also given sacks of flour and potatoes. They were supposed to be first in line for whatever housing had been patched up and deemed habitable, and their children were exempted from school fees, issued clothing coupons, and promised more milk. The veterans themselves received pensions whose size was determined by length of service, rank, and any injury. But all these scraps and packets were controlled by overworked officials of the state. Resources in each town or village were managed by local networks, bureaucrats who had spent their war at work behind the lines. To veterans, these office functionaries were a breed apart, "rats" whose priorities would never match their own. The tensions between those who had fought and those who had stayed at home found expression in quarrels over flats and heating, food and children's shoes.

The situation was even more poignant in the case of invalids. In the first months of peace, it was beyond official means to calculate the total number of these men, and many of the critically ill would die before the end of 1945. But by the spring of 1946, the state estimated that there were roughly 2.75 million surviving invalids of the war.[74] Like everything this government would touch, these people were ranked in categories, depending on the extent of their disability and their need for hospital care. All received pensions as a form of compensation for their inability to work, and many were entitled to parcels containing delights like kasha, dried fish, and eggs. They were also supposed to receive the best available medical attention, and here things became more difficult. Many hospitals were housed in shacks or former schools; there were few sound buildings left.[75] Then there were shortages of doctors, nurses, drugs, and prosthetic limbs. Young men who had lost their legs were forced to trundle around on their own homemade carts, and maimed beggars became a common sight in Russian towns.

The disabled were handicapped in several cruel ways. True, the Soviet Union was desperately poor, unable to meet the most basic needs for lack of funds. But the blind, the deaf, and the crippled might have tolerated that, at least for a time. It was the public attitude that hurt. This was a haunted nation, but it was also a nation trying to forget. The jazz and foppish clothing that enjoyed an unofficial vogue among the young in 1946 were part of a larger quest for release, for deliverance from the shadow of wartime austerity. Disabled people were a nuisance, an embarrassment. Since most had once been foot soldiers, they usually lacked education, influence, or cash.[76] Instead of gratitude, these Ivans often met with resentful silence. The more they talked about the war, the more they made their case, the more unwelcome they became, the more irrelevant. The last blow fell in 1947, when Stalin ordered the streets of Soviet cities cleared of beggars, many of whom were amputees. Maimed veterans who had chosen urban life were herded back onto trains, this time bound for the north and especially for Valaam, an island on the far side of Lake Ladoga. Stalin's untouchables often died in exile.[77]

For those who lived in the remoter villages, the peasant riflemen, a disability of any sort was a different kind of trap. A man with one leg or no arms could not get on a horse and ride.[78] But it might be scores of miles to the nearest rail station. The peasant hut became a prison. An invalid could be deprived for years of medical attention, company, and work. The state occasionally proposed new training programs, but the details were an insult to men who had fought. Blind veterans, for instance, were encouraged to learn to play musical instruments. The idea was to lift them out of depression, to help them earn their keep. But many had no aptitude for music, or no desire to learn it, let alone to busk like beggars on the street.[79] People's real skills were left to rot for want of more imaginative help. For their part, invalids began to avoid medical care. Faced with imprisoning hospital walls, the petty tyranny of orderlies, they preferred to stay at home, nurse memories, and soothe the pain with *samogon*.[80]

Drink was the remedy of choice for pain of a more universal kind, the shock and trauma that followed the war. There was little official recognition of war's psychological effects, and almost none of the condition that is now called post-traumatic stress disorder. For one thing, everyone had nightmares. The entire nation had suffered, even children. To complicate matters still more, the violence, though new in scale and vehemence, was not unprecedented in a country that had seen both civil war and state repression over several decades. It was not clear where the line should be drawn between the shock, depression, and exhaustion that everyone felt and genuine psychological disorder. Physicians went on noting cases of contusion, and they also responded to the most acute problems, with diagnoses of neurosis, schizophrenia, and mania piling up on hospital desks. But veterans were unlikely to get treatment for battle shock. They might be given vitamins, and in extreme cases they might be locked away. But most were urged to think of duty and get on with life.[81] Madness carried a real stigma, and dependency of any kind was treated as weakness.

Conscientious doctors still observed and noted changes that official dogma was unable to explain. For a few months after the war's end, problems with blood pressure, digestive complaints, and even heart disease increased.[82] But these could readily be dismissed as the universal effects of wartime life. Moreover, the postwar hospitals to which sufferers were referred were so uninviting, and the treatments so uncertain, that the number of sufferers who were prepared to report symptoms dropped rapidly from 1946.[83] When veterans talk of the good old days, the great communal struggle, they never mention the sleeplessness and long-term malnutrition that afflicted almost everyone. They also forget the untreated toothache, the chronic infestations of lice, the diarrhea and boils. The soldiers who survived to tell their stories for this book were a small elite in physical terms. War injuries, poor diet, and strain would shorten millions of lives.

No fantasy of the good war, however, was stronger than the idea that the people pulled together. It was tempting, of course, to look for hidden benefits to balance the war's obvious cost, to hope that all the suffering had brought out something good. And it is true that singleness of purpose—and achievement—gave some people an extraordinary inner strength. But the idea of a warm community was either propaganda or wishful thinking. For those whom the state punished, postwar life was cruel. For all the rest, it was a time when relief was tinged with disquiet. Everyone would find, too, that Soviet society had grown harder, more brutal, and cold.

The policies and public style of Stalin's ruling clique set the tone. The vengeful treatment of liberated prisoners of war, the calls for sustained vigilance against spies, the new rounds of arrests and trials all worked to fuel suspicion, not build communities. The veterans were not to blame for Stalin's genocidal schemes. But many would connive in them, becoming willing heirs of tyranny. For those who could not face a quiet night, there were still regions where the war had yet to end. In Ukraine and the Baltic, nationalist guerrillas went on fighting until the late 1940s. Special troops, the successors of Mikhail Ivanovich's OSMBON, were ranged against them, backed up by security police. By 1950, an estimated 300,000 people had been arrested and deported from western Ukraine. Large mass graves continue to surface from beneath those pretty orchards and neat lupin fields.[84] Red Army veterans who fulfilled their wartime dream of moving to Ukraine would settle on stolen land, in empty houses that were thick with ghosts. So would the thousands who moved to the Crimea, a favored place for soldiers to retire. The crime against the Tatars was officially ignored. For veterans, the coastal villages of the Black Sea were attractive enough to soothe whatever doubts might linger in their minds. They were the conquerors, after all, and this was Soviet soil.

War itself, too, had shattered Soviet family and social networks and debased further the values of mercy, cooperation, and even simple good manners. Society was divided, and all sides viewed the others with dismay. Prisoners, ex-soldiers, and civilians were almost like unrelated tribes. Veterans like Vasily Grossman were shocked by the callousness of postwar urban life. It was, he wrote, as though "ordinary people had made an agreement to refute the view that one can always be sure of finding kindness in the hearts of people with dirty hands."[85] But the comradeship of the front line was also set to shatter in the peacetime world. Crimes like theft and drunken violence would persist even when the peace was signed. They were, if anything, made easier by the movements of people, refugees and settlers, not to mention all the guns.[86]

The family ought to have been a haven for war-damaged men. Stalinist propaganda, and much postwar writing, tried to present it that way.[87] But as they headed home on those garlanded trains, few soldiers could have anticipated the toll that war had taken on domestic life. The so-called home front had been very hard on women. Some, working like oxen, had given up on femininity for good.[88] It served no purpose, brought no joy. In rural areas, too, there were almost no males. "I was left with three sons," a widow told Alexiyevich. "They were too young to look after each other. I carried sheaves of corn on my back and wood from the forest, potatoes and hay. . . . I pulled the plough myself and the harrow, too. In every other hut or so there was a widow or a soldier's wife. We were left without men. Without horses, they were taken for the army, too."[89] These women would grow tough, unblinking. Some even nursed resentment against the army that had abandoned them to the Germans for so many months. When their invalid husbands returned home, the shelter that they gave them was not always warm. Indeed, some women deliberately married invalids in order to claim the handouts—pensions, food, fuel, and medical supplies—that their husbands' documents provided for.[90] The trick was to know where to sell them on.

"What games did we play?" A man who grew up in this grim decade thought for a moment. "We didn't play much at all. We had to grow up fast." It was the truth. Children were taught that there was more to life than games. Many had gone without schooling for several years, including Aleksandr Slesarev's young sister, Masha, and the thousands of "sons of the regiment" who were now coming home. As they recalled, no teaching now would ever buy those years of schooling back, and nothing could wipe out the images of war. Masha Slesareva, who was already laboring full-time in the fields at fourteen, was typical of the millions of children who started work as soon as they could shift a shovelful of earth. But though the war's children could not remember much fun, some pastimes had proved unforgettable. "That's it," one man recollected. "We used to play 'the ravine of terror.' We used to throw grenades into this gully near the town and wait to see which ones were live." The game had cost his best friend both his hands.[91]

Home, then, was not the haven that the soldiers conjured as they sat up writing to their wives. Even the couples who managed to rebuild their lives together were aware of a gap, of a blank space that no amount of talking could enliven. It was a cruel payment for the waiting and the letters. Vitaly Taranichev and Natalya Kuznetsova would pull through, but the journey toward reunion was difficult. Vitaly's letters grew more impatient through the summer of 1945. By August, even his army food was poorer, especially after his deployment to western Ukraine. In

September, there was a spark of hope that he might be demobilized, but instead he was moved southeast, to yet another haunted region, Chechnya, where his job was to rebuild the rail links near Groznyi. His requisitioned quarters were nearer to Ashkhabad. "Our apartment has two rooms and an enclosed veranda," Vitaly wrote home. "The second room is not a through room, and I've taken it. If you can come, we'll be really nice and comfortable; we'll even be able to cook and eat together."[92]

Vitaly could not get leave, so the traveling and the strain fell on Natalya. In October 1945, she took time off from her own engineering job, stood in line to buy tickets, left the children, and embarked on an unscheduled adventure. After the long train ride west over the semidesert to the Caspian, she crossed the inland sea by steamer, then fought her way onto another train into the foothills of the Caucasus. The journey to and from Chechnya took longer than the brief time she had with her husband. For Vitaly, so used to traveling, the price seemed well worth paying. But Natalya was left feeling unsettled. "Your silence really makes me miserable," she wrote to him when she got home. "You haven't written a single line to me since I left. You don't want to write anything. . . . Perhaps you were disappointed by the way I was, and you have already stopped thinking about me the way you used to do before our meeting in Groznyi?" It was the November holiday, and Vitaly was, in fact, writing at the same moment. "My landlady and I talk about you all the time," he began. "I have become so used to your being here that every time I come home I half expect to find you." He was unable to imagine her insecurity before the uniformed, preoccupied stranger he had become. "Can it be, Vitya," she wrote, "that you are not the same as you once were, and I am no longer dear to you anymore? It's so hard for me to think like that. I'm waiting impatiently for you at home," she finished. "I need to know by looking in your eyes exactly who you really are."[93] Ten months later, she was still waiting.

Vitaly and Natalya's story was about as good as homecomings got. Another story, that of a woman named Valentina and her husband, was probably more typical of younger couples. As Valentina explained, she and her husband, married just before the war, had spent almost no time together before he was called up. They were still almost strangers, and the war would perpetuate the gulf. His letters home were regular, but they arrived at intervals, in bundles, scored through by the censor's pen. They also had to find Valentina at the munitions factory to which, as a chemist, she had been evacuated. She worked there for the war's duration, supervising a production line that hummed without a break. Her shifts could be ten hours long, or twelve, and all that time the NKVD watched her every move. As she recalled the war, the strain was still clear in her voice, although a bit of light relief came from an unexpected source. "The German prisoners were nice," she said, referring to the prisoners of war who worked near her site. "They were so clean. They even swept the shelves they kept potatoes on." I asked her if she ever talked to one. "Talked?" she replied. "We danced with them. They were the only men for miles, and they were such good dancers, too."

Her husband had his own experience of Germans. Valentina's file of wartime papers contains photographs of him, sometimes in uniform, sometimes half naked, lolling in a boat. Berlin was a good billet for the young man. It would be 1946 before he would come home. Again, the reunion worked, or rather, it did not end in divorce. He and Valentina lived together until his death in 2001. Eventually, they even had a son, although the young man, like so many others, had died before his father, a victim of the Soviet scourge of heart disease. The family was comfortable, respectable, and privileged to live in a private, three-bedroom flat in the heart of Moscow.

Valentina let me read her husband's wartime letters. She even invited me to dictate some of them into my tape recorder as she busied herself making tea. And then I noticed that she was sobbing, as if the memory were too painful to bear. I thought at once it was my fault. I put the recorder away and went to comfort her, guilty that I had revived old grief. "Oh no," she said as we carried the cups and biscuits from the kitchen. "I don't mind the old letters. But they were such lies. All that stuff about love and homesickness. All the time he was with her, the German woman. They even had a child. He left her the day after their baby was born." Valentina's rage was murderous. She didn't want the man back, but apartments were difficult to get, and married couples— especially veterans' families—took precedence. All the same, when she became pregnant at the end of 1946, Valentina could not bear to carry the child. Abortion was illegal, dangerous. But somehow she managed to find a doctor who would perform one, and somehow she went through with it.

Stories like this would lie beneath so many tight-lipped silences after the war. The sacrifice, the epic hope, would peter out in the quest for a larger room in the communal flat, a holiday in newly Russified Crimea, or maybe a collection of kitsch ornaments made from tank parts (clocks made from dials were briefly in demand).[94] The flurry of altruism that had livened the first weeks of the victory, like the vogue for jazz, soon faltered. The favored veterans were privileged, and it would be these small advantages, the knowledge that the neighbors envied them, that bound them, like a sort of postwar middle class, to Stalinism. Little advantages, that is, and the terror of chaos, disorder, arrest, and vengeance from anyone that postwar politics chose to exclude. The war that the heroes had fought had not been a campaign for holidays or sausage. It was a betrayal, albeit small, when the soldiers' passion was allowed to dissolve into small lies, vodka, and homemade jam. But the real tragedy, the perfidy of Stalin's final years, was the theft that forced decent citizens to acquiesce in tyranny because of fear, the theft of almost every grand ideal that they had fought to save.

It was not a question of the long term: the Soviet Union's collapse, Communism's ultimate defeat. Those problems waited for the veterans' old age. The first betrayals were immediate. At the top of the list were the collectives. They would stay, and it would be the veterans themselves, often, who would have the job of trying to make agriculture work. They even helped to export the detested model to the reconquered Baltic and western Ukraine, as well as watching it become established in Soviet-controlled territories like Poland, Hungary, and Czechoslovakia. Then there was Soviet brotherhood, the hope that everyone would pull together to build a society where class, religion, and ethnicity were no longer divisive. That one was trampled by the hate campaigns, the deportations, and the racist language that Soviets learned from their Nazi invaders. Among the victims of the new Soviet chauvinism, cruelly, were Jews.[95] The Gulag swelled, hungrily drawing new contingents—including veterans themselves—into its twilight of forced labor.[96] Even the arts, so dear to soldiers at the front, were subject to obscene and stifling attack, as were many of the poets and writers whose work had tried to capture the truth of the war.[97] Once more, Stalin's dictatorship relied on exclusion and fear, and the people with the most to lose (albeit pitifully little) became its strongest supporters.

There is no doubt that Russia—and much of the Soviet Union— would have suffered terribly if Hitler had succeeded in capturing Moscow back in 1941, if Stalingrad had fallen, or wartime Soviet government dissolved. Just as seriously, the whole of Europe, and even the United States, would have faced an unthinkable catastrophe. Stalingrad, Kursk, and Berlin were real victories, and not for Moscow only but for its allies, too. Their human cost was paid by Stalin's people, and whether they were willing soldiers or not, all but a small minority believed that they were on the right side in a true just war. There had not been one kind of soldier, one Ivan, but there was one aspiration, and it was not served by fostering a tyranny no less oppressive than the one all had been fighting to destroy. Unfortunately, the Soviet people, who had acquiesced, however unwillingly, in the emergence of Stalinism, and who had also fought and suffered to defend it, would now permit the tyrant to remain. The motherland was never conquered, but it had enslaved itself.

ELEVEN

AND WE REMEMBER ALL

★

The myth of Ivan began in the midst of war. It was a product of the Sovinformburo, of wartime songs and poetry, and of the stories people loved to read. Even the troops, sometimes, imagined themselves as romantic volunteers, heroes who would do battle for the motherland. Real combat did not coincide with the ideal, but the propagandists' wooden soldier was a useful figure to invoke before an operation and again when the survivors had to struggle with their exhaustion and shock. The simple hero and his skillful, selfless officers were models that gave the men a sense of purpose, glorified the brutal business of killing, and offered a cloak of indemnity for crimes that no one wanted to acknowledge. Given the soldiers' love of irony, such mythic figures also—and simultaneously—served as the objects of crude, self-deprecating jokes, for Ivan was not always master of his weapons or his body, let alone of the latest party directive. But though men mocked the stuffy rules and the solemnity, wartime propaganda keyed into some basic human needs. And it was just as important after the firing stopped. When the conscript army dispersed and soldiers rejoined the civilian world, the notion of the brave and simple rifleman gave them dignity, a public face, whatever private stories they kept to themselves.

The slogans that the men had used acquired an almost holy resonance with time. The Soviet motherland was an inviolable space, its people bound together in their loyalty. But the repetition of familiar words concealed real changes in their meaning. Patriotism, in 1941, was a radical, liberating, and even revolutionary ideal. The notion, in fact, received a moral boost when Hitler's troops invaded. At last true patriots had an invader to repel, rather than shadow traitors conjured by the secret police. The surge of faith in 1941 even revived the ghost of internationalism, for to be patriotic, in the Soviet sense, was once again to be the proud leader of the proletarian campaign for universal brotherhood. It was to be opposed to Fascism, the very cruelty of which, as it became manifest, forced millions to place their hope in socialism. More immediately, patriotism was a matter of self-defense, the collective struggle of the entire Soviet people against aggression. For those who entered into it—the majority of Russian, and probably even Soviet, citizens—the mood was self-righteous. "Our cause is just," Molotov assured the Soviet people in 1941. However far their army marched, and whatever atrocities it committed, most did not stop believing that.

Mass death and suffering rendered the patriotic impulse sacred. The worst outcasts of the postwar years were the supposed betrayers of the motherland. But while it lost none of the sanctimonious passion of 1941, the meaning of patriotic pride had changed by the war's end. The cause turned inward, focusing on Stalin's state and also, above all, on Russia.[1] Instead of aspiring to freedom, patriots would henceforth—wittingly or not—become complicit in the repression of minorities, large-scale arrests, and a bleak and deadly dogma that had almost nothing in common with the libertarian promises that had drawn such crowds to Palace Square in the revolutionary months of 1917. The new Soviet patriotism would be used to condemn and exclude all kinds of dissidents in the years to come. War veterans, many of them still intoxicated with the original idealistic brew and still breathing the old pietism, were trapped. They could not be unpatriotic and they could not stand against the government. This was the country (and, in the early postwar years, the leader) in whose name oceans of blood had been spilled. It did not take the veterans long to turn into conservative bastions of Soviet rule.

The process was not smooth, and there were always issues that made former soldiers boil with rage. Among them was a campaign launched by Nikita Khrushchev, Stalin's successor, to cut the size of the army.[2] Coming on the heels of his famous denunciation of Stalin, the so-called secret speech of 1956, which confused and appalled many ex-soldiers, the apparent betrayal of the armed forces caused widespread disquiet.[3] But the Indian summer of the veterans' long affair with their state was soon to come. Leonid Brezhnev, whose own war record would not have merited a footnote if chance—including the wartime loss of his more talented potential rivals—had not propelled him into the political elite, emerged as the Soviet leader after 1965. His dedication to Bolshevik ideology was slight, his drive for power far stronger. Rather than trying to revive flagging Soviet unity by appealing directly to revolutionary ideals, he used the war myth to rebuild the nation's faltering sense of purpose. The Brezhnev years would turn into a golden age of concrete and hot air, an era of state-sponsored multivolume histories of the war, of solemn speeches of commemoration, handouts, new medals, and the mass design and construction of memorials.[4] The message was that the nation had fought as one, that young lives had been lost, and that new generations owed the past (and also their current leaders) limitless loyalty and gratitude.

The veterans, now in their middle age, were called upon to play a patriotic role again. They had always gathered to remember the war, but now they were encouraged to go into schools, talk of their battles, and fire the romantic imaginations of young citizens.[5] The purpose was to bind a generation that had never known the war more closely to the Soviet ideal. A mythic soldier, the Soviet hero, returned to stake his claim upon the nation's loyalty. This man was stern, moral, and unflinchingly courageous. In many stories, conveniently, he was also dead. Although most veterans remember the great anniversary of 1965, the twentieth year after the victory, as the high point of war commemoration, the historical phoenix that rose from Stalingrad and Kursk in the 1960s was emblematic, two-dimensional.[6] And real pressures worked to keep it so.

Once the official histories had been passed by the censor, for instance, it was forbidden to publish any fact about the war that was not already in print.[7] The archives themselves, those cities of manila files, were closed to almost everyone, and certainly to scholars. Whole areas of wartime life, including desertion, crime, cowardice, and rape, were banned from public scrutiny. And several specific crimes, such as the Katyn massacre, were buried under mountains of denial.[8] In place of the truth, so complex and so comprehensibly human, the state built a glittering and specious edifice of myth.

Few veterans had much to gain by challenging this. For one thing, the myth suited them. Many used their war records as proof of character in the careers they later chose. War service, or at least the loyal kind, earned soldiers generous pensions, while denigrating what became known as "the great exploit" would always seem like insulting the dead. The hero myth was also partly true, or true enough to make successive generations grateful. To rummage through it all in search of weaknesses and crimes might end in collective tragedy; it might even raise questions about the value of Soviet power itself. Brezhnev's regime would never lack for foreign critics, and that gave its supporters an excuse to advocate strict unity at home. "War is war," the veterans would say. And then it would be time to sing the songs again, get out the photographs, and reminisce. The shadows of the past were dispelled by the glamour of collective glory, the accusations dissolved into euphemism. After all, even Stalin had referred to rape, famously, as "having a bit of fun with a woman."[9]

The set and props for Brezhnev's remake of the war epic are still in use across his former empire. When it came to monumental masonry, Soviet output, even in the years of stagnation, was prodigious. The densest concentrations were clustered around former battlefields, and famous sites are still the best places to look for them. There is a granite monument, for instance, on the Sapun rise outside Sevastopol. It is composed of overbearing lumps of polished rock, like a prefabricated cathedral without a roof or even like a giant crematorium, since gas jets feed a pallid line of eternal flames and prerecorded music pipes out from loudspeakers hidden in the walls. Like most other memorials, this one commemorates a triumph, the recapture of Crimea, not the defeats of 1941. In Kiev, the scene of the Red Army's great humiliation that year, a giant Mother Russia celebrates the city's liberation in the same spirit. She towers over the banks of the Dnepr, her drawn sword raised to guarantee that she exceeds in height all other landmarks, including the nearby cupolas of the medieval Caves Monastery. Her skirts swirl above another staple item of Brezhnevite mass production, the war museum. This one is the usual squat, graceless agglomeration of pointlessly extensive red-carpeted spaces. A visitor who is determined to see everything must walk for hours, mostly in semidarkness, tramping the corridors that link the rooms where medals, blown-up photographs, and guns molder beneath the dusty flags.

The irony, in these two cases, is that the Kiev and Sevastopol memorials stand on the territory of independent Ukraine, a country that is no longer part of the Soviet Union and whose links with Russia itself have been weakened since the Orange Revolution of January 2005. There is, in fact, no political home anywhere for the patriotism that these buildings commemorate. Some young Ukrainians, and certainly the descendants of populations in the west, around Lvov, resent the monstrous presence of monuments that celebrate a war that brought them nothing except pain. And this is also true in other former Soviet states. If the concrete had been lighter, if there had been less of it, the national governments in several former Soviet republics might have thought of clearing the great lumps away when they toppled the Lenins and Dzerzhinskys in their public squares. But the memorials are too massive, too heavy to dismember. Their removal might also leave a crater that could not be filled. Russia is not the only country that paid a high price for Hitler's war. It continues to matter that Ukrainians were the national group that bore the largest number of civilian casualties on the Soviet side. In Belarus, too, some cities lost one in four of their population. Whatever the citizens of these republics think of Soviet power, the memory of those deaths remains important, and it is bitter and personal for the millions of survivors. Commemoration is not an irritant to be swept aside.

For Russians, the story is slightly different, for this was largely Russia's war and it remains a touchstone for those who are struggling, in the confused postimperial present, to find anything to celebrate in their country's last hundred years. The Museum of the Revolution in Moscow is a good place to see how these tensions are playing out. Formerly a shrine to the achievements of the Communist Party, the museum was refitted after 1991, when the very idea of Communist achievement had become an oxymoron. Today's museum displays the bitter fruit of the utopian project. In one room there are photographs of food lines; in another, scraps and relics from the Gulag. Two further rooms display a selection of the presents that Stalin received from comrades all around the world. The cabinets are stuffed with kitsch: painted china, woven rugs, cut glass, and inlaid hunting knives. For some reason, the gift that his admirers in Mexico selected for the great leader was a stuffed, gold-plated armadillo, which stands on fragile golden feet in its glass case.

Most of the exhibits in the museum are new, but two of its rooms have not been touched. The first houses formal cabinets of medals, portraits, and regimental flags. The second, where the light is always low, is draped with camouflage netting. There are helmets and rifles caught up in the web, and recorded gunfire echoes in the gloom. "People seem to need it," the curator explained. "We have never been asked to change those rooms." The opposite may well be true: there may still be a real demand. Another Moscow attraction, the Park of Victory in the Great Patriotic War on Pokhlonnaya Hill, was under construction when Communism fell. At that moment, some critics urged planners to allow the site to revert to pine forest.[10] But the work continued, and the park is now complete, an eclectic fantasy of gold-leaf and marble in the Disneyland style. Its vast war museum, which sprawls around the parade ground, is a white monster whose faux-classical colonnade would have delighted Mussolini.

An industry has taken over the business of war commemoration. The beneficiaries of its peculiar economy are seldom veterans themselves. Instead, they tend to be state functionaries, soft fleshed and middle aged. Their self-importance is nourished by frequent anniversary dinners, large-scale planning meetings, and even by the arrogance of sixty-year-old triumph. "British," a woman in uniform remarked as she checked my passport at the door to the administrative block behind the museum in the Park of Victory. "They were on our side, weren't they?" I nodded meekly, biting back a comment about 1939. It is absurd to argue about decisions that were made by strangers who are so long dead. "You can go up," she said. "But it was not good that it took Churchill so long to open the second front."

To criticize this cult of patriotic war still sounds like carping. "If you do not like the war the way it was," the poet Boris Slutsky writes, addressing the young, "try winning it your way."[11] It is a refrain that war veterans of many different points of view can echo. Soviet history has been a battleground since the archives were opened in the 1980s, but the soldiers claim to hold true to the real war. The Russian state, however, has abandoned the old dogma in at least one important way. Faced with the loss of an empire and, with it, of a mobilizing creed, Gorbachev's successors in the Kremlin chose to turn to one of the ancient pillars of Russian identity, the Orthodox Church. "I call those politicians *podsvechniki*," a veteran quipped in disgust. He was punning on the Russian word for candle, *svechka*, and the effeminate associations of *podsnezhniki*, snowdrops. Today's Russian leaders are always well represented at church festivals. Vladimir Putin carries his pious candle at the great ceremonies in the cathedral of Christ the Savior in Moscow, a building that is an exact replica of a church that his Bolshevik predecessors blew up in 1931. And just as they bless former agents of the KGB in their new role as statesmen, priests of the Orthodox Church must now pray for Red Army dead.

Religious faith was not widespread among soldiers during the war. There were a few believers, but most used prayers and ritual gestures out of superstition, as spells, crossing themselves to ward off death. After two decades of godless socialism, most Red Army soldiers fought without looking for priests, and many rejected religion absolutely. It is incongruous, then, that today's Park of Victory in Moscow should include a cathedral. Several hundred miles away, at Prokhorovka, the builders have just finished another, designed to look exactly like the kind of nineteenth-century Russian church that 1930s komsomols liked to demolish. In place of traditional frescoes, the walls inside are decorated with the names of the Soviet soldiers who died in the battle for Kursk. The vault is massive, too high to capture in a single photograph. The cruciform shape also defies the camera, for the church is a traditional one, octagonal within and built around a central dome. And though the lettering for every name is small, there is not an inch of plaster on its eight walls that is not covered in writing. The numbers overwhelm imagination, and the monument at least ensures that visitors will be aghast. But every soldier's name is now a hostage in the Russian church.

The Orthodox Church's claim might well have provoked a clash of dogmatisms, but few veterans have complained. Some even find that churches suit their taste more than the offerings of socialist realism that were favored in the Brezhnev years. Incense and priests seem fitted to the grim business of mourning, and in its guise as the soul of the nation, the Orthodox Church offends today's elderly far less than does pornography or the materialism of the new rich. But the new piety also has a way of troubling the very old. When they look back on the war, they remember how death seemed simple, part of the patriotic fight. The comrades of their youth died for a cause, whatever happened afterward. By contrast, their own deaths, as they approach, have become confusing. It is hard to be sure what lives spent under Communism mean now that the ideology has gone. It is even harder, for the grand old men, to make sense of post-Soviet death.

It was Anatoly Shevelev who described this dilemma best. "My wife was dying," he explained. "She had throat cancer. They made her have nine operations in the end. She became a Christian believer because of that. I don't have any time for it myself, I am an absolute atheist. I go to church sometimes because I like the music. But anyway, my wife asked me to pray for her. It was a problem because I don't know a single prayer, and I hadn't been to church, really, in my life. But when I came back from the cathedral that day and told her what I'd said, she threw her arms round me. She was so grateful that she wept. She knew, you see, that I'd done the best that I could."

Shevelev cleared his throat and began to recollect that prayer. " 'Dear God,' " he began, " 'forgive me that I have been an atheist all my life—not because I chose to be but because from my childhood no one took me to the church. I was brought up in an atheist world. I admire the Russian Orthodox Church, and these days I've started to value it because if it had not been for the church there would have been no Muscovy, and that was the foundation of our state. So I have no quarrel with the church really, and in my own defense, please remember that I, along with millions of other atheists, saved our motherland. By doing that, indirectly, we saved your orthodox church. I've come to pray for the recovery of my wife, please God. And forgive me.'" He paused. "How did I finish? . . . That's right. 'Forgive me because for my entire life I have been a member of the Communist Party of the Soviet Union.'"

The changing context of politics has influenced the way that the war is commemorated and even imagined in today's Russia. It is the same with soldiers' memories, most of which incorporate gleanings from later war stories, from cinema and poetry, as well as from the distant past. The only evidence that has not changed—the depredations of mice, damp, insects, and sixty years of dust notwithstanding—is that of documents. Archival sources echo with authentic voices from the past, the idiom of soldiers and their government as it was recorded in the very midst of war. It would be a mistake to see these records as the bearers of objective truth. Whole areas of soldiers' lives never found their way into print, including most front-line humor, many impious grievances, and the details of excess and atrocity. But archived letters and other papers are a welcome corrective to the prim reverence that seems to surround most public discussion of the war in Russia. They offer the best means of understanding the character of the army and the spirit in which the soldiers fought, especially as these changed over time. The main problem is not lack of material but the need to follow shifts in meaning. Words and ideas that looked clear in 1945 often began the war with other connotations and darker prospects.

A classic instance is the idea of the motherland. From Tolstoy onward, all writers have noted Russian soldiers' love for Russian soil. The same might be said for others—Georgians, for instance—although each culture differs in its sense of home.[12] The concept is now plain enough again, at least for people who were never Soviet at all. But motherland, for the early Soviet generations, was a troublesome idea with no defined boundaries or single meaning. It may have been a village or a region, but it was also the entire space, a multinational empire in all but name, in which "we" Soviets lived. Ethnic diversity, in Soviet culture, was more likely to generate confusion than pride. As with patriotism, the invasion of 1941 made things clearer, at least at first. Motherland became the space that the invaders sought to take from "us." The arrogance of Hitler's Germany, and its implied assumption that backward Russia would buckle and collapse, inspired real anger among Soviet troops, and that by itself helped some endure the first terrible weeks.[13]

Strong as it was, however, the notion of the motherland would change. It continued to be something that a man could love, but Red Army soldiers learned new ways to imagine it as the war progressed. Peasants from rural backwaters came to glimpse the ruins of Pskov, to see the mountains of Crimea, the cliffs along the Dnepr. Their sense of what they were defending widened as they marched and fought. It mattered, naturally, that after 1943 the march was westward, toward Berlin. Home must have seemed less glamorous before, when it was clouded by the enemy's pungent smoke. From the beginning of 1943, as the army moved on from Stalingrad, the image of the motherland, an abstraction, acquired a fresh, intense connection with political geography. Soviet borders would soon cease to be distant ideas, becoming wide rivers and real hills instead. It was all "ours," from the vineyards of the Black Sea to the dunes of the Baltic. But "ours," at a time of intense national chauvinism, gradually came to mean "Russia's." The idea that a republic in this great empire might choose independence, to the veterans who still gather in their close-knit clubs and associations, remains almost insulting.[14]

At the time, beyond the myth, there were conscripts of other types, and many of the kind that had to be coerced and threatened. The myths of Ivan and of motherland take little account of western Ukrainians or even of the ragtag of Belorussian teenagers swept up into the colors in the summer of 1944. They take little note of ethnic loyalties that were not Russian ones, and none of simple reluctance to fight. The Red Army used threats and bullets to force many of the doubters into uniform and keep them in the field. Brutality, physical and verbal, was always part of front-line culture. Violence and terror were used after the war to quell insurgency across the Baltic and western Ukraine. These stories have reemerged since the Soviet Union's collapse, they are documented in archives, but have yet to be fully explored. They suggest that some soldiers, the forgotten ones, must have been driven almost entirely by fear.

Here at last is a notion that anyone can understand, or so it is tempting to think. Fear seems so natural in this appalling world that someone who did not know the region's history might use it to explain almost everything. But it is a mistake to assume that these Soviet people, survivors in a universe of violence, would respond like a nation used to peace. This is not to say that fear was unimportant—it was ubiquitous—or even that life was simply cheap, but in this brutal, lethal world, fear was relative. It required weighing, a habit that Red Army men had often learned from childhood. As deserters showed in 1941, for instance, mere threats were not enough when the Germans appeared more terrible than any commissar, and death most certain under enemy fire. By 1944, the balance had changed, and it was clear that the Red Army had the upper hand in the regions where new recruits were being drafted. This was the era of the "1943 partisan" and others who opted, despite justifiable fear, to join the winning side before it was too late.

The war created a landscape where every choice was potentially deadly for soldiers and civilians alike. To join the army, ironically, may even have looked like a way of taming the nightmares. It was less dangerous, for many, than the genocidal regime of the Nazis. It was less unpredictable, and less brutal, than wartime labor camps. And above all, military service had a meaning, a value. This was clear enough in the case of members of guards regiments and the Communist Party, but the sense of collective purpose extended far beyond this small elite. The army scarcely bothered to train members of its punishment battalions, for instance. Indeed, its whole approach was calculated to humiliate them, to make them feel less than human. They could also be almost certain that their next battle would end in death. Some deserted, others panicked, and the vast majority would die. It is a testimony to the culture of the times (and to the power of the postwar hero myth) that some survivors should remember pride, a sense of purpose, amid their recollections of slaughter and fear.[15] They were victims, outcasts, wretched men. But hatred of the enemy was a sure way—their own, not the army's—of putting their fear and outrage to work.

If fear was not enough to make men fight, then neither, on its own, was ideology. It, too, was something that would change, another word whose meaning needs careful reconstruction. The idioms of progress and morality were central to many Soviet people's sense of themselves. Ideology encompassed a range of different things, not a simple and universal code. "We believed," officers, soldiers, and surviving NKVD officers insist. Mikhail Ivanovich, the young OSMBON officer, believed for his entire life, indeed believed his way into the ranks of the KGB. Even at his death, in 2002, he demanded a Communist funeral. His belief sustained him when he had to shoot at fellow Muscovites. It reinforced the physical strength that enabled him to complete a forced march across 150 miles of icy swamp behind the German lines. He was, in that sense, typical of other former peasants who found adventure and promotion through military service. It would be unwise to assume much love for Communism among the rural population as a whole, but where the new ideas struck root, they could be embraced with a fanaticism that calls to mind the Inquisition or the new jihad. This kind of ideology was really faith, and it was ruthless and personal.

Stalinist ideology had shaped the language of the time, becoming part of everybody's universe by 1941. Even a semiliterate conscript could recognize a *politruk* and know what role he played; even a peasant would have learned to pronounce the clumsy adjective *proletarian.* But the more formal, systematic kinds of ideological understanding of the prewar era were accessible only to those with the education to grasp them. At the extreme, such beliefs now appear absurd. "Please send me something I can read," a wounded cadet wrote home from his hospital bed in 1941. "Something that's not about the war. One of the classics, maybe Lenin's *State and Revolution.*"[16] The war itself exposed the naïveté, even the irrelevance, of bookish Marxism-Leninism. As the fighting unfolded, a cruder set of beliefs took hold, ones that almost any soldier could share. It was one thing to sign up in a haze of patriotism, after all, and another to go on thinking about classlessness and dialectics as the order came to rush the guns. No rifleman was likely to resort to Marx as the air started vibrating and the screams began.

Moskvin's reflections trace the path that many Communists of the prewar era would follow. Initially, though he was reasonably thoughtful and already a soldier of some experience, the *politruk* subscribed to a kind of fantasy, the dream of all those prewar films. In the first hours of the war, he believed that his own side had to win—that was the judgment of history, and individual lives counted for little beside it. Faith in that old lie would shatter in the blast of German guns. The credulous utopianism of 1938 either dissolved or it gave way to something else. In Moskvin's case, and that of thousands like him, belief survived because to die for nothing was unthinkable. There was no easy alternative, either. If a Soviet Communist was going to have faith, it would be shaped somehow by Soviet paradigms, and even nonbelievers in the party's lore borrowed from its vocabulary. For all that, however, wartime belief was grimmer, less sophisticated, and more immediate. It was better, through those bleak nights in the forest, to cheer for Zhukov and Stalin than to have nothing in which to place a faltering faith. Ideas were less important than a sense of purpose, and in combat itself, mere survival was probably utopia enough.

Victory, and even the first signs that defeat had been postponed, changed the nature of belief again. As Stalin pointed out in 1943, the army's progress was proof that Soviet Communism worked. There were all those tanks, those heaps of shells, those planes, those skilled young men to use them. But front-line soldiers made their own judgments about meaning. Their brand of Communism was a far cry from the gray world of the theoretical manuscripts. The soldiers put their faith in progress, in the collective, and in the value of acquiring skills. What they called Communist belief was about the victory of a just cause over the darkness. It was proof that, with enough will and effort, all the pain of the prewar decades would work out right, and it was also a kind of membership pass. If a person was a good soldier, a good comrade, then small misdeeds were unimportant.

By the end of 1942, moreover, prewar concepts of ideology were less important to a soldier's sense of his place in Soviet destiny than military experience and training. Even after the demotion of the political officers, ideologically based pep talks continued at the front, but now nation and leader were calling on soldiers to know tactics, to learn the proper use of weapons and the value of commands. The turn to professionalism was crucial to the army's success, and the party, for a while, was openly subordinated to the army's own commanders. But for a soldier—whether an officer or a technician with a single task to master—the image of a "good" soldier, the personal goal, was a combination of patriotism and manliness (a word much used in wartime poetry), loyalty to the collective, and professional skill. The skill gave soldiers their confidence, the collective the warmth, often the love, that sustained them through battle. If those feelings shaded into an affinity for the Communist Party, joining would have been a relatively small step in their minds. But it was not the ideology of 1937, or even the teaching of purist political commissars, that wartime recruits would have had in mind as they took their new party oaths.

After the war (and even before Zhukov had accepted Germany's surrender), front-line collectivism would become a target for Stalin's regime. According to the state's own reckoning, the veterans were heroes, but it was never likely that the dictator would allow them to apply their hard-won confidence and public spirit to the task of governing at home. The tragedy of the veterans, or part of it, was that their sacrifice counted for almost nothing in the shaping of postwar politics. True, their symbolic value was enormous. But they were used, not consulted. An ideal soldier took the place of all the diverse, the opinionated and self-confident fighters who came back from the front. While this hero was praised, the real veterans were misunderstood, idealized in ways they did not choose, and ignored or rebuffed everywhere else. In Brezhnev's time, it suited those in power to turn old soldiers into tame, even boring, paragons of developed socialism. No doubt future regimes will evolve uses of their own for the symbols of patriotic war. When the last veteran is dead, there will be no limit to the words and ideas that the heirs of Russia's victory can attribute to its heroes. But for a little longer, there remains a check. While the soldiers are alive, they can still speak out for themselves.

The place to find the old soldiers in Kursk is in a chilly-looking building that is still referred to as the Officers' Club. The mansion, now somewhat neglected, stands in the shadow of the former cinema, a building that, in 2003, was being restored to its original status of cathedral. The whole site was a maze of scaffolding and heaps of sand when I visited, although it was the very eve of the sixtieth anniversary of the tank battle. The local veterans' association was holding a meeting, as it always did, in a large room around the back. To step inside was like crossing some fault in time, for Lenin frowned from the walls and there were dismal rows of memoirs in the glazed shelves underneath. The room could not have changed in twenty, maybe thirty years. A huge table occupied most of the space, as if the people were an afterthought. But there they were, stern and austere, failing to hear the chairman as he spoke amid the din of tractors and drills. It was nine o'clock in the morning and they had all arrived promptly, used to discipline.

Their chairman had offered to give me five minutes of the meeting's time. The idea was that I would say my piece, take down some names, and then sit quietly while the meeting transacted its other business. The arrangement was awkward, for it put me in the role of interloper, but it was probably my foreignness that rankled most. I explained that I was looking for volunteers to interview. As ever, I said that I wanted people to tell me what they remembered, and I promised not to pry for secrets. There was a hesitation, then somebody told me that I should go back to Moscow. There were books, he said, to tell people like me whatever stuff we seemed to need to know. The faces around the table closed as quickly and decisively as sea anemones around a rock pool. But then, as always, someone called me over to his chair and asked me to explain again. It was the marvelous Anatoly Shevelev, and when I had described what I was doing for a second time (and promised cognac in the place of tea), he agreed to come to my room the next morning. His generosity inspired the others. The next day, when I had set a banquet out in my hotel room, borrowed a samovar, and piled up blank cassette tapes on a desk, I found a line in the lobby downstairs. The first person arrived for a late breakfast around nine o'clock. It would be nearly fourteen hours before the last group left.

That night, I dreamed of shelling, saw the bodies, woke up in a knot of Russian words. Part of my mind had picked up the horror that was always implied in the soldiers' tales. But though my own imagination had supplied the blood and flames, the veterans had not dwelled on the grotesque when we talked. As they recounted life before the war, life between battles, and their individual tales of adaptation to the peace, the soldiers could be vivid raconteurs, but their battle stories were as bland as any formal histories of war, the horror disembodied, safe. Even the veterans who talked for hours—and to one another, for the interviews tended to overlap—kept the worst details out of their accounts of violence. Rather than trying to relive the grimmest scenes of war, they tended to adopt the language of the vanished Soviet state, talking about honor and pride, of justified revenge, of motherland, Stalin, and the absolute necessity of faith. When it came to accounts of fighting, the individual was set aside, shut off, as if we were all looking at the story through a screen. There were bodies, and there were tears, but there was no blood, no shit, no nervous strain.

This reticence had troubled me when I began the research for this book, but by the time I got to Kursk I had begun to understand. The veterans' detachment was not merely a feature of their old age, some weakness of psychology to be pathologized and healed, nor was it simply self-defense. Instead, the images they used, and their choice of silences and euphemisms, hinted at the secret of their resilience. Back then, during the war, it would have been easy enough to break down, to feel the depth of every horror, but it would also have been fatal. The path to survival lay in stoical acceptance, a focus on the job at hand. The men's vocabulary was businesslike and optimistic, for anything else might have induced despair. Sixty years later, it would have been easy again to play for sympathy or simply to command attention by telling bloodcurdling tales. But that, for these people, would have amounted to a betrayal of the values that have been their collective pride, their way of life.

The war gave veterans very little. The assumption, beloved of a certain kind of well-nourished romantic conservative, that war makes nations stronger and more positive, would not stand two minutes' exposure to the reality of Stalingrad. I asked every veteran I met if his army service had improved his life, and most told me about the things that they had lost. The list included youth, years of freedom, health, and then the scores of people: comrades, parents, families. True, many soldiers received useful training, but most believe (correctly or not) that their skills could more easily have been acquired in peacetime. As for the loot, the feather pillows and the children's shoes, they were poor compensation for material loss and scant comfort for veterans' families in the lean years after the war. War pensions used to be worth a great deal. In the hard times of the 1990s some veterans helped adult children and grandchildren support themselves by sharing their benefits, but these days even the handouts have started to lose value, turned to cash in an inflationary world. The only gain that significant numbers of the old soldiers acknowledged was that the misery of war itself had made them value their survival more. This love of life is one of the most attractive qualities they share.

The veterans of Kursk were winners. They were neither former prisoners nor convicts from a punishment battalion. Their silences defended them from memories of injustice, though it would be impertinent to tell them so. But none of them sailed through the war undamaged. It is a measure of their strength, and of their survival, that they can talk at all about shelling, sniping, decomposing limbs, and wounds. It is a measure of an entire generation that it kept its dignity. Perhaps their very reticence helped these soldiers to victory. Morale, after all, is largely based on hope. And memory, for them, is sacred, live. "What do the old men talk about when they come back to remember?" I asked the curator of the museum at Prokhorovka, Russia's greatest battle site. "They don't talk much," she answered. "They don't seem to need to. Sometimes they just stand and weep."

CHRONOLOGY OF MAIN EVENTS

★

1938

13 March: Germany declares Austria to be part of the Third Reich
29 September: Munich conference agrees to the transfer of the Sudetenland to Germany but guarantees the remaining borders of Czechoslovakia

1939

15 March: Germans invade "post-Munich" Czechoslovakia
31 March: Britain guarantees Poland's defense
23 August: Nonaggression pact signed between Germany and the Soviet Union
1 September: German troops invade Poland and annex Danzig
3 September: Britain and France declare war on Germany
17 September: Red Army enters Poland from the east
28 September: German troops capture Warsaw
30 November: Russians invade Finland
14 December: Soviet Union expelled from the League of Nations

1940

11 February: Soviets attack the Mannerheim Line in Finland
3 March: Red Army captures Vyborg (Viipuri)
12 March: Finland signs peace treaty with USSR, ceding the Karelian Isthmus and the shores of Lake Ladoga
10 May: Germans invade Holland, Belgium, and Luxembourg
29 May: British begin evacuation from Dunkirk (continue until 3 June)
14 June: Germans enter Paris
17–23 June: Russians occupy Baltic states
22 June: France signs armistice with Germany
11–18 August: Peak of the Battle of Britain
7 September: First blitz over London
9 December: Eighth Army begins offensive in North Africa

1941

22 June: Germany invades the Soviet Union; Finland attacks Soviet Karelia
27 June: Romania declares war on Russia
28 June: Germans capture Minsk
3 July: Stalin's first wartime broadcast to the Soviet people
16 July: Germans reach Smolensk
25 July: Germans capture Tallinn
30 August: Mga, the last rail link to Leningrad, is captured by the Germans
17 September: Encirclement of Soviet troops near Kiev
30 September: Battle of Moscow begins
2 October: Germans capture Orel
12 October: Germans capture Kaluga
13 October: Germans capture Kalinin (Tver')
16 October: Height of the "Moscow panic"
20 October: State of siege declared in Moscow
30 October: Siege of Sevastopol begins in Crimea
3 November: Germans capture Kursk
22 November: Germans break into Klin
26 November: Germans capture Istra
6 December: Soviet counteroffensive begins near Moscow
7 December: Japanese bomb Pearl Harbor and raid British Malaya
8 December: United States and Britain declare war on Japan
15 December: Soviets recapture Klin and Istra
25 December: Russians begin to establish bridgehead in eastern Crimea
30 December: Soviets recapture Kaluga

1942

15 February: Singapore falls to Japanese
8 May: Germans attack in eastern Crimea
12 May: Soviets open unsuccessful offensive near Kharkov
20 May: Germans retake the Kerch peninsula
3 July: Fall of Sevastopol
30 July: Stalin's order no. 227, "Not a Step Back"
23 August: Forty thousand killed in air raid on Stalingrad
13 September: Germans launch offensive to take Stalingrad
23 October: Battle of El Alamein (North Africa) begins
19 November: Soviet counteroffensive launched near Stalingrad

1943

31 January: Paulus surrenders at Stalingrad
2 February: Final German surrender at Stalingrad
8 February: Soviets recapture Kursk
14 February: Soviets take Rostov
16 February: Soviets take Kharkov
15 March: Germans recapture Kharkov

5 July: Germans begin offensive at Kursk
12 July: Soviet counteroffensive launched near Kursk
5 August: Russians take Orel and Belgorod
23 August: Soviets capture Kharkov
3 September: Allies invade Italy
25 September: Smolensk recaptured by Red Army
6 November: Soviets recapture Kiev

1944

27 January: Final relief of Leningrad
2 April: Soviets enter Romania
9 May: Liberation of Sevastopol
13 May: Final defeat of Germans in Crimea
18 May: NKVD troops round up Crimean Tatars, who are exiled to Central Asia
6 June: Allies invade Normandy
22 June: Operation Bagration launched in Belorussia
3 July: Soviets recapture Minsk and take about 100,000 German prisoners
18 July: Red Army troops under Rokossovsky enter Poland
1 August: Warsaw uprising begins
25 August: Paris liberated
2 October: Polish nationalist forces surrender in Warsaw

1945

17 January: Soviet troops take the ruined city of Warsaw
4 February: Yalta conference begins
13 February: Budapest falls to Soviets
9 April: Germans surrender Königsberg to Soviets
13 April: Russians take Vienna
16 April: final offensive for Berlin launched
23 April: Russians reach Berlin
30 April: Hitler and his closest aides commit suicide
2 May: Berlin surrenders to Russians
8 May: VE Day. Keitel surrenders to Zhukov near Berlin (final documents signed just after midnight on 9 May).
9 May: Russians take Prague. Official Victory Day in Soviet Union.
17 July: Potsdam conference opens
6 August: Atomic bomb dropped on Hiroshima
8 August: Soviet Union declares war on Japan
9 August: Atomic bomb dropped on Nagasaki
14 August: Japan agrees to surrender
2 September: Japan signs capitulation on board USS *Missouri*

SOURCES

★

This book draws on extensive comparative literatures on soldiers, combat, and the Second World War. The bulk of it, however, is based on several kinds of primary source. Most of the detail comes directly from archives in the former Soviet Union and Germany. A list of these, together with the abbreviations used in the notes to the text, appears below.

The sets of documents involved include soldiers' letters and diaries, the reports of political officers and secret police operatives, reports intended for use as the basis for political agitation, military intelligence reports, and the evidence of prisoner of war interrogations. In addition, I have used Soviet government sources, including documents associated with the trials of former soldiers accused of antigovernment agitation in the immediate postwar years. Many of these include evidence gathered from semiliterate respondents, so they provide insights into the world of soldiers who could not—or chose not to—write. Finally, I have gathered evidence from civilian sources about the army's impact on the regions it liberated or occupied and about the conditions and morale of civilian members of soldiers' families. I have often found myself reading documents that have not been opened—except for routine checking at the archive—since they were filed sixty years ago. In every case, whatever the source, I have changed the names of all parties unless the material has already been published elsewhere.

I have also used a range of published sources, notably the multivolume editions of wartime documents that have appeared in Russian bookshops in the last ten years. Tens of thousands of individual documents are involved, and although the most sensitive material has been withheld, such volumes constitute a formidable primary source in their own right.

I have been more circumspect in the use of memoirs, war novels, and other literary sources. War memoirs are notoriously unreliable whoever writes them, and this is especially true in a regime where the censor wields a heavy pen. In the Soviet Union, purportedly ethnographic material, even the texts of songs, was collected on a selective, controlled basis. Novels and films about the war were never spontaneous. What literature can do, however, is to provide a clue about the style and content of surviving veterans' accounts. A reading of Konstantin Simonov, for instance, or an awareness of the extensive range of war films of the 1960s and 1970s can enable us to decode the testimonies of veterans who have come to believe that the public tale—the story that the state has woven over many years—is actually their own.

Those testimonies have been my other source. I collected approximately two hundred interviews in writing this book, most of which I conducted myself, alone, or with the help of a Russian assistant. The interviews usually took place in the veterans' homes, whether in Moscow, the Russian provinces, Ukraine, or Georgia. In some cases, I was privileged to talk to the same person several times, building friendships that remain among the greatest pleasures of my working life. Many former soldiers were able to correct my misapprehensions as I worked, while others brought documents and photographs from their own collections for us to discuss. I am grateful to them all.

I was surprised by the willingness of elderly people to revisit wartime memories and delighted by the wealth of detail, much of it about daily life, that former combatants recall. Much has been forgotten or suppressed and much, no doubt, embellished, but the value of testimony lies in the human link that it provides with the war itself and also with the long years of adaptation and recollection that have followed it. The story of postwar remembering—and of selective oblivion—is itself part of the larger story of survival. Suspicion, or at least a reasonable degree of caution, is another. For many veterans, I was an outsider in every respect—a woman, a civilian, an academic, and a foreigner. In answer, as a way of checking the bias that my presence imposed, I asked a male ex-soldier to collect some additional interviews, and another set was gathered in Ukraine by a native Ukrainian speaker. Accordingly, I have been able to consider a range of types of testimony and a broad spectrum of political opinions. If the interviews convey a largely uncritical and patriotic, Soviet, view, it is because that is how most survivors see this war even today. That imaginative hold, too, is part of the story I must tell.

LIST OF ARCHIVES

Moscow

GARF Gosudarstvennyi arkhiv Rossiiskoi Federatsii (State Archive of the Russian Federation)

RGAKFFD Rossiiskii gosudarstvennyi arkhiv kinofonofotodokumentov (Krasnogorsk, Moscow region) (Russian State Archive of Cinema, Recording, and Photography)

RGALI Rossiiskii gosudarstvennyi arkhiv literatury i iskustva (Russian State Archive of Literature and Art)

RGASPI Rossiiskii gosudarstvennyi arkhiv sotsial'no-politicheskoi istorii (Russian State Archive of Social-Political History)

RGASPI-M Rossiiskii gosudarstvennyi arkhiv sotsial'no-politicheskoi istorii–molodezh (Archive of the Komsomol)

RGVA Rossiiskii gosudarstvennyi voennyi arkhiv (Russian State Military Archive)

TsAMO Tsentral'nyi arkhiv ministerstva oborony (Podolsk, Moscow region) (Central Archive of the Ministry of Defense)

Kursk

GAKO Gosudarstvennyi arkhiv Kurskoi oblasti (State Archive of Kursk Oblast)

GAOPIKO Gosudarstvennyi arkhiv obshchestvenno-politicheskoi istorii Kurskoi oblasti (State Archive of Social and Political History of Kursk Oblast)

Smolensk

GASO Gosudarstvennyi arkhiv Smolenskoi oblasti (State Archive of Smolensk Oblast)

TsDNISO Tsentr dokumentatsii noveishei istorii Smolenskoi oblasti (Center for the Documentation of Contemporary History, Smolensk Oblast)

Freiburg

Bundesarchiv-Militärarchiv (State Military Archive)

NOTES

★

Introduction: True War Stories

1. John Garrard and Carol Garrard, eds., *World War 2 and the Soviet People: Selected Papers from the Fourth World Congress for Soviet and East European Studies*, Houndmills, 1993, pp. 1–2.
2. G. F. Krivosheev, gen. ed., *Grif sekretnosti snyat: Poteri vooruzhennykh sil SSSR v voinakh, boevykh deistviyakh i voennykh konfliktakh*, Moscow, 1993, p. 127.
3. Ibid., p. 141.
4. It remains impossible to give precise figures for the number of Soviet prisoners of war the Germans captured, not least because so many of the captives died. German figures are still around 2,561,000 for the first five months of the war (Krivosheev, *Grif sekretnosti snyat*, p. 336). The total for the entire war may be higher than 4,500,000 (ibid., p. 337). N. D. Kozlov (*Obshchestvennye soznanie v gody Velikoi Otechestvennoi Voiny*, St. Petersburg, 1995, p. 87), gives a figure of over 5,000,000.
5. Krivosheev, *Grif sekretnosti snyat*, p. 161.
6. John Erickson, "The System and the Soldier," in Paul Addison and Angus Calder, eds., *Time to Kill: The Soldier's Experience of War in the West, 1939–1945*, London, 1997, p. 236.
7. The figure that commands the most support is a "demographic loss" (i.e., excluding returned POWs) of 8,668,400. For a discussion, see Erickson, "The System," p. 236. Statistics in this war are notoriously unreliable, and it is possible that the true figure is higher by several million.
8. Antony Beevor, *Stalingrad*, London, 1998, p. 30.
9. Krivosheev (*Grif sekretnosti snyat*, p. 92) gives a figure of 34,476,700 for the women and men who "donned military uniform during the war."
10. The classic American accounts include S. L. A. Marshall, *Men against Fire: The Problem of Battle Command in Future Wars*, New York, 1947, and Samuel A. Stouffer and others, eds., *The American Soldier*, 2 vols., Princeton, 1949.
11. Among the first postwar studies was E. Shils and M. Janowitz, "Cohesion and Disintegration in the Wehrmacht in World War II," *Public Opinion Quarterly* 12 (1948): 280–315. The Wehrmacht's performance is examined comparatively in Martin van Creveld, *Fighting Power: German and US Army Performance, 1939–1945*, London and Melbourne, 1983. A more recent but classic account is Omer Bartov, *Hitler's Army: Soldiers, Nazis, and War in the Third Reich*, New York, 1992.

12. Cited in Catherine Merridale, *Night of Stone: Death and Memory in Russia*, London, 2000, p. 218. For a moving account of the famine, see Robert Conquest, *The Harvest of Sorrow: Soviet Collectivization and the Terror-Famine*, Oxford and New York, 1986.

13. The story of this violence is explored in my *Night of Stone*.

14. Richard Overy, *Russia's War*, London, 1997, pp. xviii–xix.

15. For a more detailed commentary on wartime poetry, see Katharine Hodgson, *Written with the Bayonet: Soviet Russian Poetry of World War Two*, Liverpool, 1996.

16. Grossman himself was condemned when his great war novel, *Life and Fate*, was judged to be "devoid of human feelings, friendship, love and care for children." The banning of *Life and Fate*, including the references that his critics made to the needs of veterans, is discussed in Merridale, *Night of Stone*, pp. 319–20.

17. The phrase is used as the title for one of the tales in Tim O'Brien, *The Things They Carried*, London, 1991.

18. Among the most energetic exponents of this renewal is Elena Senyavskaya, of the Academy of Sciences in Moscow, whose generous help and warm encouragement of colleagues, including me, has fostered an entire school of new research. See, for example, her *Psikhologiya voiny v XX veke: Istoricheskii opyt Rossii*, Moscow, 1999.

19. The most treasured series is Russkii Arkhiv's *Velikaya Otechestvennaya*, a set of reprints of wartime laws, regulations, and military orders whose numerous volumes have been published in Moscow since the 1990s. Its striking scarlet bindings came to seem like a trophy of true veteran status, at least in the capital.

20. Some essays, such as the winners of the 2000–01 competition, have been published. See *Rossiya-XX vek, sbornik rabot pobeditelei*, Moscow, 2002.

21. Oksana Bocharova and Mariya Belova, a social scientist and an ethnographer respectively, at different times also carried out interviews alone, as well as staying in touch with the veterans afterward. In several cases, the result was a correspondence that continued for months.

22. Cited in John Ellis, *The Sharp End of War: The Fighting Man in World War II*, London, 1980, p. 109.

23. For a discussion, see Nina Tumarkin, *The Living and the Dead: The Rise and Fall of the Cult of World War II in Russia*, New York, 1994.

24. The surviving fruits of those interrogations and inquiries, which I was able to consult thanks to the help of German colleagues, are archived in the military section of the Bundesarchiv in Freiburg.

25. Donald S. Detwiler and others, eds., *World War II German Military Studies*, 24 vols., New York and London, 1979, vol. 19, document D–036.

26. *Russian Combat Methods in World War II*, Department of the Army pamphlet no. 20–230, 1950. Reprinted in Detwiler and others, *World War II German Military Studies*, vol. 18.

27. The observation, by Lieutenant General Martel, applied to Soviet troops in 1936. Cited in Raymond L. Garthoff, *How Russia Makes War*, London, 1954, p. 226; see also p. 224.

28. Some people used this designation to answer the question on "nationality" in the census of 1937. At the other extreme were individuals who answered "anything but Soviet." See Catherine Merridale, "The USSR Population Census of 1937 and the Limits of Stalinist Rule," *Historical Journal* 39, no. 1 (1996): 225–40.

29. This democratic army—or quasi-democratic one—is the subject of Mark von Hagen's *Soldiers in the Proletarian Dictatorship: The Red Army and the Soviet Socialist State, 1917–1930*, Ithaca and London, 1990.

30. David Samoilov, "Lyudi odnogo varianta: Iz voennykh zapisok," part 2, *Avrora* 2 (1990): 51.

31. See Omer Bartov's important book *The Eastern Front, 1941–45: German Troops and the Barbarisation of Warfare*, London, 1985.

32. First discussed in the 1940s, the theory was placed on the policy agenda by Shils and Janowitz, "Cohesion and Disintegration."

33. This argument is developed in Bartov, *Hitler's Army*.

34. Beevor, *Stalingrad*, p. 173.

35. The problem did concern postwar authorities. See Vera S. Dunham, *In Stalin's Time: Middle-Class Values .in Soviet Fiction*, Cambridge, 1976, especially pp. 214–224.

ONE: Marching with Revolutionary Step

1. The music was composed by Dmitry and Daniil Pokrass, but it was Lebedev-Kumach whose name people remembered.

2. There is an account of just such a screening in O. V. Druzhba, *Velikaya otechestvennaya voina v soznanii sovetskogo i postsovetskogo obshchestva: Dinamika predstavlenii ob istoricheskom proshlom*, Rostov on Don, 2000, p. 22.

3. John Erickson, *The Road to Stalingrad*, vol. 1 of *Stalin's War with Germany*, London, 1975, pp. 27–28.

4. Druzhba, *Velikaya*, pp. 22–23.

5. In round figures, roughly 1,700,00 Russian soldiers died in World War I, compared with 1,686,000 Germans, although Germany fought for ten months longer and was waging war on two fronts for most of the time. Troops of the British Empire lost about 767,000 killed, and those of the United States about 81,000.

6. Sheila Fitzpatrick, *Stalin's Peasants: Resistance and Survival in the Russian Village after Collectivization*, Oxford, 1994, pp. 80–81.

7. The children of former kulaks were permitted to join the front line from April 1942.

8. Lev Kopelev, *No Jail for Thought*, trans. Anthony Austin, London, 1977, p. 13.

9. Cited in Conquest, *Harvest of Sorrow*, p. 233.

10. Varlam Shalamov, *Kolyma Tales*, trans. John Glad, Harmondsworth, 1994, p. 43.

11. Alexander Werth, *Russia at War*, London, 1964, pp. 112, 136.

12. Stephen J. Zaloga and Leland S. Ness, *Red Army Handbook, 1939–1945*, Stroud, 2003, p. 157. The number of armored vehicles in the Soviet tank pool was just over twenty-three thousand.

13. See also Stephen Kotkin, *Magnetic Mountain: Stalinism as a Civilization*, Berkeley and Los Angeles, 1995, p. 238.

14. Sheila Fitzpatrick, *Everyday Stalinism: Ordinary Life in Extraordinary Times; Soviet Russia in the 1930s*, Oxford, 1999, p. 18.

15. Fitzpatrick, *Everyday Stalinism*, pp. 90–91.

16. See Kotkin, *Magnetic Mountain*, p. 246.

17. Vyacheslav Kondrat'ev, "Oplacheno krov'yu," *Rodina* 6–7 (1991): 6.

18. The details are taken from the excellent biographical summaries in Harold Shukman, ed., *Stalin's Generals*, London, 1993.

19. They were, in fact, more likely to have been Dornier 17s or Heinkel 111s. Kirill's memory suggests that *Messer* was a generic term for German planes before people began to know them all too intimately.

20. Werth, *Russia at War*, p. 200.

21. In his classic history of the years leading up to Stalingrad, Antony Beevor suggests that Soviet Jews did not suspect the Fascists' genocidal plans (*Stalingrad*, p. 56). In reality, while there was little reference to German antisemitism after the Molotov-Ribbentrop Pact of 1939 and while no one suspected the full extent of the Final Solution, Soviet citizens had been bombarded with evidence of German racism, including antisemitism, before 1939, and many Polish and Austrian Jews fleeing Nazi rule confirmed their Soviet cousins' fears.

22. Detwiler and others, *World War II German Military Studies*, vol. 19, D–036, pp. 3–4.

23. This claim involved downgrading the achievements of late tsarism. See Jeffrey Brooks, *When Russia Learned to Read: Literacy and Popular Literature, 1861–1917*, Princeton, 1985.

24. Druzhba, *Velikaya*, pp. 9–10.

25. Ibid., p. 29.

26. Fitzpatrick, *Everyday Stalinism*, p. 69.

27. On the quality of the training, see William E. Odom, *The Soviet Volunteers: Modernization and Bureaucracy in a Public Mass Organization*, Princeton, 1973. See also Reina Pennington, *Wings, Women, and War: Soviet Airwomen in World War II*, Lawrence, 2001.

28. Fitzpatrick, *Everyday Stalinism*, p. 75.

29. Zaloga and Ness, *Red Army Handbook*, p. 147.

30. This one was from May 1941. Rossiskii gosudarstvennyi arkhiv sotsial'no-politicheskoi istorii (RGASPI), 17/125/44, 57.

31. Angelica Balabanoff, cited in Merridale, *Night of Stone*, p. 148. The same perception has been voiced by citizens of other ideological dictatorships, including the Iranian Azar Nafisi.

32. Gosudarstvennyi arkhiv obshchestvenno-politicheskoi istorii Kurskoi oblasti (GAOPIKO), 1/1/2807, 14.

33. The NKVD's own figure for 1939 is 1,672,438. For a discussion of numbers, see Anne Applebaum, *Gulag: A History of the Soviet Camps*, London, 2003, pp. 515–22.

34. Kopelev, *No Jail*, p. 92.

35. V. M. Sidel'nikov, comp., *Krasnoarmeiskii fol'klor*, Moscow, 1938, pp. 142–43.

36. On irony in war narratives, see Samuel Hynes, *The Soldier's Tale: Bearing Witness to Modern War*, London, 1998, especially p. 151.

37. Druzhba, *Velikaya*, p. 29.

38. Ibid.

39. E. S. Senyavskaya, "Zhenskie sud'by skvoz' prizmu voennoi tsenzury," *Voenno-istoricheskii arkhiv* 7, no. 22 (2001): 82.

TWO: A Fire through All the World

1. Reports of atrocities are frequent through the war. See Rossiskii gosudarstvennyi voennyi arkhiv (RGVA), 9/31/292, 315 (December 1939). On the unburied dead, see RGVA, 9/36/3821, 56. As the reporter comments, the sight "influenced the political-moral condition of soldiers on their way into attack."

2. Krivosheev, *Grif sekretnosti snyat*, p.78. The figure he gives is 126,875 for "irrecoverable losses," a category that includes those who died in action or of wounds and disease as well as those who were reported missing in action.

3. Ibid., p.79

4. Ibid., p.78.

5. Ibid., p.64.

6. Carl van Dyke, "The Timoshenko Reforms: March–July 1940," *Journal of Slavic Military Studies* 9, no. 1 (1996): 71.

7. The interview was for a documentary shown on Russian television in 2002.

8. RGVA, 9/31/292, 257 (December 1939); 9/36/3821, 7 (December 1939).

9. RGVA, 9/31/292, 318.

10. Ibid.

11. Detwiler and others, *World War II German Military Studies*, vol. 19, p.5.

12. Ibid.

13. See Roger R. Reese, *Stalin's Reluctant Soldiers: A Social History of the Red Army, 1925–1941*, Lawrence, pp.2–3.

14. See von Hagen, *Soldiers in the Proletarian Dictatorship*, pp.21–50.

15. Erickson, "The System," p.234.

16. RGVA, 9/31/292, 137.

17. RGVA, 9/36/3818 (information from Chita), 292–93, 309.

18. O. S. Porshneva, *Mentalitet i sotsial'noe povedenie rabochikh, krest'yan i soldat v period pervoi mirovoi voiny*, Ekaterinburg, 2000, p.221.

19. Von Hagen, *Soldiers in the Proletarian Dictatorship*, p.273.

20. The research was collected for I. N. Shpil'rein, *Yazyk krasnoarmeitsa*, Moscow and Leningrad, 1928. I am grateful to Dr. V. A. Kol'tsova of the Moscow Psychological Institute for introducing me to this material.

21. See Mark von Hagen, "Soviet Soldiers and Officers on the Eve of the German Invasion: Towards a Description of Social Psychology and Political Attitudes," *Soviet Union/Union Sovietique* 18, nos. 1–3 (1991): 79–101.

22. Victor Kravchenko, cited in Reese, *Stalin's Reluctant Soldiers*, p.13.

23. Porshneva, *Mentalitet*, p.110.

24. Anna Politkovskaya, *A Dirty War*, trans. John Crowfoot, London, 2001, p.44.

25. Reese, *Stalin's Reluctant Soldiers*, p.51.

26. Gabriel Temkin, *My Just War: The Memoirs of a Jewish Red Army Soldier in World War II*, Novato, 1998, p.104.

27. Reese, *Stalin's Reluctant Soldiers*, p.4.

28. Ibid., p.42.

29. RGVA, 9/31/292, 2.

30. Ibid., 9.

31. The Belgorod military district housing crisis, which was typical, is described in GAOPIKO, 1/1/2114, 13.

32. For examples of all these problems, see GAOPIKO, 1/1/2772, 16–17.

33. RGVA, 35077/1/6, 16.

34. Ibid., 18.

35. KPA, 1/1/2776, 85.

36. RGVA, 9/31/292, 14–21.

37. RGVA, 9/36/3818, 142; 9/36/4263, 29.

38. RGVA, 9/31/292, 69.

39. Reese, *Stalin's Reluctant Soldiers*, p. 50.
40. RGVA, 35077/1/6, 53.
41. Reese, *Stalin's Reluctant Soldiers*, p. 47.
42. Ibid., p. 44; Gosudarstvennyi arkhiv Smolenskoi oblasti (GASO), 2482/1/12, 8.
43. RGVA, 35077/1/6, 403.
44. Tsentral'nyi arkhiv ministerstva oborony (TsAMO), 308/82766/66, 25.
45. PURKKA order no. 282, cited in RGVA, 9/362/3818, 48.
46. RGVA, 9/36/4229, 77–92.
47. Reese, *Stalin's Reluctant Soldiers*, p. 55, citing regulations.
48. RGVA, 9/36/4229, 150.
49. These examples are from RGVA, 9/36/4282, 147–49.
50. RGVA, 9/31/292, 43.
51. RGVA, 9/36/3818, 292.
52. P. N. Knyshevskii and others, *Skrytaya pravda voiny: 1941 god; Neizvestnye doku-menty*, Moscow, 1992, pp. 14–21.
53. See Zaloga and Ness, *Red Army Handbook*, pp. 189–91; RGVA, 9/36/4262, 40–42.
54. RGVA, 9/36/3818, 206.
55. RGVA, 9/36/4262, 40.
56. RGVA, 350077/1/6, 403.
57. RGVA, 9/31/292, 91.
58. RGVA, 9/36/3818, 249, 292–93.
59. Cited in Reese, *Stalin's Reluctant Soldiers*, p. 63.
60. Ibid., p. 124.
61. Shukman, *Stalin's Generals*, p. 255.
62. Knyshevskii and others, *Skrytaya pravda voiny*, p. 218.
63. Roger R. Reese, "The Red Army and the Great Purges," in J. Arch Getty and Ro-berta T. Manning, eds., *Stalinist Terror: New Perspectives*, Cambridge, 1993, p. 213.
64. RGVA, 9/31/292, 46–47. Monthly suicide statistics for 1939 appear in the same file.
65. Knyshevskii and others, *Skrytaya pravda voiny*, p. 219.
66. Reese, *Stalin's Reluctant Soldiers*, pp. 163–64.
67. RGVA, 9/36/4282, 148 (January 1940).
68. RGVA, 7/36/3818, 123–24.
69. Reese, *Stalin's Reluctant Soldiers*, p. 93.
70. Van Dyke, "The Timoshenko Reforms," p. 79.
71. Werth, *Russia at War*, p. 71.
72. Interview, Kiev, April 2003.
73. Cited in von Hagen, "Soviet Soldiers," p. 99.
74. L. N. Pushkarev, *Po dorogam voiny: Vospominaniya fol'klorista-frontovika*, Mos-cow, 1995, p. 11.
75. The Red Army's participation here is described in RGVA, 9/31/292, 160–61.
76. Ibid., 209.
77. Ibid., 181–82.
78. Rossiiskii gosudarstrennyi arkhiv sotsial'no-politicheskoi istorii-molodezh (RGASPI–M), 33/1/1406, 4.
79. M. Dean, *Collaboration in the Holocaust: Crimes of the Local Police in Belorussia and Ukraine, 1941–1944*, Houndmills, 2000, p. 9.
80. RGVA, 9/31/292, 279.
81. TsAMO, 308/82766/66, 16, refers to directive of Glav PURKKA of 14 January 1941.

82. *Vestnik arkhivista* 3 (2001): 56–59.
83. GAOPIKO, 1/1/2772, 16 (22 April 1941).
84. TsAMO, 308/82766/66, 17.
85. RGASPI, 17/125/44, 23.
86. TsAMO, 308/82766/66, 17 (15 January 1941).
87. RGVA, 9/31/292, 75.
88. For a discussion of this issue, see Garthoff, *How Russia Makes War*, p. 231.
89. RGVA, 9/31/292, 288 (15 December 1939).
90. RGVA, 9/31/292, 250–51.
91. On primary groups, see Shils and Janowitz, "Cohesion and Disintegration."
92. Reese, *Stalin's Reluctant Soldiers*, p. 171.
93. On the lack of team spirit, see RGVA, 9/36/3821, 54.
94. RGVA, 9/31/292, 245.
95. Ibid., 288 (15 December 1939).
96. RGVA, 9/36/3821, 44.
97. RGVA, 9/31/292, 255 (2 December 1939).
98. RGVA, 9/36/3821, 2.
99. RGVA, 9/31/292, 361.
100. Ibid., 351.
101. RGVA, 9/36/3821, 8.
102. Krivosheev, *Grif sekretnosti snyat*, p. 63.
103. RGVA, 9/31/292, 290.
104. Ibid., 288 (15 December 1939).
105. Ibid., 253 (2 December 1939).
106. Ibid., 363.
107. Ibid., 360.
108. Ibid., 374.
109. Garthoff, *How Russia Makes War*, p. 236.
110. RGVA, 9/36/4282, 47.

THREE: **Disaster Beats Its Wings**

1. Evseev's memoir is cited in Knyshevskii and others, *Skrytaya pravda voiny*, pp. 330–31.
2. Erickson, *Stalingrad*, p. 92.
3. Ibid., p. 112.
4. Knyshevskii and others, *Skrytaya pravda voiny*, p. 331.
5. Erickson, *Stalingrad*, p. 104.
6. Werth, *Russia at War*, p. 150.
7. Rossiiskii gosudarstvennyi arkhiv literatury i iskustva (RGALI), 1710/3/49, 8.
8. *Rossiya-XX vek: Dokumenty; 1941 god v 2 knigakh*, vol. 2, Moscow, 1998, p. 422.
9. Erickson, *Stalingrad*, p. 106.
10. RGALI, 1710/3/49, 9.
11. Erickson, *Stalingrad*, pp. 118–19.
12. Timoshenko replaced the vain and inept Voroshilov in May 1940 after the Finnish debacle.
13. Pavlov's testimony at his interrogation on 7 July, reprinted in A. N. Yakovlev, chief ed., *1941 god*, 2 vols., Moscow, 1998, vol. 2, pp. 455–68.

14. Pavlov's testimony, *1941 god*, vol. 2, p. 456.

15. Erickson, *Stalingrad*, p. 116.

16. Yakovlev, *1941 god*, vol. 2, p. 459.

17. Cited in Werth, *Russia at War*, pp. 152–53.

18. Ibid., pp. 153–54.

19. Pavlov's testimony in *1941 god*, vol. 2, p. 459.

20. Werth, *Russia at War*, p. 157; Shukman, *Stalin's Generals*, p. 49.

21. *Velikaya Otechestvennaya: Russkii arkhiv*, vol. 2, part 2, p. 58 (text of order no. 270, where Boldin is singled out for praise).

22. Yakovlev, *1941 god*, vol. 2, pp. 472–73.

23. Werth, *Russia at War*, p. 181.

24. Yakovlev, *1941 god*, vol. 2, pp. 434–45.

25. Anatoly Shevelev, interview, Kursk, July 2003.

26. GAOPIKO, 1/1/2636, 40–42.

27. M. M. Gorinov and others, eds., *Moskva voennaya, 1941–1945: Memuary; arkhivnye dokumenty*, Moscow, 1995, p. 49.

28. Ibid., p. 43.

29. Druzhba, *Velikaya*, p. 302.

30. RGASPI, 17/125/44, 70, 72.

31. Mikhail Ivanovich, interview, Moscow province, April 2001.

32. Gorinov and others, *Moskva voennaya*, p. 51.

33. GAOPIKO, 1/1/2636, 41.

34. RGASPI, 17/125/44, 69.

35. Gorinov and others, *Moskva voennaya*, p. 52.

36. Detwiler and others, *World War II German Military Studies*, vol. 19, D–036, pp. 3–4.

37. The story of one small and doomed nationalist group was related to me in a series of interviews in Tbilisi, September 2002.

38. GAOPIKO, 1/1/2636, 43.

39. Gorinov and others, *Moskva voennaya*, p. 53.

40. RGASPI, 17/125/44, 69–71.

41. Gorinov and others, *Moskva voennaya*, p. 52.

42. Ibid., pp. 53–55.

43. GAOPIKO, 1/1/2636, 51–52.

44. Knyshevskii and others, *Skrytaya pravda voiny*, p. 59.

45. Ibid., pp. 60–61.

46. RGASPI, 17/125/44, 71–73.

47. Gorinov and others, *Moskva voennaya*, p. 55.

48. They shot them all. When the Germans took the city, the bodies were exposed in the prison yards for the local people to see. It was an effective propaganda move that turned an already anti-Soviet city even more strongly against Stalin.

49. RGASPI-M, 33/1/360, 10–11.

50. Druzhba, *Velikaya*, p. 21.

51. Werth, *Russia at War*, p. 165.

52. Comments reported in Gorinov and others, *Moskva voennaya*, p. 68.

53. Ibid., p. 69.

54. GAOPIKO, 1/1/2638, 30.

55. GAOPIKO, 1/1/2807, 9.

56. GAOPIKO, 1/1/2636, 50–51.
57. GAOPIKO, 1/1/2807, 9.
58. Werth, *Russia at War*, p. 149.
59. Ibid., pp. 166–67.
60. GASO, R1500/1/1, 2–3.
61. Ibid., 6.
62. Knyshevskii and others, *Skrytaya pravda voiny*, pp. 14–16.
63. Report to Mekhlis, July 1941 (ibid., p. 66).
64. Temkin, *My Just War*, p. 38.
65. Cited in Werth, *Russia at War*, p. 148.
66. Yakovlev, *1941 god*, vol. 2, p. 499.
67. Erickson, *Stalingrad*, p. 162.
68. Zaloga and Ness, *Red Army Handbook*, p. 69.
69. Knyshevskii and others, *Skrytaya pravda voiny*, p. 204.
70. Detwiler and others, *World War II German Military Studies*, vol. 19, C–058, pp. 18–19.
71. "O boevykh deistviyakh 6 armii pri vykhode iz okruzheniya," *Voenno-istoricheskii zhurnal* 22, no. 7 (2001): 109.
72. M. B. Mirskii, *Obyazany zhizn'yu*, Moscow, 1991, p. 19.
73. Knyshevskii and others, *Skrytaya pravda voiny*, p. 65.
74. Erickson, *Stalingrad*, p. 121.
75. Knyshevskii and others, *Skrytaya pravda voiny*, p. 266.
76. Ibid., pp. 264–65.
77. *Velikaya Otechestvennaya: Russkii arkhiv*, vol. 6, p. 61. Also barred were soldiers who had escaped encirclement "in small groups or singly."
78. Krivosheev, *Grif sekretnosti snyat*, p. 114.
79. Yakovlev, *1941 god*, vol. 2, p. 469. The mass production of the crude missiles was ordered by secret order no. 631 of the GKO.
80. Knyshevskii and others, *Skrytaya pravda voiny*, pp. 104–06.
81. Detwiler and others, *World War II German Military Studies*, vol. 19, P–123.
82. *Velikaya Otechestvennaya: Russkii arkhiv*, vol. 6, pp. 42–43 (order no. 081).
83. Ibid., p. 47 (order no. 085).
84. *Vstrechi s proshlym* 6 (1988): 443.
85. RGASPI, 17/125/87, 1.
86. RGASPI, 17/25/47, 47.
87. Ibid., 23.
88. Werth's account of the battle is largely positive, describing it as the first Soviet victory of the war. For a different view, see Beevor, *Stalingrad*, pp. 28–29.
89. Cited in Werth, *Russia at War*, p. 172; Knyshevskii and others, *Skrytaya pravda voiny*, p. 203.
90. Druzhba, *Velikaya*, p. 20.
91. Martin Dean, *Collaboration in the Holocaust: Crimes of the Local Police in Belorussia and Ukraine, 1941–44*, Houndmills, 2000, p. 26.
92. Knyshevskii and others, *Skrytaya pravda voiny*, p. 55.
93. Ibid., p. 304.
94. *Velikaya Otechestvennaya: Russkii arkhiv*, vol. 2, part 2, pp. 58–60.
95. GASO, R1500/1/1, 6.

FOUR: **Black Ways of War**

1. *Velikaya Otechestvennaya: Russkii arkhiv*, vol. 15, part 4, p. 40. The captured German document is Hoepner's "Storming the Gates of Moscow: 14 October–5 December 1941," dated December 1941.
2. Ibid., p. 41.
3. Krivosheev, *Grif sekretonosti snyat*, p. 139; Erickson, "The System," p. 225.
4. S. G. Sidorov, *Trud voennoplennykh v SSSR 1939–1956 gg.*, Volgograd, 2001, p. 60.
5. Ibid., p. 61.
6. Erickson, "The System," p. 233.
7. Ibid., p. 238.
8. *Velikaya Otechestvennaya: Russkii arkhiv*, vol. 4, part 1, p. 41.
9. Werth, *Russia at War*, pp. 238–39.
10. V. I. Yukov and others, *OZNAZ: Ot brigady osobogo naznacheniya k "vympely,"* *1941–1981*, Moscow, 2001, p. 45.
11. Mikhail Ivanovich, interview, April 2001; Gorinov and others, *Moskva voennaya*, p. 103.
12. *Velikaya Otechestvennaya: Russkii arkhiv*, vol. 4, part 1, p. 56.
13. Overy, *Russia's War*, p. 118.
14. A. E. Gordon, "Moskovskoe narodnoe opolchenie 1941 goda glazami uchastnika," *Otechestvennaya istoriya* 3 (2001): 158–61.
15. GAOPIKO, 1/1/2773, 18–21.
16. Gordon, "Moskovskoe narodnoe," pp. 158–63.
17. Report dated 14 January 1942, cited in Knyshevskii and others, *Skrytaya pravda voiny*, p. 227.
18. Ibid., p. 226.
19. Bundesarchiv-Militärarchiv, Oberkommando des Heeres, RH2–1924, p. 23.
20. Overy, *Russia's War*, pp. 116–7.
21. Report from Volokolamsk front, 27 October 1941, cited in Knyshevskii and others, *Skrytaya pravda voiny*, p. 184.
22. Kozlov, *Obshchestvennye soznanie*, p. 24.
23. Knyshevskii and others *Skrytaya pravda voiny*, p. 313.
24. Gorinov and others, *Moskva voennaya*, p. 167.
25. *Velikaya Otechestvennaya: Russkii arkhiv*, vol. 2, part 2, pp. 108–9.
26. Gorinov and others, *Moskva voennaya*, pp. 167–68.
27. RGALI, 1814/4/5, 42.
28. Tsentr dokumentatsii noveishei istorii Smolenskoi oblasti (TsDNISO), 8/1/212, 4.
29. Knyshevskii and others, *Skrytaya pravda voiny*, pp. 187–8.
30. Omer Bartov, in his study of the Wehrmacht, also suggests that harsh discipline, a raw ideological belief, and the fear of death created bonds between the men. See *The Eastern Front*, pp. 144–5.
31. RGASPI–M, 33/1/360, 3–8.
32. TsDNISO, 8/2/99, 1–2.
33. E. M. Snetkova, *Pis'ma very, nadezhdy, lyubvy. Pis'ma s fronta*, Moscow, 1999, p. 1.
34. RGASPI–M, 33/1/276, 4.
35. *Stroki, opalennye voiny. Sbornik pisem voennykh let, 1941–1945*, 2nd ed. Belgorod, 1998, pp. 115–6.
36. Gordon, "Moskovskoe," pp. 160–61.

37. Alexander Nevsky defeated the Teutonic knights in 1242. Dmitry Donskoi's defeat of the Tatars followed in 1380. Minin and Pozharsky drove out the Poles in the seventeenth century, and the last two generals, Suvorov and Kutuzov, led the campaign against Napoleon in 1812.
38. Stalin "Rech' na parade krasnoi armii," *O velikoi otechestvennoi voine Sovetskogo Soyuza*, Moscow, 1947, pp. 37–40.
39. Gorinov and others, *Moskva voennaya*, pp. 44–45.
40. Werth, *Russia at War*, p. xvi.
41. Kursk NKVD report, GAOPIKO, 3605/1/307, 1–3.
42. TsDNISO, 8/1/25, 7–8.
43. GASO, 1500/1/1, 16–18.
44. See Vasil Bykov, "Za Rodinu! Za Stalina!," *Rodina*, no. 5 (1995): 30–37.
45. On swearing, see E. S. Senyavskaya, *Frontovoe pokolenie: Istoriko-psikhologicheskoe issledovanie, 1941–1945*, Moscow, 1995, p. 83.
46. Memorial essay no. 2272: "Memoirs of Valish Khusanovich Khabibulin," ed. Nina Pavlovna Bredenkova, Tyumen', 2002.
47. TsDNISO, 1555/1/3, 3–5.
48. Knyshevskii and others, *Skrytaya pravda voiny*, p. 355.
49. TsDNISO, 1555/1/3, 5.
50. Gorinov and others, *Moskva voennaya*, p. 167.
51. RGASPI–M, 33/1/1395, 6.
52. *Velikaya Otechestvennaya: Russkii arkhiv*, vol. 2, part 2, p. 155.
53. Sidorov, *Trud voennoplennykh*, p. 60.
54. *Velikaya Otechestvennaya: Russkii arkhiv*, vol. 2, part 2, p. 114–15.
55. Ibid., p. 155.
56. Ibid., pp. 114–5; 193–94.
57. Ibid., p. 166; vol. 6, p. 120.
58. Werth, *Russia at War*, p. 370.
59. *Velikaya Otechestvennaya: Russkii arkhiv*, vol. 2, part 2, p. 73.
60. Ibid., pp. 252–53; 166 (on thieving).
61. For an example from the Battle of Moscow, see Knyshevskii and others, *Skrytaya pravad voiny*, p. 184.
62. Ibid., p. 164.
63. TsDNISO, 1555/1/3, 3.
64. *Velikaya Otechestvennaya: Russkii arkhiv*, vol. 6, p. 97 (order no. 307 of Glav PURKKA).
65. TsAMO, 206/298/2, 15, 49–50.
66. Bundesarchiv-Militärarchiv, RH2–1924, p. 22.
67. Werth, *Russia at War*, p. 422.
68. GASO, 1/1/1500, p. 15.
69. TsDNISO, 8/2/82, 50.
70. Werth, *Russia at War*, pp. 705–07.
71. RGASPI, 17/125/169, 5–8.
72. TsDNISO, 8/1/25, 12.
73. Stalin, "Vystuplenie po radio" (3 July 1941), *O velikoi otechestvennoi voine*, p. 15.
74. TsDNISO, 8/1/25, 12.
75. See John A. Armstrong, ed., *Soviet Partisans in World War II*, Madison, 1964, p. 3.

76. On field post in general, see *Velikaya Otechestvennaya: Russkii arkhiv*, vol. 6, pp. 76, 134.

77. Ponomarenko's figures, from RGASPI 69/1/19, 129.

78. The "big country"—*bol'shaya zemlya*—was the partisans' term for the unoccupied part of the USSR.

79. GASO, 1500/1/1, 25–35; TsDNISO, 8/2/99, 17.

80. Armstrong, *Soviet Partisans*, p. 170.

81. *Pis'ma s fronta i na front 1941–1945*, Smolensk, 1991, pp. 77 and 94–95.

82. Stalin, *O velikoi otechestvennoi voine*, p. 43.

83. Bundesarchiv-Militärarchiv, RH2–1924, p. 21.

84. Overy, *Russia's War*, p. 117.

85. V. L. Bogdanov and others, eds., *Zhivaya pamyat': Pravda o voine*, vol. 1, Moscow, 1995, pp. 392–96.

86. *Rodina*, no. 5 (1995): p. 68.

87. RGALI, 1814/4/5, 32.

88. Werth, *Russia at War*, pp. 388–89.

89. Information from the Adzhimuskai museum and from local people in Kerch.

90. Evseev, cited in Knyshevskii and others, *Skrytaya pravda voiny*, pp. 334–37.

91. Werth, *Russia at War*, p. 398.

92. *Rodina* 6–7 (1991): p. 68.

93. Ibid., p. 60 (testimony of Dolotsev).

94. *Zhivaya pamyat'* (diary of Vladimir Ivanov), p. 388.

FIVE: **Stone by Stone**

1. RGVA, 32925/1/504, 34.

2. See Vasily Chuikov's account in Werth, *Russia at War*, pp. 444–45.

3. *Rodina* 5 (1995): 60.

4. Lev Lvovich, interview, Moscow, April 2002; RGVA, 32925/1/504, 34.

5. I have cited one respondent for each of these explanations of wartime cowardice. In fact, almost every veteran interviewed blamed generic Central Asians or Ukrainians for the army's failures at different points in the war. Most also gave examples of "good" representatives of those groups. Indeed, few could name a "bad" one among the people they knew personally.

6. Special orders concerning the national minorities in the army, 17 September 1942, *Velikaya Otechestvennaya: Russkii arkhiv*, vol. 6, pp. 173–74.

7. See Beevor, *Stalingrad*, pp. 84–85.

8. *Velikaya Otechestvennaya: Russkii arkhiv*, vol. 6, p. 153.

9. *Velikaya Otechestvennaya: Russkii arkhiv*, vol. 2, part 2, pp. 276–77. According to more recent Soviet figures, the true number was at least ninety million. See Sidorov, *Trud voennoplennykh*, p. 60.

10. Cited in Vasily Chuikov, *The Beginning of the Road*, trans. Harold Silver, London, 1963, p. 175.

11. *Velikaya Otechestvennaya: Russkii arkhiv*, vol. 2, part 2, p. 278.

12. GASO, 1/1/1500, 31.

13. Cited in Roger R. Reese, *The Soviet Military Experience: A History of the Soviet Army, 1917–1991*, London, 2000, p. 115.

14. All figures cited by Overy, *Russia's War*, p. 160.

15. Erickson, "The System," p. 244.

16. *Rodina* 5 (1995): p. 61.

17. Gorin's story featured in a television documentary shown in Moscow in 2002, but he was kind enough to repeat it for me and to answer questions, in Moscow, that year.

18. Erickson, "The System," p. 236. This figure is almost certainly too low. At least a million prisoners were released from the Gulag and sent to the front, and most of these served in penal units of some kind, though some were drafted into regular units and used for dangerous tasks like clearing mines by hand.

19. *Velikaya Otechestvennaya: Russkii arkhiv*, vol. 6, pp. 176–77.

20. Ibid., p. 157.

21. *Velikaya Otechestvennaya: Russkii arkhiv*, vol. 2, part 2, 351.

22. See also Overy, *Russia's War*, p. 160.

23. Krivosheev, *Grif sekretnosti snyat*, pp. 125–26; Werth, *Russia at War*, p. 408.

24. TsAMO, 1128/1/4, 61.

25. See Volkogonov's biographical essay in Shukman, *Stalin's Generals*, pp. 317–21.

26. Erickson, *Stalingrad*, p. 349.

27. Anfilov's biographical essay in Shukman, *Stalin's Generals*, p. 64.

28. *Velikaya Otechestvennaya: Russkii arkhiv*, vol. 6, p. 176.

29. Ibid., p. 161

30. *Velikaya Otechestvennaya: Russkii arkhiv*, vol. 2, part 2, pp. 372–73.

31. Order no. 307 of the defense commissariat, *Velikaya Otechestvennaya: Russkii arkhiv*, vol. 2, part 2, pp. 326–27.

32. Chuikov, *Beginning*, p. 284.

33. TsAMO, 1128/1/4, 61.

34. *Velikaya Otechestvennaya: Russkii arkhiv*, vol. 2, part 2, p. 359.

35. For examples, see *Velikaya Otechestvennaya: Russkii arkhiv*, vol. 2, part 2, pp. 281–83, 318–20.

36. TsAMO, 206/298/4, 6. For more on the play, see also Werth, *Russia at War*, pp. 423–26.

37. Temkin, *My Just War*, p. 137; Werth, *Russia at War*, p. 622. The T–34 had a diesel engine, which made it less prone to combustion than most previous Soviet models, although plenty of T–34s would burn in combat conditions throughout the war.

38. See Overy, *Russia's War*, p. 195.

39. Ibid., p. 197. Veterans remember both these brands by name today.

40. *Velikaya Otechestvennaya: Russkii arkhiv*, vol. 2, part 2, p. 287.

41. Svetlana Alexiyevich, *War's Unwomanly Face*, trans. Keith Hammond and Lyudmila Lezhneva, Moscow, 1988, p. 128.

42. RGASPI–M, 33/1/1454, 36.

43. Garthoff, *How Russia Makes War*, p. 249.

44. Van Creveld, *Fighting Power*, p. 112; RGASPI, 17/125/78, 123.

45. On decorations, see *Velikaya Otechestvennaya: Russkii arkhiv*, vol. 2, part 2, pp. 360–61; on shoulder boards, see vol. 2, part 3, pp. 30–31.

46. TsAMO, 523/41119s/5, 51 (relates to an artillery regiment).

47. Bundesarchiv-Militärarchiv, RH–2, 2467, p. 127.

48. V. V. Pokhlebkin, *Velikaya voina i nesostoyavshiisya mir: 1941–1945–1994*, Moscow, 1997, p. 150.

49. Cited in Werth, *Russia at War*, p. 474.

50. Alexiyevich, *War's Unwomanly Face*, p. 96.

51. Stalin and the GKO approved the recruitment of women into male combat roles in April 1942. See *Velikaya Otechestvennaya: Russkii arkhiv*, vol. 2, part 2, pp. 212–13, 214–15.

52. RGASPI–M, 1/47/26, 175.

53. For a telling discussion, see Chuikov, *Beginning*, pp. 221–34. The marshal describes the work of women, but always with the condescending tone of one who saw them as mere girls.

54. RGASPI–M, 1/47/49, 87.

55. *Velikaya Otechestvennaya: Russkii arkhiv*, vol. 2, part 2, 285.

56. Alexiyevich, *War's Unwomanly Face*, pp. 46–47.

57. The first women snipers were trained from February 1943.

58. Alexiyevich, *War's Unwomanly Face*, p. 14.

59. R. Pennington, *Wings, Women, and War: Soviet Airwomen in World War II*, Lawrence, 2001, includes a chapter tracing Raskova's career.

60. Gosudarstvennyi arkhiv Rossiiskoi Federatsii (GARF), R9550/6/62.

61. Interview, Kaluga, August 2002.

62. RGASPI–M, 33/1/563, 7.

63. *Pis'ma s fronta i na front*, p. 87.

64. Van Creveld, *Fighting Power*, p. 73.

65. Samoilov, "Lyudi," part 1, pp. 52–53.

66. GASO, 2482/1/12, 12.

67. RGASPI–M, 33/1/19, 52.

68. Ibid., 72.

69. Ibid., 85.

70. Ibid., 84.

71. GASO, 2482/1/12, 7.

72. RGASPI–M, 33/1/19, 101.

73. *Velikaya Otechestvennaya: Russkii arkhiv*, vol. 2, part 2, 281.

74. RGASPI–M, 33/1/19, 36.

75. Samoilov, "Lyudi," part 1, p. 56.

76. RGASPI–M, 33/1/1454, 6.

77. *Po obe storony fronta: Pis'ma sovetskikh i nemetskikh soldat, 1941–1945*, Moscow, 1995, p. 43.

78. RGASPI–M, 33/1/360, 106.

79. Chuikov, *Beginning*, p. 66.

80. Ibid., pp. 78–79.

81. Werth, *Russia at War*, pp. 448–49; Beevor, *Stalingrad*, pp. 104–6.

82. Cited in Werth, *Russia at War*, p. 450.

83. Cited in Beevor, *Stalingrad*, p. 201.

84. I. K. Yakovlev and others, eds., *Vnutrennye voiska v velikoi otechestvennoi voine, 1941–45 gg., dokumenty i materialy*, Moscow, 1975, p. 16.

85. The version I heard, related by a retired general, was allegedly based on research in secret military archives. Until scholars can see the documents, the rumors will persist.

86. Krivosheev, *Grif sekretnosti snyat*, p. 125. The total death toll for Soviet troops and airmen is estimated at 470,000 (Overy, *Russia's War*, p. 212). For the entire campaign, 17 July 1942 to 2 February 1943, the total number of Soviet servicemen killed, wounded, and missing, according to Krivosheev, was 1,129,619.

87. I heard this from several veterans, and a politer version appears in Temkin, *My Just War,* p. 90.

88. Viktor Astaf'ev, "Snachala snaryady, potom lyudi," *Rodina* 6–7 (1991): 55.

89. Alexiyevich, *War's Unwomanly Face,* p. 59. The translator may have meant a mortar rather than a mine.

90. Interview, Kiev, May 2003.

91. RGASPI–M, 33/1/1454, 8.

92. Ibid., 18–19.

93. Chuikov, *Beginning,* p. 159.

94. For an analogy, drawn from a different war, see Philip Caputo's brilliant account in *A Rumor of War,* London, 1978, p. 268.

95. John Garrard and Carol Garrard, *The Bones of Berdichev: The Life and Fate of Vasily Grossman,* New York, 1996, p. 159.

96. Werth, *Russia at War,* p. 467.

97. Beevor, *Stalingrad,* p. 195.

98. Cited in Chuikov, *Beginning,* p. 253.

99. Krivosheev, *Grif sekretnosti snyat,* p. 127.

100. Beevor, *Stalingrad,* p. 232.

101. Ibid., p. 249.

102. Ibid., p. 263.

103. TsDNISO, 8/1/25, 5.

104. *Po obe storony fronta,* p. 194.

105. Ibid., pp. 195–96.

106. See, for example, Werth, *Russia at War,* p. 554.

107. *Velikaya Otechestvennaya: Russkii arkhiv,* vol. 2, part 3, pp. 36–37.

108. Werth, *Russia at War,* p. 560.

109. *Po obe storony fronta,* p. 213.

110. Werth, *Russia at War,* p. 468.

111. TsAMO, 206/298/4, 11.

112. Cited in Werth, *Russia at War,* p. 490.

113. *Politruks* agree on this, and so, in an assessment of morale, does the historian of Soviet warfare Amnon Sella. See *The Value of Human Life in Soviet Warfare,* London, 1992, p. 170.

114. RGVA, 32925/1/504, 29.

115. RGASPI, 17/125/214, 97.

116. See Peter Kenez, "Black and White," in Richard Stites, ed., *Culture and Entertainment in Wartime Russia,* Bloomington, 1995, p. 162.

117. *Pis'ma s fronta i na front,* p. 88.

118. RGASPI–M, 33/1/1454, 66.

119. Bundesarchiv-Militärarchiv, RH2–2467, p. 54.

120. Cited by Vasil Bykov in "Za Rodinu! Za Stalina!"

121. RGASPI–M, 1/47/24, 26–34.

122. RGVA, 32925/1/514, 48.

123. RGVA 32925/1/504, 4 and 20.

124. Ibid., 31.

125. Tens of thousands of Gulag inmates applied to be permitted to serve at the front for the same reason. Their service would not only redeem them but reinstate their families as well. See Kozlov, *Obshchestvennye soznanie,* p. 11; Druzhba, *Velikaya,* p. 30;

Amir Weiner, *Making Sense of War: The Second World War and the Fate of the Bolshevik Revolution*, Princeton, 2001, p. 148.

126. Viktor Astaf'ev's novel *Proklyaty i ubity* (reissued Moscow, 2002) presents this point of view in harrowing detail.
127. The first attacks in November were actually aimed at Romanians, but the point was to get at the enemy. On hatred of the Germans, see L. N. Pushkarev, "Pis'mennaya forma bytovaniya frontovogo fol'klora," *Etnograficheskoe obozrenie* 4 (1995): 27–29. Pushkarev, an ethnographer and historian, was at the front himself.
128. See Werth, *Russia at War*, pp. 411–14.
129. Werth quotes Simonov's "Kill Him!" (ibid., p. 417).
130. RGALI, 1828/1/25, 35.
131. Beevor, *Stalingrad*, p. 219.
132. Belov's diary, "Frontovoi dnevnik N. F. Belova," is published in full in *Vologda* 2 (1997): 431–76. For this comment, see pp. 446–47.
133. Ibid., p. 442.
134. GASO, 1/1/1500, 37–38.
135. RGVA, 32925/1/504, 94; Beevor, *Stalingrad*, p. 264.
136. RGASPI–M, 33/1/157, 2.
137. Sidorov, *Trud voennoplennykh*, pp. 83–85.
138. RGASPI–M, 33/1/157, 3–4.
139. RGASPI–M, 33/1/1454, 73.

SIX: A Land Laid Waste

1. Stalin, "Prikaz verkhovnogo glavnokomanduyushchego" (23 February 1943), in *O velikoi otechestvennoi voine*, pp. 89–90.
2. *Velikaya Otechestvennaya: Russkii arkhiv*, vol. 2, part 3, p. 97.
3. At Stalingrad itself, German losses were 91,000 prisoners of war and 147,000 dead. Meanwhile, the November–February counteroffensive at Stalingrad alone, excluding the losses sustained in August–October, cost the Red Army approximately 485,735 killed, missing, or wounded. Figures from John Erickson and Ljubica Erickson, *The Eastern Front in Photographs*, London, 2001, p. 137.
4. TsAMO, 223 SD/1/6, 10, gives details of the nonreporting practices of rifle divisions in January–February 1943.
5. Merridale, *Night of Stone*, p. 274.
6. For an example relating to fear among the Panfilov men, see RGASPI, 17/125/185, 23. More generally, see D. L. Babichenko, *Literaturnyi Front: Istoriya politicheskoi tzenzury, 1932–1946 gg*, Moscow, 1994.
7. Ilya Nemanov, interview, Smolensk, October 2002.
8. Druzhba, *Velikaya*, pp. 33–34.
9. Samoilov, "Lyudi," part 2, pp. 50–51.
10. Lev Lvovich, second interview, Moscow, July 2003.
11. Samoilov, "Lyudi," part 2, p. 57.
12. E. S. Senyavskaya, *Psikhologiya voiny v XX veke: Istoricheskii opyt Rossii*, Moscow, 1999, p. 80; RGALI 1814/6/144, 21 (Diaries of Konstantin Simonov).
13. Stouffer, *The American Soldier*, vol. 2, p. 186.
14. *Rodina* 6–7, (1991): 53.

15. L. N. Pushkarev, *Po dorogam voiny: Vospominaniya fol'klorista-frontovika*, Moscow, 1995, pp. 34–42.
16. Sidelnikov, *Krasnoarmeiskii fol'klor*, p. 9.
17. Translation by Lubov Yakovleva, *Twentieth-Century Russian Poetry*, ed. A. C. Todd and M. Hayward, London, 1993, pp. 623–24.
18. Ya. N. Gudoshnikov, ed., *Russkie narodnye pesny i chastushki Velikoi Otechestvennoi Voiny*, Tambov, 1997, p. 6.
19. Alexiyevich, *War's Unwomanly Face*, p. 46.
20. Nina Emil'yanova, interview, Moscow, 1998.
21. Sidelnikov, *Krasnoarmeiskii fol'klor*, p. 9; Alexiyevich, *War's Unwomanly Face*, p. 46.
22. Pushkarev, *Po dorogam voiny*, pp. 22–23.
23. Kozlov, *Obshchestvennye soznanie*, p. 105.
24. "The Crossing," trans. April FitzLyon, in Todd and Hayward, *Twentieth-Century Russian Poetry*, pp. 561–67.
25. Gudoshnikov, *Russkie narodnye*, pp. 83–89.
26. Ibid., p. 5.
27. RGALI, 1828/1/25, 35.
28. Temkin, *My Just War*, p. 90.
29. Interview, Kursk, July 2003.
30. Van Creveld, *Fighting Power*.
31. Erickson, "The System," p. 239.
32. On the United States Army, see van Creveld, *Fighting Power*, especially pp. 77–79.
33. Testimony cited in Senyavskaya, *Frontovoe pokolenie*, p. 85.
34. The petitions often served as evidence in alleged cases of desertion. See, for example, RGVA, 32925/1/526.
35. Samoilov, "Lyudi," part 1, p. 69.
36. See *Rodina* 5 (1995): 60. Gorin related similar stories to me in 2002. See also Viktor Astaf'ev's controversial novel, *Proklyaty i ubity*.
37. Ivan Gorin, interview, November 2002.
38. *Rodina* 5 (1995): 63.
39. *Velikaya Otechestvennaya: Russkii arkhiv*, vol. 2, part 3, pp. 109–10.
40. Temkin, *My Just War*, p. 34.
41. Shukman, *Stalin's Generals*, p. 354.
42. *Velikaya Otechestvennaya: Russkii arkhiv*, vol. 4, part 4, pp. 17–18.
43. Erickson, "The System," p. 246.
44. Mirskii, *Obyazany zhizn'yu*, p. 193.
45. *Velikaya Otechestvennaya: Russkii arkhiv*, vol. 4, part 4, p. 7; Overy, *Russia's War*, p. 201; K. K. Rokossovsky, *Soldatskii dolg*, Moscow, 1972, pp. 207–10.
46. Viktor Suvorov [pseud.], *Inside the Soviet Army*, New York, 1982, p. 99.
47. RGASPI–M, 33/1/1405, 1.
48. *Pis'ma s fronta i na front*, p. 90
49. Belov, "Frontovoi dnevnik," p. 452.
50. Ibid., p. 453.
51. Bundesarchiv-Militärarchiv, RH2–2624.
52. Gosudarstvennyi arkhiv Kurskoi oblasti (GAKO), R 3322/10/21, 15.
53. Ibid., pp. 1–39.

54. Ibid., 1–3.

55. GAOPIKO, 1/1/3478, 14–15.

56. GAKO, R3322/10/5, 44.

57. GAKO, R3322/10/4, 511; 3322/10/5, 44.

58. GAKO, R3322/9/106, 12–13.

59. GAKO, R3322/10/8, 27–33.

60. GAKO, R3322/10/14, 58–64.

61. GARF, R9550/6/339 (on nettles) and 527 (wild meat).

62. RGASPI–M, 33/1/1404, 16.

63. GAKO, R3322/10/1, 55.

64. *Stroki, opalennye voiny*, p. 71.

65. *Velikaya Otechestvennaya: Russkii arkhiv*, vol. 4, part 4, p. 7.

66. Zaloga and Ness, *Red Army Handbook*, pp. 163–80; *Velikaya Otechestvennaya: Russkii arkhiv*, vol. 4, part 4, p. 7.

67. Zaloga and Ness, *Red Army Handbook*, p. 169.

68. In 1943, Soviet factories produced 15,529 of the standard T–34 tanks and (in December) 283 of the modified T–34–85s. Ibid., p. 180.

69. Ibid., p. 174.

70. See John Erickson, *The Road to Berlin*, vol. 2 of *Stalin's War with Germany*, London, 1983, p. 109.

71. *Velikaya Otechestvennaya: Russkii arkhiv*, vol. 4, part 4, p. 7; Erickson, "The System," p. 239.

72. *Po obe storony fronta*, p. 52.

73. Erickson, "The System," pp. 239–40.

74. Detwiler and others, *World War II German Military Studies*, vol. 19, C–058, p. 23.

75. Ibid., p. 23.

76. *Po obe storony fronta*, p. 52.

77. Pushkarev, "Pis'mennaya forma," p. 30.

78. *Po obe storony fronta*, p. 51.

79. Krivosheev's figures for 1943–45 suggest that losses among tank crews were roughly half those among riflemen (although the catastrophic months of 1941–42 are not included for lack of information), but in view of the enormous death rates in both cases, the statistic is not comforting. See Krivosheev, *Grif sekretnosti snyat*, pp. 218–19, table 79 (Red Army Losses by Arm of Service).

80. Erickson, "The System," p. 239; see also Reina Pennington's contribution to the volume, especially pp. 257–58.

81. For descriptions, see Ellis, *The Sharp End*, pp. 153–54.

82. *Velikaya Otechestvennaya: Russkii arkhiv*, vol. 4, part 4, p. 26.

83. Ibid., p. 33.

84. Belov, "Frontovoi dnevnik," p. 454.

85. Ibid., p. 456.

86. Overy, *Russia's War*, p. 203.

87. Ibid.

88. *Velikaya Otechestvennaya: Russkii arkhiv*, vol. 4, part 4, p. 250.

89. Belov, "Frontovoi dnevnik," p. 456.

90. Krivosheev, *Grif sekretnosti snyat*, p. 132.

91. M. V. Ovsyannikov, ed., *55 let Kurskoi bitve*, Kursk, 1998, pp. 276–77 (memoir of B. Ivanov).

92. Erickson, *Berlin*, pp. 104–05.
93. Ovsyannikov, *55 let Kurskoi bitve*, pp. 265–66 (memoir of B. Bryukhov).
94. Interview, Prokhorovka, July 2003.
95. Ovsyannikov, *55 let Kurskoi bitve*, pp. 265–66 (memoir of B. Bryukhov).
96. *Po obe storony fronta*, p. 53.
97. Ovsyannikov, *55 let Kurskoi bitve*, p. 277 (memoir of B. Ivanov); S. Drobyshev, ed., *Nemtsy o russkikh*, Moscow, 1995, p. 28.
98. Alexiyevich, *War's Unwomanly Face*, p. 107.
99. Erickson, *Berlin*, p. 108.
100. Overy, *Russia's War*, p. 211.
101. Belov, "Frontovoi dnevnik," p. 456.
102. *Pis'ma s fronta i na front*, pp. 90–91.
103. Bundesarchiv-Militärarchiv, RH2/2624.
104. Belov had observed this as early as July ("Frontovoi dnevnik," p. 453).
105. Drobyshev, *Nemtsy o russkikh*, p. 28.
106. Ibid., pp. 32–33.
107. Belov, "Frontovoi dnevnik," p. 457.
108. Cited in Werth, *Russia at War*, p. 685.
109. *Pis'ma s fronta i na front*, p. 91.

SEVEN: May Brotherhood Be Blessed

1. D. M. Glantz and J. House, *When Titans Clashed: How the Red Army Stopped Hitler*, Edinburgh, 2000, p. 180.
2. Stalin, *O velikoi otechestvennoi voine*, pp. 117–20. In his assessment of the war economy, Richard Overy, among others, follows Stalin in conceding that only a centrally planned system of this type could have delivered the levels of output needed to sustain the Soviet war effort. See Overy, *Russia's War*, p. 227. This may be true, but it neither vindicates the brutality of the system nor establishes Stalin as the Soviet Union's wartime savior.
3. RGASPI–M, 33/1/1405, 50.
4. Ibid., 109–10.
5. *Po obe storony fronta*, p. 86.
6. V. I. Ermolenko, *Voennyi dnevnik starshego serzhanta*, Belgorod, 2000, p. 37.
7. Van Creveld, *Fighting Power*, p. 83.
8. *Rodina* 6–7 (1991): 53.
9. The poem is "Remember, Alyosha," trans. Lubov Yakovleva, in Todd and Hayward, *Twentieth-Century Russian Poetry*, pp. 619–21.
10. On SMERSh, which was established on 13 May 1942 and was independent of the NKVD, see Suvorov, *Inside the Soviet Army*, p. 240.
11. *Hiwis* comes from the German *Hilfswillige*, or "willing helpers."
12. On the oppression of labor battalions, see Temkin, *My Just War*, p. 53. On *hiwis*, see Kopelev, *No Jail*, p. 98.
13. Samoilov, "Lyudi," part 1, pp. 52, 67.
14. Glantz and House, *Titans*, p. 180.
15. TsDNISO, 6/1/1484, 173 (refers to Smolensk region in April 1944).
16. Belov, "Frontovoi dnevnik," p. 465.
17. Ermolenko, *Voennyi dnevnik*, p. 36.

18. Samoilov, "Lyudi," part 2, p. 56.
19. *Po obe storony fronta*, p. 99.
20. RGASPI–M, 33/1/1454, 52.
21. GASO, 2482/1/1, 35.
22. Snetkova, *Pis'ma very*, p. 38.
23. RGASPI–M, 33/1/1454, 107.
24. Leave was sometimes used as a reward for outstanding bravery, but it was usually granted only after a man was so badly wounded that he would no longer be needed. At the time of Stalingrad (9 October 1942), provision was made for more regular leave (especially for officers), but in practice it was treated as a reward, not a right. TsAMO, 1128/1/4, 32.
25. RGASPI–M, 33/1/1189, 3
26. Ibid., p. 146.
27. *Pis'ma s fronta i na front*, pp. 95–96.
28. Ibid., p. 97.
29. GAKO, 3322/10/21, 296.
30. GAKO, 3322/10/22, 2, 9, 10.
31. GAOPIKO, 1/1/3478, 7. The CC resolution is reprinted in the same file, ll. 85ff.
32. TsDNISO, 6/1/1697, 190.
33. GAKO, 3322/10/46, 30, 41.
34. *Pis'ma s fronta i na front*, 98. A pood weighs about thirty-six pounds. Even if they supplemented their diet with potatoes, Masha's family would go through a pood of flour in two months.
35. TsDNISO, 6/1/1695, 144, 219.
36. RGVA, 32925/1/515, 70.
37. TsDNISO, 8/2/109, 15.
38. TsDNISO, 6/1/1484, 33, 39.
39. See, e.g., GAKO, R3322/10/1, which defines their role in February 1943, following the city's liberation.
40. Garrard and Garrard, *Bones*, p. 155.
41. This preference, which survivors attest, was also noted by local police and the officials in charge of trophies.
42. RGASPI–M, 33/1/1406, 52.
43. RGASPI–M, 33/1/1208, 71.
44. TsAMO, 136/24416/24, 275.
45. RGASPI–M, 33/1/1494, 48.
46. *Stroki, opalennye voiny*, p. 182.
47. RGVA, 32925/1/514, 47.
48. Yu. N. Afanas'ev, ed., *Drugaya voina, 1939–1945,* Moscow, 1996, p. 433. This source claims that the comparable increase among British troops was 200 percent.
49. J. A. Armstrong, ed., *Soviet Partisans in World War II,* Madison, 1964, p. 164.
50. For an example, see RGVA, 32925/1/515, 267.
51. GAKO, R3322/9/93, 15.
52. RGASPI–M, 33/1/1454, 78.
53. Alexiyevich, *War's Unwomanly Face*, p. 65.
54. Pennington, *Wings*, p. 67.
55. Temkin, *My Just War,* p. 202.
56. RGASPI–M, 33/1/1494, 48.

57. Ibid., 78–79.
58. RGASPI–M, 33/1/1405, 100.
59. Ibid., 64–65.
60. Hunger was especially severe in the countryside, as rural people often had no right to ration cards. The theft of food anywhere in the Soviet Union was punishable by death. See William Moskoff, *The Bread of Affliction: The Food Supply in the USSR during World War II*, Cambridge, 1990, pp. 108–9.
61. RGASPI–M, 33/1/1404, 7.
62. Ibid., 8, 5.
63. Ibid., 3.
64. RGASPI–M, 33/1/1405,17.
65. RGASPI–M, 33/1/1454, 61.
66. Alexiyevich, *War's Unwomanly Face*, p. 79.
67. On blood donors, see Overy, *Russia's War*, p. 227.
68. RGASPI–M, 33/1/493, 1–6.
69. Samoilov, "Lyudi," part 1, p. 70.
70. RGASPI, 17/125/80, 3.
71. GAKO, 5166/1/24, 4–7.
72. Reina Pennington, "Women in Combat in the Red Army," in P. Addison and A. Calder, eds., *Time to Kill: The Soldier's Experience of War in the West, 1939–1945*, London, 1997, p. 257.
73. GAKO, 5166/1/24, 4.
74. Reese, *Soviet Military Experience*, p. 110.
75. Leonid Piterskii, "Deti na voine," *Istochnik* 1 (1994): 54–60.
76. Samoilov, "Lyudi," part 2, p. 79.
77. Soldiers seem to crave the companionship of animals. On other armies, see John Keegan, *The Second World War*, London, 1989, p. 242. On other front-line dogs, see Vasil Bykov, "Ataka s khody," in *Povesti raznykh let*, Moscow, 1990, p. 189.
78. Samoilov, "Lyudi," part 2, pp. 68–70.
79. V. A. Zolotarev, G. N. Sevost'yanov, and others, eds., *Velikaya otechestvennaya voina, 1941–1945*, Moscow, 1999, book 4, pp. 189–90.
80. For figures relating to Ukraine, see Weiner, *Making Sense*, p. 173.
81. Zolotarev and others, *Velikaya otechestvennaya voina*, book 4, p. 190.
82. One such band was liquidated near Smolensk on the grounds that it had refused to "accept the leadership of the Communist Party." GAOPIKO, 8/1/36, 14–16.
83. Werth, *Russia at War*, p. 792.
84. Afanas'ev, *Drugaya voina*, pp. 318–9. The Gulag awaited Aleksandr Solzhenitsyn, for instance, and also Lev Kopelev.
85. TsDNISO, 8/1/9, 10.
86. GASO, 1500/1/1, 42.
87. Overy, *Russia's War*, pp. 130–31.
88. RGASPI, 17/125/94, 34–36; 17/125/165, 46, 46r.
89. Early in the war, Ukrainian nationalists had worked with the German army, since both appeared to share the goal of driving out the Bolsheviks. The fragile alliance was already in tatters by 1942.
90. Shukman, *Stalin's Generals*, pp. 296–97; Overy, *Russia's War*, p. 311. It was in revenge for acts like this that suspected guerrilla nationalists, as well as prominent collaborators, would be hanged in public in Kiev in 1944.

91. See Weiner, *Making Sense*, pp. 248–50.

92. RGASPI-M, 33/1/73, 1–5.

93. See the report reproduced in Armstrong, *Soviet Partisans*, p. 735.

94. GASO, 1500/1/1, 40.

95. Ibid., 39.

96. Armstrong, *Soviet Partisans*, p. 731.

97. GASO, 1500/1/1, p. 44.

98. See Armstrong, *Soviet Partisans*, p. 45.

99. GASO, 1500/1/1, 46.

100. Ibid., 52.

101. Cited in Armstrong, *Soviet Partisans*, p. 738.

102. GASO, 1500/1/1, 52.

103. Cited in Armstrong, *Soviet Partisans*, p. 737.

104. Werth, *Russia at War*, p. 827.

105. Ibid., p. 830.

106. RGASPI–M, 33/1/1406, 57.

107. As the guides tell you when you walk up to the ridge, *sapun* derives from the Turkish word for soap.

108. Excavations in today's Crimea still bring the bodies of soldiers to light. As a man who spends his life exhuming such corpses told me, the Soviet dead were much better equipped by 1944 than those of the Germans they were fighting.

109. Werth, *Russia at War*, pp. 838–39.

110. Ibid., p. 835; Erickson, *Berlin*, p. 195.

111. Brian Glyn Williams, "The Hidden Ethnic Cleansing of Muslims in the Soviet Union: The Exile and Repatriation of the Crimean Tatars," *Journal of Contemporary History* 37 (2002): 325–27.

112. Most of the Tatars in the so-called Tatar legion, which amounted to no more than seven battalions by the autumn of 1943, were from the Volga, not the Crimea. See S. I. Drobyazko, "Sovetskie grazhdane v ryadakh vermakhta," in the essay collection *Velikaya otechestvennaya voina v otsenke molodykh*, Moscow, 1997, p. 128.

113. The figure that most sources quote is N. F. Bugai's estimate of just over 191,000 people, or 47,000 families. See P. Polyan, *Ne po svoei vole*, Moscow, 2001, p. 126; Williams, "The Exile," p. 334.

114. On the deportations from the Caucasus, see Polyan, *Ne po svoei vole*, pp. 116–27.

115. Williams, "The Exile," p. 333.

116. For a discussion of Tatar "guilt," see Alan Fisher, *The Crimean Tatars*, Stanford, 1978, pp. 153–64.

117. Ibid., p. 166.

EIGHT: Exulting, Grieving, and Sweating Blood

1. Accounts of the precise starting point vary because of the scale of the operation. In some places, the first shots were fired on 21 June. Elsewhere the starting date is taken as 22 or 23 June.

2. The front itself was about 450 miles long. Werth, *Russia at War*, pp. 860–61.

3. Bundesarchiv-Militärarchiv, RH2–2338, 1 (January 1944).

4. Belov, "Frontovoi dnevnik," p. 468 (21 March 1944).

5. Ibid., p. 462 (28 November 1943).

6. Ibid., p. 465 (12 January 1944).

7. Ibid., p. 468 (13 March 1944).

8. Ibid., p. 470 (7 April 1944).

9. Bundesarchiv-Militärarchiv, RH2–2338 (monthly report, March 1944, pp. 1–2).

10. Belov, "Frontovoi dnevnik," p. 464 (12 December 1943), p. 465 (17 January 1944).

11. Ermolenko, *Voennyi dnevnik*, p. 39.

12. See Catherine Merridale, "The Collective Mind: Trauma and Shell-Shock in Twentieth-Century Russia," *Journal of Contemporary History* 35 (2000): 41.

13. Generally, they were lumped together with other "amoral" or "extraordinary" incidents. If they were explained at all, it was with reference to any suicide note or final remark that existed. Since the soldiers themselves did not know the word *trauma*, they naturally attributed their agony to more immediate causes, often unrequited love or political disappointment. For examples from Belarus in 1944, see RGVA, 32925/1/516, 177.

14. For a parallel discussion of the death penalty in the British army at this time, see David French, "Discipline and the Death Penalty in the British Army in the War against Germany during the Second World War," *Journal of Contemporary History* 33, no. 4 (1998): 531–45.

15. I am grateful to Professor Simon Wessely for drawing my attention to the correlation between the statistics for Soviet mental casualties and the average incidence of adult-onset schizophrenia.

16. Richard A. Gabriel, *Soviet Military Psychiatry*, Westport 1986, p. 47. This estimate is based on interviews with survivors and their psychologists, as a result of which Gabriel produced a rough figure of six mental casualties per thousand men for the Red Army as a whole. However crude, this figure contrasts strikingly with the equivalent thirty-six to thirty-nine per thousand in the US Army in World War II.

17. See Merridale, *Night of Stone*, p. 304. The consensus among psychiatrists in Russia had shifted by 2002, when I asked these questions again. Contact with European and American medicine had clearly changed the prevailing wisdom, at least among doctors currently in practice. But retired wartime medical staff, including nurses and psychiatrists interviewed in Kursk, Smolensk, and Tbilisi, had not changed their position.

18. The point is made in Amnon Sella's optimistic book, *The Value of Human Life*, p. 49.

19. Gabriel, *Soviet Military Psychiatry*, p. 56.

20. I am grateful to Dr. V. A. Koltsova, of the Moscow Institute for Military Psychology, for sharing this unpublished material with me in 2002. See also Albert R. Gilgen and others, *Soviet and American Psychology during World War II*, Westport, 1997.

21. Gabriel, *Soviet Military Psychiatry*, p. 63.

22. Some were released, although they carried the stigma of mental illness forever and many ended up in prison camps later in life. Others joined the colonies of the crippled in the White Sea and lived out their lives in isolation. The worst fate, probably, was to remain in a Soviet psychiatric hospital of this era.

23. Gabriel, *Soviet Military Psychiatry*, pp. 42–48.

24. Vyacheslav Kondrat'ev, cited by George Gibian, "World War 2 in Russian National Consciousness," in Garrard and Garrard, *World War 2 and the Soviet People*, p. 153.

25. Order of the deputy defense commissar, no. 004/073/006/23 ss (26 January 1944), *Velikaya Otechestvennaya: Russkii arkhiv*, vol. 2, part 3, p. 241.

26. On the use of convicts for this work, see the captured report of the Fourth Tank Army, Bundesarchiv-Militärarchiv, RH-2471, p. 16 (4 August 1944). See also RH-2471, 33 (prisoner of war reports). Temkin in *My Just War* (p. 124) also recalls that a convicted murderer was used for reconnaissance work in his own unit.

27. Viktor Astaf'ev, "Tam, v okopakh," *Pravda*, 25 November 1985.

28. Examples are to be found in GARF, 7523/16/388, which contains the records of the commission that dealt with the reinstatement of medals to soldiers who had been convicted of crimes at the front.

29. Drobyshev, *Nemtsy o russkikh*, p. 94.

30. For a parallel from the British army in World War 1, see Frank Richards, *Old Soldiers Never Die*, London, 1933, p. 194.

31. Drobyshev, *Nemtsy o russkikh*, p. 94.

32. Vasily Chuikov, *The End of the Third Reich*, trans. Ruth Kisch, London, 1967, p. 40.

33. Drobyshev, *Nemtsy o russkikh*, p. 94.

34. *Velikaya Otechestvennaya: Russkii arkhiv*, vol. 14, p. 619 (report dated 1 October 1944).

35. Kopelev, *No Jail*, p. 38.

36. *Velikaya Otechestvennaya: Russkii arkhiv*, vol. 2, part 3, pp. 265–66.

37. Ibid., p. 295.

38. *Velikaya Otechestvennaya: Russkii arkhiv*, vol. 6, p. 247 (on the sorry state of the kitchens in the reserve political units of the Second Baltic Front).

39. TsAMO, 523/41119s/1, 17; see also similar reports from German intelligence, Bundesarchiv-Militärarchiv, RH2–2338, 10 (1944).

40. RGVA, 32925/1/516, 177 (April 1944).

41. RGVA, 32925/1/515, 139–40.

42. RGVA 32925/1/516, 4, 178.

43. *Velikaya Otechestvennaya: Russkii arkhiv*, vol. 14, p. 590.

44. TsAMO, 523/41119s/1, 169.

45. Ermolenko, *Voennyi dnevnik*, p. 52.

46. See Overy, *Russia's War*, pp. 238–39; Erickson, *Berlin*, 198–200.

47. Chuikov, *Third Reich*, p. 27.

48. Belov, "Frontovoi dnevnik," p. 469 (31 March 1944).

49. Ibid., pp. 473–74 (18 June 1944).

50. Glanz and House, *Titans*, p. 209.

51. Cited in Garthoff, *How Russia Makes War*, p. 237.

52. Erickson, *Berlin*, p. 225.

53. Bundesarchiv-Militärarchiv, RH2–2338, 44–07, 1–2.

54. GASO, R1500/1/1, 63.

55. Chuikov, *Third Reich*, p. 28.

56. See RH2–2467, 118, for leave. For cash incentives for planes and "tongues," see Bundesarchiv-Militärarchiv, RH2–2338.

57. Sidorov, *Trud voennoplennykh*, pp. 99, 108.

58. *Pravda*, 19 July 1944; Werth, *Russia at War*, p. 862.

59. Ermolenko, *Voennyi dnevnik*, p. 46.

60. Ibid., p. 50.

61. *Pis'ma s fronta i na front*, p. 92.

62. Stalin, *O velikoi otechestvennoi voine*, pp. 145–46.
63. Bundesarchiv-Militärarchiv RH2–2338, March–April 1944.
64. See, for example, *Pravda*, 26 August 1944.
65. German intelligence reports consistently stressed this. See, eg., Bundesarchiv-Militärarchiv, RH2–2338, 44–08 (monthly intelligence report for August 1944).
66. On ethnically based Ukrainian nationalism, see Weiner, *Making Sense*, pp. 240–41.
67. See Leo J. Docherty III, "The Reluctant Warriors: The Non-Russian Nationalities in Service of the Red Army during World War II, 1941–1945," *Journal of Slavic Military Studies* 6, no. 3 (1993): 432–33.
68. Bundesarchiv-Militärarchiv, RH2–2468, 35.
69. Ibid., 80.
70. Ibid., 35, 38.
71. Details from RGASPI, 17/125/241, 93–94.
72. Bundesarchiv-Militärarchiv, RH2–2468, 35.
73. A point specifically made—and understandably believed—by German intelligence. See RH2–2338, 44–09, 1.
74. This finding confirms the comments in RH2–2468, 80.
75. RGASPI, 17/125/241, 88.
76. Ibid., 89.
77. Ibid., 91–92; 95.
78. Ibid., 95.
79. *Velikaya Otechestvennaya: Russkii arkhiv*, vol. 6, pp. 292–95.
80. Ermolenko, *Voennyi dnevnik*, 59, 62.
81. Kopelev, *No Jail*, p. 53.
82. The agitation department's concern was fully justified. See Senyavskaya, *Frontovoe pokolenie*, p. 91.
83. For other evidence of this, see Bundesarchiv-Militärarchiv, RH2–2338, 45–02, 2–3.
84. Beevor, *Berlin*, p. 34.
85. Their comments were faithfully collected. For examples from the summer of 1944, see RGVA, 32925/1/515.
86. Chuikov, *Third Reich*, p. 34.
87. Bundesarchiv-Militärarchiv, RH2–2468, 6–7, 27.
88. See, for example, the assessment in Glantz and House, *Titans*, p. 214. A more detailed account is given in Erickson, *Berlin*, pp. 247–90.
89. Weiner, *Making Sense*, p. 149.
90. RGVA, 32925/1/516, 176 (April 1944).
91. Bundesarchiv-Militärarchiv, RH2–2337, 58.
92. Bundesarchiv-Militärarchiv, RH2–2337, 70–71.
93. These jokes are among those recalled for me by veterans, and they came up in more than one interview. They can also be found, lovingly collected, in Bundesarchiv-Militärarchiv, RH2–2337, the Wehrmacht's own report on Soviet antisemitism.
94. For a 1943 soldier's letter to exactly this effect, see Senyavskaya, *Frontovoe pokolenie*, p. 83.
95. In fact, civilian casualties were highest among Ukrainians and proportionately, though not numerically, highest of all in Belorussia.
96. Werth, *Russia at War*, pp. 702–06.
97. Bartov, *The Eastern Front*, p. 132.

98. Zolotarev and others, *Velikaya otechestvennaya voina*, book 4, p. 289.
99. Ibid. See also *Vserossiiskaya kniga pamyati, 1941–45*, Moscow, 1995; *Obzornyi tom*, p. 406; Glantz and House, *Titans*, p. 51.
100. Werth, *Russia at War*, pp. 387–88.
101. Ibid., 702; Bundesarchiv-Militärarchiv, RH2–2337, 104.
102. Garrard and Garrard, *Bones*, p. 174.
103. Weiner, *Making Sense*, p. 260.
104. For a discussion of this, see Garrard and Garrard, *Bones*, pp. 180–87.
105. *Pravda*, 3 August 1944.
106. Werth, *Russia at War*, p. 890.
107. Ibid., p. 892.
108. Ibid., p. 702.
109. RGVA, 32925/1/515, 2.
110. RGASPI, 17/125/190, 16.
111. I have heard a number of explanations for the pogrom in the city's Podol district. This one was offered to me by Antony Beevor and is based on archival documents he saw in Moscow.
112. Overy, *Russia's War*, pp. 309–11. On the "doctors' plot," see Louis Rapoport, *Stalin's War against the Jews*, New York, 1990; Jonathan Brent and Vladimir P. Naumov, *Stalin's Last Crime: The Plot against the Jewish Doctors, 1948–1953*, London, 2003.

NINE: Despoil the Corpse

1. Chuikov, *Third Reich*, p. 18.
2. RGASPI–M, 33/1/261, 9 and 24.
3. RGASPI–M, 33/1/1409–19, 6.
4. RGASPI–M, 33/1/261, 29.
5. Intercepted field post, Bundesarchiv-Militärarchiv, RH2–2688, 51 (January 1945).
6. Christopher Duffy, *Red Storm on the Reich: The Soviet March on Germany, 1945*, London, 1991, p. 274.
7. Cited in Werth, *Russia at War*, p. 965.
8. See Beevor, *Berlin*, p. 34.
9. Bundesarchiv-Militärarchiv, RH2–2467, 82.
10. *Khronika chuvstv*, Vladimir, 1991, pp. 175–76.
11. *Pis'ma s fronta i na front*, p. 93. Letter dated 26 February 1945.
12. Bundesarchiv-Militärarchiv, RH2–2467, 86.
13. Werth, *Russia at War*, p. 944.
14. RGASPI–M, 33/1/261, 27.
15. Kopelev, *No Jail*, p. 14.
16. Ibid., p. 13.
17. Julius Hay, cited in Norman Naimark, *The Russians in Germany: A History of the Soviet Zone of Occupation, 1945–1949*, Cambridge, 1995, p. 70.
18. See Naimark, *Russians in Germany*, p. 70; RH2–2686, 37.
19. See Glantz and House, *Titans*, p. 235.
20. Bundesarchiv-Militärarchiv, RH2–2338, 45–01.
21. Bundesarchiv-Militärarchiv, RH2–2686, 33.
22. Kopelev, *No Jail*, p. 36.

23. Bundesarchiv-Militärarchiv, RH2–2467, 9.
24. Ibid.
25. Stalin, *O velikoi otechestvennoi voine*, p. 100 (23 February 1945). This formula echoed a time-honored phrase about capitalism used in the harsh years of class war (collectivization). Then, the catchword was that the class enemy would resist with greatest desperation as the victory of the proletariat approached.
26. Ermolenko, *Voennyi dnevnik*, p. 105.
27. RGASPI–M, 33/1/261, 35.
28. Ibid., 38.
29. Bundesarchiv-Militärarchiv, RH2–2688, 13 (captured letter).
30. For a parallel story of captivating inhumanity, see the account of the slaughtered buffalo in O'Brien, *The Things They Carried*, pp. 75–76.
31. Leonid Rabichev, "Voina vse spishet," *Znamya* 2 (2005): 163.
32. Ibid.
33. Ibid., p. 159.
34. Ibid., p. 165.
35. Kopelev, *No Jail*, p. 37.
36. Bundesarchiv-Militärarchiv, RH2–2338, 44–10, 3.
37. Kopelev, *No Jail*, p. 50.
38. Werth, *Russia at War*, p. 964.
39. Bundesarchiv-Militärarchiv, RH2–2688, 12.
40. Kopelev, *No Jail*, p. 39.
41. Ibid., pp. 46–53.
42. Naimark, *Russians in Germany*, p. 74.
43. This seems clear despite the bland statement by Werth (p. 964) that the rapes were just an outlet for the soldiers' sexual frustration.
44. Bundesarchiv-Militärarchiv, RH2–2688, 13.
45. Overy, *Russia's War*, p. 260.
46. For discussions, see Susan Brownmiller, *Against Our Will: Men, Women, and Rape*, London, 1975; Sylvana Tomaselli and Roy Porter, eds., *Rape: An Historical and Social Enquiry*, Oxford, 1986.
47. RGASPI–M, 33/1/1409–19, 6.
48. Rabichev, "Voina vse spishet," p. 164.
49. Set in a culture of almost total denial, Rabichev's article and Kopelev's book are, to date, among the only discussions of this question in Russian. The time for an honest assessment of the war is still far off, as the Victory Day celebrations in Moscow in 2005 testified.
50. Atina Grossman, "A Question of Silence: The Rape of German Women by Occupation Soldiers," *October* 72 (1995): 51.
51. Bundesarchiv-Militärarchiv, RH2–2688, 13.
52. Cited in Naimark, *Russians in Germany*, p. 112.
53. Anonymous, *A Woman in Berlin: Eight Weeks in the Conquered City*, trans. Philip Boehm, New York, 2005, p. 173.
54. Temkin, *My Just War*, p. 197.
55. Beevor, *Berlin*, p. 326.
56. *A Woman in Berlin*, pp. 50–51.
57. Temkin, *My Just War*, p. 202.
58. Igor Kon and James Riordan, *Sex and Russian Society*, London, 1977, pp. 25–26.

59. For a more recent parallel, see Gilles Kepel's comments about Algerian Islamists, those "impoverished young men" whose crowded family conditions forced them into abstinence and who, in consequence, "condemned the pleasures of which they had been so wretchedly deprived." Cited in Jason Burke, *Al Qaeda: The True Story of Radical Islam*, London, 2004, p. 133.

60. RGASPI–M, 33/1/261, 27.

61. N. Inozemtsev, *Tsena pobedy v toi samoi voine: Frontovoi dnevnik N. Inozemtseva*, Moscow, 1995, p. 108.

62. GARF, 7523/16/79, 56.

63. For an example of such propaganda, see *Pravda*, 13 July 1944, p. 3 (account of Olga Ivanovna Kotova and her ten children).

64. Pushkarev, *Po dorogam voiny*, p. 154.

65. Belov, "Frontovoi dnevnik," p. 469.

66. RGASPI–M, 33/1/1414, 57.

67. RGASPI–M, 33/1/1405, 67.

68. Kopelev, *No Jail*, p. 29.

69. GARF, 7523/16/79, 59, has another letter demanding that soldiers have control over their children.

70. Exotic German women's clothes—"Gretchen knickers"—would often scandalize the soldiers' wives who received them as gifts from their husbands. See Beevor, *Berlin*, p. 407.

71. Cited in Naimark, *Russians in Germany*, p. 108.

72. RH2–2688, 51.

73. Ibid., 52.

74. On this aspect of rape, see Ruth Harris, "The 'Child of the Barbarian': Race, Rape, and Nationalism during the First World War," *Past and Present* 141 (1993): 170–206.

75. *A Woman in Berlin*, pp. 196–97.

76. The most comprehensive figure, from Barbara Johr, is a total of two million in the whole of Germany. See Naimark, *Russians in Germany*, p. 133. See also Helker Sander, "Remembering/Forgetting," *October* 72 (1995): 21.

77. Grossman, "Silence," p. 46.

78. Statistics on venereal disease are available in NKVD files and also in the records of hospitals near the front throughout and just after the war. Although it generally maintained a cool attitude toward the epidemic, the NKVD occasionally noted the pace of infection, as in RGVA, 32925/1/516, 178.

79. *A Woman in Berlin*, p. 5.

80. RGVA, 32925/1/526, 43. See also Naimark, *Russians in Germany*, p. 74.

81. *Velikaya Otechestvennaya: Russkii arkhiv*, vol. 2, part 3, p. 304 (order of 11 July 1944).

82. For example, the three cases of gang rape dating from April 1945 are cited in RGVA, 32925/1/527, 132. The guilty men were turned over to SMERSh.

83. Rabichev, "Voina vse spishet," p. 164.

84. Kopelev, *No Jail*, p. 51; Temkin, *My Just War*, p. 201.

85. GARF, 7523/16/424, 85, 98, for example.

86. See Douglas Botting, *In the Ruins of the Reich*, London, 1985, pp. 23–24.

87. Naimark, *Russians in Germany*, p. 10.

88. Botting, *Ruins*, p. 99.

89. Snetkova, *Pis'ma very*, p. 47.

90. GARF, R7317/6/16, 89.
91. This confirmed the GKO's resolution of 23 December 1944. *Velikaya Otechestvennaya: Russkii arkhiv*, vol. 2, part 3, 344–45.
92. Temkin, *My Just War*, p. 199.
93. *Velikaya Otechestvennaya: Russkii arkhiv*, vol. 2, part 3, 344.
94. Kopelev, *No Jail*, pp. 39–40.
95. Beevor, *Berlin*, p. 35.
96. RGASPI–M, 33/1/1405, 146.
97. Snetkova, *Pis'ma very*, p. 47.
98. See Beevor, *Berlin*, pp. 407–8.
99. RGASPI–M, 33/1/1405, 157.
100. Ibid., 152.
101. Ibid., 158.
102. GAOPIKO, 1/1/3754, 5–9.
103. RGASPI–M, 33/1/1454, 139.
104. TsAMO, 233/2354/1, 28.
105. *A Woman in Berlin*, p. 60.
106. For an account from Poland, see RGVA, 32925/1/527, 86–87.
107. RGVA, 32925/1/527, 108.
108. RGASPI–M, 33/1/1454, 125.
109. Beevor, *Berlin*, pp. 177–78. For a different perspective, see Glantz and House, *Titans*, p. 255.
110. The numbers given are two and a half million Red Army and Polish troops and roughly a million German defenders. Glantz and House, *Titans*, p. 261; Overy, *Russia's War*, p. 266.
111. Glantz and House, *Titans*, p. 260
112. *Pis'ma s fronta i na front*, p. 160.
113. Chuikov, *Third Reich*, p. 146.
114. Beevor, *Berlin*, p. 218.
115. Chuikov, *Third Reich*, p. 147.
116. Overy, *Russia's War*, p. 268.
117. Beevor, *Berlin*, p. 222.
118. Chuikov, *Third Reich*, p. 184.
119. *A Woman in Berlin*, pp. 1, 5.
120. See Beevor, *Berlin*, p. 412. As a military nurse who worked in Belorussia told me, "They were all infected with venereal diseases. All of them!" She was exaggerating, naturally, but she must have wondered when she would see a patient who was not.
121. A version appears in RGVA, 32925/1/527, 10–11.
122. *A Woman in Berlin*, pp. 90–91.
123. Overy, *Russia's War*, p. 273; Beevor, *Berlin*, p. 372; Chuikov, *Third Reich*, pp. 242–49.
124. Glantz and House, *Titans*, p. 269.
125. Chuikov, *Third Reich*, p. 251.
126. Beevor, *Berlin*, p. 405.
127. Belov, "Frontovoi dnevnik," p. 476.
128. Glantz and House, *Titans*, p. 269. The higher figure is based on Krivosheev's global estimate for the campaign on three fronts (First and Second Belorussian, First Ukrainian).

129. RGASPI–M, 33/1/1405, 137.

130. RGASPI–M, 33/1/1454, 146.

131. Samoilov, "Lyudi," part 2, p. 96.

132. RGVA, 32925/1/527, 50–53.

133. Other cases occur on almost every page of this same file. See, e.g., RGVA, 32925/1/527, 48, 233.

134. Ermolenko, *Voennyi dnevnik*, p. 126.

TEN: **Sheathe the Old Sword**

1. Werth, *Russia at War*, p. 969.

2. RGASPI–M, 33/1/1406, 70.

3. One reason for the greater proportionate loss was the annihilation of Polish Jews, which reduced the population by approximately three million. Poland's total loss, approximately six million people, amounted to about 20 percent of the prewar total. See Keegan, *The Second World War*, p. 493.

4. Figures vary, and to some extent, since all are estimates, it is impossible to compare the scale of losses. But a recent Russian account suggests that the ratio of Soviet to German military losses was 1.3:1 (even taking into account the losses of each adversary's allies). In terms of battlefield deaths, the true figure may be higher than 1.6:1. See Zolotarev and others, *Velikaya otechestvennaya voina*, book 4, p. 292; Glantz and House, *Titans*, pp. 292, 307; Krivosheev, *Grif sekretnosti snyat*, pp. 152–53, 384–92.

5. Overy, *Russia's War*, pp. 287–88.

6. The official exchange rate in 1940 was 5.3 rubles to the dollar, but the figure has little real meaning given the currency controls in operation throughout the Soviet era. *Velikaya otechestvennaya voina*, book 4, p. 294; Overy, *Russia's War*, p. 291.

7. Vsevolod Vyshnevsky, cited in Werth, *Russia at War*, p. 942.

8. See Dunham, *In Stalin's Time*, p. 11.

9. Cited in Afanas'ev, *Drugaya voina*, p. 298.

10. GARF, 7523/16/79, 173.

11. Ibid.

12. One letter, for example, demands general amnesty and numerous others request review of the penal code (GARF, 7523/16/79).

13. Ibid., 17.

14. Overy, *Russia's War*, p. 292.

15. Dunham, *In Stalin's Time*, p. 9; Merridale, *Night of Stone*, p. 323.

16. The rumor was repeated even in the soldiers' letters home. See, for example, Snetkova, *Pis'ma very*, p. 48.

17. E. Yu. Zubkova, *Obshchestvo i reformy, 1945–1964*, Moscow, 1993, p. 43.

18. On adaptation, see Ben Shephard, *A War of Nerves: Soldiers and Psychiatrists, 1914–1994*, London, 2000, pp. 328–29.

19. Gorinov and others, *Moskva voennaya*, p. 708.

20. Ibid., p. 707.

21. Lists of the military participants occupy an entire number of *Voenno-istoricheskii arkhiv* 12, no. 3 (2000). The instructions for the day are printed in vol. 12, no. 8 (2000), pp. 259–77.

22. Werth, *Russia at War*, pp. 1002–3.

23. RGASPI–M, 33/1/1405, 157–58.
24. Ermolenko, *Voennyi dnevnik*, p. 143.
25. For details of the campaign, see Glantz and House, *Titans*, pp. 278–82.
26. For an account, see Joseph Polowsky's testimony in Studs Terkel, *A Good War: An Oral History of World War II*, New York, 1984, pp. 444–50.
27. GARF, 7077/1/19, 7–10.
28. GARF, 7399/1/3, 126.
29. Cited in Naimark, *Russians in Germany*, p. 74.
30. GARF, 7317/7/147, 7317/7/118, 31.
31. GARF, 7077/1/19, 13.
32. Ibid.
33. GARF, 7399/1/3, 153–54.
34. Ibid., 125–27.
35. Ibid., 34; 7317/7/147, 76.
36. GARF, 7399/1/3, 98.
37. GARF, 7077/1/178, 10–11.
38. GARF, 7399/1/3, 95.
39. GARF, 7399/1/1, 2.
40. Ibid., 14–15.
41. An example among many was Frankfurt on the Oder (GARF 7399/1/3, 11–15), where discipline had "become better than before" by early July. See also GARF, 7317/7/124b, 36–39, on Berlin.
42. GARF, 7317/10/23, 48–49.
43. Naimark, *Russians in Germany*, p. 74.
44. GARF, 7399/1/1, 16.
45. GARF, 7317/7/124b, 5.
46. On the duty of Germans to die for the cleanup, see GARF, 7523/16/79, 215.
47. *Velikaya otechestvennaya voina*, book 4, p. 191.
48. Ibid.
49. GARF, 7077/1/178.
50. *Velikaya otechestvennaya voina*, book 4, 191–92; Overy, *Russia's War*, pp. 302–03. For a discussion of the repatriations in general, see Nikolai Tolstoy, *Victims of Yalta*, London, 1977.
51. Incidents and interviews appear in GARF, 7317/20/15, 42–68.
52. *Velikaya otechestvennaya voina*, book 4, pp. 192–93.
53. GARF, 5446/48a/13, 9–11.
54. Ibid., 26–27.
55. Ibid., 27.
56. Overy, *Russia's War*, p. 302.
57. GARF, 7317/7/124v, 18–19.
58. GARF, 7317/20/13, 76.
59. GARF, 7399/1/3, 42; 7317/20/13, 74.
60. GARF, 7184/1/65, 180.
61. GARF, 7523/16/79, 163.
62. TsAMO, 136/24416/24, 19–21.
63. GARF, 7184/1/57, 347–48.
64. *Velikaya Otechestvennaya: Russkii arkhiv*, vol. 2, part 3, p. 378.
65. GARF, 7184/1/57, 347.

66. Pushkarev, *Po dorogam voiny*, p. 160.
67. GAOPIKO, 1/7/3755, 53.
68. TsDNISO, 6/1/2005, 16.
69. GAOPIKO, 1/13755, 5.
70. GARF, 7523/16/54, 1.
71. Smolensk figures from oblast records (TsDNISO, 6/1/2005, 12–16) and district reports (6/1/2005, 24, 47).
72. This story is told in N. Tumarkin, *The Living and the Dead: The Rise and Fall of the Cult of World War II in Russia*, New York, 1994, p. 104; Garrard and Garrard, *Bones*, pp. 215–16.
73. On the fulfillment (or otherwise) of Sovnarkom resolutions on war graves, see GAKO, R3322/10/81, 33–4. Konstantin Simonov's call for a kind of Soviet orderliness in place of the soldiers' own tastes in memorials is noted in RGALI, 1814/6/144, 52.
74. GARF, 5446/48a/2657, 161.
75. Of 1,913 buildings commandeered as hospitals by May 1945, 333 were former educational institutions and 84 their former halls of residence. GARF, 5446/48a/2657, 161.
76. TsDNISO, 37/1/264, 8.
77. Tumarkin, *The Living and the Dead*, p. 98.
78. GARF, 8009/35/20, 2.
79. Ibid., 2–3.
80. Merridale, *Night of Stone*, p. 315.
81. For literary examples, see Dunham, *In Stalin's Time*, pp. 10–11.
82. Report from Leningrad hospitals, Central State Archive of St. Petersburg, 9156/4/321, 14–15.
83. Merridale, *Night of Stone*, p. 305, also referring to reports from postwar Leningrad.
84. See Overy, *Russia's War*, p. 312.
85. Vasily Grossman, *Life and Fate*, trans. Robert Chandler, London, 1985, p. 141.
86. On Leningrad, see Ilya Ehrenburg, *Post-War Years, 1945–1954*, trans. Tatiana Shebunina and Yvonne Kapp, London, 1966, p. 11.
87. See Dunham, *In Stalin's Time*, especially chapter 13, pp. 214–24.
88. Doctors working in rural areas near Leningrad at the time would also report amenorrhea in peasant women, which they ascribed to a kind of mourning but which may as easily have been the result of poor diet and heavy manual work. See Merridale, *Night of Stone*, pp. 312–13.
89. Alexiyevich, *War's Unwomanly Face*, p. 206.
90. GARF, 8009/35/20, 2–3.
91. Merridale, *Night of Stone*, p. 314; see also Werth, *Russia at War*, p. 520.
92. RGASPI–M, 129.
93. RGASPI–M, 33/1/1404, 131; 33/1/1405, 118.
94. For Vera Dunham's tart summary, see *In Stalin's Time*, p. 214.
95. See Overy, *Russia's War*, pp. 309–11; Garrard and Garrard, *Bones*, pp. 219–28; Merridale, *Night of Stone*, p. 273.
96. Applebaum, *Gulag*, pp. 414–23.
97. Merridale, *Night of Stone*, pp. 317–19. See also Robert Service, *A History of Twentieth-Century Russia*, London, 1997, p. 319.

ELEVEN: **And We Remember All**

1. On Stalinism and Russian nationalism among veterans after 1945, see Druzhba, *Velikaya*, p. 43.
2. Like Stalin, he also sacked Zhukov. See Service, *Twentieth-Century Russia*, p. 372.
3. Khrushchev attacked what he described as the cult of Stalin's personality and, with it, many of the excesses of Stalin's dictatorship. See N. S. Khrushchev, *Khrushchev Remembers*, trans. Strobe Talbott, London, 1970, pp. 559–618.
4. For the memorials, see Michael Ignatieff, "Soviet War Memorials," *History Workshop Journal* 17 (1984): 157–63.
5. For further evidence, see Ignatieff, "Soviet War Memorials," and Tumarkin, *The Living and the Dead*, which traces the Second World War cult over forty years.
6. On 1965 in the veterans' memories, see *Kolomenskii almanakh*, no. 4, Moscow, 2000, p. 238.
7. R. W. Davies, *Soviet History in the Gorbachev Revolution*, Houndmills, 1988, p. 101.
8. For the story of Katyn, which emerged only after 1990, see R. W. Davies, *Soviet History in the Yeltsin Era*, Houndmills, 1997, pp. 18–19.
9. This was a comment made to the Yugoslav diplomat Milovan Djilas. See Djilas, *Conversations with Stalin*, New York, 1962, p. 111.
10. For an account, see Nina Tumarkin, "Story of a War Memorial," in Garrard and Garrard, *World War 2 and the Soviet People*, pp. 125–46.
11. See Gibian, "World War 2 in Russian National Consciousness," pp. 147–60.
12. Georgian veterans tended to be even more "Soviet" in their outlook than Russians, not least because the notion of a Georgian homeland is fragmented and still troubled by ethnic hatreds inside the republic's territory.
13. Werth, *Russia at War*, p. 155.
14. Druzhba, *Velikaya*, p. 43. The persistence of this kind of nationalism was apparent in the interviews I carried out in Georgia and eastern Ukraine in 2002 and 2003.
15. The testimonies in *Rodina* 6–7 (1991), especially pp. 61–63, confirm what surviving members of punishment battalions said to me.
16. M. Gefter, ed., *Golosa iz mira, kotorogo uzhe net: Vypuskniki istoricheskogo fakul'teta MGU 1941 g. v pis'makh i vospominaniyakh*, Moscow, 1995, p. 41.

BIBLIOGRAPHY

★

Addison, P., and A. Calder, eds. *Time to Kill: The Soldier's Experience of War in the West, 1939–1945*. London, 1997.

Afanas'ev, Yu. N., ed. *Drugaya voina, 1939–1945*. Moscow, 1996.

Alexiyevich, S. *War's Unwomanly Face*. Trans. Keith Hammond and Lyudmila Lezhneva. Moscow, 1988.

Andreyev, C. *Vlasov and the Russian Liberation Movement: Soviet Reality and Emigré Theories*, Cambridge, 1987.

Anonymous. *A Woman in Berlin: Eight Weeks in the Conquered City*. Trans. Philip Boehm. New York, 2005.

Applebaum, A. *Gulag: A History of the Soviet Camps*. London, 2003.

Armstrong, J. A., ed. *Soviet Partisans in World War II*. Madison, 1964.

Astaf'ev, V. "Tam, v okopakh." *Pravda*, 25 November 1985.

———. "Snachala snaryady, potom lyudi," *Rodina* 6–7 (1991): 55.

———. *Proklyaty i ubity*. Moscow, 2002.

Babichenko, D. L., ed. *Literaturnyi front: Istoriya politicheskoi tsenzury, 1932–1946 gg.* Moscow, 1994.

Bacon, E. *The Gulag at War: Stalin's Forced Labour System in the Light of the Archives*. Houndmills, 1994.

Bartov, O. *The Eastern Front, 1941–45: German Troops and the Barbarisation of Warfare*. London, 1985.

———. *Hitler's Army: Soldiers, Nazis, and War in the Third Reich*. New York, 1992.

Beevor, A. *Stalingrad*. London, 1998.

———. *Berlin: The Downfall, 1945*. London, 2002.

Belov, N. F. "Frontovoi dnevnik N. F. Belova, 1941–1944." *Vologda* 2 (1997): 431–76.

Bogdanov, V. L., and others, eds. *Zhivaya pamyat': Pravda o voine*. 3 vols. Moscow, 1995.

Botting, D. *In the Ruins of the Reich*. London, 1985.

Brent, J., and V. P. Naumov. *Stalin's Last Crime: The Plot against the Jewish Doctors, 1948–1953*. London, 2003.

Brooks, J. *When Russia Learned to Read: Literacy and Popular Literature, 1861–1917*. Princeton, 1985.

Brownmiller, S. *Against Our Will: Men, Women, and Rape*. London, 1975.

Bukov, K. I., M. Gorinov, and A. N. Ponomarev, eds. *Moskva voennaya: Memuary i arkhivnye dokumenty, 1941–1945*. Moscow, 1995.

Burke, J. *Al Qaeda: The True Story of Radical Islam*. London, 2004.

Bykov, V. *Povesti raznykh let.* Moscow, 1990.

———. "Za Rodinu! Za Stalina!," *Rodina* 5 (1995): 30–37.

Caputo, P. *A Rumor of War.* London, 1978.

Chuikov, V. I. *The Beginning of the Road.* Trans. Harold Silver. London, 1963.

———. *The End of the Third Reich.* Trans. Ruth Kisch. London, 1967.

Conquest, R. *The Harvest of Sorrow: Soviet Collectivization and the Terror-Famine*, Oxford and New York, 1986.

Creveld, M. van. *Fighting Power: German and US Army Performance, 1939–1945*, London and Melbourne, 1983.

Dallin, A. *German Rule in Russia, 1941–1945: A Study in Occupation Politics.* 2nd ed. London and Basingstoke, 1981.

Davies, R. W. *Soviet History in the Gorbachev Revolution.* Houndmills, 1988.

———. *Soviet History in the Yeltsin Era.* Houndmills, 1997.

Dean, M. *Collaboration in the Holocaust: Crimes of the Local Police in Belorussia and Ukraine, 1941–1944.* Houndmills, 2000.

Detwiler, D. S., and others, eds. *World War II German Military Studies.* 24 vols. New York and London, 1979.

Djilas, M. *Conversations with Stalin.* New York, 1962.

Docherty, L. J. III. "The Reluctant Warriors: The Non-Russian Nationalities in Service of the Red Army during World War II." *Journal of Slavic Military Studies* 6, no. 3 (1993): 426–45.

Drobyazko, S. and A. Karashchuk. *Vostochnye legiony i kazach'i chasti v Vermakhte.* Moscow, 1999.

Drobyshev, S., ed. *Nemtsy o russkikh.* Moscow, 1995.

Druzhba, O. V. *Velikaya otechestvennaya voina v soznanii sovetskogo i postsovetskogo obshchestva: Dinamika predstavlenii ob istoricheskom proshlom.* Rostov on Don, 2000.

Duffy, C. *Red Storm on the Reich: The Soviet March on Germany, 1945.* London, 1991.

Dunham, V. S. *In Stalin's Time: Middle-Class Values in Soviet Fiction.* Cambridge, 1976.

Dyke, C. van. "The Timoshenko Reforms, March–July 1940." *Journal of Slavic Military Studies* 9, no. 1 (1996): 69–96.

———. *The Soviet Invasion of Finland, 1939–1940.* London, 1997.

Ehrenburg, I. *Russia at War.* Trans. Gerald Shelley. London, 1943.

———. *The War, 1941–1945.* New York, 1964.

———. *Post-War Years, 1945–1954.* Trans. Tatiana Shebunina and Yvonne Kapp. London, 1966.

Ehrenburg, I., and V. Grossman, eds. *The Black Book.* New York, 1981.

Ellis, J. *The Sharp End of War: The Fighting Man in World War II.* London, 1980.

Erickson, J. *The Road to Stalingrad.* Vol. 1 of *Stalin's War with Germany.* London, 1975.

———. *The Road to Berlin.* Vol. 2 of *Stalin's War with Germany.* London, 1983.

Erickson, J., and L. Erickson. *The Eastern Front in Photographs.* London, 2001.

Ermolenko, V. I. *Voennyi dnevnik starshego serzhanta.* Belgorod, 2000.

Evdokimov, E. L. *Politicheskie zanyatiya v Krasnoi Armii.* Leningrad, 1933.

Fisher, A. *The Crimean Tatars.* Stanford, 1978.

Fitzpatrick, S. *Stalin's Peasants: Resistance and Survival in the Russian Village after Collectivization.* Oxford, 1994.

———. *Everyday Stalinism: Ordinary Life in Extraordinary Times; Soviet Russia in the 1930s.* Oxford, 1999.

———, ed. *Stalinism: New Directions.* London, 2000.

French, D. "Discipline and the Death Penalty in the British Army in the War against Germany during the Second World War." *Journal of Contemporary History* 33, no. 4 (1998): 531–45.

Gabriel, R. *The Mind of the Soviet Fighting Man: A Quantitative Survey of Soviet Soldiers, Sailors, and Airmen.* Westport, 1984.

———. *Soviet Military Psychiatry.* Westport, 1986.

———. *The Painful Field: The Psychiatric Dimension of Modern War.* New York, 1988.

Garrard, J., and C. Garrard, *The Bones of Berdichev: The Life and Fate of Vasily Grossman.* New York, 1996.

Garrard, J., and C. Garrard, eds. *World War 2 and the Soviet People: Selected Papers from the Fourth World Congress for Soviet and East European Studies, Harrogate, 1990.* Houndmills, 1993.

Garthoff, R. A. *How Russia Makes War.* London, 1954.

Gefter, M., ed. *Golosa iz mira, kotorogo uzhe net: Vypuskniki istoricheskogo fakul'teta MGU 1941 g. v pis'makh i vospominaniyakh.* Moscow, 1995.

Geiger, H. K. *The Family in Soviet Russia.* Cambridge, 1968.

Getty, J. A., and R. T. Manning, eds. *Stalinist Terror: New Perspectives.* Cambridge, 1993.

Getty, J. A., and O. V. Naumov. *The Road to Terror: Stalin and the Self-Destruction of the Bolsheviks.* New Haven and London, 1999.

Gilgen, A. R., and others. *Soviet and American Psychology during World War II.* Westport, 1997.

Glantz, D. M. *From the Don to the Dnepr.* London, 1991.

———. "From the Soviet Secret Archives: Newly Published Soviet Works on the Red Army, 1918–1991. A Review Essay." *Journal of Slavic Military Studies* 8 (1995).

Glantz, D. M., and J. House, *When Titans Clashed: How the Red Army Stopped Hitler.* Edinburgh, 2000.

Goncharova, A. V., ed. *Voiny krovavye tsvety: Ustnye rasskazy o voine.* Moscow, 1979.

Gordon, A. E. "Moskovskoe narodnoe opolchenie 1941 goda glazami uchastnika." *Otechestvennaya istoriya* 3 (2001): 158–63.

Gorinov, M. M., and others, eds. *Moskva voennaya, 1941–1945: Memuary; arkhivnye dokumenty.* Moscow, 1995.

Gozman, L., and A. Etkind. *The Psychology of Post-Totalitarian Russia.* London, 1992.

Grinker, R., and J. Spiegel. *Men under Stress.* Philadelphia, 1945.

Gross, J. T. *Revolution from Abroad: The Soviet Conquest of Poland's Western Ukraine and Western Belorussia.* Princeton, 1988.

Grossman, A. "A Question of Silence: The Rape of German Women by Occupation Soldiers." *October* 72 (1995): 43–63.

Grossman, V. *Life and Fate.* Trans. Robert Chandler. London, 1985.

———. *Forever Flowing.* Trans. Thomas P. Whitney. New York, 1986.

———. *Gody voiny.* Moscow, 1989.

Guderian, H. *Panzer Leader.* London, 1977.

Gudoshnikov, Ya. N., ed. *Russkie narodnye pesny i chastushki Velikoi Otechestvennoi Voiny.* Tambov, 1997.

Gudzovskii, I. "Iz voennogo dnevnika 1941–2." *Rodina* 6–7 (1991): 66–67.

Gusev, S. I. *Uroki grazhdanskoi voiny.* Moscow, 1921.

Hagen, M. von. *Soldiers in the Proletarian Dictatorship: The Red Army and the Soviet Socialist State, 1919–1930.* Ithaca and London, 1990.

———. "Soviet Soldiers and Officers on the Eve of the German Invasion: Towards a Description of Social Psychology and Political Attitudes." *Soviet Union/Union Sovietique* 18, nos. 1–3 (1991): 79–101.

Harris, R. "The 'Child of the Barbarian': Race, Rape, and Nationalism during the First World War." *Past and Present* 141 (1993): 170–206.

Herr, M. *Dispatches.* New York, 1977.

Hirschfeld, G., ed. *The Politics of Genocide: Jews and Soviet Prisoners of War in Nazi Germany.* London, 1986.

Hodgson, K. *Written with the Bayonet: Soviet Russian Poetry of World War Two.* Liverpool, 1996.

Holmes, R. *Acts of War: The Behavior of Men in Battle.* New York, 1987.

Hynes, S. *The Soldier's Tale: Bearing Witness to Modern War.* London, 1998.

Ignatieff, M. "Soviet War Memorials." *History Workshop Journal* 17 (1984): 157–63.

Inozemtsev, N. *Tsena pobedy v toi samoi voine: Frontovoi dnevnik N. Inozemtseva.* Moscow, 1995.

Ivanov, F. I., ed. *Voennaya psikhiatriya: Uchebnik dlya slushatelei akademii i voenno-meditsinskikh fakul'tetov meditsinskikh institutov.* Leningrad, 1974.

Keegan, J. *The Face of Battle.* London, 1977.

———. *The Second World War.* London, 1989.

Keep, J. L. *Soldiers of the Tsar.* Oxford, 1985.

Kellett, A. *Combat Motivation: The Behavior of Soldiers in Battle.* Boston, 1982.

Khrushchev, N. S. *Khrushchev Remembers.* Trans. Strobe Talbott. London, 1970.

Knyshevskii, P. N., ed. *Skrytaya pravda voiny: 1941 god. Neizvestnye dokumenty.* Moscow, 1992.

Kolomenskii almanakh. Moscow, 2000.

Kon, I., and J. Riordan. *Sex and Russian Society.* London, 1993.

Kondrat'ev, V. "Oplacheno krov'yu," *Rodina* 6–7 (1991): 6–7.

Kopelev, L. *No Jail for Thought.* Trans. Anthony Austin. London, 1977.

Kotkin, S. *Magnetic Mountain: Stalinism as a Civilization.* Berkeley and Los Angeles, 1995.

Kozhurin, V. S., ed. *Narod i vlast' 1941–1945: Novye dokumenty.* Moscow, 1995.

Kozlov, N. D. *Obshchestvennye soznanie v gody Velikoi Otechestvennoi Voiny.* St. Petersburg, 1995.

Krivosheev, G. F., ed. *Grif sekretnosti snyat: Poteri vooruzhennykh sil SSSR v voinakh, boevykh deistviyakh i voennykh konfliktakh.* Moscow, 1993 (also trans.: "Soviet Casualties and Combat Losses in the Twentieth Century," London, 1997).

Krupyanskaya, V. Yu. *Frontovoi fol'klor.* Moscow, 1944.

Krupyanskaya, V. Yu., and S. I. Mints. *Materialy po istorii pesny Velikoi Otechestvennoi Voiny.* Moscow, 1953.

Lebedeva, N. S. *Katyn': Prestuplenie protiv chelovechestva*. Moscow, 1994.

Levasheva, Z. L. *Moral'nyi oblik sovetskogo voina: Rekomendatel'nyi ukazatel' literatury*. Moscow, 1950.

Linz, S. J., ed. *The Impact of World War II on the Soviet Union*. Totowa, 1985.

Littlejohn, D. *Foreign Legions in the Third Reich*. San Jose, 1987.

Lukov, G. D. *Psikhologiya: Ocherki po voprosam obucheniya i vospitaniya sovetskikh voinov*. Moscow, 1960.

Lynn, J. *The Bayonets of the Republic: Motivation and Tactics in the Army of Revolutionary France, 1791–1794*. Urbana, 1984.

Marshall, S. L. A. *Men against Fire: The Problem of Battle Command in Future Wars*. New York, 1947.

Merridale, C. "The USSR Population Census of 1937 and the Limits of Stalinist Rule." *Historical Journal* 39, no. 1 (1996): 225–40.

———. "The Collective Mind: Trauma and Shell-Shock in Twentieth-Century Russia." *Journal of Contemporary History* 35, no. 1 (2000): 39–55.

———. *Night of Stone: Death and Memory in Russia*. London, 2000.

Mirskii, M. B. *Obyazany zhizn'yu*. Moscow, 1991.

Moskoff, W. *The Bread of Affliction: The Food Supply in the USSR during World War II*. Cambridge, 1990.

Mosse, G. *Fallen Soldiers: Reshaping the Memory of the World War*. Oxford, 1990.

Naimark, N. M. *The Russians in Germany: A History of the Soviet Zone of Occupation, 1945–1949*. Cambridge, 1995.

"O boevykh deistviyakh 6 armii pri vykhode iz okruzheniya." *Voenno-istoricheskii zhurnal* 22, no. 7 (2001): 108–12.

O'Brien, T. *The Things They Carried*. London, 1991.

Odom, W. E. *The Soviet Volunteers: Modernization and Bureaucracy in a Public Mass Organization*. Princeton, 1973.

Overy, R. *Russia's War*. London, 1997.

Ovsyannikov, M. V., ed. *55 let Kurskoi bitve*. Kursk, 1998.

Pennington, R. *Wings, Women, and War: Soviet Airwomen in World War II*. Lawrence, 2001.

Pervyshin, V. G. "Lyudskie poteri v VOV." *Voprosy istorii* 7 (2000): 116–22.

Pesennik. Edited collection. Moscow, 1950.

Pis'ma s fronta i na front, 1941–1945. Edited collection. Smolensk, 1991.

Piterskii, L. "Deti na voine," *Istochnik* 1 (1994): 54–60.

——— "Syn polka." *Rodina* 2 (1995): 63–68.

Pokhlebkin, V. V. *Velikaya voina i nesostoyavshiisya mir, 1941–1945–1994*. Moscow, 1997.

Politkovskaya, A. *A Dirty War*. Trans. John Crowfoot. London, 2001.

Polyan, P. *Ne po svoei vole*. Moscow, 2001.

Po obe stovony fronta: pis'ma sovetskikh i nemetskikh soldat, 1941–1945. Moscow, 1995.

Porshneva, O. S. *Mentalitet i sotsial'noe povedenie rabochikh, krest'yan i soldat v periode pervoi mirovoi voiny*. Ekaterinburg, 2000.

Pushkarev, L. N. "Pis'mennaya forma bytovaniya frontovogo fol'klora," *Etnograficheskoe obozrenie* 4 (1995): 27–29.

———. *Po dorogam voiny: Vospominaniya fol'klorista-frontovika*. Moscow, 1995.

Rabichev, L. "Voina vse spishet." *Znamya* 2 (2005): 142–67.

Rapoport, L. *Stalin's War against the Jews.* New York, 1990.

Reese, R. R. *Stalin's Reluctant Soldiers: A Social History of the Red Army, 1925–1941.* Lawrence, 1996.

———. *The Soviet Military Experience: A History of the Soviet Army, 1917–1991.* London, 2000.

Richards, F. *Old Soldiers Never Die.* London, 1933.

Rokossovsky, K. K. *Soldatskii dolg.* Moscow, 1972.

Rossiya-XX vek: Dokumenty; 1941 god v 2 knigakh, vol. 2. Moscow, 1998.

Rzhevskaya, E. M. *Vechernyi razgovor: Povesti, rasskazy, zapiski.* St. Petersburg, 2001.

Samarin, G. *Patrioticheskaya tema v pesennom tvorchestve russkogo naroda.* Frunze, 1946.

Samoilov, D. "Lyudi odnogo varianta. Iz voennykh zapisok." *Avrora* 1 (1990): 42–83; 2 (1990): 50–96.

Sander, Helker. "Remembering/Forgetting," *October* 72 (1995): 22.

Sella, A. *The Value of Human Life in Soviet Warfare.* London, 1992.

Senyavskaya, E. S. *Frontovoe pokolenie: Istoriko-psikhologicheskie issledovanie, 1941–1945.* Moscow, 1995.

———. *Psikhologiya voiny v XX veke: Istoricheskii opyt Rossii.* Moscow, 1999.

———. "Zhenskie sud'by skvoz' prizmu voennoi tsenzury." *Voenno-istoricheskii arkhiv* 7, no. 22 (2001): 81–107.

Serdtsova, A. P., and G. D. Karpov. *22 iyunya 1941 goda: Istoriya i sud'by lyudei.* Moscow, 1995.

Service, R. *A History of Twentieth-Century Russia.* London, 1997.

Shalamov, V. *Kolyma Tales.* Trans. John Glad. Harmondsworth, 1994.

Shalit, B. *The Psychology of Conflict and Combat.* Westport and London, 1988.

Shapkin, Ya. M., and I. A. Al'man, eds. *Khronika chuvstv.* Yaroslavl, 1990.

Shchepetov, K. *Nemtsy—glazami russkikh.* Moscow, 1995.

Shcherbakova, I. L., ed. *Chelovek v istorii: Rossiya-XX vek; Vserossiiskii konkurs istoricheskikh issledovatel'skikh rabot starsheklassnikov.* Moscow, 2002.

Shephard, B. *A War of Nerves: Soldiers and Psychiatrists, 1914–1994.* London, 2000.

Shils, E., and M. Janowitz. "Cohesion and Distintegration in the Wehrmacht in World War II." *Public Opinion Quarterly* 12 (1948): 280–315.

Shindel', A. D., ed. *Po obe storony fronta: Pis'ma sovetskikh i nemetskikh soldat.* Moscow, 1995.

Shpil'rein, I. N. *Yazyk krasnoarmeitsa.* Moscow and Leningrad, 1928.

Shukman, H., ed. *Stalin's Generals.* London, 1993.

Sidel'nikov, V. M., ed. *Krasnoarmeiskii fol'klor.* Moscow, 1938.

Sidorov, S. G. *Trud voennoplennykh v SSSR 1939–1956 gg.* Volgograd, 2001.

Simonov, K. *Soldatskie memuary.* Moscow, 1985.

———. *Glazami cheloveka moego pokoleniya.* Moscow, 1989.

Snetkova, E. M. *Pis'ma very, nadezhdy, lyubvy: Pis'ma s fronta.* Moscow, 1999.

Stafonovskii, G. A., ed. *Poslednye pis'ma s fronta.* 3 vols. Moscow, 1991.

Stalin, I. V. *O velikoi otechestvennoi voine Sovetskogo Soyuza.* Moscow, 1947.

Stites, R., ed. *Culture and Entertainment in Wartime Russia.* Bloomington, 1995.

Stone, N. *The Eastern Front, 1914–1917.* London, 1975.

Stouffer, S. A., and others, ed. *The American Soldier.* 2 vols. Princeton, 1949.

Stroki, opalennye voiny: Sbornik pisem voennykh let., 1941–1945. 2nd. ed. Edited collection. Belgorod, 1998.

Suvorov, V. *Inside the Soviet Army.* New York, 1982.

———. *Den' M: Kogda nachalas' vtoraya mirovaya voina?* Moscow, 1994.

Sword, K. *Deportation and Exile: Poles in the Soviet Union, 1939–1948.* Houndmills, 1994.

Temkin, G. *My Just War: The Memoirs of a Jewish Red Army Soldier in World War II.* Novato, 1998.

Terkel, S. *The Good War: An Oral History of World War II.* New York, 1984.

Thomson, A. *Anzac Memories: Living with the Legend.* Melbourne, 1994.

Todd, A. C., and M. Hayward, eds. *Twentieth-Century Russian Poetry.* London, 1993.

Tolstoy, N. *Victims of Yalta.* London, 1977.

Tomaselli S., and R. Porter, eds. *Rape: An Historical and Social Enquiry.* Oxford, 1986.

Tumarkin, N. *The Living and the Dead: The Rise and Fall of the Cult of World War II in Russia.* New York, 1994.

Velikaya Otechestvennaya: Russkii arkhiv. Multivolume edition. Moscow, 1997–2005.

Velikaya Otechestvennaya Voina, 1941–1945: voenno-istoricheskie ocherki. 4 vols. Various editors. Moscow 1998–99.

Velikaya otechestvennaya voina v otsenke molodykh. Various contributors. Moscow, 1997.

Vestnik arkhivista 3 (2001): 56–59.

Volkova, N. B. "Materialy velikoi otechestvennoi voiny v fondakh TsGALI SSSR." *Vstrechi s proshlym* 6 (1988): 435–459.

Vserossiiskaya kniga pamyati, 1941–1945. Moscow, 1995.

Vyltsan, M. A. "Deportatsiya narodov v gody velikoi otechestvennoi voiny." *Etnograficheskoe obozrenie* 3 (1995): 26–44.

———. "Prikaz i propoved: Sposoby mobilizatsii resursov derevni v gody voiny." *Otechestvennaya istoriya* 3 (1995): 69–80.

Weiner, A. *Making Sense of War: The Second World War and the Fate of the Bolshevik Revolution.* Princeton, 2001.

Werth, A. *Russia at War.* London, 1964.

Williams, B. G. "The Hidden Ethnic Cleansing of Muslims in the Soviet Union: The Exile and Repatriation of the Crimean Tatars." *Journal of Contemporary History* 37 (2002): 322–347.

Yakovlev, A. N., chief ed. *1941 god.* 2 vols. Moscow, 1998.

Yakovlev, I. K., and others, eds. *Vnutrennye voiska v velikoi otechestevnnoi voine 1941–1945 gg., dokumenty i materialy.* Moscow, 1975.

Yukov, V. I., and others. *OZNAZ: Ot brigady osobogo naznacheniya k "vympely," 1941–1981.* Moscow, 2001.

Zaloga, S. J., and L. S. Ness. *Red Army Handbook, 1939–1945.* Stroud, 2003.

Zhukov, G. K. *Vospominaniya i razmyshleniya.* 13th ed. 2 vols. Moscow, 2002.

Zubkova, E. Yu. *Obshchestvo i reformy, 1945–1964.* Moscow, 1993.

ACKNOWLEDGMENTS

★

The opportunity to research and to write this book was a privilege, and I am indebted to many people for their generosity, their patience, learning, and support. The greatest burden was carried by a succession of research assistants and guides in the former Soviet Union, and in particular by the sociologist Oksana Bocharova and the ethnographer Mariya Belova. Elena Stroganova offered wise and imaginative support at all stages, and I am also grateful to Ekaterina Pushkina and Aleksei Shimchuk in Moscow, to Khatuna Chkheidze in Tbilisi, and to Larisa Shipico in Yalta. The material from German archives was collected with the skillful assistance of Carsten Vogelpohl in Freiburg and Thomas Greis in Bristol.

No project on this scale can succeed without funds, and I was particularly fortunate to secure the support of the United Kingdom's Economic and Social Research Council, whose generosity enabled me to work and travel extensively in the former Soviet Union and then to read, reflect, and write without the distractions of my normal university duties. The Council's research support was invaluable in every way, and I am also grateful to the anonymous assessors who commented on my initial proposal. When I was in the process of completing the manuscript, a further period of leave, funded by the Arts and Humanities Research Board, allowed me several more months' peace of mind; I am also grateful to the University of Bristol and to Queen Mary, University of London, for their patience and generous financial support. I owe a particular debt to the British Broadcasting Corporation, and especially to Tim Dee, one of its senior producers, for commissioning the programs on Stalinism in Georgia and on the Crimea that enabled me to travel and work in two beautiful locations while benefiting from stimulating company and sparkling creative advice.

One of the rewards of my travels was the opportunity to work in a range of archives and libraries. I would like to record my thanks to the staffs of the State Public History Library in Moscow, the Cambridge University Library, the British Library, and the London Library. I would also like to thank the helpful staffs of the State Archive of the Russian Federation, the Russian State Military Archive, the Russian State Archive of Literature and Art, and the Russian State Archive of Social-Political History and its affiliate, the Archive of the Komsomol. In Kursk, I was fortunate to work in both the State Archive of Social and Political History and the State Archive of Kursk Oblast, and a similar kindness enabled me to work efficiently in both the State Archive of Smolensk Oblast and the Center for the Documentation of Contemporary History in Smolensk during my short stay there. I owe a great deal to the two researchers who found documents for me in the Central Archive of the Ministry of Defense in Podolsk and should like to thank the Bundesarchiv-Militärarchiv in Freiburg for providing rich information from documents relating to German military intelligence. Finally, I am grateful to the staff of the Russian State Archive of Cinema, Recording, and Photography for enabling me to find and allowing me to reproduce so many of the photographs that illustrate this book.

The lives of soldiers in war were a new field of research for me. Fortunately, experts have been on hand at every stage to offer advice and comment. Among the many people whose conversation has enlivened my thinking, I thank Ian Collins, Ira Katznelson, Vladimir Kozlov, Norman Naimark, David Reynolds, Artem Sheinin, Ben Shephard, Steve Smith, and Simon Surguladze. Elena Senyavskaya in Moscow, whose own work continues to be an inspiration, was especially helpful in the early stages of research, as was her mentor, the ethnographer and war veteran Lev Pushkarev. I am also grateful to everyone who participated in the two workshops on culture and combat motivation that were held at the Centre for History and Economics at King's College, Cambridge, in 2004 and 2005. Thanks to Inga Huld Markan for organizing both meetings and, above all, as ever, to Emma Rothschild for her unfailing encouragement.

The process of turning such abundant material into a single book was always likely to be daunting. Fortunately, I have been able to count on two prodigiously gifted editors, Neil Belton at Faber and Sara Bershtel at Metropolitan Books, both of whom offered comments and encouragement from the very first. The finished book owes a great deal to each of them, while the writing of it was sustained by their friendship and enthusiasm. I am also indebted to their assistants and talented staff. My agent in London, Peter Robinson, has regularly astonished me with his willingness to read, and comment on, drafts, sort out tangles, and supply wine and sympathy at difficult moments. I have also been fortunate to work with Emma Parry in New York, whose sympathy—and perceptive conversation—more often seems to come with tea. My father, Philip Merridale, a veteran himself, read a first draft and fearlessly reminded me whenever I was missing the point. Jasper Kingston provided companionship throughout the long process of drafting and editing. Finally, I owe profound thanks to Antony Beevor and Sir Rodric Braithwaite, each of whom made time, in the course of a busy spring in 2005, to read the finished manuscript, to add their expert comments, and to correct some of the most egregious mistakes.

To work with any of these people would be privilege enough, but the unique aspect of this research was the opportunity it provided to meet and get to know the members of an extraordinary generation, the men and women who fought in the Red Army during the Great Patriotic War. I am indebted to them all, not least for the inspiration of their stories of lives well lived, of new hope and reconciliation at the end of so much pain. Two men in particular must be remembered here. Unlike most of their comrades, whose names were altered in the text in order to preserve their privacy, these two, Lev Lvovich Lyakhov and Ilya Natanovich Nemanov, appear without disguise. For one thing, each had said that he was happy to be named, and even that he would be proud to be. They both contributed so much that nothing less was justified. It was with great regret, therefore, that I learned, as I was writing, of their deaths. I hope that in some way their stories here will serve as memorials to their courage, intelligence, humor, and wisdom.

The images that the old soldiers invoked still bring Russia, and even Stalin's Russia, to life in my mind. I only have to reach for the tape of one of our conversations, for one of their admonitory letters, for a photograph, and the whole world that they described for me unfolds again in memory. For a singularly unmilitary woman, I have developed a surprising taste for old Red Army songs. The thought of the Crimean steppe or of the Dnepr cliffs brings on a sort of homesickness, as does the slightest whiff of archive dust. I have worn out a passport and two pairs of boots in the pursuit of Russia's war, and even back in England I have often disappeared behind a wall of red-bound volumes printed with Cyrillic text. It is an odd life to ask anyone to share, let alone to understand. For all these reasons, and a great deal more, I owe an incalculable debt to Frank Payne.

INDEX

★

Entries in *italics* refer to illustrations.